Relational Database Management for Microcomputers:

Design and Implementation

Jan L. Harrington

Bentley College
Department of Computer Information Systems

HOLT, RINEHART AND WINSTON, INC.
New York   Chicago   San Francisco   Philadelphia
Montreal   Toronto   London   Sydney   Tokyo
Mexico City   Rio de Janeiro   Madrid

Publisher: Ted Buchholz
Editor: DeVilla Williams
Production Manager: Paul Nardi
Production Supervision: Publishers Network, Morrisville, PA
Layout and typesetting: Black Gryphon Enterprises, Waltham, MA

7 8 9   016   9 8 7 6 5 4 3 2

Printed in the United States of America

ISBN 0-03-008542-X

Library of Congress Cataloging in Publication Data

Harrington, Jan L.
      Relational database management for microcomputers.

      Includes index.
      1. Relational data bases. 2. Microcomputers--
Programming.   I. Title
QA76.9.D3H365   1988   005.75'6   87-8450

Holt, Rinehart and Winston, Inc.
The Dryden Press
Saunders College Publishing

Relational Database
Management
for Microcomputers:

Design and Implementation

Table of Contents

PART III: APPENDICES

To the Instructor

Not so long ago, the author of this book was invited to submit a bid for a database design and implementation contract. The young man who made the initial contact over the phone admitted that he didn't know too much about databases and that he really had a problem—his file had 405 fields. Though it may not be a comfort to the business that is going to have to pay for a consultant to create its database system, that young man is not alone. There are a great many people in the business world who, while recognizing that they need a database system to capture and manage information, are also aware that they don't have the knowledge to design and implement that system.

This book was written to help those who are given the responsibility of developing database systems by filling the gap between computer-science-oriented database texts and short seminars that teach the use of database packages. Its organization and topic coverage are based on two assumptions: (1) many small to medium-sized businesses are implementing their database management systems on microcomputers, and (2) nearly all microcomputer database management systems are based on the relational model. This book is primarily intended to be used as a text in a database management course that approaches the subject as a business application. It can also be the basis for a short, intensive database design seminar or can be read independently by an individual who wishes to create an effective database system for his or her business.

The first part of the book contains two major themes: the process used to design a database system and the theory of relational database design. It has been written to teach readers the following:

1. The difference between file and database management systems
2. The activities that make up the systems development process
3. The foundations of the relational model for databases
4. Techniques for creating relations that will avoid the most common problems of poor relational design
5. Operations for manipulating relations

Chapter 2 covers material not found in most introductory database texts—the systems development cycle. Too often we forget that database design is only a part of the entire systems development process. This chapter is a review of the systems development cycle that reinforces the idea that even the best database design is of little use if it was created without regard for the needs of the users or was part of an ill-conceived implementation plan. Students should preferably have taken a course in systems analysis before coming to a database course. However, students who have only been exposed to systems analysis and design in a freshman computer literacy course should still find Chapter 2 an adequate review. The chapter ends by showing students the needs assessment phase of a case study that will appear throughout the book, using IPO (Input-Process-Output) as a general problem-solving model.

The discussion of normalization in Chapter 4 takes students through third normal form. Although further normal forms are of great theoretical interest, they are difficult for students to understand and of diminishing practical use as they move beyond 3NF. The book, therefore, does not deal with Boyce/Codd through fifth normal form. It does, however, present DK/NF to give students a feeling for the current state of normalization theory and to show them the ultimate design objective.

Part I is missing something found in older, more traditional database texts—a discussion of file and data structures. This omission was made with great care. The driving philosophy behind this book is that what we are trying to do is teach business computing students to view a database as a logical construct, as a shared pool of data, regardless of the physical implementation. Students don't need to know the details of data structures such as linked lists and B-trees to be able to design and implement effective, useful database systems. In fact, teaching file and data structures may make it more difficult for business students to divorce the physical file layouts from the logical database structure.

Examples are taken from two case studies: the relatively simple Small Bank and the more extensive Federated Taxi Company. Two additional case studies, Margaret Holmes, D.M.D. (Appendix A) and University Archaeological Museum (Appendix B) form the basis for the exercises at the end of the chapters.

Translating relational theory to actual implementation presents problems all of its own. No microcomputer database package currently available conforms strictly to the terminology of relational theory. Though most packages provide standard relational operations, they do not necessarily do so in an obvious or straightforward manner. The second portion of this book therefore includes chapters dealing with three major relational database management systems for microcomputers (*dBase III Plus*, *R:base System V*, and *Oracle*). The first two of these packages have been selected because they are widely used in business and not necessarily because they represent exemplary relational database software. *Oracle* has been included because it supports a complete implementation of SQL, the national standard query language, and because it is virtually identical to the *Oracle* DBMS available on minis and mainframes.   Readers are expected to have been previously exposed to the packages, since these chapters are not intended as tutorials but, instead, focus on how a database designer can implement the relational concepts discussed in Part I. For schools using the Macintosh, a Macintosh supplement is available as part of the *Instructor's Resource Manual* which accompanies this text.

The chapters dealing with *dBase III Plus* and *R:base System V* include sample code written in each DBMS's programming language. While these chapters do not attempt to teach programming, they do provide an overview of the languages provided by these two packages so that students can follow the sample code. Students should therefore have had some exposure to a high-level programming language, such as BASIC, Pascal, or COBOL. In particular, readers should be familiar with variables as well as the three basic program structures—sequence, selection, and iteration.

Part II also includes three chapters (6, 7, and 12) that look at more general implementation issues, including the characteristics of relational DBMSs, data orgranization (the logical concepts behind indexing and searching), multi-user databases, database security, and database administration. In particular, Chapter 6 discusses in detail the 12 theoretical rules for a fully relational database. While the importance of these rules for practical imple-mentation is still a topic for debate, they will nonetheless give students a yardstick against which they can measure relational database software.

Each chapter throughout the book is followed by THINGS TO THINK ABOUT and/or EXERCISES. THINGS TO THINK ABOUT are discussion questions, most of which have no single correct answer. Their intent is to encourage students to view the con-cepts about which they have been reading in a number of different contexts. The EXERCISES are included to give students hands-on practice with the skills presented in the chapters. They will give students practice in assessing user needs, formulating good relational designs, and creating effective queries.

Acknowledgements

A number of people contributed to making this book possible. In particular, I'd like to thank my editor at Holt, Rinehart and Winston, Inc.—DeVilla Williams—whose commitment to this project made all the difference in the world, and Paul Nardi, Production Manager, who decided to take a chance and let me do my own layout.

The reviewers, too, were an essential part of the development process. They included the following people:

- William Anderson (Montgomery College)
- Paul Bartolomeo (Community College of Rhode Island)
- Harvey Blessing (Essex Community College)
- William Brandt (Defiance College)
- John Cary (George Washington University)
- Christopher Carlson (George Mason University)
- Carl Evert (Xavier University)
- John Gallagher (Duke University)
- Alan Hevner (University of Maryland)
- Wojtek Kozaczynski (University of Illinois, Chicago)
- Anthony Mann (Sinclair Community College)
- Albert Napier (Rice University)
- Ravi Nath (Memphis State University)
- Richard Scamell (University of Houston)
- John Windsor (North Texas State University)

We also received valuable information from the following individuals, who participated in a marketing survey which helped us identify the type of text for which instructors were searching:

- Medhi Beheshtian (Loyola University)
- Glenn B. Dietrich (University of Texas San Antonio)

- Don Drake (Seminole Community College)
- Gordon Everest (University of Minnesota)
- Nelson Ford (Auburn University)
- Ella Gardner (George Mason University)
- Wojtek Kozaczynski (University of Illinois, Chicago)
- John McCann (Duke University)
- Joe McGrath (University of Florida)
- Cameron Mitchell (University of Houston)
- David Naumann (University of Minnesota)
- Robert Peterson (Notre Dame University)
- Dennis Severence (University of Michigan)
- Charles Snyder (Auburn University)
- Richard Spinetto (University of Colorado Boulder)
- Bin Yao (University of Maryland)

Finally, I'd like to thank the people at Publishers Network (especially Maricarol Cloak) who worked very closely with me while I was doing the layout for this book. They finalized a simple but elegant design, coordinated the production process, and answered all my questions about everything from reading the copyeditor's marks to how thick rules should be.

JLH

Design

Introduction

CHAPTER OUTLINE:

CHAPTER OBJECTIVES

After reading this chapter, you will:

1. Understand the characteristics of a file management system
2. Understand the problems associated with file management systems
3. Know the definition of a database system
4. Understand how database systems provide answers to many of the problems of file management systems
5. Understand the drawbacks associated with database systems

There is probably no more valuable commodity in the business world than information. Information can help us decide when to introduce a new product line, which marketing strategy to adopt, when to attempt a takeover of another company, or even when it's time to close up and declare bankruptcy. However, merely having timely, accurate information is often not enough. An organization must be able to have access to the right information at the right time. In other words, information must be organized in some way so that retrieval is easy and efficient.

This book will introduce you to the principles of one technique for organizing information using a computer as the primary storage device. The technique is referred to as *database management*, and the place where data are stored is known as a *database*. (This is an extremely simplistic definition which will be expanded later in this chapter.) You will find a discussion of the concepts behind the design of database systems in Chapters 2–5. Chapters 6–11 look at the practical sides of databases and Chapter 12 deals with managing a database installation.

Although the concepts behind databases are not new, database systems are only now beginning to replace older forms of computer data storage known as *file management systems*. File management systems and database management systems are fundamentally different. The nature of this difference is essential to an understanding of database systems and why they are increasingly being viewed as the best way to manage corporate information.

SOME INTRODUCTORY TERMINOLOGY

In order to understand the differences between file management systems and database systems, there are a few terms you should understand. These are *file*, *record*, and *field*. Be aware that these definitions come from the realm of computer science; they may not match what you find in the documentation that accompanies the database software you have purchased. (Much more on this terminology problem will follow in Part II.)

A *file* is a physical entity generally located on either a magnetic tape or a magnetic disk. It has a name and may contain the text of a document, the code for a computer program, or data organized in some known structure. The latter are often called *data files*. It is important to realize that the term *file* refers to the physical location of data on a physical storage medium. As you will see later in this chapter, it is possible to impose a logical organization on data that bears little resemblance to its physical layout in a file.

The data stored in data files are organized into *records*. A record represents data about a single person, object, or activity (the *entities* about which we are storing data). While it may take more than one record to contain all the data pertaining to any given entity, a single record rarely contains data about more than one entity.

Records can also be viewed as a group of *fields* that describe a single entity. A field is one data item.

To bring these terms into focus, let's look at a simple example—a mailing list. We wish to store the name, street address, city, state, and zip code for a group of people. The name, street address, city, state, and zip code are fields, since each represents one piece of data about the entities (people) described in the mailing list. If we group together the fields for any given individual, we have assembled a record, a complete set of data for that person. The data file that contains the entire mailing list consists of many identical records, each of which describes a different person.

Physical files made up of records with identical structure form the basis of traditional file management systems.

FILE MANAGEMENT SYSTEMS

A business that uses file management to process its data will maintain a single file for each data processing application. There will be a separate set of *application programs* associated with each file. Application programs are programs that do useful business work. They may print paychecks for an insurance company, record that a videotape has been rented at the local video outlet, print overdue notices for the library, or record an order for ski boots for a mail order sports equipment company.

As an example of a file processing system, consider Small Bank. This imaginary bank provides five major services to its customers: interest-paying checking (NOW accounts), passbook savings, certificates of deposit, loans for cars and homes, and safe-deposit boxes. The bank's data processing department therefore maintains five major files and associated programs (see Figure 1.1).

Table 1.1 shows the data contained in each file and the programs which have been written to maintain it. There are several features of file processing systems that are apparent from this table. The most important one is the great deal of *redundant data* (the same data about the same entity is stored more than once within the system; multiple copies exist of the same data). A customer's name, address, phone number, and social security number are repeated for each account of each type that he or she may have.

Also notice that each type of account has its own maintenance program to take care of changes in those customer description fields. In fact, since the file that supports each type of account is physically separate from all of the others, there is nothing to ensure that the formats of the customer description fields are the same throughout the system.

Each application program is intimately tied to the file on which it operates. Access to data in that file is based on the program's knowledge of how the data are physically stored (e.g., the order, type, and length of each field within its record). Any change in the physical structure of that file will therefore necessitate a change in the application programs that support it.

File management systems generally arise with little overall planning. For Small Bank, it was a seemingly simple matter to accommodate NOW accounts when they became

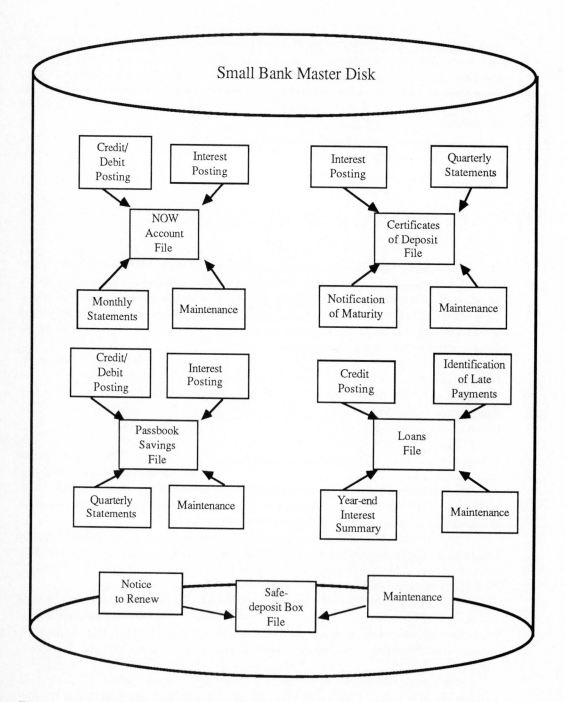

Figure 1.1 Small Bank's File Processing System

Table 1.1
Data Files, Data, and Application Programs for a Bank Using a File Management System

File	Data	Application Programs
NOW accounts	Customer name Customer address Customer phone number Customer social security number Account number Checks cashed Deposits made Interest earned Service charges Current balance	Credit/debit posting Interest posting Monthly statements Maintenance (add new accounts, change addresses, etc.)
Passbook savings	Customer name Customer address Customer phone number Customer social security number Account number Withdrawals made Deposits made Interest earned Current balance	Credit/debit posting Interest posting Quarterly statements Maintenance
Certificates of deposit	Customer name Customer address Customer phone number Customer social security number Account number Current balance Date of maturity	Interest posting Quarterly statements Notification of maturity Maintenance
Loans	Customer name Customer address Customer phone number Customer social security number Account number Current balance Payment amount Date payment due Date of last payment	Credit posting Identification of late payments Year-end interest summary Maintenance
Safe-deposit boxes	Customer name Customer address Customer phone number Customer social security number Account number Box number Box fee Renewal date	Notice to renew Maintenance

legal by merely creating a new file and the necessary application programs. Certificates of deposit were added to the system in the same manner only a few years earlier.

File management systems, especially those that have been in place for a long time, tend to store their files on tape. Using tape is cheaper than using disk, but it has one major restriction in terms of access: files stored on tape must be processed sequentially, starting at the first record and moving to the second, third, fourth, and so on until the end of the file is reached. There is no way to randomly jump to a specific record without passing over those in front of it. It is therefore more economical to assemble a group of changes or retrieval requests for the file, sort them in the same order as the file, and process them all at once; many modifications and retrievals can then be made with one pass through the file. This particular kind of processing, where activities against the file are grouped together, is known as *batch processing*.

Batch processing is generally very fast, especially when there are a large number of changes to be made in the file. Large investment brokerage houses, for example, store data about their clients' stock portfolios on tape. Every morning, before the stock market opens, they update the entire tape to reflect changes based on the previous day's closing prices. Since every single record on the tape must be updated, batch processing is very efficient. However, a customer wishing to know the current value of his or her portfolio may have to wait until the next business day, until after another batch run has been made, to get that information.

On the surface, a file management system appears simple, logical, and clean. It does, however, present a number of serious problems for both the business that uses one and the customers it serves.

PROBLEMS WITH FILE MANAGEMENT SYSTEMS

Consider Jon Dough, the average Small Bank customer. He has a NOW account, a passbook savings account, and a safe-deposit box, all at the Small Bank. He receives a monthly statement for his NOW account, a quarterly statement for his passbook savings account, and a notice once every two years when the time comes to renew his safe-deposit box rental. Small Bank has served Mr. Dough for six years without an error, but now Mr. Dough has moved across town.

Mr. Dough calls the bank and gives them his change of address. That one phone call triggers three computer system actions: Mr. Dough's new address becomes a part of the batch runs that do maintenance on (1) the NOW accounts file, (2) the passbook savings accounts file, and (3) the safe-deposit box file. Since Mr. Dough's address is stored in three places, it must be changed in three places. The redundant data does consume disk storage space that could be reclaimed if the data were only stored once and shared by the entire system. However, the inefficient use of disk space is generally not the most serious consequence of redundant data.

Assume that the NOW and passbook savings accounts maintenance programs function properly, but there is a bug in the program that maintains the safe-deposit box file; the safe-deposit box file retains Mr. Dough's old address. As far as Mr. Dough is concerned, all is well with his bank accounts. He receives his NOW and passbook savings account statements regularly at his new home. Eighteen months after his move, however, Mr. Dough suddenly remembers his safe-deposit box; he should have received a renewal notice three months ago. Unfortunately, Mr. Dough's renewal notice went to his old address. Since more than a year has elapsed since his move, the forwarding address he left with the post office has expired and the notice was returned to the bank. When he calls the bank to find out what happened, he learns that the contents of his safe-deposit box have been turned over to the state.

File management systems, as Jon Dough found out the hard way, have major problems with *data integrity*. In the narrowest sense of the term, a system that has data integrity can verify that all copies of redundant data items are identical. (The problem Jon Dough is facing might be referred to as *data distintegrity*.) Since redundant data in file management systems are stored in physically separate locations, it is exceptionally difficult to ascertain whether or not the contents of those data items are consistent (i.e., the same) throughout all the files in the system.

Data integrity, however, has implications for more than redundantly stored data. Assume, for the moment, that Small Bank decides to keep a customer master file, one that simply contains a listing of all customers who have any accounts with the bank. There is one record in the file for each customer. If Small Bank's file processing system is to have data integrity, then no person can be entered in any of the account files unless that person is also entered in the customer master file. In this case, the data integrity is *logical*, not physical. The customer master file will be of little use if Small Bank can't ensure that every customer in the account files appears in the customer master file.

Verifying this kind of logical data integrity is very difficult in a file processing environment. If they are to do so, each of Small Bank's account file maintenance programs must at least perform the following:

1. Search the customer master file to determine if the customer is already in the file.
2. If the customer has no record in the file (i.e., this is the customer's first account with Small Bank), add the customer to the customer master file.
3. Add the customer to the account file.

File processing systems cannot store data integrity rules. Since data are in separate physical files, there is no way to capture information about relationships between the files or the data in them. If file processing systems are to maintain data integrity, it must be enforced from within application programs, a procedure that is chancy at best. Even if Small

Bank's maintenance programs do verify that a customer appears in the customer master file before adding a new record to an account file, there is nothing to prevent any other application program from modifying the account files in some way that violates the rule that no customer can have an account without first having an entry in the customer master file.

Jon Dough is understandably angry with Small Bank, but he overcomes his anger long enough to apply for a car loan. (The interest rate is one-half point below the prime rate.) In order to process the loan application, the loan officer needs a history of all of Mr. Dough's accounts with the bank. She therefore asks the data processing department to prepare a single report that summarizes Mr. Dough's data. The data processing manager tells her that it will take at least two days to generate her report. Someone will have to manually search each file in the system; there is no way to know exactly which files contain data pertaining to Mr. Dough.

Small Bank's file management system, like other file management systems, has difficulty processing *one-of-a-kind requests*. A one-of-a-kind request, sometimes also called an *ad hoc query*, is a requirement for information that arises at the spur of the moment, cannot be predicted, and in all likelihood will never be repeated. Satisfying one-of-a-kind requests is especially complicated when the data are stored in more than one file, since there is generally no easy way to determine which files contains relevant data; each file must be searched. It is also expensive in terms of programmer resources, especially when files are stored in such a way that a special program must be written to do the data retrieval.

While Jon Dough is wrestling with his problems with Small Bank, the manager is replaced. The new manager sees what appears to be an easy way to save a significant amount of money on postage by switching from five-digit to nine-digit zip codes. He instructs the data processing department to replace all five-digit zip codes with the appropriate longer code. He's recently taken a couple of computer courses at night and believes that the conversion should be a simple process.

Reality, however, has nothing to do with the new manager's expectations. In the first place, the length and type of the zip code fields are not the same throughout the system; some zip codes are stored as characters, other as numbers. This problem is referred to as a lack of *data consistency*. It means that data which represent the same thing (e.g., a zip code) are not stored in the same way throughout the file processing system. Generally, this arises because the files were not developed with any consistent, overall plan; each file was created as needed, in complete isolation from other files. As a result, making the same change across all files in the system is very difficult. In our example, changing the size of the zip code field will require the following:

1. Determining exactly how and where the zip code is stored in each file
2. Determining what changes must be made to each file to allow the extra space for the expanded zip codes
3. Writing one or more programs that will make the changes in a manner appropriate to each individual file

Actually changing the files is only one small part of the problem. Because the application programs are so closely tied to the physical layout of the records in the files, any change in those files will require changes in the application programs that process them. For example, the application program that prints monthly NOW account statements assumes that each record is 256 characters long. To find the beginning of any given record, the application program multiplies the record number by 256. (This tells the program how many characters the required record is offset from the beginning of the file.) However, if the length of the record changes, then the program will have to be altered to reflect that new length in its computations. This situation is called a lack of *logical-physical data independence.*

If a system *has* logical-physical data independence, then it is possible to change the physical structure of the files without changing any application programs that use the data in those files. However, the application programs that use data stored in a file management system must locate the data by their physical position within a file; there is no intermediary program that can translate a more general request (e.g., record number 605 or Jon Dough's record) into a location within a file. The bank manager's idea to cut costs by using the longer zip codes may well end up costing more in programmer salaries to implement than the savings it would generate.

Small Bank may discover that changing to longer zip codes is only the tip of the iceberg when it comes to problems due to the lack of logical-physical data independence. Eventually, Small Bank's files will absorb all the space allocated to them. The data processing department will have to undertake a major reorganization of the entire physical storage system. In most cases this will also require modifications to all application programs.

DATABASE SYSTEMS

Database systems arose out of the many difficulties engendered by file management systems. A database system logically places all its data in a single, communal pool along with definitions of the relationships that exist between those data. Physically, the data are stored on a disk in one or more files, but the user can think of that data as if they were all in a single location.

The most important implication of this is that data can be shared. For example, Small Bank need only store a customer's name, address, phone number, and social security number once; any application that needs the information can retrieve it from the common data pool (see Figure 1.2). Each customer's account data can then be related in some way to the customer's name. The nature and structure of data relationships is basic to the design of database systems and is the topic of Chapter 3.

Access to the data is through a program called a *database management system* or *DBMS*. A DBMS sits between the user and the files where data are physically stored. The user issues requests to the DBMS, which in turn takes care of storing and retrieving the data. DBMSs designed for serious business use support application programs. These programs

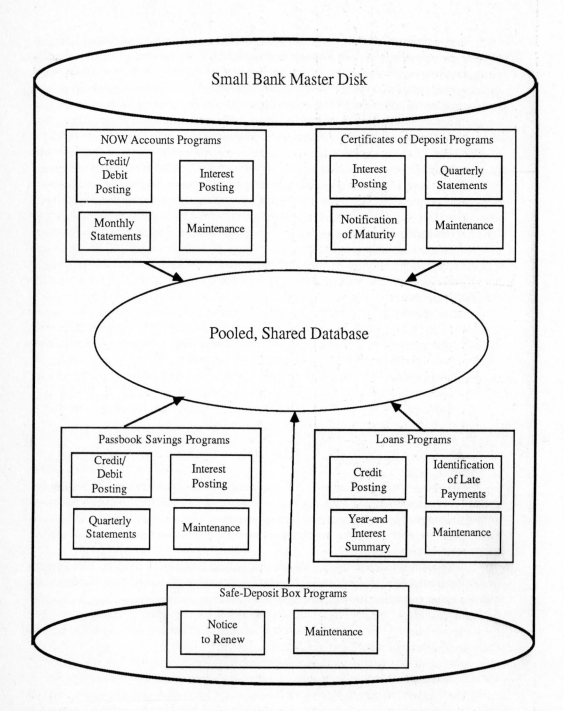

Figure 1.2 A Database System for Small Bank

contain commands to the DBMS embedded within a high-level host language. The host language may be a general programming language like COBOL, C, or BASIC (as with *Oracle*) or may be a language specific to the DBMS, such as the languages that are available with microcomputer DBMSs like *dBase III Plus* and *R:base System V*. Examples of those two languages can be found in Chapters 10 and 11.

A DBMS user can also search the data directly using an *on-line query language*. An on-line query language, often referred to as a *fourth-generation language*, is a special set of commands that a DBMS understands. A user enters the commands one at a time from the keyboard; the DBMS executes each command immediately. A full-featured query language allows a user to define database structure, to enter, edit, and delete data, to retrieve data, and to format and print reports. While query languages are usually easier to learn than high-level programming languages, their use nonetheless requires specialized user training. Early in 1986, *SQL* (pronounced "sequel") was accepted by the American National Standards Institute (ANSI) as the national standard query language for relational databases. SQL is discussed in Chapter 8 along with *Oracle*, which supports a full implementation of that query language. Other DBMSs have query languages specific to the DBMS. This is the case for *dBase III Plus* and *R:base System V*. (*R:base*'s query language, however, is "SQL-like.") Examples of these query languages are scattered throughout Chapters 10 and 11.

Unlike file management systems, a well-designed database system cannot be developed in bits and pieces; it requires planning. The overall logical organization of a database, as it appears to those who develop and administer the database, is known as a *schema*. A database schema contains definitions of all the data items that the database will contain as well as the relationships between those data. Though database schemas can change, an initial schema must be completely designed before the database system is implemented on a computer. Creating database schemas is discussed in Chapters 3 and 4.

The schema is described in what is known as a *data dictionary*, or *catalog*. In its most primitive form, a data dictionary may be nothing more than a notebook that records information about the schema. More sophisticated systems have on-line data dictionaries. Some are simply text files that record the same information that is kept on paper in a three-ring binder, but others are integrated with the database system itself. In a system with an integrated data dictionary, any change made to the definition of a data item in the data dictionary will cause a corresponding change in the database. Data dictionaries are discussed in terms of specific DBMSs in Chapters 8, 10, and 11.

Responsibility for administering and maintaining database schemas falls to a *database administrator* (DBA). The extent of the DBA function within any given organization depends, to a great extent, on the size and complexity of the organization's database system. At the very least, the DBA controls any changes that are to be made to the database schema. In large organizations, the DBA function may be handled by a group of people, working not only to ensure the integrity of the schema, but to manage activities such as application program development and system backup as well. More details about database administration can be found in Chapter 12.

Most applications that use any given database will not need to use every data item in the database. Therefore, many DBMSs allow the user to define a *subschema*, or *view*. A subschema is a subset of the schema including only as much of the schema as is needed by a particular application. Generally, the subschema is a user's logical view of the database. Theoretically, there is no limit to the number of subschemas that can be defined from any schema.

A database system therefore supports three ways of looking at the data:

1. The schema—the global logical view of the entire system used primarily by system designers and database administrators
2. The subschema—a logical view of the data related to one particular application used by application programmers and end-users
3. The physical—the actual way in which data are physically stored in files on a disk (generally of interest to systems programmers and those who write DBMSs)

A word of caution is in order about microcomputer database management systems: there are a great many software packages on the market that are advertised as database management systems but that are, in reality, file management systems. Any package that allows you to manipulate only a single file at a time is not a database manager but a file manager. It is important to remember that no matter what the software vendors state in their documentation, *a file is not a database;* a file is a physical entity whereas a database is a collection of files that contain data and definitions of the relationships between the data in those files.

Microsoft File, *pfs:File*, *DBMaster*, and *PC-File*, for example, are rather powerful file management programs. Although they provide advanced on-line query features, sorting, and report generation, they can handle only one file at a time. Such software is most useful for stand-alone applications, such as maintaining a mailing list. It cannot, however, efficiently support more complex data processing without encountering one or more of the problems discussed above that are endemic to file management systems. For an excellent overview of current microcomputer file and database management software, see "File Management Software" (Mace, 1986).

A spreadsheet package, such as *Lotus 1-2-3*, is also not a database management system. Spreadsheets do allow users to manipulate blocks of data, providing some sophisticated file management capabilities including the ability to sort data on one or more fields. However, like file management software, no spreadsheet has the ability to logically pool data and store information about data relationships.

THE DATABASE ADVANTAGE

Database systems provide solutions to many of the problems generated by file management systems primarily because of the sharing of data and the common interface provided by the DBMS.

Because data can be shared, database management systems require less redundant data than file processing systems. Database systems do not necessarily eliminate *all* data redundancy; in some cases, as you will see in Chapter 3, some data redundancy is essential to capture meaning about data relationships. On the whole, however, they do decrease the amount of duplicated data. While this certainly decreases the amount of disk space that is required, it has far more important consequences.

When data are stored only once, rather than in many different places, the problem of data integrity can be somewhat reduced. For example, if Small Bank had been using a database system when Jon Dough phoned in his address change, Mr. Dough's address would have been maintained in only one location (the common data pool used by the entire database system) and therefore changed only once. Since each of Mr. Dough's accounts would be using the single copy of Mr. Dough's address, there is no chance that any two accounts could have a different address.

Pooling the data to eliminate some redundancy does not, however, solve problems of logical data integrity. (Think back to the problem caused by the introduction of a customer master file into Small Bank's file processing system.) Ideally, a database management system should permit data integrity rules to be stored within its data dictionary. Then, whenever data are modified, the DBMS should automatically consult those rules and take action to ensure that they are enforced. As you will see in Chapters 8–11, DBMSs vary widely in how well they handle logical data integrity.

Problems with data consistency can also be avoided by reducing data redundancy. Data inconsistency arises when redundantly stored data have incompatible data formats. Therefore, storing a given piece of data only once ensures that there is no possibility of an alternative data format appearing within the database system. When data redundancy is either unavoidable or desirable, data consistency can be maintained by building it into the schema; that is, since the entire schema is defined before the database is implemented, instances of redundant data items can be identified while the database is still in the planning stages. The designers can then ensure that duplicated data items have identical data formats.

The existence of the DBMS provides solutions to other file management problems. Since the DBMS provides a common access route to data that appear to the user as if they were in a single pool, one-of-a-kind requests are easy to accommodate. Using the DBMS's query language, a user can formulate a request for data retrieval without having to write an application program. The DBMS will take care of locating the requested data, regardless of where or how it is physically stored.

For example, assume that you have a database that stores the names of all the magazines to which you subscribe (TITLE), the address to which renewals should be mailed, the yearly cost, and the expiration date (EXPIRES). Every so often, you want to see a list of all the magazines that are due to expire shortly. You could certainly write an application program to do the retrieval, but it is simpler to issue a command in whatever query language is being used by your database management system.

If you were using *dBase III Plus*,

LIST TITLE FOR EXPIRES <= 12/31/86

would display the titles of all magazines that had expiration dates before January 1, 1987.

The same query, written in *R:base*'s query language, would appear as:

SELECT TITLE   FROM MAGS WHERE EXPIRES <= 12/31/86

The SQL query might be written as:

SELECT   TITLE
FROM   MAGS
WHERE EXPIRES <= '31-DEC-86';

The DBMS also provides logical-physical data independence. Since the DBMS performs the actual storage and retrieval of data, the user of a database management system does not need to be concerned with how the data are stored on disk. A variety of subschemas, for example, can be created off a single database without ever modifying the files that underlie the database system. In other words, the same files can support many different logical views of the data.   Conversely, it is possible to modify and even change the physical layout of data files without affecting the schema, subschemas, or application programs.   The degree of logical-physical data independence does, however, vary between DBMS packages.

DRAWBACKS TO DATABASE SYSTEMS

It would be misleading to think that a database system is the cure for all ills. Database systems bring with them a few problems of their own (Schroeder, 1986).

Database systems are more costly in terms of hardware and software than file management systems. Though software prices have dropped dramatically, a DBMS is still the most expensive type of software you can buy for a microcomputer (i.e., a DBMS costs relatively more than a file management program, a word processor, or a spreadsheet).

Database systems generally require more hardware than file management systems. While file management systems can operate off floppy disks, perhaps keeping each file on a separate disk, meaningful database applications require both the added storage space and increased speed of a hard disk. DBMS programs tend to be rather large and often require more main memory than file management systems. As hardware prices drop, however, this becomes less and less of a drawback.

Database systems are also more difficult and more costly to develop than file management systems. Because a database system needs a great deal of planning before you ever get to the computer, it absorbs a significant amount of human time, the most expensive part of most computer systems. The design of database systems requires people with special knowledge, which may mean that an organization must hire an outside consultant.

Once they are operational, database systems are more vulnerable to failure than file management systems. If something happens to one file in a file management system, the rest of the system can continue to function. However, if a central database goes down, all data processing within the organization grinds to a halt.

This vulnerability to failure means that businesses using database systems must be very careful to keep adequate backup materials and to establish workable recovery procedures. Database backup and recovery does, however, tend to be more complicated than similar procedures in file management systems.

SUMMARY

Database management systems are an alternative to file management systems for the organization, storage, and retrieval of corporate data resources.

File management systems store data for each application within an organization in a separate, physical file. Each file supports its own set of application programs. Because data are duplicated and separated throughout file management systems, they are prone to a number of major problems:

1. Lack of data integrity (Multiple copies of a single data value are not identical and logical cross-references between files are not maintained.)
2. Difficulty handling one-of-a-kind requests (There is no easy or quick way to answer requests for information that arise on the spur of the moment, that cannot be predicted, and that are not likely to be repeated.)
3. Lack of data consistency (The same data items in different files are stored with different data formats.)
4. Lack of logical-physical data independence (Changes to the physical storage of data requires changes in all application programs using those files.)

Database systems provide solutions to these problems by logically viewing the data as if they were stored in a single, unified pool. Database systems therefore provide increased:

1. Data integrity (When only one copy of a data value is stored, multiple copies that do not agree cannot exist. Since data are logically pooled, integrity rules can be stored in the data dictionary and enforced by the DBMS when data modifications are made.)
2. Ease in handling one-of-a-kind requests (Since the data are pooled, all data are available to answer unpredictable, spur-of-the-moment requests for information.)
3. Data consistency (Since a global plan for the database is produced before it is implemented, redundant data items can be identified and the consistency of their formats ensured.)
4. Logical-data independence (DBMS software provides an interface between the user and the physical storage media; it is therefore possible to change the physical

storage structures without altering application programs or the way in which on-line queries are formulated.)

Database systems do have a few drawbacks:

1. They require more hardware than file management systems.
2. DBMS software is relatively costly.
3. They are more difficult to develop and cost more to develop than file management systems because they must be thoroughly planned before they are implemented.
4. They are more vulnerable to failure than file management systems; if the database goes down, all processing must stop.

REFERENCES

Ahituv, Niv and Michael Hadass. (1980) "Identifying the need for a DBMS." *Journal of Systems Management*. August:30-33.

Fry, J.P. and E.H. Sibley. (1976) "Evolution of data base management systems." *ACM Computing Surveys*. 8(1). March.

Mace, Scott. (1986)   "File management software." *InfoWorld*. September 8: 29-37.

Patterson, Albert C. (1972) "Data base hazards." *Datamation*. 18(7):48-50. July.

Schroeder, Matthew T. (1986). "What's wrong with DBMS." *Datamation*. December 15: 27-30.

Stonebraker, M.R. (1974) "A functional view of data independence." *Proceedings of the 1974 ACM SIGMOD Workshop on Data Description, Access, and Control*. May.

THINGS TO THINK ABOUT

1. Consider your bank. Do you get a single statement for your checking account and another for your savings account? Or do you get one integrated statement for all of your accounts at the bank? What clues do these different kinds of statements give you about the type of system the bank might be using (i.e., file management vs. database management)?

2. Of all the problems associated with file management systems, which do you consider to be the most devastating for an organization? Why? When formulating your answer, consider the impact of the problems in terms of tangibles such as hardware costs, software costs, and programmer salaries. Then look at the implications for intangibles such as customer satisfaction.

3. A large insurance company is considering exchanging their current file processing system for a database system. Their major concern in making the change is the volume of data they must process every day (*thousands* of separate activities). They are worried that a database system will be too slow. What arguments might you make to the management of this company to convince them that they will gain more by living with the decrease in speed than by staying with their file processing system?

4. A lumber mill has hired you to evaluate their information system. You discover that they have a file management system to keep track of inventory. The inventory is updated once a week. The manager says that this works just fine, since even though the mill produces cut lumber throughout the work week, all orders are shipped on Mondays. What advantages does the file management system afford the lumber mill? What might they gain by switching to a database system?

5. File management software can be a useful business tool for managing stand-alone applications such as a mailing list. What other application areas can you think of that might be adequately handled by a file manager rather than a DBMS?

6. Some file management software packages support an on-line query language. Can an on-line query language be used if files are stored on tape? Why or why not? By the same token, is it possible to use a DBMS without disk storage? Why or why not?

7. The introduction of a database system into a large organization has often frightened the application programmers in the organization's data processing department. They fear that the DBMS's on-line query language will mean that there will no longer be a need for as much application programming, and they will either lose their jobs or be downgraded. What arguments might you make to calm their fears?

The Design Process

CHAPTER OUTLINE:

CHAPTER OBJECTIVES:

After reading this chapter, you will:

1. Understand that database design requires more than the skill to work with a specific piece of software
2. Be reacquainted with the activities that make up the systems development cycle
3. Have seen the needs assessment phase of a systems development project whose ultimate goal is the installation of a database system

There are really two ways to view the problem of designing a database system. In its narrowest sense, database design is concerned with creating the "best" logical structure for a given set of data items. In fact, Chapters 3 and 4 of this book deal with just exactly that. However, to assume that database design means merely putting data items together in some optimal way is somewhat shortsighted.

To take a broader, more complete view of database design, the designer must investigate the environment that the database system will serve. In other words, it is difficult to create a useful, efficient, logical design for data storage and retrieval without knowing the requirements of the people who will be using the database. By the same token, someone must select and purchase hardware and software for the system. Someone must implement the database and train the users. Together, these activities are part of what is known as the *systems development cycle*.

When a database system is the intended product of a systems development project, the entire project is often referred to as a database design project. Therefore, to avoid confusion between the logical design of a database schema and the overall development of an information system, we will refer to the former as *database design* and the latter as *systems development*. The purpose of this chapter to is to review the systems development cycle and to show you where database design fits within it.

THE SYSTEMS DEVELOPMENT CYCLE

The systems development cycle is a set of procedures used by organizations to develop computer information systems. While there are many schemes for describing the steps in the cycle, they usually include the following:

1. Performing a needs assessment. The purpose of the needs assessment is to identify the strong and weak points of the current system and to define what improvements should be made, either by designing a completely new system or by modifying the old, to create a system that meets the current needs of the organization. The result of this phase is a document that details the requirements of the new or improved system.
2. Generating alternative proposals for the new or improved system and evaluating and selecting the most cost effective strategy. The alternative proposals are not specific design proposals but general strategies for meeting the requirements of the organization as identified during the needs assessment.
3. Creating the detailed system design.
4. Implementing the system. This includes acquiring and testing the necessary hardware and software as well as actually putting the system to work within the organization.

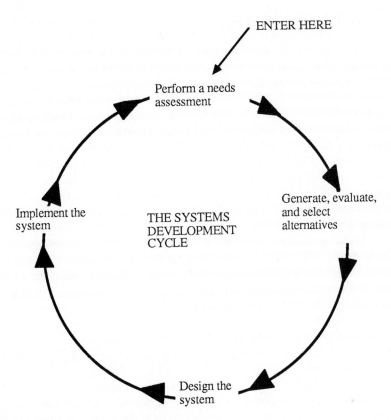

ENTER HERE

Perform a needs
assessment

Implement the
system

THE SYSTEMS
DEVELOPMENT
CYCLE

Generate, evaluate,
and select
alternatives

Design the
system

Figure 2.1 The Systems Development Cycle

Figure 2.1 is drawn as a circle for a very important reason. The four steps are part of a continuous process that, once begun, should be continued indefinitely by an organization. Good systems designs contain provisions for redoing the needs assessment at regular intervals. If the system is satisfactory, then no further action is required until the next scheduled needs assessment. However, if the needs assessment indicates that the system should be modified, the organization follows the remaining steps in the cycle.

The database design itself fits within step three of the systems development cycle. Working from the document prepared at the end of step one and with details of the implementation alternative selected at the end of step two, designers create the database schema, user views, and design application programs to manipulate the data. Though it is not necessarily part of the database design process, step three may also include the design of the physical storage mechanisms needed to support the database system.

The development of a computer-based information system can be a complex task. If you wish to explore the process in greater depth, consult the following resources: Burch, 1983; Fitzgerald, 1981; Nordbottom, 1985; Ostle, 1985; Zmud, 1983.

THE NEEDS ASSESSMENT

Another term for the needs assessment phase of the systems development process is *systems analysis*. The person who coordinates and/or performs the analysis is a *systems analyst*. Systems analysts are trained in interviewing and other data-gathering techniques, which they use to form a picture of an organization's current information system and to identify how well that system is meeting the organization's information needs. In particular, a systems analyst will attempt to create a picture of how information moves through an organization. A *data-flow* diagram (discussed later in this chapter) is often used as a summary tool.

When approaching a systems development project, it is essential to realize that developing an information system is really solving a business problem. It is therefore possible to use a general problem-solving model as a framework for conducting the needs assessment. A model commonly used by systems analysts and computer programmers alike is the input-process-output model (IPO).

IPO assumes that most information-processing activities involve taking some input, processing it in some way, and producing some desired output. An analyst working with this model first identifies the output of an information system. During the needs assessment phase, the analyst will identify both current outputs and outputs that the organization currently doesn't have but would like to have. Once he or she knows what the outputs are or should be, the analyst can identify the input needed to produce those outputs. The final step is to describe the process that transforms the input into output.

Identifying output before specifying input and how that input should be processed may seem a bit backwards. Consider, however, this simple analogy: you want to make some dessert to serve after dinner. The problem you are solving is "making dessert." Since you have few groceries in the house, you will have to go to the market regardless of what dessert you choose to make. Before you can go to the market, you must decide what dessert you will make; otherwise, how can you know what items to purchase? The recipe that governs the transformation of raw ingredients (even if it means merely opening a box and mixing) is the last detail with which you will be concerned. In other words, if you don't know what you want out of a project, how can you possibly know what should go in?

The first step in a systems analysis using the IPO model is, therefore, to specify the output the current system produces. Usually, this involves spending time with the individuals who are using the system. The systems analyst asks those individuals to identify the results of information-handling procedures currently in place. Often, this means looking at forms, reports, and files. Then the analyst gathers data on what input is used to produce the output. He or she attempts to identify which input documents, along with other sources of input (e.g., data files kept on disk), contribute to the production of each individual output. Finally, the analyst asks current system users to demonstrate and/or describe the procedures they follow to transform input into output.

The movement of data from input, through processing, to output is often summarized in a data-flow diagram. While there is more than one way to draw a data-flow diagram, commonly it has three symbols: squares for sources of input (people or departments, not the input itself), circles for processes, and open-ended rectangles for places where data are stored. Arrows connect the symbols to show the way in which data move from one to the other.

Labels are added to the diagram to identify symbols. Specific inputs and outputs are identified by labeling the data-flow arrows, showing exactly what is traveling along a given path.

Figure 2.2 contains a data-flow diagram that shows Small Bank's procedure for establishing a new NOW account using their file processing system. At the top of the diagram, the New Accounts Clerk is the source of input that initiates the entire process. The New Accounts Clerk transmits new accounts forms, which are then used in a data-entry process which builds a transaction file. The transaction file is a place for data storage (it appears in a rectangle). The transaction file and the existing NOW accounts file are both used to create an updated NOW accounts file. The process also produces another output—the New Accounts Summary Report—which is transmitted back to the New Accounts clerk.

The data-flow diagram shown in Figure 2.2 is a picture of Small Bank's current system. Once the diagram has been completed, the analyst must identify where this system works well and where it doesn't. He or she asks those who are using the system to specifically evaluate their current system: What does it do right? What output would they like to retain in the new system? Where does the current system fall down? What output would they like to see added to the new system? In situations in which new outputs are requested, the analyst must also identify the input needed to produce those outputs and at least get a general overview of the processes needed to create them. The analyst can then modify, or perhaps completely redraw, the data-flow diagram to show new patterns of information flow.

Figure 2.3 presents a data-flow diagram that might be created to show how accounts could be created if Small Bank were to upgrade to a database system. The New Accounts Clerk still completes a new accounts form. However, the update requests are no longer batched. In fact, they are sent directly to an update program that operates on the existing database to produce an updated database. The system continues to produce a paper summary of new accounts which is returned to the New Accounts Clerk.

After completing a data-flow diagram of a new or improved system, the analyst reports to corporate management. Together, they rank the outputs the system might provide in order of importance. (This is often referred to as *prioritizing*.) Generally, the database designer proposes a set of priorities which are then taken to management for approval. The database designer must be familiar enough with databases in general, with the limitations placed on data retrieval by existing software, and with the environment in which the database will operate in order to justify his or her recommendations.

The issue of communication between the person doing the systems development and management cannot be overemphasized. There are many horror stories in the business world about systems development projects that have gone awry, costing organizations hundreds of thousands of dollars. The common denominator in most of these tales is a lack of communication between the people developing the system and those who will benefit from the information the system is expected to provide. At the very least, a systems developer should present his or her proposals for system output for management approval before proceeding any further with system development.

Finally, using all the data he or she has gathered, the analyst prepares a *requirements document* that will be transmitted to management for approval. This extensive report includes details of all outputs the new or improved system must provide. It may also specify

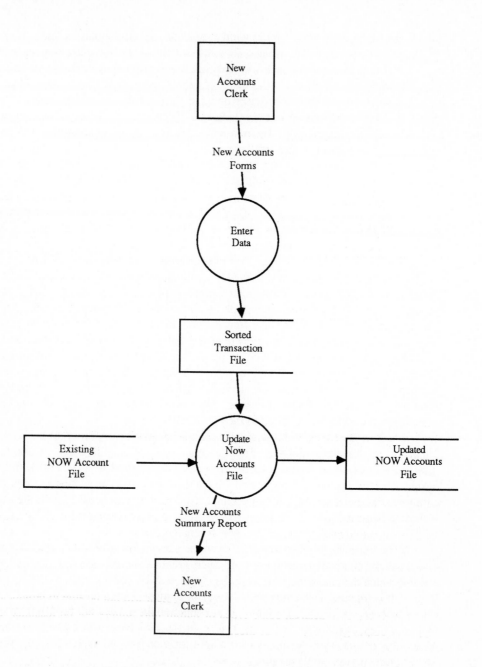

Figure 2.2 A Data-Flow Diagram for Creating New NOW Accounts at Small Bank with a File Processing System

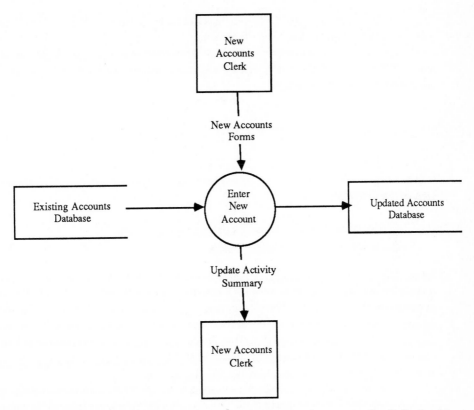

Figure 2.3 A Data-Flow Diagram for Creating New NOW Accounts at Small Bank with a Database System

the inputs associated with each output, the processes to transform input to output, and the resources (people, time, and money) needed to implement various outputs. The requirements document may include paper samples of all *reports* (information-bearing documents) the system should produce to formalize the hard copy output which the new system will provide. It may also contain paper samples of CRT screen formats for data display to define the on-line output which the new system will provide.

It is important to realize that a database system will not be able to provide every output that every user desires; some types of output may simply not be feasible. Infeasible types of output generally include those things that consume amounts of resources disproportionate to their value. In other words, they may require excessive development time in terms of the current goals set for database implementation, or they may be tasks with limited usefulness that consume large quantities of database processing time. Note that "infeasible" isn't the same as "impossible"; impossible output is output that cannot be generated from the database, regardless of how much time or effort is expended.

There are no hard and fast guidelines as to what constitutes feasible and infeasible output. The decision must be based on factors unique to each particular database environment. In most cases, however, output that users have requested will be evaluated in terms of the ratio between the importance of the particular output to the organization as a whole and the cost of creating the particular output.

GENERATING AND EVALUATING ALTERNATIVES

There will always be more than one way to implement the specifications delineated in a given requirements document. Any systems development process will have at least two design alternatives:

1. Keep the old system (this is *always* a possibility)
2. Install a new or modified system

More often, however, the systems analyst will present management with several ways in which the old system can be changed to better meet the needs of the organization. The alternatives will include various types of hardware (e.g., one size of computer vs. another or one brand of computer vs. another) and various sources for software (e.g., purchased off-the-shelf or custom programmed specifically for the organization). The alternatives will also deal with which of the feasible outputs should be developed and in which order they should be developed; a development time line may also be included.

Each alternative has a variety of costs associated with it. Costs for hardware and software can be estimated relatively easily. The difficult portion of the analysis is trying to assign values to the benefits each alternative will bring to the organization. Often, affixing dollar values to intangible benefits (e.g., better customer satisfaction) is based on the knowledge of experienced managerial personnel. The final decision is made by comparing costs to benefits and then applying human judgment. Many decisions about the type of system that is to be implemented are made on "gut feelings," a process which is not necessarily wrong; experienced managers often have knowledge about their market which cannot be easily expressed in words, much less quantified.

DETAILED SYSTEMS DESIGN

It is at this point in the development cycle—after a general design strategy has been approved—that the actual design of a database begins. If not included in the requirements document, paper samples of output formats can be used to identify the data items that are necessary to produce each individual output; these form the pool of data upon which the database system will be built.

However, merely knowing the types of data that need to be stored in the database is not enough to produce an effective design. A database schema consists of not only the pool of data items but definitions of the relationships between those data. Therefore, the systems designer must be able to assemble a set of rules that describe how the data interact; these are known as *constraints*. Constraints emerge as the systems analyst conducts interviews with an organization's personnel. Further information about database constraints appears throughout the rest of this book.

Having both a pool of data items and a set of constraints, the database designer is ready to create an effective logical organization for the data. While most database design textbooks begin their discussions of database design at this point in the systems development process, it is important to remember that the needs assessment, alternative generation, and alternative selection must be performed before schema creation is possible.

IMPLEMENTATION

The implementation of an information system generally involves the following activities:

1. Purchasing, installing, and testing hardware
2. Purchasing off-the-shelf software. If the information system includes a database, then the major software item will be the DBMS. An organization may also decide to purchase application or utility programs which have been written specifically for their DBMS.
3. Tailoring off-the-shelf-software. In some cases, it may be necessary to modify off-the-shelf software to better meet the needs of the organization.
4. Writing application programs
5. Testing all software
6. Writing documentation
7. Training users
8. Final implementation of the system

While the activities above are listed as if they were a series, they do not always occur in sequence. Steps one and two can occur simultaneously. Once the hardware and purchased software are available, steps three to seven can be performed concurrently. Step eight, placing the system in actual use, cannot begin until all other activities are completed.

Even if a system has been superbly designed, its software tailored perfectly to the organization, and all hardware and software thoroughly tested, it can still fail if the implementation is not handled properly. The most successful implementation schemes are based on the premise that if something can go wrong, it will. Therefore, most new computer systems are implemented using a *parallel* approach.

With the parallel approach to implementation, the new system is run along with the old system (i.e., the two systems are run in parallel). This continues through at least one complete business cycle. There are two major advantages to this strategy that offset the additional effort of doing everything twice:

1. Output from the new system can be checked against output from the old to verify that the new system is performing accurately.

2. If, for some unforeseen reason, it becomes necessary to shut down the new system, the organization still has an operational, up-to-date old system that can be used until the new system is repaired.

The opposite of the parallel approach is often referred to as the *plunge* approach, since an organization plunges into the new system, completely discontinuing the old. A plunge implementation is an invitation to disaster, since any failure of the new system will cause major disruption in the operation of the organization.

CONDUCTING A NEEDS ASSESSMENT

To better understand the idea of a needs assessment, imagine that you have been hired to develop a database system for the Federated Taxi Company. FTC is owned and operated by Joe and Mary Kelly. Until recently, the business has been profitable but small. However, the City Council has just made 500 more taxi licenses available, 200 of which were acquired by FTC. With the added taxis on the road, FTC's manual record keeping has become unwieldy and therefore inaccurate. The Kellys are astute businesspeople and realize that computerizing their record keeping is the only realistic answer to their problem. They are also intelligent enough to recognize that they don't have the necessary computer skills to handle the project themselves. Therefore, they decided to seek the help of an outside consultant—you.

CONDUCTING INTERVIEWS

On your first visit to FTC you are met by Mrs. Kelly. Once the two of you are comfortably seated in the office, you ask her to describe in general terms how the company operates:

"FTC owns all of its cabs," Mrs. Kelly explains. "We have a full-time maintenance staff that handles all repairs except major body work. However, our drivers are not on the FTC payroll. A driver rents a cab from us for a fixed fee for each shift; the fee for a given shift is based on the earning potential for that time period. For example, fees for a day shift—8 a.m. to 4 p.m.—are higher than those for the graveyard shift—12 a.m. to 8 a.m. Drivers also pay for all their own gas. In order to make a profit, then, a driver must take in more money than the rental fee and the cost of the gas. This arrangement benefits a driver who consistently finds fares and who can drive economically.

"For new drivers, the rental fee is due before the driver takes the cab out on the road. We allow drivers who have been with us for a while to pay when they return from their shift.

"The rental arrangement also simplifies management of the company. Our payroll is small; we pay the three-person office staff, a janitor for the garage and the office, our five mechanics, and the six dispatchers.   We make our profit by keeping as many cabs on the road as we can.   Therefore, adding all these new cabs hasn't placed much of a strain on our payroll system—the current one-write system is still working pretty well—but handling information about the cabs has become a nightmare.

"We keep records on each of the cabs, both to make sure they get regular preventative maintenance and to identify any cabs that are being mistreated by their drivers. Every so often we do have to refuse a driver's request for cab rental because of a poor driving record. Therefore, we also keep records on each of the drivers: which cab they rented, how far they drove, and so on. One of the things we need to be able to do with our new record-keeping system is to match up drivers with cabs that develop major problems so we can identify which driver is responsible.

"We're also having trouble with our parts inventory. The new cabs aren't the same make as the older cabs (you can't buy the big Checker cabs any more!), which means that we now have to stock two sets of everything. And by the same token, our accounts payable and accounts receivable systems are overwhelmed by the new workload. The bookkeeper is ready to quit, but I don't think it's quite that bad. The clerk who schedules drivers for cabs isn't particularly happy either.

"Like most cab companies, ours are radio dispatched. We have three dispatchers that work a regular five-day week, one on each shift, and three part-timers for the weekends. The dispatchers are responsible for checking drivers in and out, answering phone calls, and sending cabs to make pickups. When a dispatcher comes in for a shift, we give that person a list of the cabs that are scheduled to be driven that shift. The dispatcher then uses a grid on the office whiteboard to keep track of where each cab is at any time. It's been working quite well while the number of cabs has been small, but some days now there isn't room on the board to list all the cabs on the road. However, I'm concerned that our dispatchers won't take to a computer easily; most of them are retired people. I'm also afraid that a computer won't be fast enough for them, that it won't give them an overview of all the cabs at once. I think a bigger whiteboard is the answer, at least for the time being."

There is only one thing that Mrs. Kelly has said that you don't quite understand. If the driver's pay the rental fees for their cabs either before their shift or directly afterwards, why does FTC have any accounts receivable?

"Oh, I forgot," she replies. "We have 10 unmarked cabs that we rent to local businesses when they need to expand their fleets temporarily. These are established customers; we bill them and they pay regularly." This answer clears up your confusion.

Although the conversation you had with Mrs. Kelly was a great start, it didn't give you enough detail to create a requirements document. You need to make another visit to FTC so that you can talk to some of the employees. Cab scheduling and maintenance records are handled by two people, an office clerk and the chief mechanic. To understand how they interact and share data, you must speak with both of them.

The chief mechanic shows you a 5-by-8-inch card file that is kept on the ledge of a pass-through (a window without a window pane) between the office and the garage. Noting the physical placement of the file may at first seem like an unnecessary detail, but it is important in terms of who has access to the data. The chief mechanic and the office clerk both need to use the data in that card file regularly, and any computer system that ultimately replaces the card file must provide the same sort of access.

The card file is divided into two sections. In the first section is one card for each cab. The data on the card includes:

1. Cab number
2. Manufacturer
3. Model
4. Year
5. License number
6. Date of last tune-up
7. Mileage at last tune-up

The cards are kept in order by the date of last tune-up. In order to determine which cars are due for regular maintenance, the chief mechanic merely checks those cards at the front of the box. He orders tune-ups for any car whose date of last tune-up is more than three months prior to the current date. He decides on any further required maintenance by checking the cab once it is in the garage. Cabs are also scheduled for maintenance whenever a driver reports a specific problem.

The back portion of the card file also contains one card per cab, but these are kept in order by cab number. Each card contains the cab's maintenance record and the result of random inspections of the cab's condition. The last entry on the card is always a short statement of the cab's present condition.

The chief mechanic has no set procedure for deciding which cabs will be inspected. In most cases, it depends on who is driving the cab. In other words, cabs driven by new, inexperienced drivers will be inspected far more frequently than cabs driven by drivers who the chief mechanic knows and trusts. He relies on experienced drivers to report mechanical problems as they arise.

The clerk who actually schedules drivers uses two loose-leaf notebooks in addition to the card file. One notebook contains one or more sheets for each driver, listing the driver's history with the company. The sheets of paper are kept in alphabetical order by driver name, and data pertaining to individual drivers are kept in chronological order. The clerk records:

1. Date the activity occurred
2. Type of activity (e.g., the shift for which a cab is rented, any traffic tickets received, any accidents in which the driver was involved)
3. Additional notes and comments (in the case of a traffic ticket or accident, the clerk includes details of the incident)

Unless something unusual occurs (e.g., a serious accident), the driver-history notebook is reviewed by Mr. or Mrs. Kelly once a week. The owners make decisions on how specific drivers should be handled. For example, they may decide that a particular driver has established a safe record and is no longer required to pay the cab rental prior to taking a cab out onto the street.

Cab scheduling is done in the second loose-leaf notebook. The notebook, so crammed with paper that the rings barely stay closed, is divided into two sections. The first section has one page for each shift in the next 30 days (there are three shifts per day), organized by shift within each day. The second section contains one page for each cab, organized by cab number. The clerk established the notebook in this manner so that it was possible to not only assign drivers to cabs, but to know which cabs and drivers were on the street for any given shift.

The clerk handles the cab reservation process as follows:

1. A driver requests a cab for a specific shift on a specific day. (A number of drivers have standing reservations—they drive the same cab for the same shift five or six days a week.)
2. The clerk turns first to the driver-history notebook. If the driver's status has changed in any way, the driver is informed. If the Kellys have decided that the driver's record is unsatisfactory, the request for a reservation will be refused.
3. Unless the driver has requested a specific cab, the clerk assigns the driver to a cab. In either case, the driver's name, the date, and the shift are written in the notebook. Before assigning a cab, however, the clerk must check the back portion of the chief mechanic's card file to ensure that the cab is in working condition. Since there is a maximum number of cabs that can be on the road during any given shift, the clerk must also check the front portion of the notebook to be sure that the day and shift in question aren't completely filled. When selecting cabs for drivers who do not request a specific vehicle, the clerk makes an effort to rotate the cabs, ensuring that usage is spread evenly throughout the fleet. Decisions on which cab to assign are generally made by looking at which cab has logged the fewest miles in the given week.
4. Assuming that the reservation can be made, the cab number and driver are transferred to the sheet corresponding to the appropriate day and shift in the front portion of the notebook. The data are also written on the driver's sheet in the driver-history notebook.

Each morning the clerk checks the reservation sheets to determine if enough cabs are scheduled to be on the streets. If the number of cabs is too low, the clerk will begin to call drivers to see if any are interested in working.

When a driver comes in before a shift, he or she requests the keys for the cab from the dispatcher. The dispatcher verifies the reservation by checking the appropriate sheet in the front of the schedule notebook, collects the prepaid cab rental if required, and hands over the keys. The dispatcher must then indicate that the driver has shown up for a reserved shift. The notation is made in three places: on the page for the specific shift for the specific day, on the page for the cab, and on the driver-history page.

Listening to the clerk's description of this procedure, two things occur to you in your role as a systems analyst. First of all, this procedure has been very well thought out. Whoever designed it paid special attention to the ways in which people needed to access the data. On the other hand, while this manual system worked well when the number of cabs was small, the sheer volume of paper required to cope with the increased fleet and increased pool of drivers has made the entire process unmanageable. The process suffers from those problems generally associated with data redundancy—increased storage space and more important, a lack of data integrity.

Now that the interviews are completed, you can draw a data-flow diagram for FTC. Part of that diagram appears in Figures 2.4.1–2.4.4. The figures show the inputs, processes, and outputs for making reservations for shifts, for distributing cabs to drivers as they arrive for reserved shifts, for recording the return of cabs after shifts, for summarizing shift data, and for dispatching cabs to customers.

MEETING WITH MANAGEMENT

While FTC is a small business, its information needs are nonetheless complex. Before you write a requirements document, you would really like some information on what parts of the system are most important to the management. Therefore, you schedule a meeting with Mr. and Mrs. Kelly. At that meeting you identify the major modules within FTC's information system:

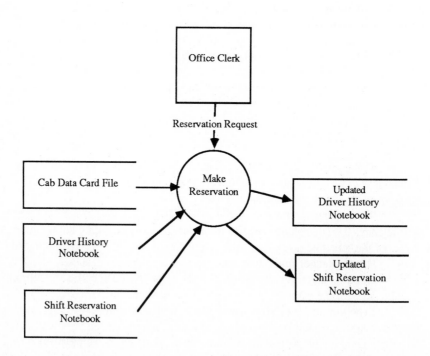

Figure 2.4.1 Data-Flow Diagram for the Federated Taxi Company—Making a Reservation

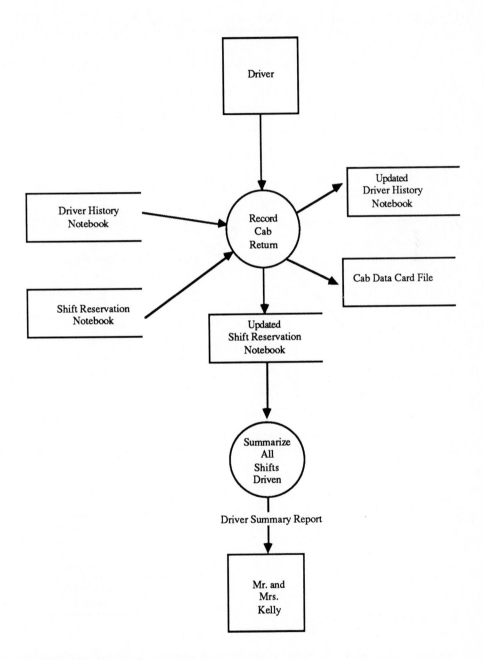

Figure 2.4.2 Data-Flow Diagram for the Federated Taxi Company—Recording the Return of a Cab

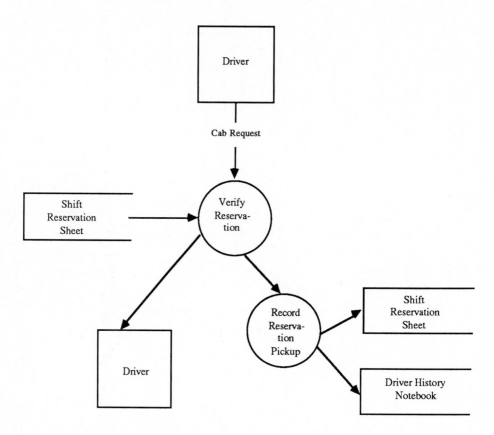

Figure 2.4.3   Data-Flow Diagram for the Federated Taxi Company—Issuing a Cab to a Driver

1. Payroll
2. Cab/Driver scheduling
3. Cab maintenance
4. Driver history
5. Cab dispatching
6. Spare parts inventory
7. Accounts payable
8. Accounts receivable

Not all of these areas are of equal priority in terms of computerized implementation. From what Mrs. Kelly said during your interview with her, payroll is probably the least important at the current time. While dispatching probably could benefit from being computerized, the

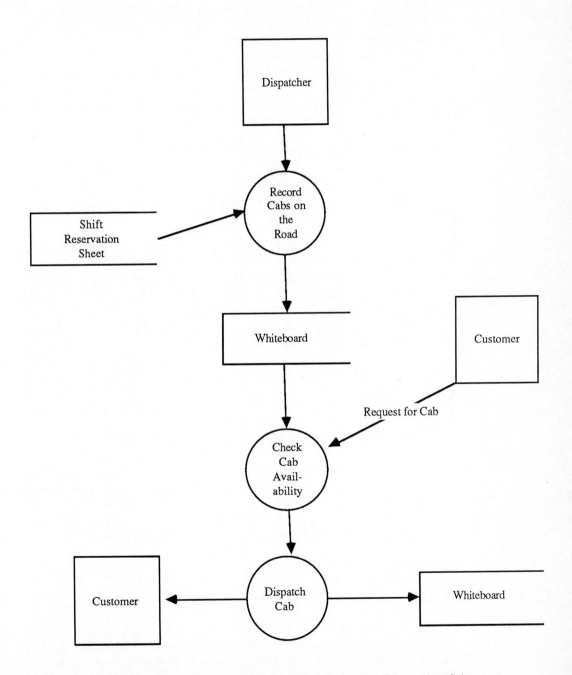

Figure 2.4.4 Data-Flow Diagram for the Federated Taxi Company—Dispatching Cabs

Kellys seem to be reluctant to proceed in that area at this time. Cab maintenance, driver history, and the spare parts inventory would appear to be the most important, and accounts payable and receivable are of slightly less importance.

There is a very important issue that should be considered at this point: one way to ensure that a computerization project will fail is to attempt to computerize an entire organization at one time. Successful system designers propose implementation plans that introduce computers in successive phases. In the case of Federated Taxi, the applications that lend themselves to computers fall into five broad groups:

1. Cab scheduling and maintenance, including driver history
2. Cab dispatching
3. Spare parts inventory
4. Accounting
5. Payroll

Considering the priorities set by the company's owners, the cab scheduling and maintenance is by far the most important and therefore should be implemented first. A computerized inventory system should not be installed until the cab scheduling and maintenance system has been implemented successfully. The accounting functions can be computerized after the inventory. Logically, the cab dispatching should be computerized immediately after the cab scheduling and maintenance functions. However, until the Kellys change their minds about wanting it on the computer, there is nothing that you can do.

Unless the owners come to feel that payroll is not being handled adequately by their manual system, there is no need to include plans for payroll in an implementation schedule. It is essential to realize that sometimes there are processes within an organization that do not need to be computerized. Successful system developers try to be aware of processes that are functioning optimally without computers and generally will propose no modifications in those processes. The old aphorism—if it ain't broke don't fix it—applies in full measure to systems development.

You discuss with the Kellys the problems involved with attempting to implement the entire system. They agree with your recommendation that cab scheduling and maintenance be implemented first. Your requirements document will therefore be limited to the specifics for these two modules, though it will consider carefully where the cab scheduling and maintenance modules will interface with those parts of the system that will be implemented at a later date.

PUTTING TOGETHER THE REQUIREMENTS DOCUMENT

You've decided to organize your requirements document by drawing sample output formats. Along with each desired output, you'll list the inputs needed to produce that output. To organize the document, outputs are documented by the people who will be their primary users.

For the chief mechanic:

1. Screen display of the current status and/or history of a specific cab. A sample screen appears in Figure 2.5.

DATA ITEMS
- Cab number
- Make
- Model
- Year of manufacture
- Date of purchase
- License number
- For each time maintenance is done on the cab
    - Date of work
    - Type of work
    - Odometer reading
- For each accident in which the cab has been involved
    - Date of accident
    - Description of damage incurred
- Summary of condition of the cab
- Cab status (e.g., road-safe or not road-safe)

```
Cab Number: 1Ø6       Make/Model: Checker      Model year: 1968

Plate: 496 AAA        Odometer: 2Ø6777         Status: road-safe




                          MAINTENANCE


DATE               TYPE OF SERVICE
Ø6/12/86           Standard tune-up
Ø6/1Ø/86           Repair right rear tire
Ø3/1Ø/86           Standard tune-up
Ø2/17/86           Replace master brake cylinder
12/11/85           Standard tune-up
12/11/85           Replace seat covers
Ø9/11/85           Standard tune-up
Ø6/15/85           Standard tune-up

                        -MORE-
```

Figure 2.5 Sample Cab-Info Screen

2. Paper listing of those cabs needing regular maintenance (see Figure 2.6)

DATA ITEMS
- Cab number
- License number
- Date of last maintenance
- Type of work last performed
- Date of last tune-up

For the scheduling clerk:

1. Screen display of the current status and/or history of a specific driver (see Figure 2.7)

DATA ITEMS
- Driver name
- Driver address
- Driver phone number
- Chauffeur's license number
- Date chauffeur's license expires
- For each time the driver rents a cab
    - Date and shift
    - Cab number
- For each incident in which the driver is involved
    - Date

```
                  MAINTENANCE LIST
                     Ø7/15/86

              LAST        TYPE OF                 LAST
  CAB#  PLATE#  MAINT      WORK                    TUNE-UP

  1Ø4   356 QLT Ø6/23/86  Replace windshield      Ø4/12/86
  1Ø5   111 ABC Ø4/12/86  Tune-up                 Ø4/12/86
  144   29Ø AAQ Ø4/14/86  Tune-up                 Ø4/14/86
  238   98Ø JAM Ø7/Ø3/86  Replace wiper blades    Ø4/12/86
  378   771 TOW Ø4/14/86  Tune-up                 Ø4/14/86
  404   206 TTL Ø4/14/86  Tune-up                 Ø4/14/86
```

Figure 2.6 Sample Printed Output of Cabs Needing Regular Maintenance

```
Driver: Aaron Wells                        Phone: 617-555-2434

Status: pay after




                              SHIFTS


              Date       Shift     Cab#        Driven

              07/14/86    day       205          no
              07/13/86    day       205          yes
              07/12/86    day       387          yes
              07/11/86    day       205          yes
              07/08/86    day       205          yes
              07/07/86    day       205          yes
              07/07/86    eve       387          yes
              07/06/86    day       205          yes
              07/05/86    day       205          no
                             -MORE-
```

Figure 2.7 Sample Driver-Info Screen

            - Nature of incident (e.g., traffic ticket or accident)

     • Driver status

2. Screen display of the cabs available for a given shift on a given day (see Figure 2.8)

DATA ITEMS

     For each cab with a Cab status of "road-safe" and no reservation for the requested day and shift

     • Cab number
     • License number
     • Number of miles driven in the past week (Note that this is a computed data item. It assumes that the database stores odometer readings for each cab taken at the start of each shift for which the cab is in use.)

3. Screen display of days and shifts available for a specific cab (see Figure 2.9)

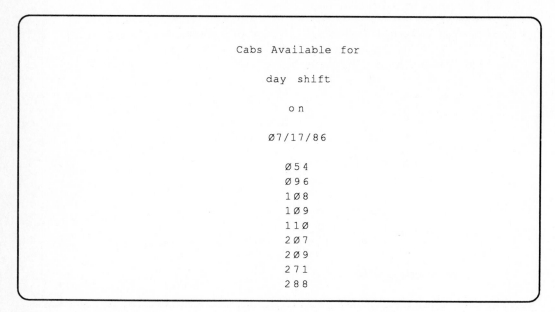

```
                    Cabs Available for

                       day shift

                          o n

                      Ø7/17/86

                         Ø54
                         Ø96
                         1Ø8
                         1Ø9
                         11Ø
                         2Ø7
                         2Ø9
                         271
                         288
```

Figure 2.8 Sample Display of Cabs Available for a Single Date and Shift

```
                            Cab#  Ø51

     Miles last seven days: 189Ø




                      SHIFT  AVAILABILITY


            DATE        DAY        EVENING      NIGHT

            11/12/86     x            x           x
            11/13/86                  x
            11/14/86                  x
            11/15/86                  x           x
            11/16/86     x            x
            11/17/86     x            x           x

                             -MORE-
```

Figure 2.9 Sample Cab-Availability Screen

DATA ITEMS
> Assuming the cab has a Cab status of "road-safe"
> - Date and number of each available shift in the next 12 months
> - Number of miles driven in the past week

4. Screen display of the cabs and drivers scheduled for a given shift on a given day (see Figure 2.10)

DATA ITEMS
> - Date and shift number
> - For each cab that has been reserved,
>> - Cab number
>> - Cab license number
>> - Driver name
>> - Comments about driver

One report for the dispatcher of each shift:

Paper listing of the cabs and drivers scheduled for a given shift on a given day (see Figure 2.11)

```
    SHIFT: Evening        Date: Ø7/17/86



    DRIVER            CAB#      PLATE#          COMMENTS

    Bailey, Max       ØØ2       345 YAO         pay before
    Baker, MaryAnn    ØØ6       997 IUF         pay after
    Lewis, John       Ø45       867 POP         pay before - ticket Ø7/14/86
    Miller, Pat       1Ø8       76Ø PLP         pay after
    Miller, Phyllis   215       776 IKL         pay before
    Phong, Quen       318       333 IPO         pay after
    Wong, David       341       285 KKN         pay after
    Young, Leslie     49Ø       249 LKL         pay before
    Zilog, Charlie    492       888 IOA         pay after
```

Figure 2.10 Sample Cab Schedule Screen

```
                    Shift  Schedule  for
                     August  12,  1986
                          Evening

Cab # Plate       #Driver              Notes

023   256 POZ     Erlich, Martin       2 tickets last week— give
                                       warning
025   808 IIK     Kowalski, Pete       pay after
045   008 IKL     French, Janice       first shift—pay before
106   802 UWQ     Thieu, Lin Van       pay after
277   172 OIY     Jackson, Rafael      pay before
318   181 JHG     Kolson, Jan          pay after (notify of status
                                       change)
```

Figure 2.11   Sample Shift Schedule

DATA ITEMS

Same as for the screen display of cabs and drivers scheduled for a given shift on a given day.

While there are many kinds of summary output that can be created from the data pool under design for Federated Taxi, the weekly driver summary report examined by the owners is of vital importance. Since that information is used for decision making on a regular basis, it should be included in the original design. The report might appear as in Figure 2.12. The data items required to construct it are:

- Driver name
- For each shift the driver has completed
    - Date and shift number
    - Cab number
    - Miles driven
    - Comments (e.g., notes about incidents, excessive cab wear noticed by maintenance personnel, etc.)

The data items listed for each of the eight outputs that Federated Taxi's database system will provide are only those that will be visible on either a CRT screen or a piece of paper. However, there are "hidden" data items that, while they may not appear as an output item, must be retained in the database in order to produce visible outputs. For example, in order to maintain a driver's history record and to compile the driver history summary report, there must be a data item that indicates whether or not a driver actually drove a shift for which he or she reserved a cab. In order to compute the number of miles a cab travels in

```
                    Driver  Summary
                 08-20-86 to 08-26-86


Driver           Date    Shift Cab#   Miles  Comments

Abelman,  John   08-20   day   356    204
                 08-21   day   356    287    speeding ticket
                 08-22   day   356    225
                 08-25   day   356    197
                 08-26   day   356    201


Erlich,  Martin  08-20   eve   244    156
                 08-22   eve   244    197
                 08-23   eve   244    106    rear-ended a bus
                 08-24   eve   018    188
                 08-25   eve   018    057    stuck in a freeway jam



Jackson, Rafael  08-20   eve   013    252
                 08-21   eve   013    233    rear seat fabric slashed
                 08-22   eve   013    211
                 08-23   eve   013    290    one out-of-town run
                 08-24   day   029    106    too tired for whole shift
```

Figure 2.12 Sample Weekly Driver Summary Report

each shift or in a given week, the database must also store the odometer readings of each cab at the beginning of each shift.

The definition of the output formats and the identification of the additional "hidden" data items needed to create those outputs provides enough information for you, the systems analyst, describe the pool of data items that will form the shared data pool upon which the database system will be based. There are three general groups of data:

1. Data items that describe a cab (see Table 2.1)
2. Data items that describe a driver (see Table 2.2)
3. Data items that describe cab reservations (see Table 2.3)

Note that while the same data items may appear in more than one of the three data item groups, this does not mean that the data must be stored redundantly; rather, this only indicates data that will be shared.

The outputs which have been described above are predictable outputs that will be used repeatedly. However, there will certainly be times when either the chief mechanic or the

Table 2.1
Data Items Describing Cabs for the Federated Taxi Company

Data Item Name	Contents
CABNUM	A unique number assigned to the cab and painted on its side
MAKE	Name of the manufacturer
MODEL	Model name
YEAR	Model year
PURDATE	Date cab was acquired by Federated Taxi
LICNUM	License number
CURODOM	Odometer reading at end of last shift
MAINDATE	Date some type of maintenance was performed
MAINTYPE	Type of maintenance performed
MAINODOM	Odometer reading when maintenance was performed
INCIDATE	Date of incident (traffic citation or accident) in which cab was involved
INCITYPE	Type of incident
DETAILS	Details about an incident
CONDITN	Summary of condition of cab
CABSTAT	Status of cab (either "road-safe" or "not road-safe")

Table 2.2
Data Items Describing Drivers for the Federated Taxi Company

Data Item Name	Contents
DRVNUM	Unique number assigned to each driver
DRVNAM	Driver's name
DRVSTR	Street address
DRVCSZ	City, state, and zip code
DRVPHONE	Phone number
DRVLIC	Chauffeur's license number
DRVLEXD	Date chaffeur's license expires
WKDATE	Date for which a cab is reserved
WKSHIFT	Shift for which a cab is reserved
CABNUM	Cab number for which a reservation has been placed
WKFLAG	"True" if driver works a shift he or she has reserved, "False" if he or she does not
INCIDATE	Date on which a driving incident occurred
INCITYPE	Description of the incident
DETAILS	Specific info about an incident
DRVSTAT	Driver status (generally either "pay-first," "pay-after," or "do not reserve")

Table 2.3

Data Items Describing Cab Reservations for the Federated Taxi Company

Data Item Name	Contents
CABNUM	Cab number
LICNUM	License number
WKDATE	Date for which the cab is reserved
WKSHIFT	Shift for which the cab is reserved
DRVNAME	Name of driver who has reserved the cab
WKFLAG	"True" if the driver completes the shift, "False" if he or she does not
ODOMRDG1	Odometer reading at the beginning of a shift
ODOMRDG2	Odometer reading at the end of a shift

scheduling clerk have a need for information which either cannot be predicted or which may never be needed again. If the Kellys wish these two employees to be able to satisfy such information needs on their own, then the mechanic and the clerk must be trained in the syntax of whatever query language their DBMS supports.

The Kellys must also be told that the system will work most efficiently if the dispatchers are trained to input data indicating which drivers have driven their shifts, the odometer readings at the start and end of shifts, and the amount of cab rental paid. If they are still adamant that the dispatchers not interact with the computer at all, then some alternative procedure must be established to ensure that the data are captured on paper and kept for the clerk to handle during normal business hours.

SUMMARY

Database design is more than identifying an optimal way of arranging the data items in a database. It is part of a larger set of activities known as the systems development cycle. The systems development cycle is used by organizations to implement successful computer systems.

The steps in the systems development cycle can be described as follows:

1. Conduct a needs assessment (systems analysis) which includes evaluating the current system and identifying how it should be modified to meet the needs of the organization.
2. Generate general alternatives strategies for remedying the weaknesses identified during the needs assessment; evaluate the alternatives and select one for implementation.

3. Create a detailed systems design based on the selected alternative.

4. Implement the system.

Once an organization begins the cycle, it should continue indefinitely. Effective systems designs include provisions for periodic re-evaluation.

Systems development projects are usually coordinated by systems analysts. Systems analysts use interviewing and data-gathering techniques during the needs assessment to create a picture of the current system—to identify where it succeeds and where it should be modified to better meet the organization's information needs.

A systems analysis is really solving a business problem. The process is therefore amenable to a general problem-solving model such as IPO (Input-Process-Output). A designer using IPO will first identify the outputs the system should provide. He or she will then determine what input is necessary to produce the desired outputs. Finally, the designer specifies the process to be used to transform the inputs to the outputs.

Successful systems development projects include open lines of communication between the person or people developing the system and corporate management. They do not attempt to implement an entire system at once, but instead assign priorities to parts of the system. The small parts of the systems are implemented in order of their assigned priority. Successful projects also employ the parallel method of implementation: the new system is run in tandem with the old until it is clear that the new system is accurate and reliable enough to discontinue the old.

REFERENCES

Burch, John G., Jr., Felix R. Strater, and Gary Grudnitski. (1983) *Information Systems: Theory and Practice.* 3d ed. New York: Wiley.

Edwards, Perry. (1985) *Systems Analysis, Design, and Development with Structured Concepts.* New York: Holt, Rinehart and Winston.

Fitzgerald, Jerry, Ardra F. Fitzgerald, and Warren D. Stallings, Jr., (1981) *Fundamentals of Systems Analysis.* 2d ed. New York: Wiley.

Nordbottom, Joan C. (1985) *The Analysis and Design of Computer-Based Information Systems.* Boston: Houghton-Mifflin.

Ostle, Jud. (1985) *Information Systems Analysis and Design.* Minneapolis: Burgess Communications.

THINGS TO THINK ABOUT

1. You have been hired as a consultant by an independent drug store to help computerize the pharmacy. The owner doesn't know anything about the systems development cycle. In your own words, explain to the owner the steps you will take to design the system.

2. The owner of the local fish store has been shopping and has purchased a microcomputer with 640K RAM and a 20 Mb hard drive. For software, she has purchased a word processor, a spreadsheet, and a relational DBMS (the dealer told her those were the most widely used business applications). After making the purchases, she has asked you to use the DBMS to computerize her business. What problems does this situation present to a systems designer? What kind of mistake has the fish store owner made?

3. The owner of the drug store in question one has asked you to design and implement a database system for accounts receivable, accounts payable, inventory, and prescription records. The owner wants the entire system installed at the same time. Is this a good idea? Why or why not?

4. Many systems development projects fail because of a lack of communication. In what phases of a systems development project is communication an essential element? Between which groups of people should the communication occur?

5. Not everyone is cut out to be a systems analyst. Make a list of the skills and personality traits that, in your opinion, characterize the ideal systems analyst. Is this a job you would like? Why or why not?

6. IPO (Input-Process-Output) is a general problem-solving model; it doesn't apply only to the design of a database system. To what activities in your daily life might you apply IPO to help you solve a problem or achieve some goal?

EXERCISES

In Appendixes A and B you will find transcripts of interviews conducted during the needs assessment phase of a systems development project for two different organizations, the University Archaeological Museum and the office of Margaret Holmes, D.M.D. Using the information contained in the interviews, do the following:

1. Identify the major application areas in which a database system will be useful.
2. Assign developmental priorities to the application areas.
3. Design output formats for the major applications.
4. List the data items that must be stored in the database in order to produce the outputs you have designed.

3

Data Models

CHAPTER OUTLINE:

CHAPTER OBJECTIVES

After reading this chapter, you will:

1. Understand the idea of a logical data model
2. Be familiar with the traditional hierarchical and network data models
3. Understand thoroughly the basic concepts behind the relational data model

LOGICAL DATA MODELS

A *data model* is a framework used to describe the logical relationships between data in a database. For example, when designing a database for Small Bank, we need some way to indicate that a particular account belongs to a particular customer. That ownership of an account by a customer constitutes a logical relationship between the data item CUSTOMER NAME and the data item ACCOUNT NUMBER.

It is important to realize that data models are not concerned with the specific values that a data item might assume. They deal with data items as generic entities which might, at some later date, assume any number of specific values. To distinguish between actual data values and the generic term describing a data item, data values are often spoken of as *occurrences* or *instances* of a data item type.

There are three major data models:

1. Hierarchical (or tree)
2. Networks (simple and complex)
3. Relational

Most DBMSs will support a single data model, though some mini and mainframe packages do support two (these are generally older hierarchical or network systems which have added relational features in an attempt to bring them up-to-date). Whichever data model the software supports is used to describe database schemas.

The majority of microcomputer databases are based on the relational model. It is the newest of the data models (it was first described in 1970) and the theory is still maturing. Though it is not strictly necessary for someone working with a relational database to be familiar with the earlier models, it will enhance the ability to capture the meaning in a database environment if the person understands how data relationships are described in hierarchies and networks and why many people consider the relational model to be both simpler and more powerful. If you wish to read beyond this text about any of the data models, see Bradley, 1983; Cardenas, 1985; or McFadden and Hoffer, 1985.

THE HIERARCHICAL MODEL

Figure 3.1 presents a *hierarchy*, or *tree* structure, that Small Bank might use to describe the relationships between its branches, their customers, customer accounts, and transactions processed by each account. This drawing is referred to as an *occurrence diagram*, since each box represents actual data values. The boxes represent *record types*, each of which is given a name. A record type describes a single entity about which the database is storing data. Within each record type are any number of fields, though the field names are rarely included.

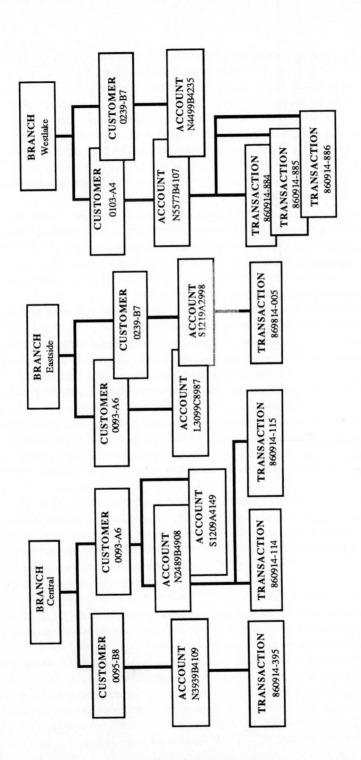

Figure 3.1 Occurrences of a Hierarchy

The lines connecting the boxes represent data relationships. In Figure 3.1, any record occurrence is related to only one record occurrence above it (i.e., at a higher level in the hierarchy). However, it may have no, one, or more occurrences below it (i.e., at a lower level in the hierarchy). Hierarchies are limited to relationships of exactly this type. Notice, for example, that customer 0093-A6 has accounts at both Central and Eastside branches. Because occurrences in a hierarchy can only be related to one occurrence at a higher level, there is no way to take a single occurrence of customer 0093-A6's record and relate it to two different branches. The only alternative is to duplicate the record occurrence, which is exactly how the situation is handled in Figure 3.1. This restriction means that hierarchies contain a significant amount of redundant data.

Record occurrences in a hierarchy may be *path dependent*. A path-dependent record has no identity independent of its parent in the hierarchy. For example, if transaction numbers are unique only within an account, then a transaction record has no meaning unless we know which account is its parent. In other words, a path dependency exists between transaction and account. This situation is sometimes referred to as *attribute inheritance*. The transaction record *inherits* the account number from its parent.

Customer record occurrences, however, can be identified by their customer numbers alone. There is no need to know the branches at which a customer has accounts to completely describe a customer. In this case, there is no path dependency between the branch and customer records. The customer record does not inherit the branch name from its parent. The concept of path dependencies also applies to the network data models.

Occurrence diagrams like the one in Figure 3.1 are of limited usefulness in describing database structures for two reasons: (1) when the database acquires more than a handful of data, an occurrence diagram becomes unreasonably large; (2) an occurrence diagram shows only data which are actually stored in the database; it cannot demonstrate that the overall data model for the organization includes types of data for which actual values may not yet be available. Therefore, we need a better technique for generalizing what data can be stored in a database.

A generalization of the occurrence diagram from Figure 3.1 appears in Figure 3.2. The elements of the drawing make up what is known as a *Bachman diagram*. Bachman diagrams, created by Charles Bachman (Bachman, 1969), are a common tool used to graphically describe both hierarchical and network databases. Each box indicates that the database *may* store data in a given record type; it in no way indicates exactly what data are actually present in the database. The lines connecting the boxes indicate data relationships, which are usually given names. It is important to realize that these lines are describing relationships between occurrences. Since it is possible to have more than one relationship between the same two record types, relationship names allow a user to determine exactly which relationship should be used to process a particular query.

The exact nature of the data relationship is indicated by the arrows in the relationship lines. In a hierarchy, there will always be one arrow pointing up. This means that each occurrence of a given record type is related to exactly one occurrence of the record type above it. For example, in Figure 3.2, any given account belongs to only one customer (the customer is the account's *parent*); each customer occurrence belongs to only one branch (the branch is the customer's *parent*). If a customer has accounts at more than one branch, the

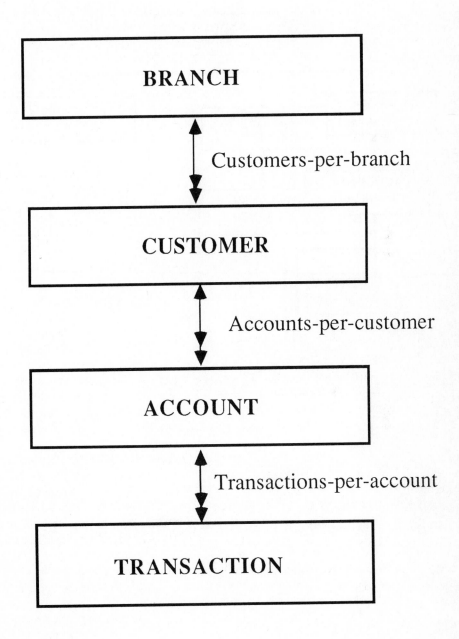

Figure 3.2 A Hierarchy to Represent Small Bank's Data

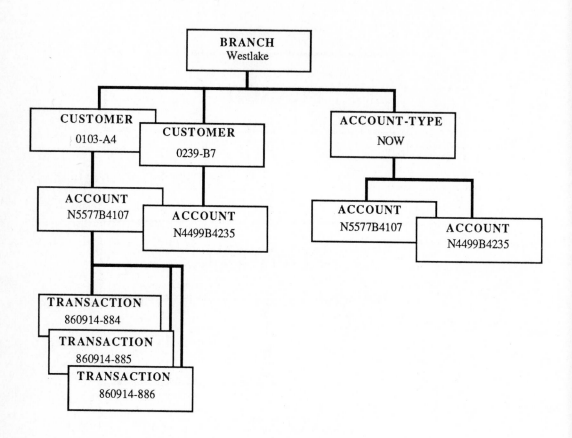

Figure 3.3 Occurrences of a Hierarchy with Multiple Child Record Types

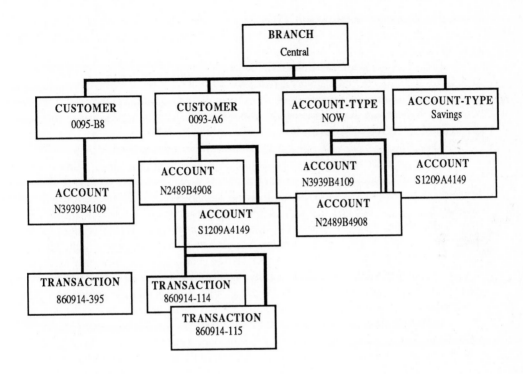

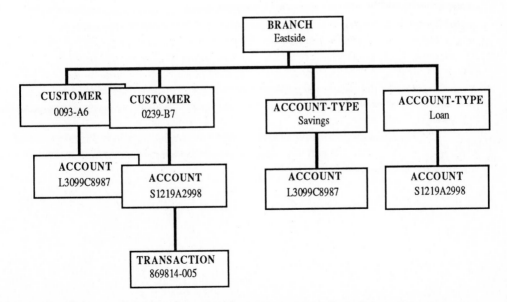

Figure 3.3 (cont.) Occurrences of a Hierarchy with Multiple Child Record Types

customer record must be duplicated. (There is no way to link a single customer record occurrence with more than one branch.) By the same token, each transaction record applies to only one account.

However, each relationship in the hierarchy shows two arrows going down. The double arrows indicate that each occurrence of a record type may be related to zero or more occurrences of the record type below it. For example, any given customer may have many accounts (accounts are the *children* of the customers); each account may have many transactions records related to it (transactions are *children* of accounts).

There is a problem with using a hierarchy to describe Small Bank's data. Certainly it is not realistic to assume that every account belongs to just one customer. What about joint accounts? In fact, the relationship between accounts and customers is what we call a *many-to-many* relationship; each customer has many accounts and each account can belong to more than one customer.   Because hierarchies limit children record occurrences to a single parent, they cannot directly represent many-to-many relationships. If we solve the problem by duplicating the account record occurrences for each customer that owns a joint account, we must also duplicate all the transaction records for each account.   Not only will we have introduced a large amount of redundancy into the database, but processing will become difficult. How might monthly statements be processed? How would an application program identify multiple owners of the same account?

Hierarchies have another limitation in addition to the inability to represent directly many-to-many relationships. Assume that Small Bank not only wants to associate accounts with their owners but would also like to classify accounts by their type. In other words, each occurrence of an account record should not only be related to a customer but to an account type as well. However, the hierarchical data model forbids any record occurrence to be related to more than any one record above it. The only solution is to store two copies of each account record, one of which belongs to a customer, the other to an account type.   In Figure 3.3, you'll see an occurrence diagram that captures the account type data. Notice that while the account record occurrences are duplicated, the transaction record occurrences aren't. The occurrence diagram can be generalized by a Bachman diagram (see Figure 3.4).

By their nature, hierarchies must include a great deal of redundant data. They are therefore more prone to data integrity and consistency problems than databases built on other data models.

The major hierarchical implementation is IBM's IMS, first introduced in 1964 (see IBM Form GH20-1260 for details). IMS runs on IBM mainframes and is widely used throughout the business community.

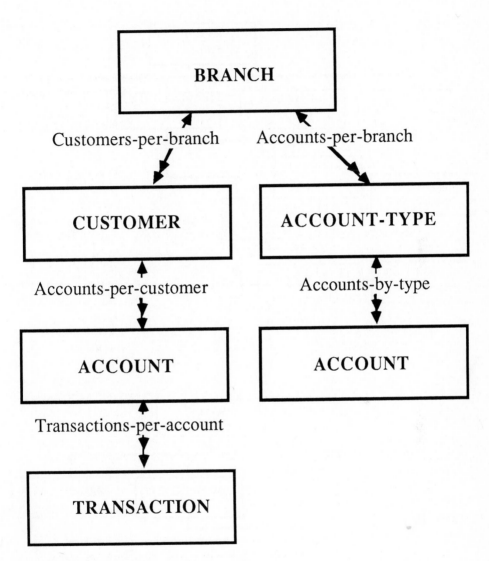

Figure 3.4 Hierarchy with Multiple Child Record Types

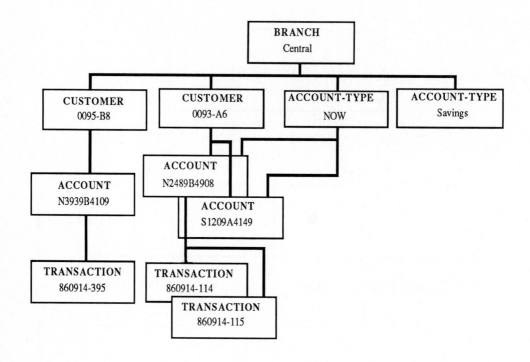

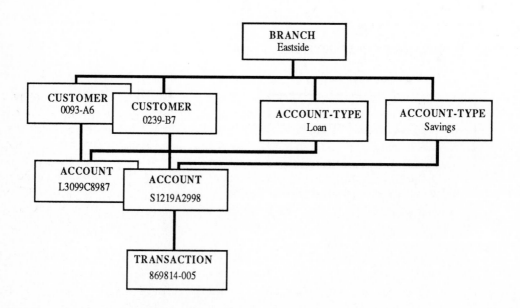

Figure 3.5 Occurrences of a Simple Network

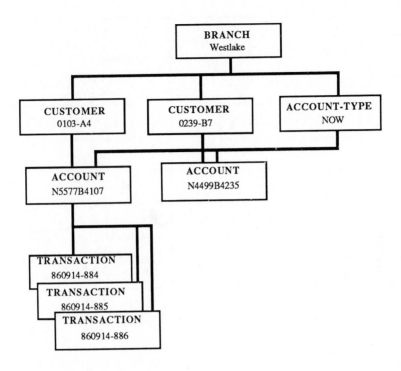

Figure 3.5 (cont.) Occurrences of a Simple Network

THE NETWORK MODELS

Network databases come in two flavors—simple and complex. Networks allow an occurrence of a record type to belong to more than one other record occurrence. In other words, an occurrence can not only have multiple children, but it can have multiple parents as well. It is the nature of the multiple parentage that determines whether a network is simple or complex.

An occurrence diagram of a simple network for Small Bank appears in Figure 3.5. There is one major difference between this diagram and the hierarchy in Figure 3.3; the account records aren't duplicated. Instead, each occurrence of an account record is related to both a customer record occurrence and an account-type record occurrence.

In Figure 3.6 (the Bachman diagram for the simple network from the occurrence diagram in Figure 3.5) look carefully at the record type ACCOUNT. You will see that there is a line directly relating account records with both customers and account types. This is what makes this data model a simple network rather than a hierarchy. Each account has two parents and each parent is of a different record type. All of the relationships within the simple network are one-to-many (i.e., they are *simple* relationships).

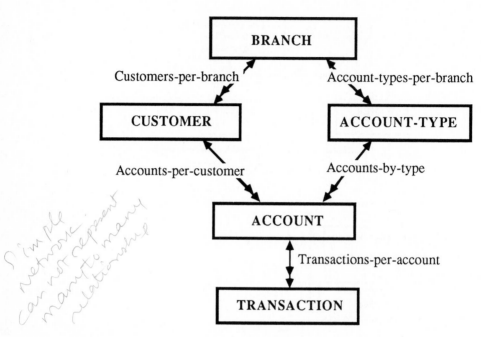

Figure 3.6 A Simple Network for Small Bank's Data

Like a hierarchy, a simple network cannot directly represent many-to-many relationships. Therefore, while some data redundancy is eliminated by allowing multiple parentage of different record types, the simple network may still have to resort to duplicate account records to handle the situation where a single account belongs to more than one customer or where customers have accounts at more than one branch. (A better solution to this problem appears shortly.)

Complex networks do allow direct representation of many-to-many relationships. An occurrence of a complex network for Small Bank can be seen in Figure 3.7. This diagram removes all data redundancy (i.e, no record occurrences are duplicated). If you look closely, you'll notice that two accounts are joint accounts and that one customer has accounts at two branches.

The Bachman diagram for the occurrence in Figure 3.7 appears in Figure 3.8. There are double arrows going in both directions between accounts and customers and between customers and branches; these are complex relationships. Complex networks, since they permit many-to-many relationships, can eliminate all data redundancy. In doing so, however, data relationships tend to become increasingly intricate. The task of following relationships through the database to retrieve a specific piece of data places a great burden on both the DBMS and the applications programmer.

While the data model in Figures 3.7 and 3.8 eliminates all data redundancy, it has a major problem in terms of capturing the meaning of the database environment. If you consider the occurrence diagram carefully, you will see that it is no longer possible to deduce

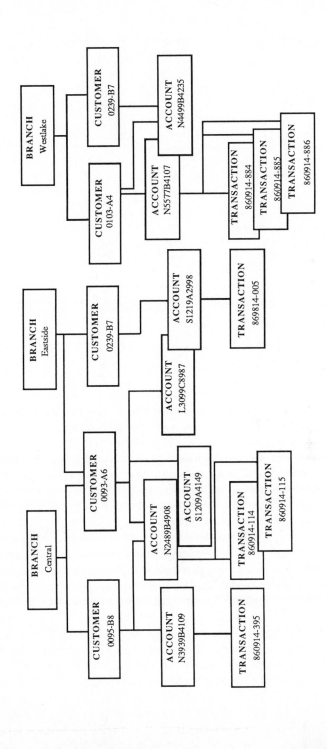

Figure 3.7 Occurrences of a Complex Network (Branch—Account Relationship is Lost)

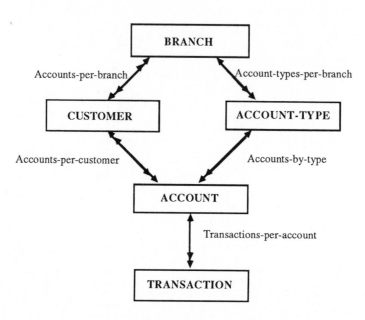

Figure 3.8   A Complex Network for Small Bank's Data (Branch–Account Relationship is Lost)

which account is carried at which branch. By eliminating the redundant customer occurrences, we have also removed some meaning from the database. In this situation, the database will provide better information if we leave the duplicated customer records. In Figure 3.9 (an occurrence diagram) and Figure 3.10 (a Bachman diagram of Figure 3.9), the complex relationship between accounts and customers has been retained, but the relationship between customers and branches has been returned to a simple relationship. This data model preserves the information about which account is carried at which branch and may therefore be a better data model for Small Bank, even though it does contain some data redundancy.

There is, however, another technique for dealing with the problem presented by Figures 3.7 and 3.8. This solution will also transform a complex network into a simple network, removing many-to-many relationships and replacing them with one-to-many relationships. The idea is to create a new record type for each many-to-many relationship in a data model. This new record type, known as an *intersection* record if it contains data items or a *link* record if it does not, is placed between the two records in a many-to-many relationship.

Figure 3.11 is a Bachman diagram of the complex network in Figure 3.8. There is now a record type between the branch and customer records (BRANCH-CUSTOMER) and another between the customer and account (CUSTOMER-ACCOUNT) records. Each many-to-many relationship has been replaced by *two* one-to-many relationships and an intersection record.

Let's look more closely at the relationship between branches and customers. There will be one occurrence of the BRANCH-CUSTOMER record for each branch at which a

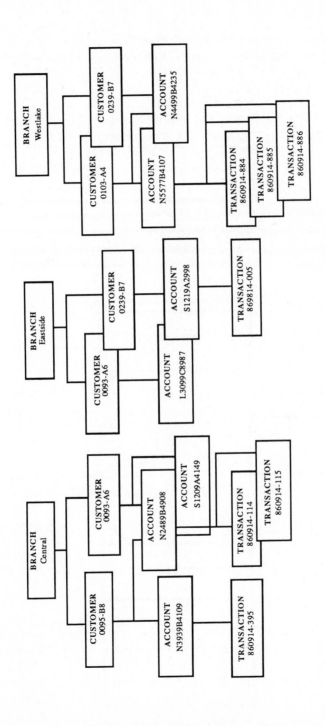

Figure 3.9 Occurrences of a Complex Network (Branch—Account Relationship is Retained)

customer has an account. Put another way, there will be one occurrence of BRANCH-CUSTOMER for each customer who has an account at a branch. To find all the customers served by a given branch, a DBMS will:

1. Find the branch record occurrence
2. Find the first BRANCH-CUSTOMER record that is a child of the branch record
3. Find the customer record that is the parent of the BRANCH-CUSTOMER record
4. Find the next BRANCH-CUSTOMER record
5. Repeat steps three and four until there are no more BRANCH-CUSTOMER records

This process is often called *database navigation*. It refers to threading through the relationships in a hierarchy or network data model to locate needed information.

The contents of an intersection record will vary. Some DBMSs permit them to be totally empty (i.e., they contain no data items). In that case, they are merely link records that indicate a relationship between their two parent records. Often, however, it makes sense

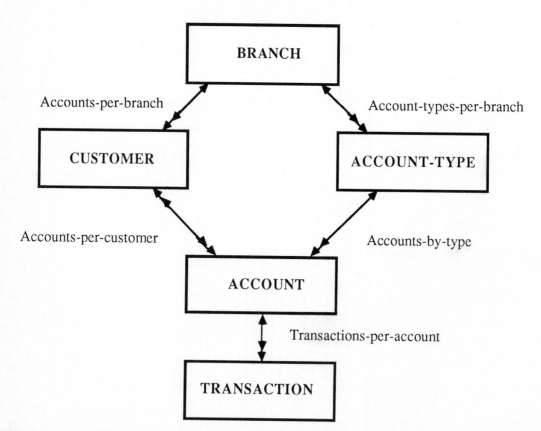

Figure 3.10 A Complex Network for Small Bank's Data (Branch–Account Relationship is Retained)

to duplicate the keys of the parent records in the intersection record. BRANCH-CUSTOMER, for example, might contain the branch name and the customer number. The presence of the duplicate keys can speed up query processing by cutting down the number of records that must be retrieved to answer an information request. In the query described above (listing all customers at a single branch), step three can be eliminated entirely if the customer number is present in the intersection record.

Intersection records are used to capture data that are meaningless except in the context of a relationship between two entities. These data, called *intersection data*, are usually associated with many-to-many relationships. For example, assume that Small Bank wants to keep records on its supply purchases. Supplies are ordered from many vendors; each vendor

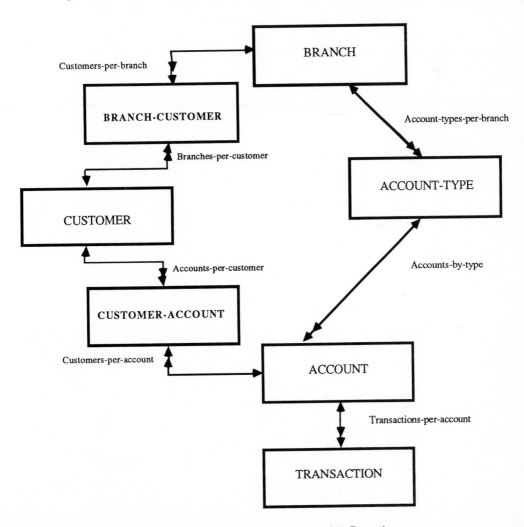

Figure 3.11 Making a Complex Network Simple with Intersection Records

can provide many supplies.   The price that Small Bank must pay for any given supply varies from vendor to vendor. In other words, it depends on the relationship between a given
vendor and a given supply. The situation is diagrammed in Figure 3.12.

Where should the price be recorded? It can't be part of the supply record, since there
isn't a single price for a given supply. It also can't be part of the vendor record, since a
vendor doesn't charge a single price for all its wares. If, however, an intersection record is
introduced to change the many-to-many relationship into one-to-many relationships, the
price can be kept in that intersection record (see Figure 3.13). Each occurrence of the intersection record indicates that a given supply can be ordered from a given vendor. While the
price isn't related to either the supply or the vendor, it is related to the supply/vendor relationship.

There are two special kinds of relationships between records that can occur in networks. One is known as a *loop*, the other as a *cycle*. Figure 3.14 expands the supply-
ordering portion of Small Bank's database. In this situation, each branch orders supplies
individually. Supplies come from many vendors and each vendor supplies many branches.
This diagram contains a cycle, since the relationship from the lowest level in the network
cycles around to the top. Though each of the relationships are many-to-many, they can be

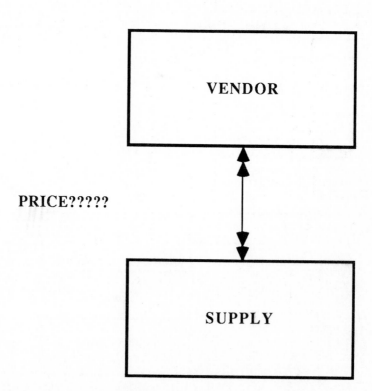

Figure 3.12   Small Bank's Supply Line

reduced to one-to-many relationships with intersection records. Cycles, therefore, can be handled by DBMSs that use either complex or simple networks.

A loop occurs when a record type is related to itself. Figure 3.15 contains a portion of Small Bank's personnel database. This Bachman diagram is designed to capture data about supervisor/supervisee relationships. In other words, some employee record occurrences are parent occurrences (the supervisors); other employee record occurrences are child occurrences (the supervisees). The same employee can be both a supervisor and a supervisee. DBMSs based on complex networks can handle loops; not all simple networks can do so.

Because complex networks are difficult to program, there are few complex network DBMSs in wide distribution. However, simple networks have proven to be a good compromise between hierarchies and complex networks. The national standard for a database is a simple network. It was developed by the CODASYL committee, the same people who created COBOL; their first recommendations were submitted in 1971 (see CODASYL, 1971; CODASYL, 1978; and Olle, 1980), though simple networks have been around since the mid sixties. DBMSs based on the CODASYL model even today form the majority of installed business database systems that run on mainframes and minis. One of the most widely used implementations is IDMS, a product of the Cullinet corporation (Cullinet, 1982).

The basic structure in a CODASYL database is the *set*. A set is a two-level tree (hierarchy) with one parent record type and one or more child record types. The parent record type is known as the *owner* of the set; the children are *members*. Because CODASYL databases are simple networks, any given member occurrence can be related to one owner

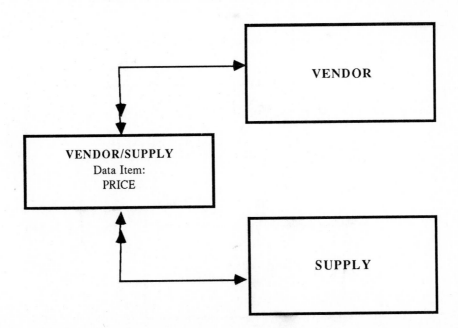

Figure 3.13 Small Bank's Supply Line—Capturing the Price in an Intersection Record

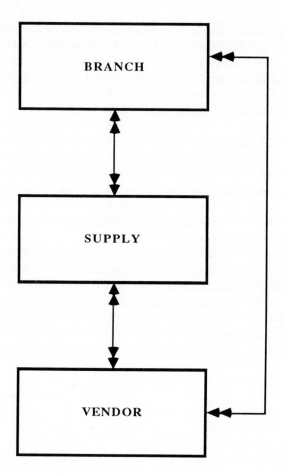

Figure 3.14 Small Bank's Supply Line by Branch—A Cycle Within a Network

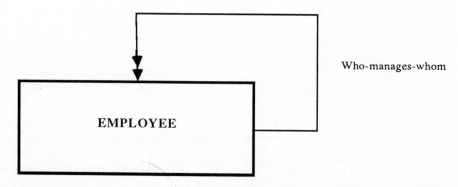

Figure 3.15 Recording Who Supervises Whom—A Loop Within a Network

occurrence in a given set. However, member occurrences can have two owners, as long as they are in different sets. The same record occurrence can also be a member of one set or more sets and the owner of other sets. The combination of these two allows the CODASYL database to build the simple network from the two-level trees.

Figure 3.16 shows the seven CODASYL sets needed to implement Small Bank's accounts database. The sets are:

1. Customers-per-branch
    - Owner: BRANCH
    - Member: BRANCH-CUSTOMER
2. Branches-per-customer
    - Owner: CUSTOMER
    - Member: BRANCH-CUSTOMER
3. Accounts-per-customer
    - Owner: CUSTOMER
    - Member: CUSTOMER-ACCOUNT
4. Customers-per-account
    - Owner: ACCOUNT
    - Member: CUSTOMER-ACCOUNT
5. Transactions-per-account
    - Owner: ACCOUNT
    - Member: TRANSACTION
6. Accounts-by-type
    - Owner: ACCOUNT-TYPE
    - Member: ACCOUNT
7. Account-types-per-branch
    - Owner: BRANCH
    - Member: ACCOUNT-TYPE

When you look at Figure 3.16, remember that the physical placement of the record types in the diagram has nothing to do with whether a record is an owner or member of a set. For example, the intersection record CUSTOMER-ACCOUNT is physically above its owner, ACCOUNT, in the customers-per-account set (set #4). The reason ACCOUNT is below its member is a purely practical one; there was no way to draw the diagram with all owner record types physically above their members and retain any clarity in the drawing.

While the network and hierarchical data models were adequate, in practice, to capture the meaning of most database environments, by the late sixties there were those working in the area of database design theory who believed that the existing models were unnecessarily complex and unnatural. Networks and hierarchies did not live up to their promise of physical-logical data independence; often the command used to retrieve a piece of data was determined by how the data had been physically stored. Developing and maintaining such systems required extensive programmer resources. Dissatisfaction with these models lead to the development of an alternative data model, the relational model.

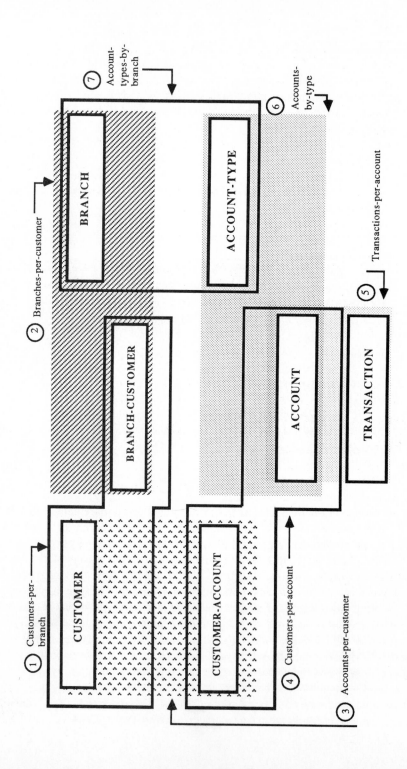

Figure   3.16   CODASYL Sets Needed to Implement Small Bank's Accounts Database

THE RELATIONAL MODEL

The relational model was first proposed by E.F. Codd in 1970 (Codd, 1970). Codd took most of his ideas from mathematics. In mathematics, a *relation* is a table with a very precise definition. For most people, however, knowledge of the rigorous math isn't essential to being able to design good databases.

A relational database views all data as if they were stored in flat, two-dimensional tables comprised of columns and rows. As an example, consider Figure 3.17. The table in that figure contains data about Small Bank's branches, customers, accounts, and account transactions. The table itself—not the data it holds—is the relation. When a table holds data, it is called an *instance* of a relation, since any given relation can theoretically hold an infinite variety of data values. An instance of a relation is much like occurrences of records in network and hierarchical databases.

A relational database is made up of a collection of relations. Logically, each table is a separate entity. Some relational DBMSs store each relation as a separate file (e.g., *dBase III Plus*). Others put the data for all relations in the database in a single file or in a set of files completely unrelated to the logical structure (e.g., *R:base System V* and *Oracle*). Regardless of how the data are physically stored, the relations are logically separate tables.

The tables that are actually stored by a relational database are called *base tables*. During processing, the DBMS may create other tables that are not stored on disk but are retained in main memory only until the application using them finishes. These temporary tables are often referred to as *virtual tables*.

Relations have a number of distinguishing characteristics. First of all, each relation has a name. In Figure 3.17, the relation might be called ACTIVITY, since it contains data on activity against Small Bank's accounts. Relation names are arbitrary, but generally they reflect the type of data stored in the relation.

A relation is made up of a collection of *attributes*. An attribute is a data item that describes an entity about which data is to be stored. When you look at a relation, the attributes form the columns. In Figure 3.17, BRANCH, CUSTOMER, ACCOUNT#, TRANSACTION#, and AMOUNT are attributes. Each attribute has a name which is generally suggestive of the data that attribute will contain.

The range of data values that are permitted for any given attribute are known as its *domain*. For example, the domain for the attribute AMOUNT is numbers expressed in the format ±XX,XXX,XXX.XX, since all amounts are expressed as dollars and cents. The domain for CUSTOMER is all characters in the English language; there is no way to define the values that comprise people's names more narrowly.

A domain is an example of a *constraint* on a relation. As you will remember from Chapter 2, a constraint is a restriction, or rule, that governs which data can be stored in a relation. You will be introduced to other constraints in this chapter.

Each row in a relation is called a *tuple*. Duplicate tuples are not permitted. It is important to realize that while the rule against duplicate tuples exists as part of relational

Primary Key →

BRANCH	CUSTOMER	ACCOUNT#	TRANSACTION#	AMOUNT
Central	0084-C5	S1304AC980	860201-146	+100.00
Central	0084-C5	N2589DF332	860201-147	-25.00
Central	0084-C5	N2589DF332	860201-148	-52.50
Central	0084-C5	N2589DF332	860202-149	+1500.00
Central	0084-C5	S1304AC980	860202-150	+100.00
Eastside	0007-A1	N3588DF246	860202-151	+2599.00
Eastside	0007-A1	N3588DF246	860202-152	-25.00
Eastside	0007-A1	N3588DF246	860203-153	-10.00
Central	0852-A1	S8045AC123	860203-154	+525.00
Central	0111-B4	N2938DF888	860203-155	-824.00
Central	0111-B4	N2938DF888	860203-156	-115.00
Westlake	0084-C5	L4512BE345	860203-157	+190.25
Westlake	0331-A4	N2714DF498	860203-158	-190.25
Westlake	0331-A4	N2714DF498	860203-159	-165.99
Westlake	0331-A4	S3456AC876	860204-160	+25.00
Eastside	0007-A1	N3588DF246	860204-161	-40.99
Eastside	0329-B6	N2287DF309	860204-162	-886.00
Eastside	0329-B6	N2287DF309	860204-163	+1920.23

Figure   3.17   A Relation Containing Small Bank's Transaction Data—Transaction Numbers Are Unique

database theory, that does not mean that relational DBMSs will automatically ensure that each tuple is unique; it may be up to the user or application programmer to enforce this constraint.

PRIMARY KEYS

Each relation in a relational database has a *primary key*. A primary key is a single attribute or a combination of attributes whose values uniquely identify each tuple in the relation. In other words, while the values of other attributes may be repeated in the relation, primary keys must be unique.

For an example, refer again to Figure 3.17. The CUSTOMER attribute cannot serve as a primary key. Customer names are repeated each time an account belonging to that customer records some activity. ACCOUNT# also cannot serve as the primary key, since the account number is repeated for every action posted to that account. However, if we know that Small Bank never reuses transaction numbers, then the TRANSACTION# can be designated as the primary key.

What if Small Bank's transaction numbers are duplicated? Assume, for example, that transaction numbers are unique only within one single account (see Figure 3.18). In that case, TRANSACTION# is not sufficient to uniquely identify each tuple in the relation. Instead, it is the combination of ACCOUNT# and TRANSACTION# that is not repeated. The primary key for the relation must then consist of the *concatenation* of the two attributes. Concatenation simply means that the value of one attribute is pasted on the end of the other to form a single value. Most DBMSs do not physically concatenate the values of multiple attributes which form primary keys; rather, they logically view the values as if they were one.

You may have noticed that which attribute or combination of attributes were needed to form the primary key depends a great deal on the database environment. It is very difficult to decide which attributes will contain unique values without knowing the rules under which the data operate. For example, there is no way to determine a primary key for Small Bank's data without knowing how transaction numbers are assigned.

Figure 3.19 contains another version of a relational database for Small Bank. (This happens to be a "better" design than that in Figures 3.17 and 3.18; you'll understand why later.) It consists of three tables, PEOPLE, ACCT and TRANS. The ACCT relation pairs customers and their accounts; it identifies the customer to which an account belongs by a new attribute—CUSTOMER#. Since each customer may have many accounts, the primary key must consist of the combination of CUSTOMER# and ACCOUNT#. This relation is what is known as *all-key*, since no attributes exist in the relation which are not part of the primary key.

The TRANS relation pairs accounts and transactions. The primary key for this relation is the combination of TRANSACTION# and ACCOUNT#.

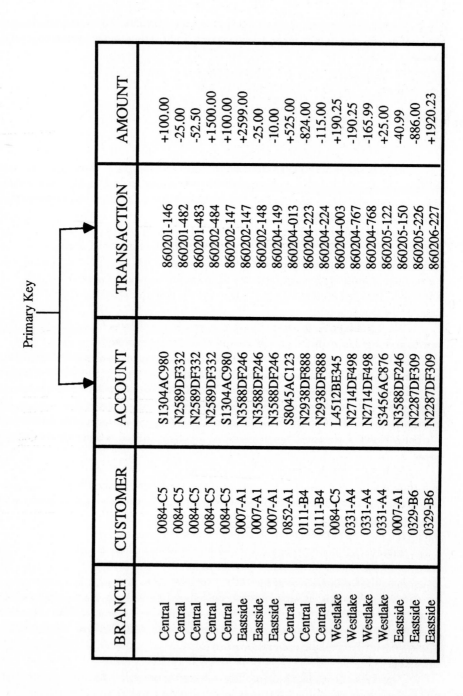

BRANCH	CUSTOMER	ACCOUNT	TRANSACTION	AMOUNT
Central	0084-C5	S1304AC980	860201-146	+100.00
Central	0084-C5	N2589DF332	860201-482	-25.00
Central	0084-C5	N2589DF332	860201-483	-52.50
Central	0084-C5	N2589DF332	860202-484	+1500.00
Central	0084-C5	S1304AC980	860202-147	+100.00
Eastside	0007-A1	N3588DF246	860202-147	+2599.00
Eastside	0007-A1	N3588DF246	860202-148	-25.00
Eastside	0007-A1	N3588DF246	860204-149	-10.00
Central	0852-A1	S8045AC123	860204-013	+525.00
Central	0111-B4	N2938DF888	860204-223	-824.00
Central	0111-B4	N2938DF888	860204-224	-115.00
Westlake	0084-C5	L4512BE345	860204-003	+190.25
Westlake	0331-A4	N2714DF498	860204-767	-190.25
Westlake	0331-A4	N2714DF498	860204-768	-165.99
Westlake	0331-A4	S3456AC876	860205-122	+25.00
Eastside	0007-A1	N3588DF246	860205-150	-40.99
Eastside	0329-B6	N2287DF309	860205-226	-886.00
Eastside	0329-B6	N2287DF309	860206-227	+1920.23

Primary Key

Figure 3.18   A Relation Containing Small Bank's Transaction Data—Transaction Numbers Are Not Unique

PEOPLE

CUSTOMER#	CUSTOMER	ADDRESS	PHONE	S S N
0093-A6	Jones, Samuel	105 W. 99th, Newtown 02899	555-0345	123-45-1234
0095-B8	Abrams, Max	2204 Nox Hill, Newtown 02845	555-1414	098-76-5432
0103-A4	Cohen, Esther	39 Summer, Newtown 02845	555-8486	019-28-3745
0239-B7	Khan, Satya	1001 N. 54th, Newtown 02898	555-7623	567-12-3489

ACCT

CUSTOMER#	ACCOUNT#
0093-A6	N2489B4908
0093-A6	S1209A4149
0093-A6	L3099C8987
0095-B8	N3939B4109
0103-A4	N5577B4107
0239-B7	N4499B4235
0239-B7	S1210A2998

TRANS

ACCOUNT#	TRANS#	AMOUNT
S1209A4149	860415-156	+100.00
L3099C8987	860415-023	+250.85
N5577B4107	860415-309	-10.00
N5577B4107	860415-310	-800.00
S1210A2998	860415-003	+1.89
N4499B4235	860415-308	+1876.00
N4499B4235	860415-309	-25.45
N4499B4235	860415-310	-52.67
S1210A2998	860416-004	+10.00
N3939B4109	860416-588	-88.00
N5577B4107	860416-311	-1077.00
N5577B4107	860416-312	-25.00
N5577B4107	860416-313	-25.00
N5577B4107	860416-314	-115.00
N3939B4109	860417-589	-105.00
N4499B4235	860417-311	-550.00
N4499B4235	860417-312	-43.25
S1209A4149	860417-157	+100.00
S1210A2998	860417-005	+5.00
N5577B4107	860417-315	+3205.00
N2489B4908	860417-012	+18056.00

Figure 3.19 Another Version of Small Bank's Transaction Data

The choice of a primary key for the PEOPLE relation is not so clear. CUSTOMER# alone would be acceptable as a primary key. So might the social security number. By the same token, a concatenated key, consisting of CUSTOMER# and SSN also meets the requirement of uniquely identifying each tuple.

The concatenated key is *redundant*. In other words, it contains more attributes than are absolutely necessary to make a valid primary key; if you remove either attribute from the key, the key will still be valid. Primary keys, however, must be *nonredundant*. That means that they must include the fewest number of attributes needed to uniquely identify a tuple. The concatenated key is therefore not an acceptable primary key.

CUSTOMER# and SSN are what is known as *candidate keys*, since either will function perfectly well as the primary key. In a situation where more than one candidate key exists in a relation, select the key that is comprised of the fewest number of attributes and is least likely to be *null*. In this case, CUSTOMER# is probably the better choice. Some people may not have social security numbers, in which case the SSN attribute might be null.

Null is a value; it is not the same as a zero or a blank. Rather, it means that the value of an attribute is unknown. If one instance of an attribute that is part of a primary key is null, there's no problem. However, if some other instance also has an unknown value, then the primary key loses its property of uniqueness. Therefore, the relational model states that no part of a primary key can be null. This rule is an example of an *integrity constraint*. This particular integrity constraint is known as *entity integrity*. (The other major integrity constraint—referential integrity—is discussed in the following section.)

FOREIGN KEYS

In Figures 3.17 and 3.18, it is very easy to see which transaction is related to which account and which account belongs to which customer. The relationships in Figure 3.19 may not appear so obvious. Consider, however, that if you look at any two of the relations in Figure 3.19, they have one attribute in common. For example, the attribute ACCOUNT# appears in both ACCT and TRANS; CUSTOMER# appears in both ACCT and PEOPLE.

This duplication is no accident. It is the technique used by relational databases to show links between relations. If, for example, customer #0073 has three accounts, each of which appears in ACCT, then the data associated with customer #0073 in PEOPLE applies to each account in ACCT. In other words, if the attribute CUSTOMER# has duplicate values in both ACCT and PEOPLE, we can assume that all data values in tuples with the same customer number refer to the same individual, regardless of the relation in which they appear.

The attribute CUSTOMER# in ACCT is a *foreign key*. A foreign key is an attribute (or the concatenation of two or more attributes) in one relation that is defined on the same logical domain as the primary key in some other relation. This means that the columns in the tables do not necessarily need the same names; they need only contain logically equivalent data. For example, if a column called CUST# contains customer numbers for Small Bank in one relation, and if the CUST-NO column of another relation also contains customer numbers for Small Bank, a primary key–foreign key relationship *could* exist between them. Matching values between foreign and primary keys form logical links between relations. In a fully relational database, there are no physical connections between relations (i.e., no pointers), just the logical connections made by duplicate values.

To get a listing of a customer's name, address, and account numbers, a relational database will use the PEOPLE relation to retrieve the customer name and address. Although the customer number is not a part of the output, it must also be retrieved. That number is then used to search the ACCT relation to find all accounts belonging to the specific customer.

Because foreign keys reference primary keys, it is essential that a primary key value exist somewhere in the database for every foreign key value. This is known as *referential integrity.*

Very few microcomputer databases can store information about primary key–foreign key relationships in their data dictionaries. They therefore cannot automatically enforce referential integrity. An exception is *Reflex*, a relational database for the Macintosh. Figure 3.20 shows a *Reflex* implementation of the Small Bank database from Figure 3.19. Like Figure 3.19, this implementation consists of three relations: PEOPLE, ACCT, and TRANS. However, notice that there are two extra attributes, one in PEOPLE, the other in ACCT.

Like most microcomputer DBMSs, *Reflex* has had to make compromises. In order to express a primary key–foreign key relation, the relation to which the primary key belongs must contain an attribute for the foreign key. Consider, for example, the relation PEOPLE.

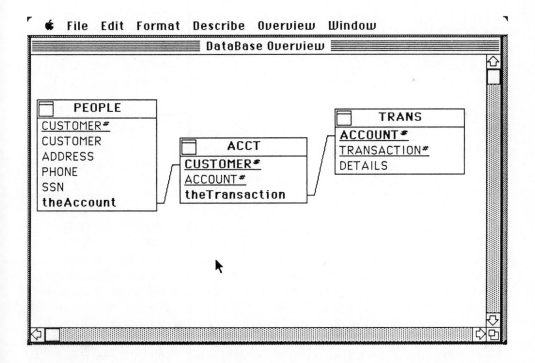

Figure 3.20 *Reflex* Database for Small Bank

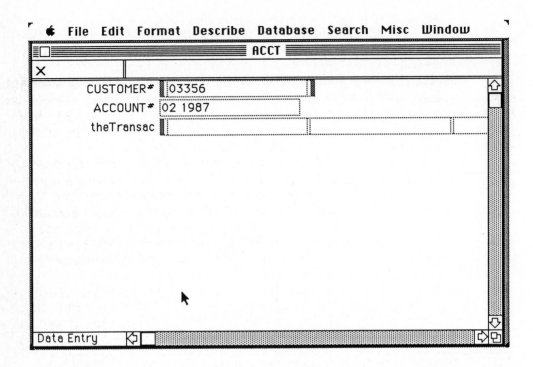

Figure 3.21 *Reflex* Data Entry Screen

The attribute theAccount indicates that there may be accounts related to any given customer. The line from theAccount to CUSTOMER# in ACCT diagrams exactly how the relationship should be interpreted.   The attribute theTransaction in ACCT indicates that there may be transactions related to any given account. Again, a line between ACCT and TRANS illustrates the relationship. However, if *Reflex* were adhering strictly to the relational model, the extra attributes would not appear and the lines would be drawn directly between matching attributes (i.e., between CUSTOMER# in PEOPLE and CUSTOMER# in ACCT).

Figure 3.21 contains a form for entering data into the ACCT relation. The user fills in the CUSTOMER# and ACCOUNT#. (Entries in theTransaction are made by *Reflex* whenever a transaction for this account is entered into TRANS.) If the customer number entered does not match an existing tuple in PEOPLE, referential integrity has been violated. *Reflex* automatically consults PEOPLE whenever an entry is made in ACCT and alerts the user if a matching tuple in PEOPLE cannot be found (see Figure 3.22). If *Reflex* detects a referential integrity violation, the user has two choices—either abandon the entry in ACCT or create a tuple in PEOPLE for the customer number. Unless the user consciously disables integrity checking, *Reflex* will not permit the entry of a tuple that violates referential integrity. *Reflex* also, by the way, enforces the constraint that primary keys must be unique.

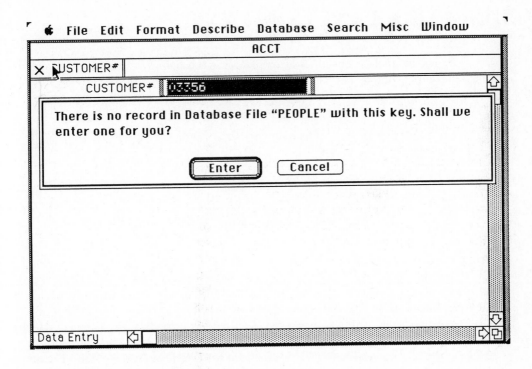

Figure 3.22 *Reflex* Notification of Violation of Referential Integrity

A NOTATION TO DESCRIBE RELATIONS

There is a simple notation that is often used to describe a relation. For example, the PEOPLE relation from Figure 3.19 would be written:

PEOPLE (<u>CUSTOMER#</u>, CUSTOMER, ADDRESS, PHONE, SSN)

The name of the relation is written first, followed in parentheses by the names of the attributes which make up the relation. While the order of the attributes in a relation is unimportant, the attributes which form the primary key are usually listed first. The primary key attributes are also underlined.

The other two relations from Figure 3.19 are expressed as:

ACCT (<u>CUSTOMER#</u>, <u>ACCOUNT#</u>)
TRANS (<u>ACCOUNT#</u>, <u>TRANS#</u>, AMOUNT)

FEDERATED TAXI COMPANY

Data to monitor Federated Taxi Company's cab scheduling and maintenance might be stored in the following set of relations:

CAB (<u>CABNUM</u>, MAKE, MODEL, YEAR, PURDATE, LICNUM, CONDITN, CABSTAT, CURODOM)

DRIVER (<u>DRVNUM</u>, DRVNAM, DRVSTR, DRVCSZ, DRVPHONE, DRVLIC, DRVLEXD, DRVSTAT)

SHIFTS (<u>WKDATE</u>, <u>WKSHIFT</u>, <u>CABNUM</u>, DRVNUM, WKFLAG, ODOMRDG1, ODOMRDG2)

INCIDENTS (<u>CABNUM</u>, <u>WKDATE</u>, <u>WKSHIFT</u>, INCITYPE, DETAILS)

MAINTENANCE (<u>CABNUM</u>, <u>MAINDATE</u>, <u>MAINTYPE</u>, MAINODOM)

The relation CAB stores basic information about each vehicle. This is information that doesn't change very often. The one exception is the current odometer reading (CURODOM); this is updated every time a cab returns from a shift. The primary key in this relation is CABNUM. These are numbers assigned to each cab when it is purchased. The cab numbers are also painted on the side of each cab.

At first glance, it might appear that LICNUM is a candidate key for the relation CAB. Each cab has only one plate number and no two cabs have the same plate. However, in FTC's operations there is a chance that the value of LICNUM could be null. If a cab is badly damaged and requires extensive repairs for which maintenance must wait for parts, the cab will sit in the garage unregistered, without a license plate. Therefore, since the value of LICNUM may be null, it is not suitable as a primary key.

Static information about drivers is stored in the relation DRIVER. Since two drivers could have the same name, each is assigned a unique driver number (DRVNUM). That number, which consists of only one attribute, makes a far more convenient key than, for example, name and address. Social security numbers are often used as keys in relations that store data about people, since they represent a unique identifier for most Americans. However, they present problems in cases in which people concerned about their privacy prefer not to disclose the social security number or when more than one person represented in the database has no social security number.

SHIFTS is used to indicate which cabs have been reserved for a given shift. The primary key consists of three attributes—WKDATE, WKSHIFT, and CABNUM. All three are essential, since each date has three shifts and many cabs are available for each shift on each date. The data item WKFLAG is what is known as a Boolean. It can take only one of two values—TRUE or FALSE. When a driver reserves a cab for a shift, WKFLAG is set to FALSE. If the driver reports for the shift, then WKFLAG is changed to TRUE. Then, to discover which drivers failed to show up for their scheduled shifts, Federated's scheduling clerk can ask the DBMS to retrieve all tuples from SHIFT with a date and shift that have already passed and a WKFLAG value of FALSE.

SHIFTS, by the way, has another candidate key—WKDATE, WKSHIFT, and DRVNUM. Since a driver can only drive one cab at a time, the combination of date, shift, and driver is enough to uniquely identify the reservation. In this case, the choice between the two candidate keys is a toss-up, since both have the same number of attributes and neither will ever have any null values (i.e., in terms of this database environment, a reservation will never be made without knowing date, shift, driver, and cab).

The relation INCIDENTS contains one tuple for every traffic citation and accident that occur. Since it is important to Federated Taxi to know exactly when incidents occurred, the relation includes not only the number of the cab involved, but the associated date and shift. The primary key therefore consists of the three attributes WKDATE, WKSHIFT, and CABNUM.

The relation MAINTENANCE records data about all work done on FTC's cabs. Since more than one type of maintenance can be performed on a single cab on a single day, the primary key must consist of the three attributes CABNUM, MAINDATE, and MAINTYPE.

There are a number of foreign keys in this set of relations:

1. The attribute DRVNUM is a foreign key in the relation SHIFTS. It makes a logical link to the relation DRIVER. Suppose, for example, that there are too few cabs on the road for a given shift. The scheduling clerk wants the phone numbers of all drivers who didn't appear to drive during that shift so that he or she can call them. First, the DBMS consults the SHIFTS relation to identify all reservations for the shift in question that have not been driven (i.e., WKFLAG has a value of FALSE). Then the driver number from each tuple retrieved from reserve is used to retrieve the matching tuple in DRIVER, where the driver's phone number is stored.

2. The attribute CABNUM is a foreign key in SHIFTS, INCIDENTS, and MAINTENANCE. In all three cases it makes a logical link to CAB. If, for example, the office clerk needs the license plate number of a cab that was involved in an accident for an insurance form, the DBMS would take the cab number from the tuple in INCIDENTS that described the accident and use it to retrieve a tuple from CAB with a matching value for CABNUM. The tuple from CAB contains the license plate number of the cab.

3. The attributes WKDATE, WKSHIFT, and CABNUM together form a foreign key that references SHIFTS from INCIDENTS. If Federated Taxi wants to know which driver was responsible for a given incident, the WKDATE, WKSHIFT, and CABNUM from INCIDENTS can be matched to a WKDATE, WKSHIFT, and CABNUM from SHIFTS. The tuple in SHIFTS contains the driver number. In this way, the driver number does not have to be duplicated in the INCIDENTS relation.

USER VIEWS

According to the theoretical relational model, relational databases should allow authorized users to create a customized subset of the base tables that contain only the parts of the relational schema that a given application will use. These subsets are known as *views*. Unfortunately, not all microcomputer relational DBMSs support user views.

A view consists of the definition of a table. The tables in a view may select and rearrange the attributes in the base tables in any way that makes logical sense to the user. It is therefore possible to use views as a security device. By including only nonsensitive attributes and/or tuples in a particular view and restricting a group of users to that view, users can be prevented from gaining access to data to which they have no rights.

Views are not stored on disk; they consist of virtual tables kept temporarily in main memory. View definitions, however, may be stored. Then whenever a user invokes a view, the virtual table to support that view is created from the base tables. The virtual table is removed from main memory when the user concludes his or her activity against the database.

SUMMARY

A logical data model is a scheme for describing the relationships between data in a database. There are three major data models:

1. Hierarchical
2. Network
3. Relational

The hierarchical model views data as a tree. A given record occurrence can be related to exactly one record above it (its parent); that same record occurrence may be related to many records below it (its children).

The network models are similar to the hierarchical model but permit a given record occurrence to have more than one parent record. Simple networks permit multiple parents only if each parent record is of a different record type. Complex networks permit the multiple parents to be of either the same or different record types.

The relational model, used for most microcomputer DBMSs, views data as a set of two-dimensional tables known as relations. The relations are logically separate entities.

A relation has the following characteristics:

1. A name
2. A set of attributes that defines the columns in the table

3. A unique, non-null primary key (one or more attributes whose value(s) uniquely identify each row in the table)

The relationships between tables in a relational database are established through the presence of foreign keys. A foreign key is one or more attributes in one relation that are defined on the same logical domain as a primary key in another relation. The foreign key–primary key reference logically links the two tables. Rows with matching foreign key–primary key values contain data describing the same entity.

REFERENCES

Bachman, C.W. (1969) "Data structures diagrams." *Data Base Journal, ACM SIGDBP*. 1(2):4-10.

Bradley, James. (1983) *Introduction to Data Base Management in Business*. New York: Holt, Rinehart and Winston.

Cardenas, Alfonso F. (1985) *Data Base Management Systems*. 2d ed. Boston: Allyn and Bacon.

CODASYL. (1971) *Data Base Task Group Report*. New York: ACM.

CODASYL Data Description Language Committee. (1978) *DDL Journal of Development*. Ottawa: Material Data Management Branch, Canadian Federal Branch.

Codd, E. F. (1970) "A relational model of data for large shared data banks." *Communications of the ACM*. 13(6):377-387.

Codd, E.F. (1979) "Extending the database relational model to capture more meaning." *ACM Transactions on Database Systems*. 4(4):397-434.

Cullinet Corporation. (1982) *IDMS Database Design and Definition Guide*. Westwood, MA: Cullent.

Delobel, C. (1980) "An overview of relational theory." *Proceedings of the IFIP Congress, 1980*. 413-426. Melbourne.

Gerritsen, R. (1975) "A preliminary study for the design of DBTG data structures." *Communications of the ACM*. (October):551-557.

IBM Corporation. *Information Management System/Virtual Storage General Information Manual.* IBM Form GH20-1260.

McFadden, Fred R. and Jeffrey A. Hoffer. (1985) *Data Base Management.* Menlo Park, CA: Benjamin/Cummings.

Olle, T. William. (1980) *The CODASYL Approach to Data Base Management.* Chichester, England: Wiley.

EXERCISES

Below you will find groups of relations that might be used to represent data for the University Archaeological Museum and Margaret Holmes, D.M.D. For each set of relations, do the following:

1. Underline the primary key attributes in each relation.
2. Draw a line between each foreign key and the primary key it references.
3. For each attribute, indicate a reasonable domain.
4. Transform the relations into a single Bachman diagram for a simple or complex network (whichever is necessary to represent the data relationships).

When necessary, refer back to the interview transcripts in Appendixes A and B to clarify the meaning of data relationships in the context of a specific database environment.

A. For the University Archaeological Museum

SLIDE (DIG, SEQ-NUM, DESCRIPTION)
SUBJECTS (SUBJECT, DIG, SEQ-NUM)
BORROWED (DIG, SEQ-NUM, BORROWER, DATE-DUE, RETURN-FLAG)

Attributes:

DIG	Unique ID# for each dig
SEQ-NUM	Sequence # for a slide (unique within dig only)
DESCRIPTION	Text description of contents of slide
SUBJECT	Subject term from a fixed list of subjects

BORROWER	Person borrowing a slide
DATE-DUE	Date when slide should be returned
RETURN-FLAG	Boolean indicating whether slide has been returned

B. For the University Archaeological Museum

ARTIFACT-LOG (ARTIFACT-NUM, DIG, GRID-NO, DATE-FOUND, DEPTH-FOUND, DESCRIPTION, SHELF-NUM)
ARTIFACTS-OUT (ARTIFACT-NUM, BORROWER, DATE-BORROWED, DATE-DUE,PLACE-TAKEN)

Attributes:

ARTIFACT-NUM	Unique number assigned to an artifact
DIG	Unique ID# for each dig
GRID-NO	Coordinates where artifact was found at the dig site
DATE-FOUND	Date artifact was found
DEPTH-FOUND	Depth at which artifact was found
DESCRIPTION	Text describing the artifact
SHELF-NUM	Location in warehouse where artifact is stored when not being used in any way
BORROWER	Person responsible for artifact taken from warehouse
DATE-BORROWED	Date artifact was taken from warehouse
LOCATION	Place where artifact was taken

C. For the office of Margaret Holmes, D.M.D.

PATIENT-MASTER (PATIENT#, NAME, ADDRESS, PHONE, SSN, AGE, SEX, WHO-PAYS, REL-TO-WHO-PAYS, PAYMENT-SOURCE)
PAYERS (WHO-PAYS, P-ADDRESS, P-PHONE, PLACE-OF-EMPLOYMENT,WORK-PHONE, INSURANCE-CARRIER)
VISITS (PATIENT#, DATE, PROCEDURE, COMMENTS)
COSTS (PROCEDURE, PRICE)
INCOME (PATIENT#, P-DATE, SOURCE, AMT, WHO-PAYS)
LEDGER (WHO-PAYS, TOTAL-AMT-OWED)

Attributes:

PATIENT#	Unique number assigned to each patient
NAME	Patient's name

ADDRESS	Patient's address
PHONE	Patient's home phone
AGE	Patient's age
SEX	Patient's sex
SSN	Patient's social security number
WHO-PAYS	Person responsible for the bills (may be the same as NAME)
REL-TO-WHO-PAYS	Relationship between patient and whoever pays the bills
PAYMENT-SOURCE	Either cash, insurance, or both
P-ADDRESS	Address of WHO-PAYS
P-PHONE	Home phone of WHO-PAYS
PLACE-OF-EMPLOYMENT	Where WHO-PAYS works
WORK-PHONE	Work telephone of WHO-PAYS
INSURANCE-CARRIER	Insurance company covering WHO-PAYS and dependents
DATE	Date when a patient received treatment
PROCEDURE	Treatment given to a patient
COMMENTS	Text of any notes the treatment provider wishes to record
PRICE	Normal cost of a procedure
P-DATE	Date a payment is received
SOURCE	Type of payment - cash, personal check, insurance check, etc.
AMT	Amount of payment
TOTAL-AMT-OWED	Amount owed by WHO-PAYS at any given time

Normalization

CHAPTER OUTLINE:

CHAPTER OBJECTIVES:

After reading this chapter, you will:

1. Understand the problems that occur when all the attributes in a database are stored in a single relation
2. Understand how third normal form alleviates the problems of first normal form
3. Be able to recognize databases that are in third normal form
4. Understand the major concepts behind the ultimate normal form—domain/key normal form

For any given set of attributes that form the central pool of data for a database, there are many different ways that those attributes can be assembled into a set of relations. Some arrangements are "better" than others. The ways in which attributes can be arranged are called *normal forms*. The theory behind the arrangement of attributes into relations is known as *normalization theory*. (Additional discussions of normalization issues can be found in Date, 1986; Korth and Silberschatz, 1986; Loomis, 1987; Salzberg, 1986; and Yang, 1986).

Normal forms provide an increasingly more stringent set of rules that relations must meet. The least stringent is first normal form, often written 1NF. Any set of attributes that are expressed in tabular form without repeating groups is in at least first normal form.

The full range of normal forms recognized by database theorists appears in Figure 4.1. They are nested in this way to indicate that if a relation, or set of relations, meets the criteria for an inner normal form, it is also in all the normal forms outside it. For example, if a relation is in Boyce/Codd normal form, then it is also in third, second, and first normal forms. The higher a normal form that a database can meet, the "better" the design, theoretically.

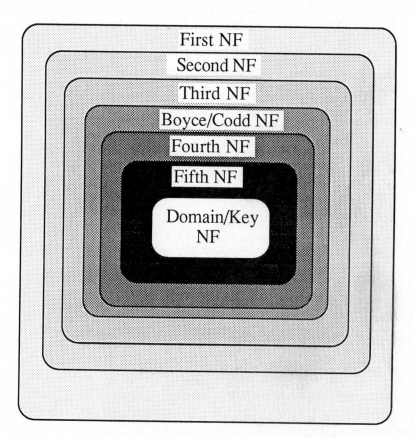

Figure 4.1 The Relationship of Normal Forms

To be honest, normal forms beyond third normal form (3NF) are of more theoretical than practical interest. In fact, if you can design and implement your database as a set of 3NF relations, then you will have avoided the large majority of database design problems. There is, however, an ultimate normal form, a design objective toward which the design of relations is aimed. This normal form, domain/key normal form (DK/NF), is discussed at the end of this chapter.

FIRST NORMAL FORM AND ITS PROBLEMS

Figure 4.2 contains a first normal form relation that captures Small Bank's transaction data. File management software such as *pfs:File*, *Microsoft File*, and *PC File*, and spreadsheets such as *Lotus 1-2-3* restrict the user to just such a design. Putting all the attributes into a single relation is conceptually simple; however, first normal form relations are prone to several significant problems.

The primary key for the relation in Figure 4.2 is CUSTOMER#, ACCOUNT#, and TRANSACTION#. What happens, then, when a customer opens a new account and no transactions have yet been posted? Is there any way to insert the customer number, customer name, and account number into the relation? That is, is it possible to record data about a customer and account before there has been activity against the account? No, because there isn't enough data to form a complete primary key. The TRANSACTION# attribute must take a value of null (unknown), yet no part of a primary key can be null. This situation is known as an *insertion anomaly*. It arises whenever a user wishes to insert data into a relation and cannot do so because it isn't possible to assemble a complete primary key.

Consider, now, what happens when Small Bank decides to purge the relation in Figure 4.2, transferring all the transaction data to archival tape storage. Not only are the data about the transactions removed from the relation, but information about customers, their names, addresses, and accounts must be deleted as well. Why? Removing the transaction number causes part of the primary key to become null, making it impossible to leave the tuple in the relation. However, Small Bank needs to retain the customer and account data; an account doesn't cease to exist if there are no transactions posted against it during any given period. This problem is what's known as a *deletion anomaly*. Whenever the deletion of a tuple causes the accidental loss of data that should be retained, the relation has a deletion anomaly.

The relation in Figure 4.2 also contains a great deal of redundant data; a customer's name is stored once for every account the customer has. What happens if the customer changes his or her name? The DBMS must locate every occurrence of the customer name and change it. First normal form relations, which by nature contain a great deal of redundant data, are therefore prone to the problems that arise from redundant data: lack of data consistency and lack of data integrity.

BANK

CUSTOMER#	CUSTOMER	ADDRESS	PHONE	SSN	ACCOUNT#	TRANS#	AMT
0093-A6	Jones, Samuel	105 W. 99th, 02899	555-0345	123451234	N2489B4908	860914-114	+1500.00
0093-A6	Jones, Samuel	105 W. 99th, 02899	555-0345	123451234	N2489B4908	860914-115	-25.00
0095-B8	Abrams, Max	2204 Nox Hill, 02845	555-1414	098765432	N3939B4109	860914-395	+500.00
0103-A4	Cohen, Esther	39 Summer, 02845	555-8486	019283745	N5577B4107	860914-884	+750.00
0103-A4	Cohen, Esther	39 Summer, 02845	555-8486	019283745	N5577B4107	860914-885	-55.25
0103-A4	Cohen, Esther	39 Summer, 02845	555-8486	019283745	N5577B4107	860914-886	-106.95
0239-B7	Khan, Satya	1001 N. 54th, 02898	555-7623	567123489	S1219A2998	860914-005	-10.00

Figure 4.2   First Normal Form Database for Small Bank

THE BENEFITS OF THIRD NORMAL FORM

If the relation from Figure 4.2 is transformed into a set of 3NF relations, then Small Bank can avoid insertion and deletion anomalies as well as many of the problems arising from redundant data. Figure 4.3 contains just such a design. It is free of insertion and deletion anomalies and contains much less redundant data than the single-relation design.

Consider again the situation where a customer opens a new account. In the 3NF design, the relationship between a customer and the accounts he or she may have is represented by the relation ACCT. ACCT has only one purpose—to link a customer to accounts; transaction data are kept elsewhere. ACCT's primary key requires only the customer number and the account number (the relation is all key); therefore, the insertion anomaly that existed in the first normal relation, which required that at least one transaction be posted before the customer and account number could be entered, is not present.

PEOPLE

CUSTOMER#	CUSTOMER	ADDRESS	PHONE	SSN
0093-A6	Jones, Samuel	105 W. 99th, Newtown 02899	555-0345	123-45-1234
0095-B8	Abrams, Max	2204 Nox Hill, Newtown 02845	555-1414	098-76-5432
0103-A4	Cohen, Esther	39 Summer, Newtown 02845	555-8486	019-28-3745
0239-B7	Khan, Satya	1001 N. 54th, Newtown 02898	555-7623	567-12-3489

ACCT

CUSTOMER#	ACCOUNT#
0093-A6	N2489B4908
0093-A6	S1209A4149
0093-A6	L3099C8987
0095-B8	N3939B4109
0103-A4	N5577B4107
0239-B7	N4499B4235
0239-B7	S1210A2998

TRANS

ACCOUNT#	TRANS#	AMOUNT
S1209A4149	860415-156	+100.00
L3099C8987	860415-023	+250.85
N5577B4107	860415-309	-10.00
N5577B4107	860415-310	-800.00
S1210A2998	860415-003	+1.89
N4499B4235	860415-308	+1876.00
N4499B4235	860415-309	-25.45
N4499B4235	860415-310	-52.67
S1210A2998	860416-004	+10.00
N3939B4109	860416-588	-88.00
N5577B4107	860416-311	-1077.00
N5577B4107	860416-312	-25.00
N5577B4107	860416-313	-25.00
N5577B4107	860416-314	-115.00
N3939B4109	860417-589	-105.00
N4499B4235	860417-311	-550.00
N4499B4235	860417-312	-43.25
S1209A4149	860417-157	+100.00
S1210A2998	860417-005	+5.00
N5577B4107	860417-315	+3205.00
N2489B4908	860417-012	+18056.00

Figure 4.3 Third Normal Form Database for Small Bank's Transaction Data

DEFINING THIRD NORMAL FORM

The 3NF design also makes it possible to record data about a customer before the customer has opened any accounts, something which could not be done in the 1NF relation. The relation PEOPLE requires only the customer number as a primary key; no accounts or transactions on accounts are necessary.

The deletion anomaly in the first normal form relation is not present in the 3NF design. If the relation TRANS is completely purged of data, or even deleted from the database, the relation ACCT is untouched. Information about which customer has which account is therefore left unaltered in the database.

 If a customer closes all of his or her accounts with Small Bank, it is still possible to retain demographic data about that person in the database. It works in this way: every time an account is closed, the tuple in ACCT that relates that account to the customer is deleted. However, the tuple in PEOPLE that describes the customer is not deleted. Therefore, even if a given customer number has no tuples in ACCT, it can still appear in PEOPLE.

It is important to recognize that the reverse is not true. While a customer number can exist in PEOPLE without having any matching tuples in ACCT, a customer number cannot exist in ACCT without having a matching customer number in PEOPLE. The latter situation is a violation of referential integrity. In other words, the customer number in ACCT is a foreign key referencing the primary key in PEOPLE. Primary key values do not need to have existing foreign key values that reference them whereas foreign key values must reference existing primary key values.

The relation PEOPLE eliminates much of the redundant data that could cause integrity and consistency problems. The demographic data about a customer is stored only once. Therefore, whenever a person changes an address or phone number, it only need to be retrieved and modified once in the database.

FULL FUNCTIONAL DEPENDENCE AND 2NF

The goal of practical relational database design is to obtain a set of 3NF relations. 3NF relations meet the following criteria:

1. They are expressed in tabular form with a unique primary key and without any repeating groups. (This qualifies them as 1NF.)
2. All non-key attributes are *fully functionally dependent* on the primary key. (This qualifies them as 2NF.)
3. All *transitive dependencies* have been eliminated. (This qualifies them as 3NF.)

There are two new terms in the definition above: *fully functionally dependent* and *transitive dependency*. These concepts are central to relational database design.

A relation is in 2NF if:

1. It is in 1NF.
2. All non-key attributes are fully functionally dependent on the primary key.

This definition relies heavily on the concept of a functional dependency. A functional dependency is a special kind of relationship between two attributes. In the relation PEOPLE from Figure 4.3, the attribute CUSTOMER is functionally dependent on the attribute CUSTOMER#. That means that for any given value of CUSTOMER#, there will be one and only one value of CUSTOMER associated with it. In other words, the value that CUSTOMER takes depends on the value of CUSTOMER#. In terms of the meaning of these attributes, that makes sense; there will be only one customer name for any given customer number. That does not mean that the customer name associated with a particular customer number will never change; it only means that at any given time, there is only one customer name for each customer number.

The functional dependency is written:

CUSTOMER# $\rightarrow$ CUSTOMER

and is read as either "CUSTOMER# determines CUSTOMER" or "CUSTOMER is functionally dependent on CUSTOMER#." In the relationship, CUSTOMER# is called the *determinant*, since its value determines the value of another attribute.

The determinant does not have to be a single attribute. For example, in the relation TRANS,

ACCOUNT# + TRANSACTION# $\rightarrow$ AMT

Why is this so? Remember that transaction numbers are sequential within each account; transaction numbers are repeated throughout the relation. Therefore, any given transaction number may have more than one amount associated with it. However, since a transaction number is used only once for a specific account, there will only be one amount associated with each unique transaction and account number pair.

It is important to realize that functional dependence is a one-way relationship. While it is true that the customer name is determined by the customer number, the reverse is not true; the customer number is not determined by the customer name. Since it is possible that two or more customers can have exactly the same name, we cannot guarantee that there will be only one customer number associated with any one customer name at any given time. For example, if there are two Jon Doughs who have accounts at Small Bank, each will have a different customer number. In that case, one name is associated with two different customer numbers, which violates the rule for a functional dependence.

The definition of 2NF talks about *full* functional dependence. If an attribute is fully functionally dependent on another attribute or combination of attributes, then the determinant is made up of the smallest number of attributes possible to retain the functional dependence.

For example, it is true that

$$\longrightarrow \text{CUSTOMER\# + CUSTOMER} \to \text{ADDRESS, PHONE, SSN}$$

For each customer number and customer name pair there is indeed only one address, phone number, and social security number that will be associated with it at any given time. However, it is also true that

$$\longrightarrow \text{CUSTOMER\#} \to \text{ADDRESS, PHONE, SSN}$$

While the address, phone number, and social security number are functionally dependent on the concatenated determinant, they are not *fully* functionally dependent on it, since it is possible to remove part of the determinant (CUSTOMER) and still preserve the functional dependence. Generally, when database people speak of functional dependence, they mean full functional dependence.

Diagrams such as those in Figure 4.4 are often used to represent the functional dependencies within a relation. Determinants are placed in a box and connected to the attributes they determine by an arrow. The direction of the arrowhead indicates the direction of the dependency.

Relations are transformed from 1NF to 2NF by *decomposing* them into a set of smaller relations. The easiest way to do so is to first create a new relation for each determinant in the 1NF relation. The determinants become the primary keys in the new relations; the non-key attributes are all attributes which are fully functionally dependent upon them. Then add any relations that are essential to capture relationships between data. That is exactly the process that was followed to create Figure 4.3 from Figure 4.2. There are two determinants in Figure 4.2 (CUSTOMER# and ACCOUNT#+TRANSACTION#). However, if the database consists of just the relations PEOPLE and TRANS (from Figure 4.3), information about which customer owns which account is lost. Therefore, ACCT must be created to capture the customer-account relationship.

Placing relations in 2NF, where all non-key attributes are fully functionally dependent on the primary key, does not necessarily remove all insertion, deletion, and update anomalies. Some may remain if *transitive dependencies* are present in the relation. For this reason, 2NF is rarely a design objective, but rather a stepping-stone to 3NF.

TRANSITIVE DEPENDENCIES AND 3NF

A relation is in 3NF if:

1. It is in 2NF.
2. All transitive dependencies have been removed.

A transitive dependency exists in a relation if:

AttributeA $\to$ AttributeB $\to$ AttributeC

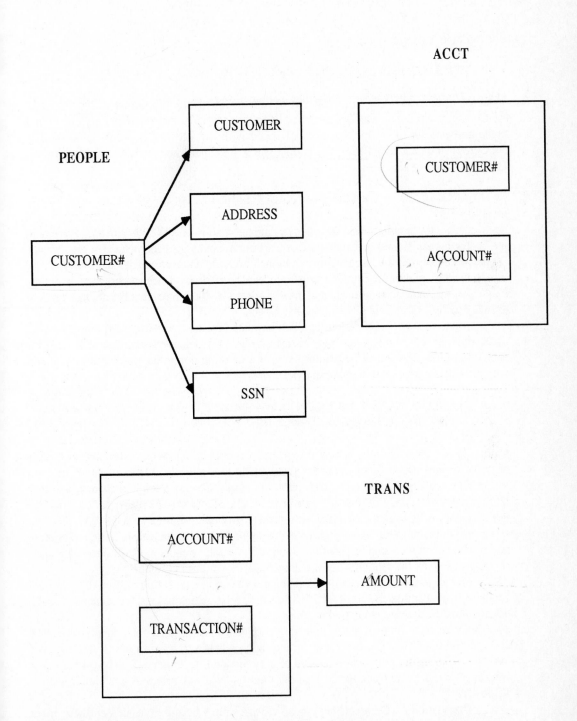

Figure 4.4 Functional Dependencies in the Relations in Figure 4.3

For example, consider the relation ACCT-ACCESS:

ACCT-ACCESS (<u>ACCOUNT#</u>, BRANCH, HOURS)

This relation is in 2NF; both BRANCH and HOURS are functionally dependent on ACCOUNT#. (Since an account is carried at only one branch, there will be only one branch name and one set of business hours associated with it.) However, while it is true that ACCOUNT# determines BRANCH and HOURS, it is also true that BRANCH determines HOURS. In other words:

$$ACCOUNT\# \rightarrow BRANCH \rightarrow HOURS$$

There are insertion, deletion, and update anomalies in ACCT-ACCESS. For example, a new branch cannot be added until at least one account has been opened at that branch. By the same token, if the last account at a branch is closed and its tuple deleted from the relation, information about the branch's operating hours are lost. Since the branch's hours are duplicated for every account located at that branch, a change in branch hours must be made in as many tuples as there are accounts at that branch.

Anomalies in 2NF relations can be eliminated by decomposing them into 3NF relations which have no transitive dependencies. As with the decomposition from 1NF to 2NF, each determinant becomes the primary key in a new relation, along with those attributes which are dependent upon it. For example:

ACCT-LOCATIONS (<u>ACCOUNT#</u>, BRANCH)
BRANCH-HOURS (<u>BRANCH</u>, HOURS)

Using the two 3NF relations above, it is possible to record data about a branch's operating hours before any accounts are opened at that branch. It is also possible to delete all accounts located at a branch without losing the operating hours data. In addition, a change in branch hours needs to be made in only a single tuple in the BRANCH-HOURS relation. In other words, the transformation to 3NF has removed the anomalies present in 2NF.

Do the set of relations in Figure 4.3 actually represent a database in 3NF? In order to make a statement to that effect, each relation in the database must meet all three 3NF criteria. Let's examine the relations to see if they really are in third normal form.

To meet the first criteria, the relations must be in tabular form (1NF). Any relational database will meet this criteria, even if it is a single relation database, since it cannot be relational unless the data are expressed in tables.

The second criteria requires that all non-key attributes be fully functionally dependent upon the primary key. To make a judgment as to whether a relation meets this rule you must first identify the primary key and all of the functional dependencies. The primary keys and functional dependencies for each of the three Small Bank relations are summarized in Table 4.1.

The relation ACCT meets the second criteria simply because it is all key (there are no non-key attributes). In the relation TRANS, there is only one non-key attribute, AMT.

Table 4.1
Summary of Functional Dependencies in the Relations in Figure 4.3

Relation	Determinants	Attributes that are determined
PEOPLE Primary key: CUSTOMER#	CUSTOMER#	CUSTOMER ADDRESS PHONE SSN
ACCT Primary key: CUSTOMER#+ACCOUNT#	none	none
TRANS Primary key: ACCOUNT#+TRANS#	ACCOUNT#+TRANS#	AMOUNT

Assuming that transaction numbers are unique only within one account, then, as discussed above, AMT is fully functionally dependent on the concatenated key of ACCOUNT# and TRANSACTION#. The relation PEOPLE contains four non-key attributes (CUSTOMER, ADDRESS, PHONE, SSN), each of which is functionally dependent on the single-attribute primary key, CUSTOMER#. Since the primary key is comprised of just one attribute, there is no question but that the functional dependencies are full functional dependencies.

The third criteria that determines 3NF requires that all transitive dependencies be eliminated. Since ACCT has no non-key attributes, it is automatically in 3NF. TRANS, with only one non-key attribute, is also automatically in 3NF. However, we must look more closely at PEOPLE.

While it is generally true that any given person has only one address, phone number, and social security number, it is likely that customer names are not unique. Therefore, it is possible that any given value for CUSTOMER in the database may be associated with more than one address, phone number, and social security number. Therefore, there are no transitive dependencies of the nature:

CUSTOMER# $\rightarrow$ CUSTOMER $\rightarrow$ ADDRESS

or

CUSTOMER# $\rightarrow$ CUSTOMER $\rightarrow$ SSN

It is also true that there is no transitive dependency involving a phone number and a social security number. (More than one person may be associated with a given phone number, and a person may be associated with more than one phone number.) The same holds for the social security number and the address. However, while the address does not determine the phone number (since an address may house more than one telephone line), does a phone number determine an address? That is, does the following transitive dependency hold?

$$CUSTOMER\# \rightarrow PHONE \rightarrow ADDRESS$$

We are faced here with a question of interpretation of the database environment. Does a phone number always belong to precisely one address? With today's telephone technology, it does not. (Consider call forwarding: someone calls a number and is automatically switched to a phone at a remote location.) Therefore, we are forced to conclude that the transitive dependency above does not exist. In that case, there are no transitive dependencies in the relation PEOPLE. The relation is in 3NF along with TRANS and ACCT, which means that the entire database is in 3NF.

THE IMPORTANCE OF MEANING

There is an important issue raised by the whole idea of functional and transitive dependence. The ability to identify the functional dependencies in a relation depends a great deal on the meaning of the database environment. What happens, for example, if we change the rules by which Small Bank assigns transaction numbers? Assume that transaction numbers are unique throughout the bank—they are never repeated. In this situation,

$$ACCOUNT\# + TRANSACTION\# \rightarrow AMT$$

no longer constitutes a full functional dependence. Since the transaction numbers are unique, each transaction number will have one and only one set of details associated with it. The full functional dependence is therefore

$$TRANSACTION\# \rightarrow AMT$$

Because the definition of functional dependencies relies so heavily on a database designer's interpretation of the environment, there are rarely any absolutes in terms of what constitutes a functional dependency. Whenever you specify functional dependencies, you must therefore also indicate the assumptions you are making about the way the database environment works.

THE FEDERATED TAXI COMPANY

Let's take another look at the set of relations that represent the data for cab scheduling and incident reporting to determine if they are in 3NF:

CAB (<u>CABNUM</u>, MAKE, MODEL, YEAR, PURDATE, LICNUM, CONDITN, CABSTAT, CURODOM)

DRIVER (<u>DRVNUM</u>, DRVSTR, DRVCSZ, DRVPHONE, DRVLIC, DRVLEXD, DRVSTAT)

SHIFTS (<u>WKDATE</u>, <u>WKSHIFT</u>, <u>CABNUM</u>, WKFLAG, ODOMRDG1, ODOMRDG2)

INCIDENTS (<u>CABNUM</u>, <u>WKDATE</u>, <u>WKSHIFT</u>, INCITYPE, DETAILS)

MAINTENANCE (<u>CABNUM</u>, <u>MAINDATE</u>, <u>MAINTYPE</u>, MAINODOM)

In order to do so we must first identify all the functional dependencies. They can be found in Table 4.2.

In the relation CAB, the primary key is CABNUM. For each vehicle that is identified by a cab number, there will be only one make, model, model year, purchase date, license plate number, status, and current odometer reading. Therefore, each of these attributes is functionally dependent on the primary key. Since the primary key is a single attribute, these functional dependencies also constitute full functional dependencies. The relation CAB does at least meet the criteria for 2NF.

To make a decision on 3NF, we have to determine whether there are any transitive dependencies. Each non-key attribute must therefore be evaluated against all the others. In most cases, this is a trivial activity. For example, it is clear that for any given make, model, model year, purchase date, or road status there can be more than one license plate number associated with it, so that transitive dependencies like CABNUM → LICNUM → MAKE do not hold. No transitive dependencies exist with make, model, and model year either, since a given make of cab has many models and is produced over many years.

Another way to look at this issue of transitive dependency is to realize that if a many-to-many relationship exists between two non-key attributes, then they cannot participate in a transitive dependency with the relation's primary key. For example, any given model year will have many purchase dates associated with it, since Federated Taxi may have purchased many cabs that were manufactured in the same year. By the same token, any given purchase date can have many different model years associated with it, since cabs manufactured during different model years may be purchased in a single day.

What about SHIFTS? The primary key consists of a combination of three attributes: the date, shift, and cab number. For any given day, shift, and cab there will only be one driver. There will also only be one WKFLAG value, since the value applies in particular to this day, shift, and cab combination. The two non-key attributes are therefore fully functionally dependent on the primary key. No transitive dependency exists between the driver and WKFLAG, since just knowing the driver number is not enough to determine the value of WKFLAG. (The day, shift, and cab determine WKFLAG's value, not the driver.) It is also impossible to determine the driver by knowing the value of WKFLAG, since the two Boolean values that WKFLAG may assume can apply to many drivers. SHIFTS is therefore in 3NF.

The relation DRIVER is also in 3NF. For any given driver number, there will only be one name, address, phone number, and status. (While it is true that there be more than

Table 4.2
Functional Dependencies in the Federated Taxi Company Database

Relation	Determinant	Attributes that are determined
CAB Primary key: CABNUM	CABNUM	MAKE MODEL YEAR PURDATE LICNUM CONDITN CABSTAT CURODOM
DRIVER Primary key: DRVNUM	DRVNUM	DRVNAM DRVSTR DRVCSZ DRVPHONE DRVLIC DRVLEXD DRVSTAT
SHIFTS Primary key: WKDATE+WKSHIFT+CABNUM	WKDATE+WKSHIFT+CABNUM	DRVNUM WKFLAG ODOMRDG1 ODOMRDG2
INCIDENTS Primary key: CABNUM+WKDATE+WKSHIFT	CABNUM+WKDATE+WKSHIFT	INCITYPE DETAILS
MAINTENANCE Primary key: CABNUM+MAINDATE+MAINTYPE	CABNUM+MAINDATE+MAINTYPE	MAINODOM

one phone number at which a driver could conceivably be reached, a driver must designate one as his or her single contact point.) It is also true that there are no transitive dependencies for the same reasons that the relation PEOPLE from Small Bank's database has no transitive dependencies.

INCIDENTS has two non-key attributes: the type of incident (i.e., accident, moving violation, parking ticket, etc.) and the details of the incident. The contents of both of these fields do depend on when the incident occurred (the day, shift, and time) and which cab was involved. There are also no transitive dependencies, since any given type of incident can have a variety of details associated with it, and any given set of details might apply to a variety of types of incidents. INCIDENTS is therefore in 3NF.

MAINTENANCE, too, is in 3NF. It has only one non-key attribute, MAINODOM, which records the cab's odometer reading at the time the maintenance was performed. Its value does depend on the full primary key—CABNUM, MAINDATE, and MAINTYPE. Even if more than one type of maintenance is performed on a single day, there is no way to ensure that the cab isn't driven between trips to the service bays. Since there is only one non-key attribute, there is no need to consider transitive dependencies. (It takes at least two non-key attributes to define a transitive dependency.) The relation therefore meets the criteria for 3NF by default.

Since all the relations in FTC's database are in 3NF, the entire database is in 3NF. However, when the database is expanded to include more of FTC's operations, each new relation added to the system must also be in third normal form to ensure that the entire database remains in 3NF.

DOMAIN/KEY NORMAL FORM

Domain/key normal form (DK/NF) was proposed in a 1981 paper by Fagin. DK/NF is considered to be the ultimate normal form. If a relation can be placed in DK/NF, then it consists of the best possible collection of attributes.

The definition of DK/NF is deceptively simple—a relation is in DK/NF if it has no insertion or deletion anomalies. However, Fagin's definitions of insertion and deletion anomalies are very different from the definitions given to those terms earlier in this chapter. (The definitions you have already learned are those in general use in the database field; Fagin's definitions apply only to DK/NF.)

According to Fagin, a relation has insertion anomalies if it is possible to insert a tuple into the relation so that the resulting instance of the relation violates some constraint on the relation. A relation has deletion anomalies if it is possible to delete a tuple from a relation so that the resulting instance of the relation violates some constraint on the relation. The entire concept of DK/NF therefore relies on the constraints applied to a relation. DK/NF recognizes two basic kinds of constraints: *domain constraints* and *key constraints*. (This is where the normal form gets its name.)

A domain constraint specifies the acceptable range of values for a given attribute; this is the same definition that was given to a domain in Chapter 3. For example, the domain for customer numbers in Small Bank's database is all possible groups of seven-digit alphanumeric characters with the format ####-A#, where # is a digit in the range 0–9 and A is an upper-case letter between A and Z. A key constraint simply indicates that one or more attributes can serve as a primary key (i.e., they form a candidate key).

Any other constraints (e.g., functional dependencies, foreign key–primary key references) that should be applied to the relation are derived from the domain and key constraints.

Therefore, if the domain and key constraints are enforced, the remaining constraints will also be automatically enforced.

As an example of an insertion anomaly under the DK/NF definition, look at Figure 4.5. The relation B-CUST has three constraints:

1. A domain constraint for B-NAME (strings of up to eight characters, taken from the group Central, Eastside, and Westlake). This domain constraint allows us to derive a foreign key–primary key constraint, since every value of B-NAME in B-CUST must also exist in BRANCH.

(a) A valid instance of B-CUST

B-CUST

B-NAME	CUSTOMER#
Central	0093-A6
Eastside	0093-A6
Central	0095-B8
Westlake	0103-A4
Westlake	0239-B7
Eastside	0239-B7

(b) An invalid instance of B-CUST (violation of the B-NAME domain constraint)

B-CUST

B-NAME	CUSTOMER#
Central	0093-A6
Eastside	0093-A6
Central	0095-B8
Westlake	0103-A4
Westlake	0239-B7
Eastside	0239-B7
North	0105-Z1

Figure 4.5 The DK/NF Definition of an Insertion Anomaly

2. A domain constraint for CUSTOMER# (strings of seven characters in the format ####-A#, as previously discussed)
3. A key constraint (B-NAME + CUSTOMER# is the primary key)

Figure 4.5(a) contains a valid instance of B-CUST; all three constraints are met. However, if we add a new tuple (North, 0105-Z1 as in Figure 4.5(b)), we are left with an invalid instance of the relation; the domain constraint (and the derived foreign key–primary key constraint) for B-NAME has been violated. It makes no difference that the insertion makes no logical sense (Small Bank has no North branch); the point is that the structure of the relation cannot prevent the insertion. B-CUST is therefore not in DK/NF.

In concept, DK/NF is very simple and elegant. However, at this time there is no way to put a relation in DK/NF, nor is it clear that it is even desirable to do so for all relations. It therefore remains a theoretical ideal, the ultimate normal form toward which a database designer might wish to work.

SUMMARY

Normalization theory deals with the way in which a given pool of attributes are grouped into relations. Normal forms, the ways in which the attributes can be arranged, provide an increasingly stringent set of rules that relations must meet. While database theorists recognize seven normal forms, many database designers consider only the first three to be of use for practical database design.

To be in first normal form, data must simply be stored in a two-dimensional table which has no repeating groups. First normal form relations, which contain a great deal of data redundancy, have three major classes of problems:

1. Insertion anomalies—data are not available to provide a complete primary key (i.e., some parts of the primary key are null), preventing the insertion of data into the relation.
2. Deletion anomalies—deletion of all or part of a primary key forces the deletion of data that should be retained.
3. Update problems—redundant data storage leads to data disintegrity.

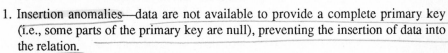

Second normal form relations must be in first normal form and have all non-key attributes fully functionally dependent on the primary key. Functional dependence is a special relationship between two attributes or groups of attributes such that one (the determinant) has one and only one value of a second associated with it at any given time. The second is functionally dependent on the first. Second normal form is rarely used as a design objective. (Second normal form relations can still contain insertion and deletion anomalies.) It is more commonly viewed as a midpoint between first and third normal form.

Third normal form relations must be in second normal form. All transitive dependencies must also be removed. A transitive dependency exists if AttributeA $\rightarrow$ AttributeB $\rightarrow$ Attribute C, where AttributeA is the primary key in the relation. Third normal form relations are generally free of anomalies and, because they contain much less redundant data than first or second normal form relations, are less prone to update problems.

The ultimate normal form is domain/key normal form (DK/NF). DK/NF relations are completely free of insertion and deletion anomalies. In terms of DK/NF, an insertion anomaly exists when it is possible to insert a tuple into a relation so that the resulting instance of the relation violates a constraint on the relation. A deletion anomaly exists when deletion of a tuple from the relation produces a resulting instance that violates a constraint on the relation. At this time, DK/NF remains a design objective. There is no way to place a relation in DK/NF nor is it known whether all relations should be placed in DK/NF.

REFERENCES

Armstrong, W.W. and C. Delobel. (1980) "Decompositions and functional dependencies in relations." *ACM Transactions on Database Systems.* 5(4):404-430.

Beeri, C. (1980) "On the membership problem for functional and multivalued dependencies in relational databases." *ACM Transactions on Database Systems.* 5(2):241-259.

Beeri, C., P.A. Bernstein, and N. Goodman. (1978) "A sophisticate's introduction to database normalization theory." *Proceedings of the Fourth International Conference on Very Large Data Bases.* West Berlin. pp. 113-124.

Carlson, C.R. and A.K. Arora. (1982) "The application of functional dependency theory to relational databases." *Computer Journal.* 25(1):68–71.

Codd, E.F. (1972) "Further normalization of the data base relational model." In: R. Rustin, ed. *Data Base Systems.* Englewood Cliffs, NJ: Prentice-Hall. pp. 33-64.

Date, C. J. (1986) *An Introduction to Database Systems, Vol. I.* 4th ed. Reading, MA: Addison-Wesley.

Deleobel, C. (1978) "Normalization and hierarchical dependencies in the relational database model." *ACM Transactions on Database Systems.* 3(3):201-222.

Fagin, R. (1981) "A normal form for relational databases that is based on domains and keys." *ACM Transactions on Database Systems.* 6(3).

Housel, B.C. et al. (1979) "The functional dependency model for logical data base design." *Proceedings of the Fifth International Conference on Very Large Data Bases.* Rio de Janeiro. pp. 1-15.

Korth, Henry F. and Abraham Silberschatz. (1986) *Database System Concepts.* New York: McGraw-Hill.

Loomis, Mary S. (1987) *The Database Book.* New York: Macmillan.

Salzberg, Betty Jean. (1986) *An Introduction to Data Base Design.* New York: Academic Press.

Yang, Chao-Chih. (1986) *Relational Databases.* Englewood Cliffs, NJ: Prentice-Hall.

EXERCISES

In the first normal form relations below (all are drawn from either the University Archaeological Museum or the office of Margaret Holmes, D.M.D), indicate the following:

1. All functional dependencies that make sense to you in terms of the database environment as described in the interviews at the end of Chapter 2
2. The insertion anomalies
3. The deletion anomalies

Then transform each 1NF relation into a set of 3NF relations. Verify that each meets the criteria for 3NF by indicating the following:

1. All functional dependencies
2. How the relations meet the criteria for second normal form (i.e., justify the claim that all non-key attributes are fully functionally dependent on the primary key)
3. How the relations meet the criteria for third normal form (i.e., justify the claim that all transitive dependencies have been removed)

A. From the office of Margaret Holmes, D.M.D

PAYMENTS (<u>VENDOR</u>, <u>DATE</u>, CHECK#, AMT-PAID, AMT-OWED)

Attributes:

VENDOR	Vendor from whom supplies or drugs are ordered
DATE	Date a payment is made
CHECK#	Number of check used to make payment
AMT-PAID	Amount of check
AMT-OWED	Amount left unpaid with this vendor

B. For the University Archaeological Museum

GRANT (GRANT-NUM, SOURCE, TOTAL-AWARD, PRINCIPAL-RESEARCHER, COST-CNTR-#, COST-CNTR-DESC, ORIG-ALLOC, AMT-AVAIL)

Attributes:

GRANT-NUM	Unique number assigned to each grant
SOURCE	Source of the funding
TOTAL-AWARD	Total amount of the grant
PRINCIPAL-RESEARCHER	Researcher in charge of the grant project
COST-CNTR-#	ID number of a cost center used by a specific grant
COST-CNTR-DESC	Text describing the cost center
ORIG-ALLOC	Amount allocated to the specific cost center
AMT-AVAIL	Amount not yet spent for a specific cost center

C. For the University Archaeological Museum

GRANT-PURCHASES (GRANT-NUM, COST-CENTER#, COST-CNTR-DESC, P-O-NUM, DATE, VENDOR, VENDOR-ADDRESS, ITEM, QUANT, COST-EACH, LINE-COST)

Attributes:

GRANT-NUM	Unique number assigned to each grant
COST-CENTER#	Number assigned to a cost center used by GRANT-NUM
COST-CNTR-DESC	Text describing the cost center
P-O-NUM	Purchase order number

DATE	Date on purchase order
VENDOR	Vendor to whom the purchase order is issued
VENDOR-ADDRESS	Vendor's address
ITEM	Line item being ordered
QUANT	Number of items being ordered
COST-EACH	Cost per item
LINE-COST	Total cost for this item

D. For the University Archaeological Museum

GRANT-PAYROLL (GRANT-NUM, COST-CENTER#, DATE, ID#, NAME, ADDRESS, PHONE, SSN, #-DEDUCTIONS, INS-PLANS, GROSS-PAY, FED-TAX, SS-TAX, STATE-TAX, INSURANCE, NET-PAY)

Attributes:

GRANT-NUM	Grant from which payment is being made
COST-CENTER#	Cost center within the grant
DATE	Date on the check
ID#	Employee ID number
NAME	Employee name
ADDRESS	Employee address
PHONE	Employee home phone
SSN	Employee social security number
#-DEDUCTIONS	Number of deductions being claimed by employee
INS-PLANS	Cost of insurance plans for which employee is enrolled
GROSS-PAY	Gross pay for this check
FED-TAX	Federal tax deducted from this check
SS-TAX	Social security tax deducted from this check
STATE-TAX	State tax deducted from this check
INSURANCE	Insurance costs deducted from this check
NET-PAY	Net pay for this check

Relational Algebra

CHAPTER OUTLINE:

CHAPTER OBJECTIVES

After reading this chapter, you will:

1. Understand the five major relational algebra operations: project, select, join, union, and difference
2. Be familiar with the less frequently used relational algebra operations: product, intersect, and divide
3. Understand how information is retrieved from relational databases using operations from the relational algebra

Relations are manipulated with either the *relational calculus* or the *relational algebra*. The relational calculus uses the notation of formal logic to express complex queries in a single command. The relational algebra is much simpler. Each command performs a single function. It may therefore require a series of relational algebra commands to complete a single query.

In order to be considered *relationally complete*, a DBMS must support at least five operations from the relational algebra: select, project, join, union, and difference. *Select* is used to retrieve tuples from a relation. *Project* is used to take a subset of the columns of a relation (often referred to as a cut). *Join* is used to paste relations together by matching values against a condition. *Union* combines all tuples from two relations, and *difference* produces all tuples from one relation that are not contained in another.

DBMSs also occasionally make use of three other relational operations: product, intersect, and divide. *Product* combines two relations by creating new tuples for all possible combinations of tuples. *Intersecting* two relations produces a result consisting of all tuples that appear in both relations. *Divide*, which works on a relation with one column (a *unary* relation) and another with two columns (a *binary* relation), extracts values from the binary relation in a manner that will be discussed later in this chapter.

It is important to realize that while full-featured DBMSs use five or more of the relational algebra operations to implement data retrieval, it is not necessarily true that the DBMS's query language contains individual commands which perform those operations. As you will see in Chapters 8, 10, and 11, many single query language commands perform more than one relational algebra operation.

The result of all eight relational algebra operations is a virtual table that is retained in main memory while an application needs it; none of the relational operations modify a base table.

Select is one major tool used for retrieval from relational databases. A select operation is qualified to return tuples that meet only a particular criteria. Join, union, difference, product, intersect, and divide are also retrieval tools.

Project, however, is a design tool as well as a retrieval tool. Third normal form databases are actually groups of projections (or subsets) of first normal form relations. In other words, the decomposition of 1NF relations to 3NF relations is accomplished by taking projections.

PROJECT

A projection of a relation is a new relation created by assembling one or more of the columns from the original relation. As an example, consider Figure 5.1. The relation TRANS is a projection of the relation BANK with the attributes CUSTOMER#, ACCOUNT#, TRANS#, and AMT.

BANK

CUSTOMER#	CUSTOMER	ADDRESS	PHONE	SSN	ACCOUNT#	TRANS#	AMT
0093-A6	Jones, Samuel	105 W. 99th, 02899	555-0345	123451234	N2489B4908	860914-114	+1500.00
0093-A6	Jones, Samuel	105 W. 99th, 02899	555-0345	123451234	N2489B4908	860914-115	-25.00
0095-B8	Abrams, Max	2204 Nox Hill, 02845	555-1414	098765432	N3939B4109	860914-395	+500.00
0103-A4	Cohen, Esther	39 Summer, 02845	555-8486	019283745	N5577B4107	860914-884	+750.00
0103-A4	Cohen, Esther	39 Summer, 02845	555-8486	019283745	N5577B4107	860914-885	-55.25
0103-A4	Cohen, Esther	39 Summer, 02845	555-8486	019283745	N5577B4107	860914-886	-106.95
0239-B7	Khan, Satya	1001 N. 54th, 02898	555-7623	567123489	S1219A2998	860914-005	-10.00

TRANS

CUSTOMER#	ACCOUNT#	TRANS#	AMT
0093-A6	N2489B4908	860914-114	+1500.00
0093-A6	N2489B4908	860914-115	-25.00
0095-B8	N3939B4109	860914-395	+500.00
0103-A4	N5577B4107	860914-884	+750.00
0103-A4	N5577B4107	860914-885	-55.25
0103-A4	N5577B4107	860914-886	-106.95
0239-B7	S1219A2998	860914-005	-10.00

TRANS = Π BANK (ACCOUNT#, TRANS#, CUSTOMER#, AMT)

Figure 5.1 Taking a Projection

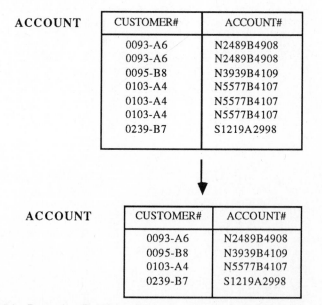

TRANS

CUSTOMER#	ACCOUNT#	TRANS#	AMT
0093-A6	N2489B4908	860914-114	+1500.00
0093-A6	N2489B4908	860914-115	-25.00
0095-B8	N3939B4109	860914-395	+500.00
0103-A4	N5577B4107	860914-884	+750.00
0103-A4	N5577B4107	860914-885	-55.25
0103-A4	N5577B4107	860914-886	-106.95
0239-B7	S1219A2998	860914-005	-10.00

ACCOUNT = $\prod$ TRANS (CUSTOMER#, ACCOUNT#)

ACCOUNT

CUSTOMER#	ACCOUNT#
0093-A6	N2489B4908
0093-A6	N2489B4908
0095-B8	N3939B4109
0103-A4	N5577B4107
0103-A4	N5577B4107
0103-A4	N5577B4107
0239-B7	S1219A2998

Figure 5.2(a)   The First Stage in Taking a Projection

ACCOUNT

CUSTOMER#	ACCOUNT#
0093-A6	N2489B4908
0093-A6	N2489B4908
0095-B8	N3939B4109
0103-A4	N5577B4107
0103-A4	N5577B4107
0103-A4	N5577B4107
0239-B7	S1219A2998

ACCOUNT

CUSTOMER#	ACCOUNT#
0093-A6	N2489B4908
0095-B8	N3939B4109
0103-A4	N5577B4107
0239-B7	S1219A2998

Figure 5.2(b)   Removing Duplicate Tuples to Obtain the Final Result of a Projection

In the relational algebra, the projection in Figure 5.1 is written:

TRANS = ∏ BANK (CUSTOMER#, ACCOUNT#, TRANS#, AMT)

∏ is the projection operator.

Projection removes duplicate tuples from the resultant relation. That means that projections may have fewer tuples than the relation from which they were taken. Figure 5.2(a) contains the intermediate result from the following projection:

ACCOUNT = ∏ TRANS (CUSTOMER#, ACCOUNT#)

Note that this relation contains duplicate pairs of customer number and account number. The final result which is returned appears in Figure 5.2(b). All the duplicate tuples are gone.

While it is theoretically possible to create projections from any combination of the columns in a relation, not all projections may be valid. In other words, some projections may produce resultant relations that contain misleading information. Consider the projection in Figure 5.3:

PLACE = ∏ BANK (ADDRESS, TRANS#)

The relation PLACE is nonsense. It implies that there is some relationship between a transaction and a physical address. In the terms of the meaning of this database environment, an address is related to a customer and a transaction number to an account, but when the customer number and account number are missing from a relation, the associations are lost.

There is no set of rules as to what constitutes a valid projection. As with determining functional dependencies, judgments as to the validity of projections depends a great deal on the meaning of the data the database is attempting to capture.

JOIN

The join operation pastes two relations together. It is used primarily to implement retrieval operations in which data are stored in two or more relations. Assume that Small Bank's account and transaction data are stored as follows:

PEOPLE (<u>CUSTOMER#</u>, CUSTOMER, ADDRESS, PHONE, SSN)
ACCT (<u>CUSTOMER#</u>, ACCOUNT#)
TRANS (<u>ACCOUNT#</u>, <u>TRANS#</u>, AMT)

BANK

CUSTOMER#	CUSTOMER	ADDRESS	PHONE	SSN	ACCOUNT#	TRANS#	AMT
0093-A6	Jones, Samuel	105 W. 99th, 02899	555-0345	123451234	N2489B4908	860914-114	+1500.00
0093-A6	Jones, Samuel	105 W. 99th, 02899	555-0345	123451234	N2489B4908	860914-115	-25.00
0095-B8	Abrams, Max	2204 Nox Hill, 02845	555-1414	098765432	N3939B4109	860914-395	+500.00
0103-A4	Cohen, Esther	39 Summer, 02845	555-8486	019283745	N5577B4107	860914-884	+750.00
0103-A4	Cohen, Esther	39 Summer, 02845	555-8486	019283745	N5577B4107	860914-885	-55.25
0103-A4	Cohen, Esther	39 Summer, 02845	555-8486	019283745	N5577B4107	860914-886	-106.95
0239-B7	Khan, Satya	1001 N. 54th, 02898	555-7623	567123489	S1219A2998	860914-005	-10.00

PLACE = Π BANK (ADDRESS, TRANS#)

PLACE

ADDRESS	TRANS#
105 W. 99th, 02899	860914-114
105 W. 99th, 02899	860914-115
2204 Nox Hill, 02845	860914-395
39 Summer, 02845	860914-884
39 Summer, 02845	860914-885
39 Summer, 02845	860914-886
1001 N. 54th, 02898	960914-005

Figure 5.3   An Invalid Projection

If the DBMS receives a request to print out the name, address, and account numbers for each of Small Bank's customers, it must not only consult both PEOPLE and ACCT to locate all the relevant data, but it must have some way to associate the right account numbers with the right names and addresses.

Tuples in PEOPLE and ACCT are linked by the value of CUSTOMER#, the foreign key in ACCT that references the primary key in PEOPLE. Therefore, tuples with matching values for CUSTOMER# can be pasted together and included in a new relation which is the result of the join. Using the relational algebra, the operation is written:

LIST = PEOPLE * ACCT (CUSTOMER, ADDRESS, ACCOUNT#)

The join operator is *. A join can include all the attributes in both relations or selected attributes from either. In this example, only three attributes will be included in the result. Note that the attribute that is being used to match the tuples (e.g., CUSTOMER#) need not be part of the new relation. Like project, join excludes duplicate tuples. The result of this join appears in Figure 5.4.

Join is a directional operation. In Figure 5.4, PEOPLE was joined to ACCT in the following manner: each value for CUSTOMER# from PEOPLE was compared to each occurrence of CUSTOMER# in ACCT. If a match was found, CUSTOMER, ADDRESS, and ACCOUNT# were copied to LIST.

While it is theoretically possible to join any two relations, the result of a join is not always valid. As an example, consider the following expanded version of the Small Bank database:

PEOPLE (CUSTOMER#, CUSTOMER, ADDRESS, PHONE, SSN)
BRANCH (B-NAME, B-ADDRESS, B-PHONE, HOURS)
B-CUST (B-NAME, CUSTOMER#)
B-ACCT (ACCOUNT#, B-NAME)
ACCT (CUSTOMER#, ACCOUNT#)
TRANS (ACCOUNT#, TRANS#, AMT)

The relation BRANCH contains data about each of Small Bank's branches (the name, address, telephone number, and customer service hours). B-CUST represents all customers who have accounts at a given branch. This is a many-to-many relationship, since any customer can have accounts at more than one branch. B-ACCT represents the association between an account and the branch where it is located; any given account can be located at only one branch.

Given these relations, is it necessary to retain the relation ACCT in the database? Surely it could be generated as the join of B-ACCT and B-CUST using B-NAME to match the tuples. The join would be written as:

ACCT = B-ACCT * B-CUST (CUSTOMER#, ACCOUNT#)

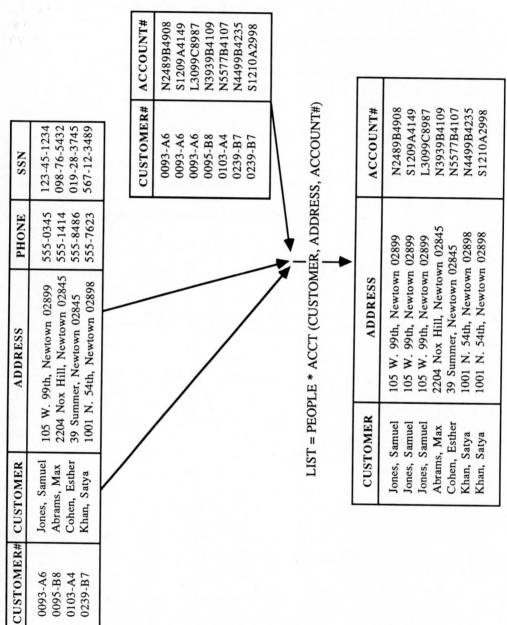

Figure 5.4   A Join

The result of this join appears in Figure 5.5. Something is clearly wrong; this relation indicates that each ACCOUNT# belongs to every customer at the account's branch. How did this happen? Remember how a join works: the DBMS takes the B-NAME associated with each ACCOUNT# in B-ACCT and looks for a match in B-CUST. Whenever a match is found, a new tuple is created for ACCT.

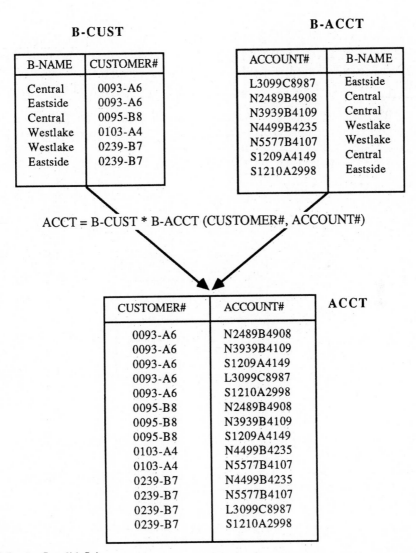

Figure 5.5 An Invalid Join

The joins that we have looked at to this point are based on matching values of an attribute held in common by the two relations being joined. This type of join is referred to as a *natural* join and is the one most commonly used. It is also possible to join relations based on other criteria, such as an inequality of values in the shared attribute.

SELECT

The select operation is often misunderstood, primarily because it is used as a retrieval operator by a number of DBMS query languages. As defined in the relational algebra, select creates a new table by copying rows from a relation that meet a specified criteria. Select copies all attributes in the relation; it has no facility for specifying which attributes should be included in the resulting table.

For example, suppose we want to retrieve the customer numbers of those customers who have accounts at Small Bank's Central branch. The operation might be expressed as:

SELECT FROM B-CUST WHERE B-NAME = "Central" GIVING ONE-BRANCH

B-CUST

B-NAME	CUSTOMER#
Central	0093-A6
Eastside	0093-A6
Central	0095-B8
Westlake	0103-A4
Westlake	0239-B7
Eastside	0239-B7

SELECT FROM B-CUST WHERE B-NAME = "Central" GIVING ONE-BRANCH

B-NAME	CUSTOMER#
Central	0093-A6
Central	0095-B8

ONE-BRANCH

Figure 5.6 Selecting Tuples

The result appears in Figure 5.6. This select does retrieve the numbers of all customers at North Central branch; however, since select cannot choose which attributes to include, the B-NAME attribute is also included in the result table, ONE-BRANCH.

UNION

Union combines all tuples from two relations into a single, resultant relation. In order for union to work, however, the two relations being combined must be *union-compatible*. That means that their structure must be identical; they must contain the same columns. The columns do not necessarily have to have the same names, but they must have the same logical domain.

For example, assume that Small Bank merges with Smaller Bank. Smaller Bank is also using a database system. The relations in their database are:

CUSTOMERS (<u>CUST#</u>, C-NAME, C-ADD, C-PHONE, C-SSN)
ACCOUNTS (<u>CUST#</u>, ACCT#)
TRANSACTIONS (<u>ACCT#</u>, <u>T-DATE</u>, <u>T-CODE</u>, AMT)

While none of these relations have the same column names as Small Bank's PEOPLE, ACCT, and TRANS relations, some union-compatibility does exist. CUSTOMERS is union-compatible with PEOPLE, since each attribute in CUSTOMERS corresponds exactly to an attribute in PEOPLE. The same is true for ACCOUNTS; it matches ACCT attribute for attribute. However, TRANSACTIONS does not match TRANS. Smaller Bank records transaction data differently from Small Bank; the date and type of transaction aren't built into the transaction number as they are in the Small Bank system. TRANSACTIONS and TRANS are not union compatible.

Small Bank can use the union operation to compile a single list of customers. Figure 5.7 shows the result of a union operation on Small Bank's PEOPLE relation and Smaller Bank's CUSTOMERS relation.

DIFFERENCE

The difference operation produces a result that consists of all tuples in the first relation that are not present in the second (i.e., it subtracts the second relation in the command from the first). Tuples which appear in the second relation but not the first are ignored. To obtain a valid result, difference should only be performed on union-compatible relations.

PEOPLE

CUSTOMER#	CUSTOMER	ADDRESS	PHONE	SSN
0093-A6	Jones, Samuel	105 W. 99th, Newtown 02899	555-0345	123-45-1234
0095-B8	Abrams, Max	2204 Nox Hill, Newtown 02845	555-1414	098-76-5432
0103-A4	Cohen, Esther	39 Summer, Newtown 02845	555-8486	019-28-3745
0239-B7	Khan, Satya	1001 N. 54th, Newtown 02898	555-7623	567-12-3489

CUSTOMERS

CUST#	C-NAME	C-ADD	C-PHONE	C-SSN
0093-A6	Jones, Samuel	105 W. 99th, Newtown 02899	555-0345	123-45-1234
0095-A4	Abrams, Max	2204 Nox Hill, Newtown 02845	555-1414	098-76-5432
0125-C1	Marx, Edward	80 Barns Road, Newtown 02811	555-3908	102-93-8475
0188-B5	Loomis, Ella	Old Mill Farm, Newtown 02845	555-8765	800-90-1000

PEOPLE UNION CUSTOMERS

ALL-CUSTOMERS

CUSTOMER#	CUSTOMER	ADDRESS	PHONE	SSN
0093-A6	Jones, Samuel	105 W. 99th, Newtown 02899	555-0345	123-45-1234
0095-B8	Abrams, Max	2204 Nox Hill, Newtown 02845	555-1414	098-76-5432
0103-A4	Cohen, Esther	39 Summer, Newtown 02845	555-8486	019-28-3745
0239-B7	Khan, Satya	1001 N. 54th, Newtown 02898	555-7623	567-12-3489
0125-C1	Marx, Edward	80 Barns Road, Newtown 02811	555-3908	102-93-8475
0188-B5	Loomis, Ella	Old Mill Farm, Newtown 02845	555-8765	800-90-1000

Figure 5.7   The Union of Two Relations

PEOPLE

CUSTOMER#	CUSTOMER	ADDRESS	PHONE	SSN
0093-A6	Jones, Samuel	105 W. 99th, Newtown 02899	555-0345	123-45-1234
0095-B8	Abrams, Max	2204 Nox Hill, Newtown 02845	555-1414	098-76-5432
0103-A4	Cohen, Esther	39 Summer, Newtown 02845	555-8486	019-28-3745
0239-B7	Khan, Satya	1001 N. 54th, Newtown 02898	555-7623	567-12-3489

CUSTOMERS

CUST#	C-NAME	C-ADD	C-PHONE	C-SSN
0093-A6	Jones, Samuel	105 W. 99th, Newtown 02899	555-0345	123-45-1234
0095-B8	Abrams, Max	2204 Nox Hill, Newtown 02845	555-1414	098-76-5432
0125-C1	Marx, Edward	80 Barns Road, Newtown 02811	555-3908	102-93-8475
0188-B5	Loomis, Ella	Old Mill Farm, Newtown 02845	555-8765	800-90-1000

PEOPLE - CUSTOMERS

SMALLER-BANK-ONLY

CUSTOMER#	CUSTOMER	ADDRESS	PHONE	SSN
0103-A4	Cohen, Esther	39 Summer, Newtown 02845	555-3908	102-93-8475
0239-B7	Khan, Satya	1001 N. 54th, Newtown 02898	555-8765	800-90-1000

Figure 5.8 Taking the Difference of Two Relations

Difference is a very handy retrieval tool. It is used primarily to answers questions involving a negative. For example, it can be used to identify all Small Bank customers who are not Smaller Bank customers by taking the difference between PEOPLE and CUSTOMERS. That operation is summarized in Figure 5.8.

INTERSECT

The intersect operation is the opposite of union. While union produces a result containing all tuples that appear in *either* relation, intersection produces a result containing all tuples that appear in *both* relations. Intersection can therefore only be performed on two union-compatible relations.

Intersection is useful for identifying entities that have some characteristic in common. For example, if Small Bank wished to know which of its customers also had accounts at Smaller Bank, they could intersect PEOPLE and CUSTOMERS. The result, seen in Figure 5.9, contains only tuples for only those individuals who have matching tuples in both PEOPLE and CUSTOMERS.

Be aware that there is a potential problem with an intersection. In order for a tuple to be included in the result, it must exist in *exactly* the same way in the two relations being intersected. In the example we have just seen, if a customer's address is stored as 105 W. 99th in PEOPLE but as 105 W. 99th Place in CUSTOMERS, the intersection will not recognize the two tuples as being equivalent.

PRODUCT

Some people say that the product of two relations is a join run wild. The product operation creates new tuples by concatenating every tuple from one relation onto every tuple in another. In other words, it creates all possible pairs of tuples. If one of the relations in the operation has 15 tuples and the other 20 tuples, the virtual table created by taking their product will contain 300 tuples.

Assume, for example, that we wish to take the product of Small Bank's relations B-CUST and B-ACCT. The result of the operation appears in Figure 5.10. Clearly, the new relation created by this operation is meaningless. It is important to realize that, while it is theoretically possible to take the product of any two relations, the result may not be valid, just as the join shown in Figure 5.5 is invalid.

PEOPLE

CUSTOMER#	CUSTOMER	ADDRESS	PHONE	SSN
0093-A6	Jones, Samuel	105 W. 99th, Newtown 02899	555-0345	123-45-1234
0095-B8	Abrams, Max	2204 Nox Hill, Newtown 02845	555-1414	098-76-5432
0103-A4	Cohen, Esther	39 Summer, Newtown 02845	555-8486	019-28-3745
0239-B7	Khan, Satya	1001 N. 54th, Newtown 02898	555-7623	567-12-3489

CUSTOMERS

CUST#	C-NAME	C-ADD	C-PHONE	C-SSN
0093-A6	Jones, Samuel	105 W. 99th, Newtown 02899	555-0345	123-45-1234
0095-B8	Abrams, Max	2204 Nox Hill, Newtown 02845	555-1414	098-76-5432
0125-C1	Marx, Edward	80 Barns Road, Newtown 02811	555-3908	102-93-8475
0188-B5	Loomis, Ella	Old Mill Farm, Newtown 02845	555-8765	800-90-1000

PEOPLE INTERSECT CUSTOMERS

BOTH-BANKS

CUSTOMER#	CUSTOMER	ADDRESS	PHONE	SSN
0093-A6	Jones, Samuel	105 W. 99th, Newtown 02899	555-0345	123-45-1234
0095-A4	Abrams, Max	2204 Nox Hill, Newtown, 02845	555-1414	098-76-5432

Figure 5.9   The Intersection of Two Relations

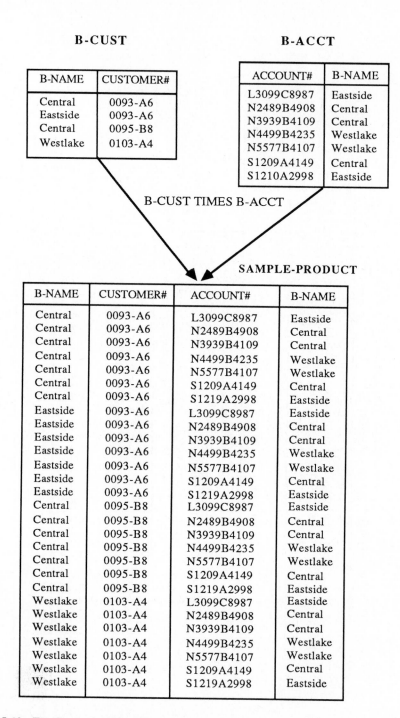

Figure 5.10 The Product of Two Relations

DIVIDE

The divide operation is perhaps the least intuitive of all the operations in the relational algebra. Division requires two relations: a *unary* relation (one with only a single column) and a *binary* relation (one with two columns).

To see how it works, assume that we have a new relation for Small Bank, B-NAMES (B-NAME). In Figure 5.11, B-NAMES contains only two tuples, one for the Central branch and one for the Eastside branch. If we divide B-CUST (the dividend) by B-NAMES (the divisor), we get a unary relation (DOUBLES) as the result. Its single column is CUS-TOMER#, the column that B-CUST and B-NAMES do not have in common. If you look at the data in DOUBLES, you will see that it contains the customer numbers of all people who have an account at *both* the Central branch and the Eastside branch.

Division retrieves values from the column of the dividend relation which it does not share with the divisor relation. However, values are selected by looking for matches between the overlapping column (e.g., B-NAME). To be included in the result, a value in the nonoverlapping column (CUSTOMER#) must be associated, in the dividend relation, with *every* value in the divisor relation. In our example, a given customer number may occur at least twice in PEOPLE; one tuple might have a value of Central for B-NAME, the other a value of Eastside for B-NAME. If those two tuples do appear, then the customer number will be placed in the result.

B-CUST

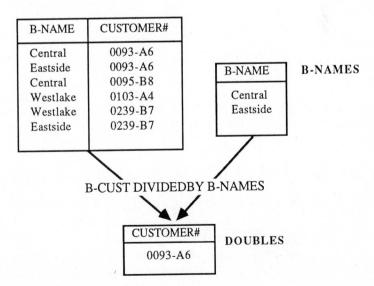

Figure 5.11 Dividing One Relation by Another

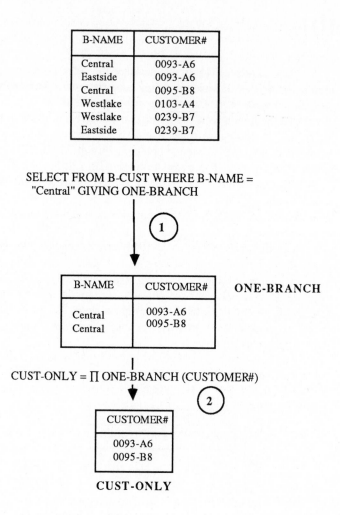

Figure 5.12 A Query Using Select and Project

RETRIEVAL WITH OPERATIONS FROM THE RELATIONAL ALBEGRA

Complex retrievals can be implemented by using a series of operations from the relational algebra. The SELECT command found in DBMS query languages works in just that way.

As a simple example, consider completing the query presented earlier in this chapter: retrieve the numbers of all customers served by Small Bank's Central branch. It's really a two-step operation:

1. Select all tuples in B-CUST that have a branch name of Central, creating ONE-BRANCH
2. Take a projection of ONE-BRANCH including only the customer number attribute, creating CUST-ONLY

This operation is summarized in Figure 5.12.

Realistically, simply retrieving customer numbers doesn't provide a great deal of useful information. A more useful query would be: retrieve the names of all the customers who have accounts at Small Bank's Central branch. This retrieval requires three steps:

1. Select tuples from B-CUST that have a branch name of Central, creating ONE-BRANCH
2. Take a projection of ONE-BRANCH including only the customer number attribute, creating CUST-ONLY
3. Join CUST-ONLY to PEOPLE, including the attributes CUSTOMER# and CUSTOMER in the result, CUST-NAMES

Look at Figure 5.13 to see the interim and final results of this query.

If a customer telephoned Small Bank's main office, asking for the operating hours of each branch at which he or she had an account, the bank's DBMS could retrieve the information with the following sequence of operations:

1. Select the tuple from PEOPLE that corresponds to the name of the person making the query, creating ONE-PERSON
2. Take a projection of ONE-PERSON, including the attribute CUSTOMER# in the result, ONE-CUST#
3. Join ONE-CUST# to B-CUST, including B-NAME in the result, BRANCHES
4. Join BRANCHES to BRANCH, including B-NAME and HRS in the result, TIMES

For a summary of the steps in the process, see Figure 5.14.

Most relational DBMSs isolate the user from part of the sequence of relational algebra operations needed to implement a query. Even if the DBMS cannot automatically execute a query that requires data from more than one table (i.e., requiring the DBMS to execute a join), it will at least have the capability of doing a select and a project in a single operation. In other words, it is generally possible to select tuples based on some criteria and to specify which attributes should be included in the result with a single instruction to the DBMS. Details of how *dBase III Plus*, *R:base System V*, and *Oracle* handle query implementation can be found in Part II of this book.

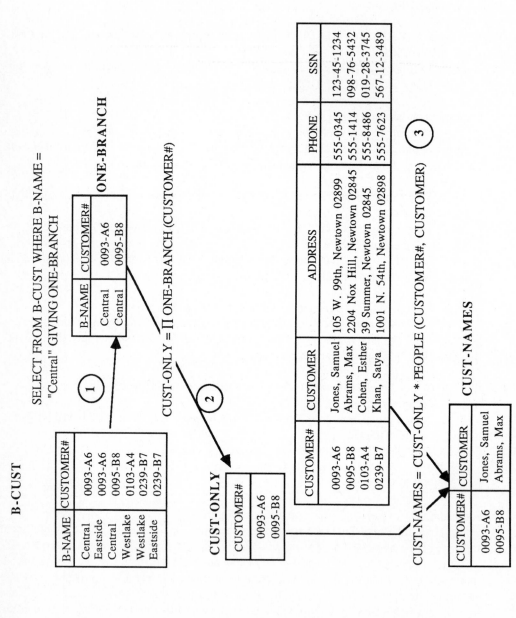

Figure 5.13   A Query Using Select, Project, and Join

PEOPLE

CUSTOMER#	CUSTOMER	ADDRESS	PHONE	SSN
0093-A6	Jones, Samuel	105 W. 99th, Newtown 02899	555-0345	123-45-1234
0095-B8	Abrams, Max	2204 Nox Hill, Newtown 02845	555-1414	098-76-5432
0103-A4	Cohen, Esther	39 Summer, Newtown 02845	555-8486	019-28-3745
0239-B7	Khan, Satya	1001 N. 54th, Newtown 02898	555-7623	567-12-3489

(1) SELECT FROM PEOPLE WHERE CUSTOMER = "Khan, Satya" GIVING ONE-PERSON

ONE-PERSON

CUSTOMER#	CUSTOMER	ADDRESS	PHONE	SSN
0239-B7	Kahn, Satya	1001 N. 54th, Newtown 02898	555-7623	567-12-3489

(2) ONE-CUST# = $\prod$ ONE-PERSON (CUSTOMER #)

ONE-CUST#

CUSTOMER#
0239-B7

BRANCHES = B-CUST * ONE-CUST# (B-NAME)

B-CUST

B-NAME	CUSTOMER#
Central	0093-A6
Eastside	0093-A6
Central	0095-B8
Westlake	0103-A4
Westlake	0239-B7
Eastside	0239-B7

(3)

BRANCHES

B-NAME
Westlake
Eastside

(4) TIMES = BRANCH * BRANCHES (B-NAME, HRS)

B-NAME	B-ADDRESS	B-PHONE	HRS
Central	100 Central Square, Newtown 02311	555-0100	830-1800 M-F
Eastside	4232 E. 44th, Newtown 02617	555-4232	0900-1200 M-S
Westlake	109 Lake Street, Newtown 02315	555-0109	0830-1630 M-F

BRANCH

TIMES

B-NAME	HRS
Westlake	0900-1200 M-S
Eastside	0830-1630 M-F

Figure 5.14 Using Select, Project, and Join to Retrieve a Branch's Operating Hours

QUERYING THE FEDERATED TAXI COMPANY DATABASE

As you will remember, the cab scheduling and maintenance records for the Federated Taxi Company are being kept in the following five relations:

CAB (<u>CABNUM</u>, MAKE, MODEL, YEAR, PURDATE, LICNUM, CONDITN, CABSTAT, CURODOM)

DRIVER (<u>DRVNUM</u>, DRVSTR, DRVCSZ, DRVPHONE, DRVLIC, DRVLEXD, DRVSTAT)

SHIFTS (<u>WKDATE</u>, <u>WKSHIFT</u>,<u>CABNUM</u>, DRVNUM, WKFLAG, ODOMRDG1, ODOMRDG2)

INCIDENTS (<u>CABNUM</u>, <u>WKDATE</u>, <u>WKSHIFT</u>, INCITYPE, DETAILS)

MAINTENANCE (<u>CABNUM</u>, <u>MAINDATE</u>, <u>MAINTYPE</u>, MAINODOM)

Operations from the relational algebra can be used to retrieve information from these relations to produce the outputs requested by the systems analysis reported in Chapter 2. The procedures described below are not the only way in which the reports can be generated but are suggestive of the steps a DBMS must take to extract information from a relational database.

CABS AVAILABLE (FIGURE 2.8)

Obtaining a list of all cabs not reserved for a particular day and shift is a fairly straightforward procedure:

1. Select all tuples from SHIFTS that match the date and shift in question.
2. Project out the cab number.
3. Project CABNUM from CAB.
4. Find the difference between the relation created in step three and the relation created in step two.

CAB INFO (FIGURE 2.5)

The Cab Info screen displays data from CAB and MAINTENANCE. To retrieve it, a DBMS must do the following:

1. Select the tuple from CAB that has a CABNUM matching the number of the cab about which data are requested.

2. Take a projection from the result of step one, including CABNUM, MAKE, MODEL, YEAR, LICNUM, CABSTAT, and CURODOM. The data from the resulting relation can be displayed to create the first output lines of the screen.
3. Select all tuples from MAINTENANCE that have a CABNUM matching the number of the cab about which data are requested.
4. Take a projection of the interim relation created by step three to capture MAIN-DATE and MAINTYPE. The resulting relation contains the data needed for the rest of the screen.

DRIVER INFO (FIGURE 2.7)

The driver info screen requires data from both DRIVER and SHIFTS. It can be created using the following steps:

1. Select the tuple from DRIVER that matches the DRVNUM of the driver about whom data is to be displayed. The result of this operation can be used to print the first two lines of the display screen using DRVNAM, DRVPHONE, and DRVSTAT.
2. Take a projection of the result of step one to include only the DRVNUM.
3. Join the relation from step two with SHIFT. This will create a new relation that contains data that pertains only to shifts the driver in question has reserved or driven.
4. Take a projection of the result of step three, including WKDATE, WKSHIFT, CABNUM, and WKFLAG. The relation created by this final step contains the data for the remainder of the screen.

TUNE-UP LIST (FIGURE 2.6)

The tune-up list is actually asking the DBMS to make a decision about which cabs need tune-ups. In order to make that sort of decision, the DBMS must be given a rule by which it should select cabs. For example, if FTC's chief mechanic has determined that cabs should be given complete tune-ups at least every three months, then the DBMS should be instructed to select all cabs whose date of last tune-up is more than three months prior to the current date.

Because the output format also includes the date and type of last maintenance, producing this particular report becomes a fairly complex process. The steps needed might be as follows:

1. Select all tuples from MAINTENANCE where (a) MAINTYPE is tune-up and MAINDATE is more than three months ago; and (b) where MAINDATE is greater than all other MAINDATEs with a MAINTYPE of tune-up for each particular

CABNUM. While this selection may seem to contain more criteria than necessary, consider this: if part (b) is not present, the resulting relation will contain tuples for *every* tune-up performed on every cab that hasn't been tuned in the last three months.

2. Take a projection from the result of step one to obtain a relation consisting only of CABNUM. This creates a table that contains the numbers of all cabs that need tune-ups, which can be used for the rest of the retrieval process.

3. Join the relation created in step two to MAINTENANCE, including only CABNUM, MAINDATE, and MAINTYPE. (This creates a relation containing the maintenance records of only those cabs needing tune-ups.)

4. Select the tuples from step three which have the latest MAINDATE for any given CABNUM.

5. Join the result of step one to the result of step four, including CABNUM, MAINDATE from step four, MAINTYPE from step four, and MAINDATE from step one. (One of the two MAINDATEs will have to be renamed.)

6. Join the relation created in step two to CAB, including CABNUM and LICNUM.

7. Join the relation from step six to the relation from step five, using all attributes.

It is important to realize that while all these steps are necessary to create the tune-up listing, most DBMSs provide a number of shortcuts for retrieving data. The number of commands a user or application program must issue is usually less than the number of operations the DBMS is performing. However, any query which must retrieve the "last" of a series of events recorded about some entity tends to be difficult.

SUMMARY

A relationally complete DBMS supports five operations from the relational algebra: select, project, join, union, and difference. The result of each of these operations is a virtual table; none modify base tables. Data retrieval from a relational database can be performed by combining sequences of these five operations.

Select extracts rows from a table based on some logical criteria. The result of select is a virtual table that contains all attributes from the original table but only those tuples that meet the logical criteria contained in the command; select cannot restrict which columns will be included in the result. Select is the most easily confused of the relational algebra operations, since many DBMSs use SELECT as a retrieval command. The retrieval command is more powerful than the relational algebra operation, since it can perform multiple relational algebra operations to implement a query.

Project extracts columns from a table. The result of a project is a virtual table that contains all tuples from the original table but only those columns specified in the project command. Project cannot restrict which tuples are included in the result. Project is the major tool used to create 3NF relations from 1NF relations. 3NF databases are sets of projections taken from a 1NF database.

Join combines two tables into one. The most common form, the natural join, creates new tuples in a virtual table by searching for matching values in the columns that the two tables have in common. Other, less frequently used types of joins create new tuples based on relationships other than equality between attributes in the two tables.

Union and difference are applicable only to tables with the same columns. (Though the columns do not necessarily require the same names, they must have the same logical domains.) Union combines two tables into a single result, including all tuples from both the source tables. The result of a difference operation is a virtual table containing all tuples from one relation that are not in the second.

The relational algebra also provides three less frequently used operations: intersect, product, and divide. Intersect, which is applicable only to union-compatible relations, produces a resultant relation that contains tuples found in both the relations being intersected. Product produces every possible pair of concatenated tuples from two relations. Divide retrieves values from the dividend relation that match all the values from the divisor relation in a column shared by both relations.

REFERENCES

Aho, A.V. et al. (1979) "The theory of joins in relational databases." *ACM Transactions on Database Systems*. 4(3):297-314.

Codd, E.F. (1972) "Relational completeness of data base sublanguages." In: *Data Base Systems*. Courant Computer Science Symposia Series, Vol. 6. Englewood Cliffs, NJ: Prentice-Hall.

Date, C.J. (1986a) *An Introduction to Database Systems, Vol I*. Reading, MA: Addison-Wesley.

Date, C.J. (1986b) *Relational Database*. Reading, MA: Addison-Wesley.

Hall, P.A.V., P. Hitchcock, and S.J.P. Todd. (1975) "An algebra of relations for machine computation." *Conference Record of the Second ACM Symposium on Principles of Programming Languages*.

Hall, P.A.V. (1984) "Relational algebras, logic, and functional programming." *Proceedings of the 1984 AMC SIGMOD International Conference on Management of Data*. June.

McFadden, Fred R. and Jeffrey A Hoffer. (1985) *Data Base Management*. Menlo Park, CA: Benjamin/Cummings.

Salzberg, Betty Joan. (1986) *An Introduction to Data Base Design*. New York: Academic Press.

EXERCISES

Given the instances of relations in Figure 5.15 (from the office of Margaret Holmes, D.M.D.), perform the relational operations indicated. Express your result as the instance of a new relation.

1. PAT-LIST = ∏ PATIENT-MASTER (PATIENT#, NAME, PHONE)
2. PAYER-LIST = ∏ PAYERS (WHO-PAYS, EMPLOYER, P-PHONE, W-PHONE)
3. PAT-HISTORY = PATIENT-MASTER * VISITS (PATIENT#, NAME, DATE, PROCEDURE)
4. COSTS-BY-PATIENT = VISITS * COSTS (PATIENT#, PROCEDURE, DATE, PRICE)
5. COSTS-BY-PAYER = COSTS-BY-PATIENT * PATIENT-MASTER (WHO-PAYS, NAME, PROCEDURE, DATE, PRICE)
6. SELECT FROM VISITS WHERE PROCEDURE = "Cleaning" GIVING WHO-CLEANED
7. PEOPLE-CLEANED = WHO-CLEANED * PATIENT-MASTER (PATIENT#, NAME)
8. SELECT FROM PAYERS WHERE INSURANCE-CARRIER = "none" GIVING NO-INS
9. CASH-PATIENTS = NO-INS * PATIENT-MASTER (PATIENT#, NAME)

Given the following set of relations for the University Archaeological Museum, list the sequence of selects, projects, and joins needed to implement the queries indicated.

SLIDE (<u>DIG</u>, <u>SEQ-NUM</u>, S-DESCRIPTION)
SUBJECTS (<u>SUBJECT</u>, <u>DIG</u>, <u>SEQ-NUM</u>)
BORROWED (<u>DIG</u>, <u>SEQ-NUM</u>, <u>S-BORROWER</u>, S-DATE-DUE, RETURN-FLAG)

GRANT (<u>GRANT-NUM</u>, SOURCE, TOTAL-AWARD, PRINCIPAL-RESEARCHER)
DIGS (<u>GRANT-NUM</u>, <u>DIG</u>)
BUDGETS (<u>GRANT-NUM</u>, <u>COST-CENTER#</u>, COST-CNTR-DESC, ORIG-ALLOC, AMT-AVAIL)
GRANT-PURCHASES (<u>P-O-NUM</u>, GRANT-NUM, COST-CENTER#,VENDOR, DATE, TOTAL-AMT)
ITEMS (<u>P-O-NUM</u>, <u>ITEM</u>, QUANT, COST-EACH, LINE-COST)
VENDORS (<u>VENDOR</u>, V-ADDRESS, V-PHONE, CONTACT-PERSON)
GRANT-PAYROLL (<u>GRANT-NUM</u>, <u>COST-CENTER#</u>, <u>DATE</u>, <u>ID#</u>, GROSS-PAY, FED-TAX, SS-TAX, STATE-TAX, INSURANCE, NET-PAY)

PATIENT-MASTER

PATIENT#	NAME	ADDRESS	PHONE	SSN	WHO-PAYS	REL-TO-WHO-PAYS	PAYMENT-SOURCE
001	Fields, Thomas	23 Oak, 18106	555-0009	543-21-0000	Fields, Joan	husband	insurance
002	Jackson, Louise	23 Oak, 18106	555-0009	123-12-1234	Fields, Joan	foster-child	insurance
003	Barsky, Harvard	45 Lincoln, 18224	555-1212	098-76-5432	Barsky, Wilson	daughter	cash
004	Waterman, Lyn	1004 S. 9th, 18106	555-0987	987-65-4321	Waterman, Lyn	self	insurance
005	Fields, Linda	23 Oak, 18106	555-0009	876-54-3210	Fields, Joan	daughter	insurance
006	Waterman, Marty	1004 S. 9th, 18106	555-0987	765-43-2109	Waterman, Lyn	son	insurance
007	Waterman, Erik	1004 S. 9th, 18106	555-0987	654-32-1098	Waterman, Lyn	son	insurance
008	Barsky, Yale	45 Lincoln, 18224	555-1212	543-21-0987	Barsky, Wilson	son	cash
009	Barsky, Wilson	45 Lincoln, 18224	555-1212	432-10-9876	Barsky, Wilson	self	cash

PAYERS

WHO-PAYS	P-ADDRESS	P-PHONE	EMPLOYER	W-PHONE	INSURANCE-CARRIER
Barsky, Wilson	45 Lincoln, 18224	555-1212	U. Archaeological Museum	555-0676	none
Fields, Joan	23 Oak, 18106	555-0009	Small Bank	555-9988	Connecticut General
Waterman, Lyn	1004 S. 9th, 18106	555-0987	Federated Taxi Co.	555-3214	Blue Cross

VISITS

PATIENT#	DATE	PROCEDURE	COMMENTS
003	10-12-86	Cleaning	
003	10-12-86	X-rays, bite-wing	
004	10-12-86	Cleaning	
005	10-12-86	Cleaning	4 fillings need replacement
005	10-12-86	X-rays, full-mouth	Overbite is getting worse
001	10-13-86	Cleaning	
006	10-13-86	Extraction, wisdom tooth	Impacted lower-left
009	10-13-86	Cleaning	Heavy smoker; much tartar
009	10-13-86	X-rays, full mouth	
009	10-13-86	Filling, bicuspid	Upper-right

COSTS

PROCEDURE	PRICE
Cleaning	45.00
Extraction, bicuspid	75.00
Extraction, eye tooth	75.00
Extraction, incisor	75.00
Extraction, molar	100.00
Extraction, wisdom tooth	150.00
Filling, bicuspid	50.00
Filling, eye tooth	50.00
Filling, incisor	50.00
Filling, molar	50.00
Filling, wisdom tooth	75.00
X-ray, bite-wing	30.00
X-ray, whole mouth	50.00

Figure 5.15 Relations for Exercises

EMPLOYEES (ID#, NAME, ADDRESS, PHONE, SSN, #DEDUCTIONS, INS-PLAN)
GRANT-ASSIGNMENTS (DIG, ID#)
INS-COSTS (INS-PLAN, INDIVIDUAL-COST, FAMILY-COST)

ARTIFACT-LOG (ARTIFACT-NUM, DIG, ID#, GRID-NO, DATE-FOUND, DEPTH-FOUND, A-DESCRIPTION, SHELF-NUM)
ARTIFACTS-OUT (ARTIFACT-NUM, A-BORROWER, DATE-BORROWED, LOCATION, A-DATE-DUE, RETURN-FLAG)

1. Given a grant number (GRANT-NUM), list all cost centers (COST-CENTER#) and the cost center descriptions (COST-CENTER-DESC) assigned to that grant.
2. List the names of all people (S-BORROWER) who have not returned slides they borrowed by the due date (S-DATE-DUE).
3. List the location (LOCATION) of all artifacts (ARTIFACT-NUM) that have been borrowed from their shelves in the warehouse.
4. List the source (SOURCE) and amounts (TOTAL-AWARD) of all grants awarded to a single person (PRINCIPAL-RESEARCHER).
5. Given a grant number, list the digs (DIG) supported by that grant.
6. Given a grant number, list the contents (ITEM) of all purchase orders (P-O-NUM) issued against that grant.
7. Given a dig identifier (DIG), list the names (NAME) and phone numbers (PHONE) of all people (ID#) working on that dig.
8. Given a dig identifier (DIG), list the number (ARTIFACT-NUM), description (A-DESCRIPTION), and the name of the finder (NAME) for each artifact.
9. List the name (NAME) and dig identifier (DIG) for any employee who has ever found an artifact on any dig.
10. Given a grant identifier, list the name (VENDOR), phone number (V-PHONE), and contact person (CONTACT-PERSON) for each vendor from which the grant has made a purchase.
11. Given a grant number, list the cost center (COST-CENTR#), payee (either VENDOR or ID#), and amount (either TOTAL-AMT or GROSS-PAY) for every cost made against the grant. This is tricky, since the costs posted to a single grant are stored in two places, GRANT-PURCHASES and GRANT-PAYROLL.
12. Given a dig identifier, list the current location for each artifact found by that dig. This will require some thought. (Remember that artifacts can be on their shelves in the warehouse, or they may be at some other LOCATION.)

Implementation

6

Relational Database Management Systems

CHAPTER OUTLINE:

CHAPTER OBJECTIVES

After reading this chapter, you will:

1. Be familiar with the theoretical characteristics of a fully relational DBMS
2. Understand the issues involved in the theory versus implementation controversy
3. Be familiar with the features of a relational database package
4. Be reacquainted with the 3NF design of the Federated Taxi Company database, on which Chapters 8–11 are based

THE FULLY RELATIONAL DBMS

If you spend a bit of time looking at software ads in computer and business publications, you'll notice that virtually every software package that handles data in tables claims to be a relational DBMS.   Some even claim to be fully relational. None, however, conform to the theoretical definition of a fully relational DBMS.

The criteria that a DBMS must meet in order to be considered fully relational were explained in an important two-part article written by E. F. Codd (Codd, 1985). The criteria include 12 rules which describe how a fully relational DBMS should define, store, retrieve, and otherwise manage data.

Rule 1: The information rule

> "All information in a relational data base is represented explicitly at the logical level in exactly one way—by values in tables."

On the surface, Rule 1 seems relatively simple—the major characteristic of the relational model is the tabular representation of data. However, Rule 1 contains the phrase "all information." This implies that not only must data be stored in tables, but any other information used by the DBMS must be stored in that way as well. This includes the description of the schema (table and attribute definitions), integrity constraints, actions to be taken when constraints are violated, and security information (descriptions of which users have what rights to which data objects within the database). Users, assuming they have the appropriate security clearance, should be able to query these tables in the same way that they query tables that store data.

Micrcomputer DBMSs that claim to be relational do store data in tables. However, many generally fail to meet this rule since they do not store all the rest of their information in that way. For example, *R:base* report formats, integrity rules, and screen forms are kept in tables, but the data dictionary is not. It cannot be queried using the SELECT syntax which is used to query tables that contain data; a user must use special commands such as LIST COLUMNS or LIST TABLES.

On the other hand, *Oracle* does adhere to Rule 1. All information, including security information, is stored in tables in the data dictionary.   Any authorized user can query the data dictionary using standard SQL syntax.

Rule 2: Guaranteed access rule

> "Each and every datum (atomic value) in a relational data base is guaranteed to be logically accessible by resorting to a combination of table name, primary key value and column name."

Rule 2 simply states that it is possible to retrieve each individual piece of data stored in a relational database by specifying the name of the table in which it is stored, the column in which it is stored (i.e., the attribute name), and the primary key which identifies the tuple in which it is stored.

The important consequence of this rule is that primary keys must be unique. If they are not, then we cannot be certain that a primary key value will identify the precise row in a table that we wish to retrieve. Instead, we could only be assured of retrieving *any* row that contained given primary key values. Therefore, any microcomputer DBMS that does not somehow enforce the requirement that primary keys be unique will violate Rule 2.

Rule 3: Systematic treatment of null values

"Null values (distinct from the empty character string or a string of blank characters and distinct from zero or any other number) are supported in the fully relational DBMS for representing missing information in a systematic way, independent of data type."

An attribute is given a value of null to indicate that its value is unknown. A fully relational DBMS will permit the inclusion of null as a value for non-primary key attributes regardless of data type. It will also have some scheme for handling the nulls when a user retrieves data.

At first it may not be apparent why the handling of nulls is important, but consider the situation in which a user formulates a SQL query against the FTC database that is based on a negative:

```
SELECT  DRVNAM
FROM  DRIVER
WHERE  DRVSTAT  <>  "do not reserve";
```

This query retrieves the names of all drivers who are eligible to reserve cabs (i.e., the value of DRVSTAT is something other than "do not reserve"). What should the DBMS do with tuples that have a value of null for DRVSTAT? Null is not equal to "do not reserve." Should those tuples be retrieved by this query, or should they be excluded? Rule 3 makes no statement about exactly how the nulls should be handled, but insists that the DBMS have some policy about them. It is equally valid to include or exclude null from retrievals. Whichever the DBMS designers decide to do, it must be consistent and it must be coded into the DBMS itself.

Most microcomputer DBMSs do not recognize nulls. (*R:base* and *Oracle* are exceptions.) An occurrence of an attribute whose value is unknown is therefore generally stored as blank (for character attributes) or zero (for numeric attributes).

Rule 4: Dynamic on-line catalog based on the relational model

"The data base description is represented at the logical level in the same way as ordinary data, so that authorized users can apply the same relational language to its interrrogation as they apply to regular data."

Rule 4 reiterates the idea that *all* information in a relational database, in this case the catalog (the relational term for a data dictionary), must be stored in tables and be queryable in the same way as tables that store data. It also specifies that the catalog must be on-line and *dynamic*. That means that when an authorized user makes some change to the schema, that change will be automatically propagated into the structure of the base tables. For example, to add an attribute to a base table the user simply issues a command that adds a tuple to one of the relations in the catalog, indicating that another attribute is part of the table in question. The user does not need to issue another command to add a column to the base table; that action is initiated by the DBMS when the change is made to the catalog.

Many microcomputer DBMSs do not support true relational catalogs (*Oracle* is a notable exception). Although *dBase III Plus* does have a catalog that is stored as a table and queryable like tables that store data, it only stores information about files and not the database schema. It also cannot initiate changes in the database structure. In fact, the precise opposite is true; entries are made in the catalog whenever files are opened or created. In other words, changes in the database structure cause changes in the catalog rather than the reverse. (For further information, see Chapter 11.)

Rule 5: Comprehensive data sublanguage rule

> "A relational system may support several languages and various modes of terminal use (for example, the fill-in-the-blanks mode). However, there must be at least one language whose statements are expressible, per some well-defined syntax, as character strings and that is comprehensive in supporting <u>all</u> of the following items:
> - data definition
> - view definition
> - data manipulation (interactive and by program)
> - integrity constraints
> - transaction boundaries (begin, commit and rollback)"

Rule 5 requires a fully relational DBMS to support a command-driven query language, regardless of any other types of command structure present in the DBMS. *Oracle*'s SQL does meet this requirement. *R:base System V* and *dBase III Plus* meet this rule in spirit, since users have a choice between selecting command actions from a menu and typing commands from the keyboard.

However, adherence to Rule 5 requires more than just the mere presence of the query language. That language must support the five major functions described in the rule itself. How do *dBase III Plus* , *R:base System V*, and *Oracle* stand up against those functions?

1. Data definition
    a. *dBase III Plus* : supported
    b. *R:base* : supported
    c. *Oracle* : supported

2. View definition
  a. *dBase III Plus* : supported
  b. *R:base* : views supported for output only
  c. *Oracle* : supported
3. Data manipulation
  a. *dBase III Plus* : supported
  b. *R:base* : supported
  c. *Oracle* : supported
4. Integrity constraints
  a. *dBase III Plus* : not supported
  b. *R:base* : supported (with some limitations—see Chapter 10 for details)
  c. *Oracle* : supported (with some limitations—see Chapter 8 for details)
5. Transaction boundaries

In a multi-user environment, actions against a database performed by application programs may be contained within *transactions*. A transaction is defined as a unit of work. The DBMS query language supports statements that indicate where a transaction begins and where it should end. Transactions can end in one of two ways: if they end in an expected manner, then they are *committed* (all changes to the database are made permanent); if they end in an unexpected or undesirable manner, then they are *rolled back* (all changes to the database are undone and the database is restored to the state it was in before the transaction began). Transactions are discussed in more detail in Chapter 7.

Single-user microcomputer DBMSs are not transaction based. Therefore, none of their query languages contain syntax to mark transaction boundaries. Of the three DBMSs discussed in this book, only *Oracle* explicitly handles transactions. SQL provides statements to explicitly end transactions. (The start of a transaction is implicit in a number of SQL commands.)

Rule 6: View updating rule

"All views that are theoretically updatable are also updatable by the system."

Rule 6 states that whenever a user creates a view that contains tables that can be updated, the DBMS must be able to propagate those updates into the base tables. Most microcomputer DBMSs fail to adhere to this rule simply because they don't allow user views. To various degrees, however, the three DBMSs discussed in this book do support views.

Oracle supports views which conform to relational database theory. Views are defined with a single SQL command and implemented as virtual tables. View definitions are stored within the data dictionary. However, the package does not check user views to determine if updates made to those views can actually be made to the base tables. *Oracle,* therefore, does not meet Rule 6.

dBase III Plus, which does support views, adheres to Rule 6 only by accident. *dBase III Plus* views (as discussed in Chapter 10) are not implemented as virtual tables. They merely restrict which base tables and which attributes within them will be available to a user at any given time. Updates are always made directly to the base tables.

R:base views are used only as output devices; updates can only be made to base tables. *R:base*, therefore, cannot adhere to Rule 6.

Rule 7: High-level insert, update, and delete

"The capability of handling a base relation or a derived relation as a single operand applies not only to the retrieval of data but also to the insertion, update and deletion of data."

The retrieval operations discussed in Chapter 5 operate on an entire relation at a time. Rule 7 states that a fully relational DBMS must also support syntax for adding, modifying, and deleting data that operate on an entire table. *Oracle*, because it uses SQL as a query language, adheres to this rule. Of the other two packages, both *dBase III Plus* and *R :base* support modification and deletion operations that work in that manner. Only *R :base*, however, also supports a data entry command (**LOAD**) that works in on the entire table.

Rule 8: Physical data independence

"Applications programs and terminal activities remain logically unimpaired whenever any changes are made in either storage representation or access methods."

Rule 8 requires that the operation of applications programs and interactive commands be unaffected by any changes made in the way data are physically stored. When microcomputer DBMSs fail this rule, they tend to fail spectacularly. Consider *dBase III Plus*, for example. Every relation must be stored as a single physical file; every view, every catalog, every report format, every screen format is a physical file. Change the name of even a single file and every application program that uses that file will fail. Even interactive commands will fail unless the user is given the new name of the file.

Rule 9: Logical data independence

"Application programs and terminal activities remain logically unimpaired when information-preserving changes of any kind that theoretically permit unimpairment are made to the base tables."

A DBMS that adheres to Rule 9 will permit changes to the schema without affecting activities that make no use of the portion of the schema that was changed. For example, adding an attribute to a base table should not disrupt programs or interactive commands that have no use for the new attribute.

In some circumstances, *dBase III Plus*, *R :base*, and *Oracle* will fail this rule. For example, all three support retrieval syntax to display all the attributes from a relation with a single keyword. If an attribute is added to a relation, then reissuing the same command will display the additional attribute as well, regardless of whether it is actually required. A programmer can get around the problem by avoiding the use of the "display all attributes" syntax and always specifying exactly which attributes should be displayed. However, this ability to enforce Rule 9 in applications software does not mean that the DBMS meets the rule; logical data independence must be enforced by the DBMS.

Rule 10: Integrity independence

"Integrity constraints specific to a particular relational data base must be definable in the relational data sublanguage and storable in the catalog, not in the application programs."

"A minimum of the following two integrity constraints must be supported:

    1. Entity integrity: No component of a primary key is allowed to have a null value.

    2. Referential integrity: For each distinct nonnull foreign key value in a relational data base, there must exist a matching primary key value from the same domain."

As you will see in Chapters 8–11, it is possible to enforce integrity constraints by using applications programs and other tricks. However, doing so does not meet Rule 10. To meet Rule 10, a DBMS must permit the integrity constraints (and actions to be taken when the constraints are violated) to be stored in the catalog.

Of the three packages discussed in this book, *R:base* comes closest to meeting this rule. Rules can be established to require primary keys to be unique and nonnull and to require primary key references to exist for foreign keys. The rules also specify the action the DBMS should take when the rule is violated. However, as you will see in Chapter 10, there are some limitations to the flexibility of these rules. *Oracle* supports checking for unique and nonnull primary keys but does not permit the definition of primary key–foreign key references. *dBase III Plus* has no features for integrity verification at all.

Rule 11: Distribution independence

" A relational DBMS has distribution independence."

A distributed database is one in which the data are stored at more than one physical location. This is different from a multi-user database, which remote users access and is stored in a single, centralized location. Rule 11 indicates that whenever a database is distributed, users should be unaware of that fact. They must be able to work with the database as if it were centralized.

There is little microcomputer software to support a distributed database. At the time this book went to press, the only distributed DMBS which would run on microcomputers was *SQL*Star* from Oracle Corporation. (*SQL*Star* also runs on larger machines.) The only other widely used distributed database is *Ingres*, which is not available for microcomputers. IBM's distributed database is still unavailable as a commerical product, though a number of other companies appear ready to announce distributed packages.

The degree to which *SQL*Star* provides distribution independence is still open to question; the initial release of the product supports distribution for retrieval only. In other words, while users are able to retrieve data using SQL from any DBMS that supports SQL without knowing where data are stored, the same is not true for updates.

Rule 12: Nonsubversion rule

> "If a relational system has a low-level (single-record-at-a-time) language, that low-level language cannot be used to subvert or bypass the integrity rules or constraints expressed in the higher level relational language (multiple-records-at-a-time)."

Rule 12 states that a DBMS musn't permit integrity constraints to be bypassed through use of a query langauge that operates on a single record at a time. *dBase III Plus* does not adhere to this rule. If, for example, a user is determined to enter a foreign key value that doesn't reference an existing primary key, then there is no way to prevent that user from doing so. The problem arises because the DBMS handles data entry one tuple at a time and at the same time cannot automatically enforce integrity constraints.

Though *R:base* also handles data entry one tuple at a time, it might appear at first glance that there is no way for an *R:base* user to get around stored integrity rules. For example, as long as rule checking is enabled, the software will stubbornly refuse to add a tuple to a relation if a rule has been established that requires unique primary keys, and the primary key value the user is attempting to enter already exists. However, a simple command (SET RULES OFF) will disable rule checking entirely, permitting the user to subvert the rules without restriction.

Oracle, too, has a way to manipulate one row at a time. This technique, which involves setting a *cursor* to point to a single tuple, cannot be used to subvert entity integrity, assuming that nonnull primary keys have been defined in the data dictionary. However, since referential integrity rules can't be included in the data dictionary, there is nothing to prevent a user from violating those constraints by updating a row that is pointed to by a cursor.

Finally, there is a caveat to the 12 relational rules known as Rule Zero:

> "For any system that is advertised as, or claimed to be, a relational data base management system, that system must be able to manage data entirely through its relational capabilities."

In other words, regardless of how well a DBMS meets the 12 relational criteria discussed above, it isn't relational if it "cheats" by performing even one data management function in a manner not described by those rules. According to Codd, there aren't any fully relational DBMSs on the market today.

THE THEORY VERSUS IMPLEMENTATION QUESTION

As you were reading the theoretical rules for a fully relational DBMS, you may have begun to wonder about the relationship of those rules to the effectiveness of database software and whether all the rules were really necessary. The publication of Codd's article stirred up a controversy over just that issue, much of which was conducted in the computer industry press (see Crawford, 1986; Gallant, 1986a; and Gallant, 1986b). The question posed by software developers was, "If product meets the needs of our customers, does it really matter if it doesn't meet the theoretical criteria for a fully relational DBMS?"

There is no easy or straightforward answer. The debate between database theorists and those who write DBMS software has been going on for years and is likely to continue for some time. Before you make up your own mind, however, there are some things on both sides of the argument that you should consider.

From the perspective of the business using a DBMS, the bottom line has always been "does it get the job done accurately, within our time constraints, and within our budget?" The business purchaser isn't concerned about whether or not the software meets a series of theoretical rules but only about whether the software performs as advertised. Certainly, the DBMSs discussed in this book, while they do not adhere strictly to Codd's rules, are powerful, effective data management tools, any of which will perform satisfactorily in a business environment.

The performance issue underlies much of software developers' reluctance to implement strict adherence to Codd's rules in their products. It is true that adding code to a DBMS to verify and enforce integrity constraints, to maintain an on-line, dynamic catalog, for example, will slow down the performance of the system. Software developers prefer to market a faster product, leaving the enforcing of constraints to applications programs written by the customer.

On the other hand, a database created by a DBMS that adheres to Codd's rules will contain far less bad data than a database that doesn't systematically enforce integrity and primary key constraints. It will be easier to maintain, since changes to the schema are made only once (in the catalog) and changes in physical storage methods don't require modifications at the applications level.

FEATURES OF A RELATIONAL DBMS

Regardless of which relational DBMS you select for your business, there are certain features and capabilities that you should expect. These include the following:

1. The ability to create multiple relations and enter data into them
2. The ability to logically reorder (*index*) or physically reorder (*sort*) the data in the

relations (Indexing and sorting will be discussed in more detail later in this chapter.)

3. An interactive query language
4. The ability to answer queries that require data stored in more than one relation (Doing so, however, may require issuing more than one DBMS command.)
5. Facilities for creating *turnkey* applications for unsophisticated and/or casual users (The idea of a turnkey application will be discussed later in this chapter.)
6. A built-in report generator

Some packages will also include the following:

1. A text editor for use in writing application programs
2. An application generator to write some kinds of application program code
3. An interpreter to run application programs while they are in the development process
4. A compiler to compile application programs (This both increases execution speed and prevents users from examining program code.)
5. A screen generator to create custom screen forms

INDEXING, SORTING, AND SEARCHING

Indexing refers to imposing a logical order on a relation without changing the physical order of the tuples. An index on a relation is very much like an index in a book. The index to a book contains a list of subjects in alphabetical order. Associated with each subject are the page numbers where more information about that subject can be found. In a way, the page numbers in the index "point to" information in the rest of the book. An index on a relation is a physical entity that contains an ordered list of subjects, called *keys*, and the computer equivalent of page numbers, *pointers*, indicating where the tuple that contains that key value can be found.

The alternative to indexing is *sorting*. Sorting refers to physically changing the order of tuples in a relation. Sorting creates a copy of the original relation (generally another base table) containing all the data from the original relation; the difference is that the tuples have been physically rearranged based on the contents of one or more attributes.

Why is ordering a relation important at all? It has implications for how the relation can be searched. Although microcomputer DBMSs vary in how intimately the user has to be concerned with search strategies, a database designer can affect retrieval speed by considering how the relations will be ordered.

A relation that is ordered can be searched far more quickly than a relation that is not ordered. Assume, for example, that we have a relation containing 1000 tuples. If the relation isn't ordered in any way, then the only way it can be searched is through a *sequential search*. A sequential search starts at the first tuple, evaluates the search criteria, and retrieves the data if they meet the criteria. Then it moves on to the second tuple. A sequential search examines every tuple in the relation in order.

As an example, take a look at the instance of the Small Bank relation PEOPLE that appears in Figure 6.1. Note that the relation is ordered on CUSTOMER#, but the customer names are in no order at all. Suppose that a teller wants to know if Philip Kagan has an account with Small Bank. He or she needs to search the attribute CUSTOMER. (If the teller knew a CUSTOMER# then there would be no need to ask the question in the first place.)

There is only one way for a DBMS to implement the search—sequentially. The DBMS will proceed in the following manner:

1. Read the next tuple of PEOPLE. (If this is the beginning of the search, then the "next" tuple is the first tuple.)
2. Compare the value of CUSTOMER to "Kagan, Philip."
3. If the value of CUSTOMER = "Kagan, Philip," the search is successful and the procedure ends.

PEOPLE

CUSTOMER#	CUSTOMER	ADDRESS	PHONE	SSN
0093-A6	Jones, Samuel	105 W. 99th, Newtown 02899	555-0345	123-45-1234
0095-B8	Abrams, Max	2204 Nox Hill, Newtown 02845	555-1414	098-76-5432
0103-A4	Cohen, Esther	39 Summer, Newtown 02845	555-8486	019-28-3745
0104-B6	Khan, Satya	1001 N. 54th, Newtown 02898	555-7623	567-12-3489
0121-A1	Weymouth, Sam	88 N. 12th, Newtown 02899	555-1020	111-22-3333
0149-A6	Anderson, Julia	2387 Nox Hill, Newtown 02845	555-3059	222-33-4444
0166-B4	Wong, Lin Sue	2300 Winter, Newtown 02899	555-1947	333-44-5555
0167-B4	O'Reilly, Brian	3578 W. 23rd, Newtown 02899	555-1896	444-55-6666
0183-A2	Cohen, Franklin	1030 N. 67th, Newtown 02898	555-3860	555-66-7777
0229-B2	Westerman, John	293 Summer, Newtown 02845	555-2882	666-77-8888
0231-A2	Langley, Paul	19 School St., Newtown 02898	555-3980	777-88-9999
0239-B7	Lloyd, Theron	347 Lake Ave., Newtown 02899	555-9138	888-99-0000
0254-A6	Maxwell, Paul	2098 W. 31st, Newtown 02898	555-1964	999-00-1111
0288-B7	Craft, Ellie	3988 E. 12th, Newtown 02845	555-7306	123-45-6789
0300-A1	Gray, Andrew	1019 N. 54th, Newtown 02898	555-8272	012-34-5678
0305-B3	Peters, Wilson	49 Church St., Newtown 02845	555-2132	234-56-7890
0308-B4	Gray, Thomas	3408 Nox Hill, Newtown 02845	555-9124	345-67-8901
0318-A3	Cohen, Elizabeth	1414 E. 35th, Newtown 02898	555-3758	456-78-9012
0321-A4	Llewelyn, Gwyn	39 Church St., Newtown 02845	555-1840	567-89-0123
0397-B4	Paine, Sam	1800 Winter, Newtown 02899	555-2948	678-90-1234
0469-A2	Kagan, Philip	79 N. 20th, Newtown 02845	555-1954	789-01-2345
0470-B4	Kahn, William	306 Summer, Newtown 02845	555-5757	890-12-3456
0472-A6	Laugherty, Mary	4522 N. 40th, Newtown 02898	555-1958	901-23-4567
0497-C3	O'Malley, Jewel	88 Church St., Newtown 02845	555-8449	987-65-4321
0533-A6	Anderson, Lyn	194 Summer, Newtown 02845	555-3768	876-54-3210

Figure 6.1 An Instance of the Relation PEOPLE

4. If all tuples in the relation have been examined, the search is unsuccessful and the procedure ends.

5. Otherwise, continue with step one.

In this case, Philip Kagan's tuple is the 21st tuple in the relation. The DBMS will therefore have to read 21 tuples to determine that Philip Kagan does indeed have an account with Small Bank. On the average, a successful sequential search on a relation of 1000 tuples will require looking at 500 tuples. The DBMS will need to look at all 1000 tuples to discover that no tuples meet the search criteria.

However, if the file is ordered, then the DBMS can use a faster search technique. One technique that might be used is a *binary search*. A binary search first looks at the middle tuple in the relation. If the middle tuple doesn't meet the search criteria, then the DBMS decides whether tuples that do meet the search criteria will be above or below the middle. In doing so, the DBMS eliminates half the tuples from the search. It then looks at the middle tuple in the half of the relation that remains. The sequence of eliminating half the remaining tuples continues until a tuple matching the search criteria is found or until it is clear that no tuple meeting the criteria exists.

Assume, now, that Philip Kagan calls Small Bank to ask about his account balance. Before any information will be given out over the phone, the caller's identity has to be verified. Therefore, Mr. Kagan is asked for his customer number. (It appears on the bank ID card he was given when he opened his first account with the bank.) The bank officer will then use that number to retrieve information about Mr. Kagan from the PEOPLE relation. If the caller can accurately give his social security number, then Small Bank assumes that he is who he says he is.

Because PEOPLE is ordered on CUSTOMER#, the DBMS can use a binary search to locate Mr. Kagan's tuple. The general procedure is:

1. Find the logically middle tuple by looking at the tuple halfway between the top and bottom of the relation.

2. Compare CUSTOMER# from the middle tuple with Mr. Kagan's customer number (0469-A2).

3. If the customer number from the middle tuple is the same as Mr. Kagan's customer number, the search is successful and the procedure ends.

4. If the customer number from the middle tuple is greater than Mr. Kagan's customer number, Mr. Kagan's tuple must be *above* the current middle tuple; the current middle tuple becomes the logical *bottom* of the relation.

5. If the customer number from the middle tuple is less than Mr. Kagan's customer number, Mr. Kagan's tuple must be *below* the current middle tuple; the current middle tuple becomes the logical *top* of the relation.

6. If the current bottom record of the relation is greater than the current top record, the search is unsuccessful and the procedure ends.

7. Otherwise, continue with step one.

The exact sequence of tuples that a DBMS must examine to find Mr. Kagan's tuple are indicated in Figure 6.2. Initially, the middle tuple is the 13th tuple. Since Mr. Kagan's customer number (0469-A2) is greater than 0254-A6 (the customer number in the 13th tuple), the tuple for which we are searching must be in the bottom half of the relation.

The second tuple that the DBMS will examine is the tuple midway between the 13th tuple (now the logical top of the relation) and the bottom of the relation. That will be the 19th tuple, which has a customer number of 0321-A4. The tuple for which we are searching is again below the current middle tuple. The logical top of the relation therefore becomes the 19th tuple.

The next middle tuple is the 22nd. This time, Mr. Kagan's tuple is above the middle. The logical bottom of the relation is moved to the 22nd tuple.

At this point, the top tuple is 19 and the bottom 22. Which tuple will be examined next will depend on how the DBMS rounds its computation of the middle tuple, since

PEOPLE

CUSTOMER#	CUSTOMER	ADDRESS	PHONE	SSN
0093-A6	Jones, Samuel	105 W. 99th, Newtown 02899	555-0345	123-45-1234
0095-B8	Abrams, Max	2204 Nox Hill, Newtown 02845	555-1414	098-76-5432
0103-A4	Cohen, Esther	39 Summer, Newtown 02845	555-8486	019-28-3745
0104-B6	Khan, Satya	1001 N. 54th, Newtown 02898	555-7623	567-12-3489
0121-A1	Weymouth, Sam	88 N. 12th, Newtown 02899	555-1020	111-22-3333
0149-A6	Anderson, Julia	2387 Nox Hill, Newtown 02845	555-3059	222-33-4444
0166-B4	Wong, Lin Sue	2300 Winter, Newtown 02899	555-1947	333-44-5555
0167-B4	O'Reilly, Brian	3578 W. 23rd, Newtown 02899	555-1896	444-55-6666
0183-A2	Cohen, Franklin	1030 N. 67th, Newtown 02898	555-3860	555-66-7777
0229-B2	Westerman, John	293 Summer, Newtown 02845	555-2882	666-77-8888
0231-A2	Langley, Paul	19 School St., Newtown 02898	555-3980	777-88-9999
0239-B7	Lloyd, Theron	347 Lake Ave., Newtown 02899	555-9138	888-99-0000
0254-A6	Maxwell, Paul	2098 W. 31st, Newtown 02898	555-1964	999-00-1111
0288-B7	Craft, Ellie	3988 E. 12th, Newtown 02845	555-7306	123-45-6789
0300-A1	Gray, Andrew	1019 N. 54th, Newtown 02898	555-8272	012-34-5678
0305-B3	Peters, Wilson	49 Church St., Newtown 02845	555-2132	234-56-7890
0308-B4	Gray, Thomas	3408 Nox Hill, Newtown 02845	555-9124	345-67-8901
0318-A3	Cohen, Elizabeth	1414 E. 35th, Newtown 02898	555-3758	456-78-9012
0321-A4	Llewelyn, Gwyn	39 Church St., Newtown 02845	555-1840	567-89-0123
0397-B4	Paine, Sam	1800 Winter, Newtown 02899	555-2948	678-90-1234
0469-A2	Kagan, Philip	79 N. 20th, Newtown 02845	555-1954	789-01-2345
0470-B4	Kahn, William	306 Summer, Newtown 02845	555-5757	890-12-3456
0472-A6	Laugherty, Mary	4522 N. 40th, Newtown 02898	555-1958	901-23-4567
0497-C3	O'Malley, Jewel	88 Church St., Newtown 02845	555-8449	987-65-4321
0533-A6	Anderson, Lyn	194 Summer, Newtown 02845	555-3768	876-54-3210

Figure 6.2 Tuples Accessed During a Binary Search

halfway between 19 and 22 is 20.5. In the worst case, assuming that the DBMS merely truncates the decimal, it will look at tuple 20. The top will be moved down to 20 and the middle computed again. This time the middle will be tuple 21, the precise tuple for which we are looking. While the sequential search for Mr. Kagan's tuple needed to read and examine 21 tuples, the binary search needed to use only five!

In a relation of 1000 tuples, a DBMS will, at most, have to look at 12 tuples to discover that no tuple meets the search criteria. A successful search will require the DBMS to consult even fewer tuples. A binary search runs about 10 times faster than a sequential search on a relation with 1000 tuples; the disparity becomes even more pronounced on larger relations.

Many microcomputer DBMSs store their indexes as *B-trees*. A B-tree is a physical storage structure that can be searched very rapidly. A discussion of the structure and traversal of B-trees is, however, beyond the scope of this book. If you wish to explore them in detail, see Ellzey, 1982; Korth and Silberschatz, 1986; or Wirth, 1986.

Most microcomputer databases conduct sequential searches on the physical relations that are stored on disk. Faster searches that require ordered lists, however, are based on indexes. Therefore, only attributes which are part of an index key can be used to conduct any type of fast search. The DBMS will evaluate the search criteria against the ordered keys in the index. When a match between the search criteria and an index key is found, the DBMS uses the associated pointer to locate the complete tuple within the relation itself.

Some microcomputer DBMSs, such as *dBase III Plus*, require the user to indicate explicitly which indexes should be used to implement a search. Others, such as *R:base* and *Oracle*, will automatically choose the index which facilitates the fastest retrieval. However, in all cases the user must explicitly instruct the DBMS to create the index.

It might seem, then, that the best strategy would be to index a relation on every attribute and combination of attributes that might possibly be used as search criteria. If disk space and update performance were of no concern, then perhaps that would be a viable alternative. However, disk space isn't unlimited. Each index does consume disk space; the more attributes in the key, the more space that is required. More importantly, indexing also slows down the update process. Not only must data be entered into or changed in a relation itself, but modification must be made to every index that exists for the relation. Therefore, designers usually compromise and create indexes for attributes or a combination of attributes that will be used frequently as search criteria.

By the same token, there are circumstances when it makes sense to sort a relation rather than to index it. If an application needs to access every tuple in a relation in order (i.e., in a sequential manner), then sorting may well be more efficient. How can this be? Finding a tuple using an index requires at least two disk accesses, one to the index and another to the relation itself; even if the index is being read in a sequential manner, without any searching required, it must still be consulted to determine which tuple in the relation is logically next. Sequential access directly to a sorted, physically ordered relation requires only one disk access per tuple. Therefore, retrieval of every attribute in order, regardless of what that order might be, will take twice as long if the file is indexed than it will if the file has been sorted.

Generally, it makes sense to sort a relation if an application needs to retrieve every tuple, in order. Included in this type of application are printing mailing labels from a mailing list, printing monthly bank account statements, and printing monthly bills to send to customers. On the other hand, sorting takes time; that time can be significant (measured in hours) if a relation contains many tuples. The sort process also precludes any activity against the relation. Therefore, indexing makes sense when the order in which tuples are retrieved is unpredictable and random and when the relation must be ordered at all times to permit fast, binary searches. The same relation may be both indexed and sorted, depending on the specific application.

TURNKEY SYSTEMS AND THE USER INTERFACE

The term *turnkey system* refers to anything that can be run by simply turning a key. A car is the ultimate turnkey system. The average driver doesn't have to understand much about what goes on under the hood; he or she simply turns the key and (hopefully) the car starts. While database applications don't have physical keys that a user can turn, it is possible to create application programs that an unsophisticated or casual user can initiate with a single, simple command or action. The user generally then selects program actions from a menu of choices (a *menu-driven* system), though some turnkey systems are controlled by a small set of commands that the user must type in (a *command-driven* system). There is no need for the user to learn the DBMS query language, to be familiar with search strategies, to know how to program, to worry about database integrity, or any of the other details that are "under the hood." Such a system is often referred to as *user-friendly*, since it is theoretically easy to use and nonthreatening.

The exact characteristics of a user-friendly application program depend a great deal on who will be using the program. Menu-driven programs are best suited to users without formal training or users who don't use the program very often. On the other hand, regular users of menu-driven systems sooner or later become frustrated with the need to go through one or more levels of menus; they know exactly what they want to do with the program and would prefer simply to enter a command to instruct the program to do it. Once they are comfortable with a program, they perceive menus as being too slow. The ideal solution is an interface that gives the user a choice between selecting program actions from a menu and entering a command.

Both *R:base* and *dBase III Plus*, for example, provide interfaces that are modeled on the idea of having two modes, one for novices and one for experts. *R:base*'s Prompt mode guides the user through most of the package's major functions. However, Prompt mode is optional; a user can enter commands at the **R>** prompt at any time. *dBase III Plus*'s Assist mode operates in the same way; the user can exit Assist at any time and enter commands at the dot prompt.

The entire issue of creating user-friendly programs has been the subject of a great deal of research. If you wish to learn more about the characteristics of good user interfaces, see: Rubenstein, 1984 (*the* book to look at if you consult only one source); Gould, 1983; Card 1983; Carroll, 1984; Norman, 1983; and Sime, 1983.

REVIEWING THE FEDERATED TAXI COMPANY

The Federated Taxi Company forms the basis of the examples used throughout the DBMS-specific implementation chapters (8–11). As presented in Part I, the database consists of the following five relations:

CAB (<u>CABNUM</u>, MAKE, MODEL, YEAR, PURDATE, LICNUM, CONDITN, CABSTAT, CURODOM)

DRIVER (<u>DRVNUM</u>, DRVNAM, DRVSTR, DRVCSZ, DRVPHONE, DRVLIC, DRVLEXD, DRVSTAT)

SHIFTS (<u>WKDATE</u>, <u>WKSHIFT</u>, <u>CABNUM</u>, DRVNUM, WKFLAG, ODOMRDG1, ODOMRDG2)

INCIDENTS (<u>CABNUM</u>, <u>WKDATE</u>, <u>WKSHIFT</u>, INCITYPE, DETAILS)

MAINTENANCE (<u>CABNUM</u>, <u>MAINDATE</u>, <u>MAINTYPE</u>, MAINODOM)

Retrieval examples are based on the instances of the relations that appear in Figure 6.3.

SUMMARY

The formal theoretical criteria for a fully relational DBMS were defined in October, 1985 by E.F. Codd, the theorist who originally proposed the relational model. To be considered fully relational, a DBMS must meet 12 criteria:

1. All information in the database must be stored in tables.
2. All information in the database must be retrievable by using only a table name, a column name, and a primary key value.
3. Null values must be handled in a systematic manner.
4. The DBMS must support an on-line, dynamic catalog.
5. The DBMS must have a query language that handles data definition, view definition, data manipulation, integrity constraints, and transaction boundaries.
6. The DBMS must be able to update any theoretically updatable views that a user can create.
7. Insert, update, and delete commands must work on entire tables.
8. Changes in physical storage methods must not affect applications activities.
9. Logical changes to the schema must not affect applications that do not use portions of the database affected by the changes.

CAB

CABNUM	MAKE	MODEL	YEAR	PURDATE	LICNUM	CONDTN	CABSTAT	CURODOM
002	Checker	4-door sedan	73	03/15/84	345 YAO	New engine - runs great!	T	0
006	Checker	4-door sedan	72	07/18/72	997 IUF	Needs new brake pads	F	485001
045	Ford	LTD	86	07/12/86	867 POP	Excellent; under warranty	T	45999
104	Checker	4-door sedan	63	05/15/67	356 QLT	Needs new seat covers	T	204998
105	Checker	4-door sedan	63	05/15/67	111 ABC	Excellent	T	286003
108	Ford	LTD	86	07/12/86	760 PLP	Excellent; warranty expired	T	56667
144	Ford	LTD	82	12/06/81	290 AAQ	Needs major body work	F	103245
215	Ford	LTD	86	07/12/86	776 IKL	Excellent; under warranty	T	23000
238	Ford	LTD	82	12/06/81	980 JAM	Excellent	T	256256
378	Checker	4-door sedan	68	02/02/68	771 TOW	Should be repainted	T	388990
404	Checker	4-door sedan	68	02/02/68	206 TTL	Excellent	T	321409

DRIVER

DRVNUM	DRVNAM	DRVSTR	DRVSCZ	DRVPHONE	DRVLIC	DRVLEXD	DRVSTAT
0001	Bailey, Max	1 North 1 St.	Anytown, US 00001	000-000-0001	US 01010101	12/15/89	pay before
0002	Baker, MaryAnn	2 South 2 St.	Anytown, US 00002	000-000-0002	US 02020202	07/30/88	pay after
0003	Lewis, John	3 North 3 Ave.	Anytown, US 00003	000-000-0003	US 03030303	10/10/88	pay after
0004	Santiago, Jorge	4 W. 4 Blvd.	Newtown, US 00004	000-000-0004	US 04040404	03/18/89	pay after
0005	Miller, Pat	1 W. 5th, Apt. 5	Newtown, US 00005	000-000-0005	US 05050505	12/01/87	pay after
0006	Miller, Phyllis	2 N. 6th, Apt. 6B	Anytown, US 00006	000-000-0006	US 06060606	02/02/89	pay before
0007	Phong, Quen	7 S.E. 7 Ave.	Newtown, US 00007	000-000-0007	US 07070707	03/12/88	pay after
0008	Wong, David	8 N. 8th	Newtown, US 00008	000-000-0008	US 08080808	05/15/88	pay before
0009	Young, Leslie	9 West East St.	Anytown, US 00009	000-000-0009	US 09090909	03/12/88	pay before
0010	Zilog, Charlie	10 W. 10th	Newtown, US 00010	000-000-0010	US 10101010	05/15/88	pay after
0011	Erlich, Martin	11th and South	Newtown, US 00011	000-000-0011	US 11111111	03/15/89	pay before
0012	Eastman, Richard	1200 N. 12th	Newtown, US 00012	000-000-0012	US 12121212	02/06/87	do not reserve
0013	Kowalski, Pete	13th and Clay	Anytown, US 00013	000-000-0013	US 13131313	12/05/88	pay before
0014	Mariott, Emily	14 W. 14 St.	Newtown, US 00014	000-000-0014	US 14141414	11/03/87	do not reserve
0015	French, Janice	1500 - 15th So.	Newtown, US 00015	000-000-0015	US 15151515	12/16/89	pay before
0016	Thieu, Lin Van	16 W. 16 Ave.	Anytown, US 00016	000-000-0016	US 16161616	04/03/88	pay after
0017	Jackson, Rafael	17000 Market	Newtown, US 00017	000-000-0017	US 17171717	03/02/89	pay after
0018	Wilson, Carter	18 Town Center	Newtown, US 00018	000-000-0018	US 18181818	04/03/87	do not reserve
0019	Kolson, Jan	19 N.E. 19th	Anytown, US 00019	000-000-0019	US 19191919	05/21/88	pay before
0020	Abelman, John	20 E. 20 Blvd.	Anytown, US 00020	000-000-0020	US 20202020	11/24/89	pay before

Figure 6.3 Sample Data for the FTC Database

SHIFTS

WKDATE	WKSHIFT	CABNUM	DRVNUM	WKFLAG	ODOMRDG1	ODOMRDG2
07/15/86	day	104	0006	T	202622	202771
07/15/86	day	238	0010	T	210965	211104
07/15/86	day	404	0020	T	319333	319487
07/15/86	eve	045	0011	F		
07/15/86	eve	104	0001	T	202771	202905
07/15/86	eve	144	0012	T	350002	350190
07/15/86	ngt	045	0016	T	48830	49190
07/15/86	ngt	108	0002	T	53885	53900
07/15/86	ngt	215	0008	F	20107	20255
07/16/86	day	104	0006	F		
07/16/86	day	238	0010	F		
07/16/86	day	404	0020	F		
07/16/86	eve	002	0004	F		
07/16/86	eve	104	0001	F		
07/16/86	ngt	002	0007	F		
07/17/86	day	104	0006	F		
07/17/86	day	238	0010	F		
07/17/86	day	404	0020	F		
07/17/86	ngt	108	0002	F		
07/18/86	day	104	0006	F		
07/18/86	day	238	0010	F		
07/18/86	eve	002	0004	F		
07/18/86	eve	045	0011	F		
07/18/86	ngt	045	0016	F		
07/18/86	ngt	108	0002	F		
07/18/86	ngt	215	0008	F		
07/19/86	day	104	0006	F		
07/19/86	eve	104	0001	F		
07/19/86	eve	238	0003	F		
07/20/86	eve	238	0003	F		

Figure 6.3   (cont.)   Sample Data for the FTC Database

INCIDENT

CABNUM	WKDATE	WKSHIFT	INCITYPE	DETAILS
104	07/15/86	day	ticket	Stopped in front of a fire hydrant to pick up a fare.
141	07/15/86	eve	accident	Front of cab crashed into Jersey barrier on I128. Driver was speeding. Claims fare was late getting to airport. Fare received minor neck injuries; driver cut by flying glass.
215	07/15/86	ngt	ticket	Speeding.

MAINTENANCE

CABNUM	MAINDATE	MAINTYPE	MAINODOM
002	05/18/86	new engine	0
002	05/18/86	tune-up	0
238	05/28/86	repack front wheel bearings	244809
238	05/28/86	tune-up	244809
104	06/12/86	tune-up	197883
215	06/12/86	tune-up	15089
404	06/12/86	replace rear upholstery	313991
404	06/12/86	replace rear windshield	313991
404	06/12/86	tune-up	313991
006	06/15/86	tune-up	485000
108	07/02/86	tune-up	55305
045	07/14/86	tune-up	40100
105	07/15/86	tune-up	286001
378	07/15/86	tune-up	388888
144	07/16/86	inspect damage	350190

Figure 6.3 (cont.) Sample Data for the FTC Database

10. The DBMS must support definition of integrity rules and consequences to be taken when rules are violated within the catalog; the DBMS must automatically check for adherence to those rules.
11. If the database is distributed, it should appear to users as if it were centralized.
12. There must be no way to get around the integrity rules specified in the catalog.

A fully relational database must also be able to manage all of its activities through its relational capabilities (Rule Zero).

A controversy has arisen between those who believe that it is important to adhere to the strict theoretical model and those who believe that it is enough to write software that meets a user's needs.

REFERENCES

Card, Stuart K., Thomas P. Moran, and Allen Newell. (1983) *The Psychology of Human-Computer Interaction.* London: Lawrence Erlbaum Assoc.

Carroll, John M. and Caroline Arrithers. (1984) "Training wheels in a user interface." *Communications of the ACM.* 27(8):800-806.

Codd, E. F. (1985) "Is your DBMS really relational?" *Computerworld.* October 14 and 21.

Crawford, Douglas B. "Can one size fit all?" *Computerworld Focus.* (February 19):13-16.

Dayal, U. and P.A. Bernstein. (1978) "On the updatability of relational views." *Proceedings of the Fourth International Conference on Very Large Databases.* West Berlin. 113-124.

Ellzey, Roy S. (1982) *Data Structures for Computer Information Systems.* Chicago: SRA.

Gallant, John. (1986a) "Strained relations: DBMS debate turns bitter." *Computerworld.* (January 13):1+.

Gallant, John. (1986b) "Sideline view: users want resolution to relational debate." *Computerworld.* (January 20):1+.

Gould, John D. and Clayton Lewis. (1983) "Designing for usability—key principles and what designers think." *Proceedings of the Conference on Human Factors in Computing Systems.* December 12–15, Boston. New York: ACM.

Hammond, Nick and Philip Bernard. (1984) "Dialogue design: characteristics of user knowledge." In *Fundamentals of Human-Computer Interaction*. Andrew Monk, ed. London: Academic Press.

Korth, Henry F. and Abraham Silberschatz. (1986) *Database System Concepts*. New York: McGraw-Hill.

Norman, Donald A. (1983) "Design principles for human-computer interface." In: *Human Factors in Computing Systems: CHI '83 Conference Proceedings*. New York: SIG-CHI.

Rubenstein, Richard and Harry Hersh. (1984) *The Human Factor: Designing Computer Systems for People*. Burlington, MA: Digital Press.

Sime, M. E. and M. J. Coombs, eds. (1983) *Designing for Human-Computer Communication*. London: Academic Press.

Wirth, Niklaus. (1986) *Algorithms and Data Structures*. Englewood Cliffs, NJ: Prentice-Hall.

THINGS TO THINK ABOUT

1. Take a good, hard look at the DBMS you are using for this class.

   a. How does it measure up to the 12 rules for a fully relational database? Which rules does it meet completely? Which rules does it meet partway? Which rules doesn't it meet at all?

   b. Of the rules that it only meets partway or not at all, which will have the most impact on the implementation of a good database (e.g., one with the least bad data, such as foreign keys that don't reference existing primary keys)?

2. In your opinion, how important are the 12 rules for a fully relational database? Should people who write DBMS software be attempting to adhere to those rules, or should they simply be attempting to write software that works? Why?

PATIENT-MASTER

PATIENT#	NAME	ADDRESS	PHONE	SSN	WHO-PAYS	REL-TO-WHO-PAYS	PAYMENT-SOURCE
001	Fields, Thomas	23 Oak, 18106	555-0009	543-21-0000	Fields, Joan	husband	insurance
002	Jackson, Louise	23 Oak, 18106	555-0009	123-12-1234	Fields, Joan	foster-child	insurance
003	Barsky, Harvard	45 Lincoln, 18224	555-1212	098-76-5432	Barsky, Wilson	daughter	cash
004	Waterman, Lyn	1004 S. 9th, 18106	555-0987	987-65-4321	Waterman, Lyn	self	insurance
005	Fields, Linda	23 Oak, 18106	555-0009	876-54-3210	Fields, Joan	daughter	insurance
006	Waterman, Marty	1004 S. 9th, 18106	555-0987	765-43-2109	Waterman, Lyn	son	insurance
007	Waterman, Erik	1004 S. 9th, 18106	555-0987	654-32-1098	Waterman, Lyn	son	insurance
008	Barsky, Yale	45 Lincoln, 18224	555-1212	543-21-0987	Barsky, Wilson	son	cash
009	Barsky, Wilson	45 LIncoln, 18224	555-1212	432-10-9876	Barsky, Wilson	self	cash

Figure 6.4   Relation for Question 3

3. An instance of the relation PATIENT-MASTER from Dr. Holmes' dental office database (Figure 6.4) appears on the next page. As you can see, the relation is ordered by patient number.

    a. Which will be faster, locating a patient by patient number or by patient name? Why?

    b. Using the data from the instance of PATIENT-MASTER, draw a table that represents an index on patient names. Use the patient number as a pointer to help the DBMS locate the appropriate tuple in PATIENT-MASTER.

4. The relation BORROWED contains data on who has borrowed slides from the University Archaeological Museum's slide library:

    BORROWED (<u>DIG</u>, <u>SEQ-NUM</u>, <u>BORROWER</u>, DATE-DUE, RETURN-FLAG)

There are many different kinds of information requests that can be answered by the data in just this relation. For example, it can tell you which slides have not been returned, or which slides have been borrowed from a specific dig, or who has borrowed a particular slide, or even which slides have been borrowed by a given individual.

    a. List three information requests for which it makes sense to sort BORROWED before commanding the DBMS to perform the data retrieval.

    b. List three information requests for which it makes sense to use an index on BORROWED to perform the data retrieval. Indicate on which attributes the index(es) should be built.

5. The Mom-and-Pop grocery has hired you to design and implement a microcomputer database to manage their inventory and ordering. Neither the owners nor their three employees have any computer experience. What advantages can you see to installing a turnkey system in this store? What disadvantages might it present?

6. Brainstorm a bit—list the characteristics that you would like to see in a user-friendly database application. Questions you might ask yourself include:

    a. Should it be menu-driven? Command-driven? Both?

    b. If there are lots of commands, should they all be placed in one menu? What about submenus?

    c. Should there be an on-line help facility? If so, how much information should it provide (i.e., should it duplicate the manual)?

    d. What happens if the user makes a mistake? How should the application respond to an error (i.e., with beeps and flashing text)?

    e. What facilities should there be for "escaping" from command sequences or menu selections that were not what the user intended?

Going Multi-User

CHAPTER OUTLINE:

CHAPTER OBJECTIVES

After reading this chapter, you will understand the following about multi-user databases:

1. The difference between networked and multi-user DBMSs
2. Transaction control
3. How concurrent use can lead to lost updates
4. How locking is used to handle concurrency problems

NETWORKED VERSUS MULTI-USER DBMSs

There are three ways in which a database management system can allow more than one user access to the same database. A DBMS may be *network compatible,* or it may be *multi-user,* or it may be both.

A *network-compatible* DBMS allows users from many microcomputers or terminals to access a centrally located database using a *local area network* (LAN). The computer on which the database is stored is known as a *server.* However, while many different users can access the database from remote locations, only one user can work with the database at any time.

A *multi-user* DBMS permits *concurrent use* of the database. In other words, many different users can simultaneously interact with the same database, performing updates and retrievals. A multi-user DBMS that is not network compatible will only support users working from multiple terminals connected to the same microcomputer. However, most multi-user microcomputer DBMSs are also network compatible and therefore support multiple users working not only from terminals connected to the server, but from terminals on a network as well.

TRANSACTION CONTROL

Many multi-user databases group activities against a database into *transactions.* A transaction, as discussed in Chapter 6, is a unit of work. It may be as small as a single retrieval command, or it may include an entire group of changes made to the database at one time. A transaction can end in one of two ways: if it is successful, if it ends in a desired manner, it will be *committed* (all changes to the database are made permanent); if it ends unsuccessfully, in an undesirable manner, the database will be *rolled-back* (all changes will be undone and the database will be restored to the state it was in before the transaction began). Of the three DBMSs discussed in this book, only *Oracle* supports transactions in this manner.

To effect transaction roll back, a DBMS must somehow save the state of the database *before* a transaction begins. This copy of the data can then be used to restore the database if a transaction fails. The data saved to be used in case of roll back are known as a *before-image* and are written to a *before-image file.* It is important to realize that the entire database is not necessarily captured in a before-image file, but only that portion of it that may be affected by the requested activity. Nonetheless, before-image files do tend to consume significant disk space. For example, an *Oracle* before-image file occupies at least one-quarter of the file space used by the entire database. (Before-image files on minis and mainframes can occupy as much as one-half the file space used by the rest of the database.)

Oracle has no command to explicitly mark the start of a transaction. Instead, it assumes that a new transaction begins immediately after the end of a previous transaction. There are three ways, however, to specify the end of a transaction: the SQL command **COMMIT** explicitly commits a transaction; the SQL command **ROLLBACK WORK** rolls back a transaction; data definition commands (i.e., those that affect the data dictionary) implicitly issue a **COMMIT** to close out the preceding transaction. The concept of a transaction is most often used with embedded SQL, the SQL used within an application program. Interactive SQL commands, commands that are entered from the keyboard for immediate execution, can each be handled as a separate transaction by setting *Oracle*'s autocommit function on. If autocommit is off, no changes will be made to base tables until the interactive SQL user issues a **COMMIT** from the keyboard..

PROBLEMS WITH CONCURRENT USE

If you have been investigating the price of DBMSs, then you will have discovered that the multi-user version of a DBMS costs nearly twice as much as the single-user version. It also requires more main memory. For example, the single-user *R:base 5000* will run on a machine with 256K RAM (assuming that you are using MS-DOS 2.1 or less). The multi-user *R:base System V* requires that the computer acting as the server and remote workstations have at least 640K. Why this price and main memory difference? Multi-user DBMSs contain extra program code that isn't needed in single-user DBMSs. The extra code is there to deal with the problems created by concurrent use of a database.

Consider the following situation: two travel agents, one located in Boston and the other in Philadelphia, are both using the same airline reservations database. A customer calls the Boston travel agent and, as part of a cross-country trip, needs three seats from Chicago to Denver on a specific date and at a specific time. The travel agent queries the database and discovers that exactly three seats are available on a flight that meets the customer's criteria. The agent reports that fact to the customer who is waiting on the phone.

Meanwhile, a customer calls the travel agent in Philadelphia. This customer also needs three seats from Chicago to Denver on the same date and at the same time as the customer in Boston. The travel agent checks the database and discovers that there are exactly three seats available. These are the same three seats that the Boston travel agent just saw.

While the Philadelphia travel agent is talking to one customer, the Boston travel agent receives an OK from the other customer to book the seats. The number of available seats on the flight is modified from three to zero.

The Philadelphia travel agent has also received an OK to book the reservations and proceeds to issue a command that reserves another three seats. The problem, however, is that the Philadelphia travel agent is working from old information. There may have been three seats available when the database was queried, but they are no longer available at the

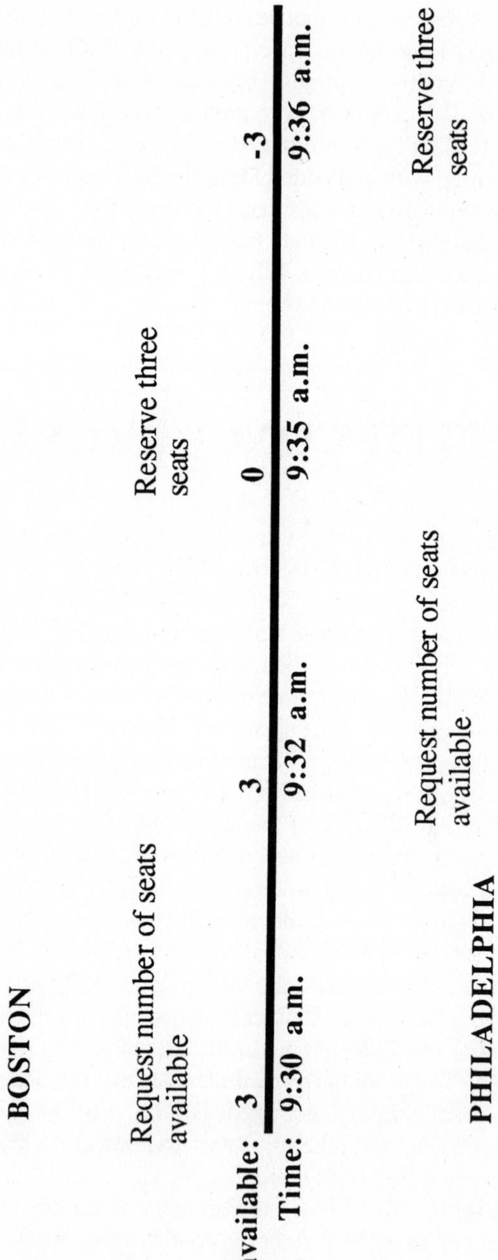

BOSTON

Request number of seats available

Reserve three seats

Seats available: 3   3   0   -3
Time: 9:30 a.m.   9:32 a.m.   9:35 a.m.   9:36 a.m.

PHILADELPHIA

Request number of seats available

Reserve three seats

Figure 7.1   A Lost Update Resulting in an Overbooked Airline Flight

time the reservations are made. As a result, the flight is now overbooked by three seats (the seats-available attribute will contain a minus 3).

This problem is known as the *lost-update problem*. It occurs when the actions of one user (in this example, the Philadelphia travel agent) cause an update made by another concurrent user (the Boston travel agent) to be lost. Figure 7.1 contains a time line that shows exactly how the Philadelphia travel agent accidentally ended up overbooking the flight.

The scheme most commonly used to handle the lost-update problem is *locking*. Locking permits each user to limit the access other concurrent users will have to the parts of the database with which he or she is working. For example, if the Boston travel agent had been able to prevent the Philadelphia travel agent from looking at the seats-available data until the Boston transaction was finished, then the Philadelphia travel agent would have seen that there were no seats available and would not have attempted to make the reservations. Locks can either be *implicit*, in which case they are placed automatically as needed by the DBMS, or they can be *explicit*, placed by a command issued by the user.

Many different data objects within a database can be locked. Locks can be placed on entire relations, on specific tuples within a relation, or on specific attributes within specific tuples within a relation. The larger the object being locked, the easier the locking scheme is to incorporate into a DBMS. However, locking large objects, such as entire relations, cuts down on the amount of concurrency the DBMS will support. Users who cannot access part of the database because another user has it locked will have to wait until the lock is released. Therefore, the more specific the objects being locked, the more opportunities for concurrent use that will exist. Some multi-user microcomputer DBMSs support locking at the row, or record; this provides an acceptable amount of concurrency for most database environments. Others lock tables and sometimes the entire database.

The most primitive and powerful type of lock is the *exclusive lock*. If a user obtains an exclusive lock on a data object, then no other user can modify or view that data until the lock is released. In other words, only one user can obtain an exclusive lock on any given data object at a given time. To see how an exclusive locking scheme would solve the travel agency problem, take a look at Figure 7.2.

In this case, the Boston travel agent receives an exclusive lock on the tuple describing the flight in question. When the Philadelphia travel agent attempts to retrieve the same tuple, the request is put in a wait state, where it remains until the Boston travel agent releases the lock. At that point, the Philadelphia request is honored and the agent retrieves data based on the update made in Boston.

While exclusive locks can solve the lost update problem, they do spawn a problem all of their own. Assume now that the Boston and Philadelphia travel agents are working with two new customers. The customer calling the Boston travel agent wants to book flights from Boston to Philadelphia and back; the customer calling the Philadelphia travel agent wants to go from Philadelphia to Boston and back. Both customers want to travel on the same day and wish to leave and return at approximately the same time.

The Boston travel agent queries the database about a Boston to Philadelphia flight and receives an exclusive lock on the tuple. While the agent is looking at the result on the terminal screen, the Philadelphia travel agent places a request for data about a Philadelphia to Boston flight and receives an exclusive lock on the tuple.

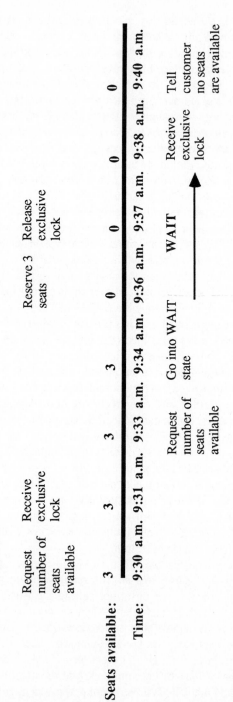

Figure 7.2 Using Exclusive Locks to Solve the Lost Update Problem

The Boston travel agent then requests data about a return flight for the customer (Philadelphia to Boston). However, the Philadelphia travel agent already has an exclusive lock on the tuple. The Boston request goes into a wait state. The Philadelphia travel agent asks for data about a return flight (Boston to Philadelphia). The Boston to Philadelphia flight, though, is locked by the Boston travel agent. The Philadelphia request also goes into the wait state. Now both travel agents are waiting for tuples on which the other has a lock. Neither can proceed until one of them releases a lock. This situation (diagrammed in Figure 7.3) is known as *deadlock*, or a *deadly embrace*.

There are two main ways that a DBMS can handle deadlock: by avoiding it or by breaking it when it occurs. Deadlock avoidance is the more difficult of the two techniques to implement, so most DBMSs choose to detect deadlock and then break it.

DBMSs detect deadlock by keeping a list of who is waiting for whom. When a cycle appears in the list (a user is waiting for someone before him or her in the list), then a deadlock has occurred. The only way to break the deadlock is to force one user in the list to release his or her locks. A DBMS will have rules by which it selects the "victim." It may, for example, choose the last user to enter the list. The victim is rolled back, which in turn releases all the victim's locks.

How the DBMS decides to release a lock depends on whether or not the user is working in a transaction-based environment. In transaction-based DBMSs, locks are retained until the DBMS encounters a statement that ends the transaction. If the DBMS is not transaction-based, then locks will usually be retained until a given operation against the database is completed.

Although exclusive locks and deadlock detection will solve the lost-update problem, the use of exclusive locks does cut down on the amount of concurrency a DBMS will support. Since there are times that a user needs to prevent other users from changing data but not necessarily from viewing it, most DBMSs support a second, less restrictive type of lock known as a *shared lock*.

A shared lock permits the user to retrieve a data object but not to modify it. A data object that is locked with a shared lock can be retrieved by users other than the one initially placing the lock. These other users also receive a shared lock on that same data object. However, no user can modify the data item (i.e., receive an exclusive lock on it) until all shared locks on it are released.

ORACLE CONCURRENCY CONTROL

Oracle supports both exclusive and shared locks on individual rows and entire tables. A user may explicitly request a lock with the SQL **LOCK** command or *Oracle* will implicitly place needed locks.

Explicit locks are placed on either single rows or entire tables. They can be placed either interactively from the keyboard or from within an application program. The locks are

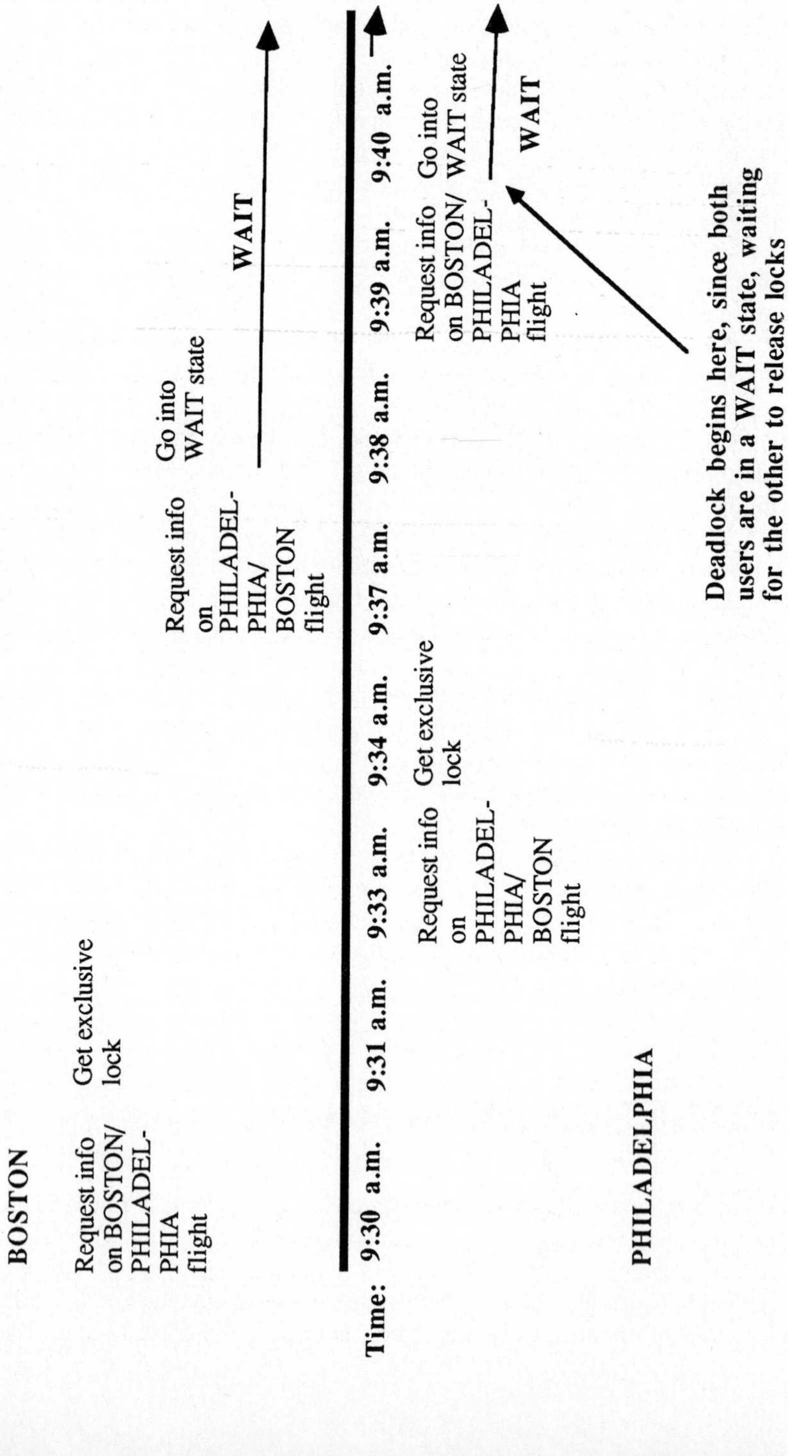

BOSTON

Request info
on BOSTON/
PHILADEL-
PHIA
flight

Get exclusive
lock

Request info
on
PHILADEL-
PHIA/
BOSTON
flight

Go into
WAIT state

WAIT

Time: 9:30 a.m.   9:31 a.m.   9:33 a.m.   9:34 a.m.   9:37 a.m.   9:38 a.m.   9:39 a.m.   9:40 a.m.

Request info
on
PHILADEL-
PHIA/
BOSTON
flight

Get exclusive
lock

Request info
on BOSTON/
PHILADEL-
PHIA
flight

Go into
WAIT state

WAIT

PHILADELPHIA

Deadlock begins here, since both
users are in a WAIT state, waiting
for the other to release locks

Figure   7.3   Deadlock

held until the user ends the transaction with **COMMIT** or **ROLLBACK WORK** or exits *Oracle*. Three types of locks are available, each of which is invoked by a single SQL command:

1. **LOCK TABLE table_name IN SHARED MODE** produces a shared lock as described earlier in this chapter. The shared lock will also allow other users to obtain a shared lock on the table but will prevent anyone from modifying the table until all locks on it are released.

2. **LOCK TABLE table_name IN SHARED UPDATE MODE** produces an exclusive lock on only those rows a user intends to update. It permits other users to concurrently update different rows in the same table. Generally, this type of lock is only useful within an application program in which rows are being fetched one at a time for update. Interactive SQL commands, which operate on an entire table at once, make it impossible for *Oracle* to determine which rows in a table "might" be updated. Therefore, interactive SQL must lock an entire table.

3. **LOCK TABLE table_name IN EXCLUSIVE MODE** produces an exclusive lock on an entire table. *Oracle*'s exclusive lock, which prevents any other user from obtaining an exclusive lock on the table and subsequently modifying it, does allow other users to view the table while the exclusive lock is held.

Normally, if an explicit lock cannot be placed, *Oracle* places the user in a wait state. However, if the keyword **NOWAIT** is appended to the **LOCK TABLE** command, *Oracle* will notify the user whenever a lock isn't available rather than entering the transaction into the wait list.

Implicit locks are placed whenever a user requests a data modification operation (the SQL commands **INSERT, UPDATE,** and **DELETE**) or whenever single rows are fetched for update. Since **INSERT, UPDATE,** and **DELETE** operate on an entire table, *Oracle* will place an exclusive lock on the table, exactly as if the user had used a **LOCK TABLE IN EXCLUSIVE MODE** command. If an application program is processing data one row at a time, *Oracle* will place an exclusive lock on only those rows that are actually retrieved. This is equivalent to using the **LOCK TABLE IN SHARED UPDATE MODE** command. Implicit locks are held until the transaction which placed the locks ends. This end may be signaled by the **COMMIT** or **ROLLBACK WORK** commands, by issuing a table modification command, by exiting *Oracle*, or by ending an application program.

If an implicit lock cannot be placed, generally because another user has a lock on the requested table and/or rows, the transaction is placed in a wait state. Because *Oracle* uses the wait list strategy, deadlock can occur.

Oracle detects deadlock and then breaks it as described earlier in this chapter. In other words, it selects one of the transactions involved in the deadlock as a victim and rolls back that transaction, forcing it to release its locks. *Oracle* selects as the victim the "youngest" transaction, the one that has been running the shortest length of time. Once the victim has been identified, *Oracle* issues a ROLLBACK WORK command to that transaction and returns an error code to the user. *Oracle* does not automatically retry the transaction; it must be resubmitted by the user.

R:BASE SYSTEM V CONCURRENCY CONTROL

R:base System V has two distinct ways of handling concurrent use problems. The first, what *R:base* calls "concurrency control," is used to alert users to the possibility of lost updates. *R:base System V* also provides both table and database locks.

The *R:base* "concurrency control" mechanism is invoked by the **ENTER USING** or **EDIT USING** commands. If two users attempt to update the same column of the same row nearly simultaneously, *R:base* will perform the first update and then send a message to the second user informing him or her of the previous update. The second user may then choose to proceed with his or her update, which will eliminate the first update, or terminate the update request. This warning system does not prevent lost updates. However, it makes users aware that the potential for a lost update exists. "Concurrency control" remains in effect for the duration of the update session, unless another user issues a command that requires a lock on the table.

R:base table locks are a combination of exclusive and shared lock. When in effect, they prevent any other user from updating the table (i.e., no other user can obtain a lock on the table). However, they do allow other users to view the data in the table. Table locks are placed implicitly by a number of commands. They are released when the command that issued the lock terminates. The following three commands will interrupt any "concurrency control" in effect at the time they are issued:

- **APPEND**
- **CHANGE**
- **DELETE ROWS**

The following commands will generate a table lock if no concurrency control is in effect:

- **EDIT ALL**
- **LOAD**
- **FORMS** (if form is being edited)
- **REPORTS** (if report is being edited)
- **VIEW** (if view is being edited)

A database lock is an exclusive lock on the entire database. When a database lock is in effect, users other than the one issuing the lock cannot interact with the database in any way. Like implicit table locks, database locks are released when the command that issued them terminates. Database locks are placed by:

- **DEFINE, EXPAND, REDEFINE, REMOVE, REMOVE COLUMN**
  (these are all database structure commands)
- **FORMS** (if the form is new)

- **INTERSECT**
- **JOIN**
- **PROJECT**
- **RENAME**
- **REPORTS** (if the report is new)
- **SUBTRACT**
- **UNION**
- **VIEW** (if the view is new)

In other words, database locks are required whenever a command is issued that modifies the structure of the database.

R:base System V supports row level access to tables from within an application program. An application can place explicit table locks with the commands **SET LOCK ON**. Locks set in this way are removed with **SET LOCK OFF**. The locks will be placed only if all tables requested by the **SET LOCK ON** command are available.

R:base System V handles the deadlock problem by limiting the amount of time a user can wait for a lock. (The default is about four seconds.) If a requested lock cannot be placed, the user is placed in a wait state. R:base will automatically periodically check to see if the requested table is available. However, if the table is not available within the limit set on the wait period, the request for the lock is aborted and the user notified. Therefore, though deadlocks may occur, they are broken when the wait period is exceeded. The wait period can be changed from the default with the **SET WAIT** command.

It is important to realize that R:base System V has no concept of a transaction. Updates are propagated to the base tables immediately after a single command is completed. There is no before image file like that used by Oracle nor is there any command to roll back update actions. Although the time out mechanism just described will break any deadlocks which occur, what happens if the lock that couldn't be obtained is somewhere in the midst of an entire series of update activities within an application program? Those updates which preceded the failed attempt to obtain a lock wil remain in the database; those updates which follow the failed attempt will not have been made. The database could quite possibly be left in an inconsistent and inaccurate state. The burden for retaining the integrity of the database in this situation rests with the applications programmer, who must explicitly write program modules that will roll back the database, undoing any changes made to the database by the program that was unable to complete its functions.

DBASE III PLUS CONCURRENCY CONTROL

Unlike Oracle and R:base, dBase III Plus, as purchased off the shelf, is not a multi-user DBMS. In order to obtain muli-user capabilities, an organization must purchase a dBase LAN pack, which allows up to five remote users to access a single centralized dBase

III Plus database. (More remote users can be added with additional LAN packs.) The discussion in this section describes the concurrency control available with the LAN pack. Note that much of *dBase III Plus*'s concurrency control must be implemented through an application program. If you are unfamiliar with the *dBase* programming language, you may wish to read the portion of Chapter 11 that introduces *dBase* programming and then return to this section.

The files in a *dBase* network environment can be opened for either exclusive or shared use. In exclusive mode, a file can be used only by a single user; concurrency control is unnecessary. Files opened in shared mode (i.e., they are opened after the **SET EXCLUSIVE OFF** command has been issued), however, are available for concurrent use and must therefore be subject to concurrency control whenever the file is updated. Like many multi-user microcomputer DBMSs, *dBase III Plus* does not provide concurrency control for retrieval activities but only for update.

dBase III Plus uses locking at the following three different levels to manage concurrent update requests:

1. Automatic file locking. Commands that affect an entire database file (e.g., **APPEND FROM, BROWSE, COPY, INDEX, JOIN, SORT**) automatically lock the entire database file, giving the user performing the command exclusive rights to that database file until the command is completed.
2. Explicit file locking. Explicit file locking allows a programmer to lock a shared database file during an update operation. Other users may continue to retrieve data in the database file but not update it until the user placing the lock releases it with the command **UNLOCK**. Explicit file locks are placed with the **FLOCK()** function, which returns a Boolean result of **.T.** if the attempt to place the lock was successful.
3. Record locking. Record locking allows a programmer to place locks on individual records within a shared database file. Since the entire database file is not locked, more than one user can simultaneously update the file so long as the update activities involve different records. Record locks are placed with either the **RLOCK()** or **LOCK()** functions, both of which return a Boolean result of **.T.** if the attempt to place the lock was successful.

dBase III Plus neither detects nor handles deadlock. This does not mean that deadlock cannot occur. In fact, deadlock is a significant danger in a networked *dBase* environment and must be carefully managed from within program code. To see how a deadlock might arise, consider the two program segments in Listing 7.1. These segments assume that two database files have been opened for use. One is in AREA1, the other in AREA2. Program1 first attempts to obtain a file lock on the database file in use in AREA1. The empty DO WHILE loop repeats the attempt until the lock is placed. Assuming that no other program other than Program2 is running concurrently, the request for the lock on the file in AREA1 will be successful At the same time, Program2 requests and successfully obtains a file lock on the database file in AREA2.

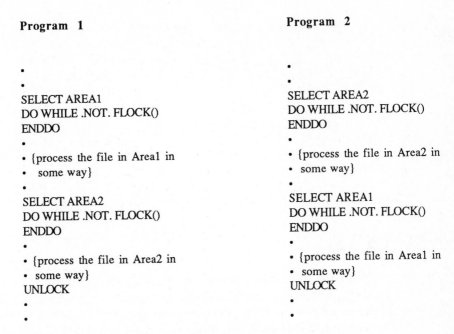

Program 1

```
•
•
SELECT AREA1
DO WHILE .NOT. FLOCK()
ENDDO
•
• {process the file in Area1 in
•  some way}
•
SELECT AREA2
DO WHILE .NOT. FLOCK()
ENDDO
•
• {process the file in Area2 in
•  some way}
UNLOCK
•
•
```

Program 2

```
•
•
SELECT AREA2
DO WHILE .NOT. FLOCK()
ENDDO
•
• {process the file in Area2 in
•  some way}
•
SELECT AREA1
DO WHILE .NOT. FLOCK()
ENDDO
•
• {process the file in Area1 in
•  some way}
UNLOCK
•
•
```

Listing 7.1 *dBase III Plus* Program Segments That Will Cause Deadlock

Each program processes data in some way. Without unlocking the database file in AREA1, Program1 then switches to AREA2 and attempts to obtain a file lock. The lock attempt is unsuccessful, since Program2 already has a lock on that database file. Program1 goes into a wait state, looping continually as long as Program2 holds its lock (i.e., **FLOCK**() will continue to return .F.). Meanwhile, Program2 finishes its processing and attempts to obtain a lock on the database file in AREA1. **FLOCK**() will return .F., since Program1 already holds the required lock. This is a classic deadlock situation. Both programs contain loops that automatically retry locking attempts; the loops are terminated only when a lock is obtained. Since *dBase III Plus* has no method for detecting this situation, the two programs might theoretically stay deadlocked indefinitely. What is more likely, however, is that a user will become frustrated and eventually terminate the program.

There are several ways in which a *dBase III Plus* programmer might avoid a deadlock. One way is to include a timer that automatically aborts a lock request after some interval has passed. For example, Program1 from Listing 7.1 might be amended as in Listing 7.2.

When the value of the variable TIMER reaches 500, the loop which attempts to place the lock will stop. In this way *dBase III Plus* can be programmed to function much like *R:base System V*, which automatically aborts a lock request after a specified interval.

Like *R:base System V*, d:Base III Plus has no concept of a transaction. If a program function must be aborted for any reason (including because a lock cannot be placed), it is up to the programmer to explicitly undo everything the program has done.

```
•
TIMER = 0
SELECT AREA1
DO WHILE .NOT. FLOCK() .AND. TIMER < 500
   TIMER = TIMER + 1
ENDDO
IF .NOT. FLOCK()
   {code for roll back goes here}
ELSE
   {process the data}
ENDIF
•
```

Listing 7.2   An Amended Program Segment That Will Avoid Deadlock

SUMMARY

Multi-user DBMSs permit more than one user to use the data at any given time (concurrent use). Concurrent use brings with it a problem known as a lost update. A lost update occurs when a user makes a change to the database based on incorrect data; another user has changed the data since the first user viewed the data. Lost updates may cause invalid data to be stored in the database.

Most multi-user databases use locking to handle the lost update problem. Users who intend to update data obtain an exclusive lock on that data, preventing any other user from even viewing the data until the lock is released.

Exclusive locks can create a problem of their own—deadlock. Deadlock occurs when a user locks a data object needed by another user *and* another user has a lock on a data object needed by the first user. A DBMS can either take measures to prevent deadlock or can wait for deadlock to occur and then break it. Most microcomputer DBMSs choose to do the latter. Breaking deadlock usually involves selecting one user as the victim. The victim's transaction is aborted, forcing the release of all of its locks.

Exclusive locks, because they prevent other users from even viewing data, cut down on the amount of concurrent activity a DBMS can support. Many DBMSs therefore use a second type of lock, the shared lock, to allow multiple users to view the same data. A shared lock prevents modification of the data until all locks on it are released (no one can obtain an exclusive lock). However, many users can hold a shared lock on the same data object.

REFERENCES

Bernstein, P.A., V. Hadzilacos, N. Goodman. (1987) *Concurrency Control and Recovery in Database Systems*. Reading, MA: Addison-Wesley.

Casanova, M.A. (1981) *The Concurrency Control Problem of Database Systems. Lecture Notes in Computer Science*. Berlin: Springer-Verlag.

Date, C. J. (1983) *An Introduction to Database Systems*, Vol. II. 2nd ed. Reading, MA: Addison-Wesley.

Kedem, Z.M. (1983) "Locking protocols: from exclusive to shared locks." *Journal of the ACM*. 30(4):787-804. October.

THINGS TO THINK ABOUT

1. Multi-user databases cause problems that aren't present with single-user databases. What are some of these problems? Though these problems exist, why might an organization choose to go to a multi-user DBMS?

2. Your best friend is writing a multi-user DBMS. Though your friend has a lot of experience with single-user DBMSs, he or she has never worked with a multi-user DBMS. You've spent three days now trying to convince your friend that record locking is needed, but a discussion of the theory hasn't gotten through. What you need is a concrete example.

      a. Describe an actual situation in which a multi-user database will suffer from a lost update problem if record locking isn't used.
      b. Show how exclusive locks might be used to solve the problem.
      c. Extend your example to show how deadlock might occur.

3. Can shared locks ever be responsible for deadlock? If so, give an example how it might occur. If not, why not?

4. In some circumstances, *R:base System V*, *dBase III Plus*, and *Oracle* lock entire tables rather than just rows within a table. Since this cuts down on the amount of concurrency a database will support, why do you think system designers chose to do it this way?

8

Oracle's SQL

CHAPTER OUTLINE:

CHAPTER OBJECTIVES

After reading this chapter, you will:

1. Be familiar with the interactive SQL commands needed to create tables and views to insert, modify, and delete data
2. Be familiar with the syntax and power of the SQL **SELECT** command

Early in 1986, SQL (for Structured Query Language) was accepted by ANSI (the American National Standards Institute) as the national standard query language for relational databases. Of the three DBMSs discussed in this book, only *Oracle* supports a full implementation of SQL. *Oracle* is different from most of the database management systems currently marketed for microcomputers. It has become available for micros only recently. The package first ran on minis and mainframes and the microcomputer implementation is virtually identical to the *Oracle* found on the larger machines.

Oracle's SQL is the same SQL query language that is used with *DB2*, IBM's relational DBMS for large mainframes. What you learn about SQL here you can transport to just about any DBMS that uses that query language; the differences in implementation between packages are generally minor syntax differences (e.g., replacement of a logical equals sign with the word **IS**).

DBMSs that support SQL refer to relations as *tables*. Attributes are called *columns*; tuples are *rows*. SQL views are implemented as virtual tables (i.e., only view definitions are stored on disk; view tables are created only when referenced). The catalog is on-line and dynamic; it is referred to as the *data dictionary*.

An *Oracle* database stores all table definitions and data in a single file. The file is created with the *Oracle* utility program *CCF* (Create Contiguous File). The only other file required to support an *Oracle* database is a before-image file, which is also created with *CCF*. The database file is initialized with another utility program, *IOR* (Initialize Oracle). The initialization removes anything previously stored in the file and rebuilds the data dictionary tables. If you wish to query the data dictionary, you must then load the data dictionary views. The on-line help facility must also be reloaded after a database file has been initialized. The programs that do the loading are run from within *Oracle* 's *UFI* (User Friendly Interface). All interactive-SQL commands are also entered from *UFI*.

USING SQL TO INSTALL A 3NF DATABASE

Base tables are defined with the SQL command **CREATE TABLE**. The general format of the command is:

CREATE TABLE table_name (column_name1 type1 [NOT NULL]
[,column_name2 type2 [NOT NULL]]...);

The notation used above places brackets around any part of the command that is optional. An ellipsis (...) indicates that a portion of the command may be repeated. Note that all SQL commands end with a semicolon. The semicolon makes it possible to split a command onto multiple lines for clarity; the DBMS does not process the command until it encounters the semicolon, regardless of how many carriage returns are present.

The following command will create the CAB relation for the FTC database:

```
CREATE TABLE cab (cabnum char (3) NOT NULL,
                  make char (15),
                  model char (15),
                  year char (2),
                  purdate date,
                  licnum char (7),
                  conditn char (25),
                  cabstat char (1),
                  curodom number (6));
```

Each attribute is given a name of up to 30 characters. Attribute names must start with a letter but can contain letters, numbers, underbars, and dollar signs.

The option **NOT NULL** is used for any columns that should not be permitted to assume a null value. Therefore, all attributes which are part of the primary key should be indicated as **NOT NULL**. Checks for violation of **NOT NULL** specifications are made when data are entered. The DBMS will not store any row which is missing data for a **NOT NULL** column. In other words, a SQL DBMS allows you to define entity integrity within the data dictionary and also automatically enforces it.

The name of each attribute is followed by a type designator, indicating what type of data will be stored in the column. *Oracle* supports four types of columns:

1. **char** columns will store any printable character. The **char** designation is followed by a number in parentheses indicating the maximum length of the column up to 240 characters.
2. **number** columns will store both integers and real numbers. If no length is specified for a **number** column, the length will default to a 22-digit integer. To store a shorter integer, a single number, corresponding to the maximum digits, is placed in parentheses after the type specification. Real numbers require a slightly more complex length specification. For example, **number (10,2)** indicates that a column should store numbers with a maximum of ten digits, two of which are to the right of the decimal place.
3. **date** columns will store dates in the format **DD-MON-YR**. For example, the 12th of May in 1988 is stored as **12-MAY-88**. This format supports date arithmetic. It can also be modified for output.
4. **long** columns are designed to store large blocks of text. There is no limit to the size of **long** columns, but there can only be one per table.

The complete set of SQL commands needed to install the FTC database appear in Table 8.1. Although the keywords in this table are printed in all upper case, SQL is not case sensitive with keywords and the names of user-created data objects (e.g., tables and views). Upper and lower case differences are, however, retained within the data themselves. The commands have been split onto multiple lines for clarity.

Table 8.1
SQL Commands Used to Create the FTC Database

```
CREATE TABLE cab (cabnum char (3) NOT NULL,
            make char (15),
            model char (15),
            year char (2),
            purdate date,
            licnum char (7),
            conditn char (25),
            cabstat char (2),
            curodom number (6));

CREATE TABLE driver (drvnum char (4) NOT NULL,
            drvnam char (25),
            drvstr char (25),
            drvscz char (25),
            drvphone char (12),
            drvlic char (11),
            drvlexd date,
            drvstat char (15));

CREATE TABLE shifts (wkdate date NOT NULL,
            wkshift char (3) NOT NULL,
            cabnum char (3) NOT NULL,
            drvnum char (4),
            wkflag char (1),
            odomrdg1 number (6),
            odomrdg2 number (6));

CREATE TABLE incidents (wkdate date NOT NULL,
            wkshift char (3) NOT NULL,
            cabnum char (3) NOT NULL,
            incitype char (15),
            details long);

CREATE TABLE maintenance (cabnum char (3) NOT NULL,
            maindate date NOT NULL,
            maintype char (15) NOT NULL,
            mainodom number (6));
```

To completely remove a table from the database, use the command DROP TABLE:

DROP TABLE table_name;

Unless you have been given database administrator privileges, you will only be able to drop tables that you have created.

SQL INDEXES

As discussed in Chapter 6, an index can enhance the retrieval performance of a database. Once an index has been created, the DBMS will automatically use it whenever that use will facilitate performance. SQL indexes can also be used to ensure that primary key values are unique. Therefore, each table should be indexed at least on its primary key.

The general form of the **CREATE INDEX** statement is:

CREATE [UNIQUE] INDEX index_name
    ON table_name (column_name1 [,column_name2]...);

If the optional keyword **UNIQUE** is present, the DBMS will not permit duplicate values within the table for the columns listed in the **CREATE INDEX** command. An index for a composite key can be built by simply including more than one attribute name within the parentheses that follow the table name. For example, the SQL command to create a unique index for the SHIFTS table is:

CREATE UNIQUE INDEX shiftkey
    ON shifts (wkdate, wkshift, cabnum);

Note that SQL has no trouble concatenating the column of type **date** (wkdate) with columns of type **char** (wkshift, cabnum); no special conversion routines are required. The complete set of **CREATE INDEX** commands for use with the FTC database is available in Table 8.2.

MODIFYING THE STRUCTURE OF A TABLE

Existing tables can be modified in one of two ways: either a column can be added to the table or the width of an existing column can be expanded. When adding a column, the format of the command is:

ALTER TABLE table_name
    ADD column_name type;

The column name and type designation must conform to the rules for column names and data types in the **CREATE TABLE** command. For example, to add a column to hold the color of a cab to the CAB table:

> **ALTER TABLE** cab
> **ADD color char (8);**

There is no command to remove a column from a table.

The syntax to expand an existing column is only slightly different:

> **ALTER TABLE** table_name
> **MODIFY** column_name type;

For example, if the 15 characters originally allocated for the INCITYPE attribute in the INCIDENTS relation proves too small, it can be expanded with:

> **ALTER TABLE incidents**
> **MODIFY incitype char (25);**

The **MODIFY** version of **ALTER TABLE** cannot make a column smaller. It can only increase the number of characters in a **char** column or change the width or number of decimal places in a **number** column. It also cannot be used to change the type of a column.

Table 8.2

SQL Commands to Index the FTC Database

```
CREATE UNIQUE INDEX cabkey
    ON cab (cabnum);

CREATE UNIQUE INDEX drvkey
    ON driver (drvnum);

CREATE UNIQUE INDEX shiftkey
    ON shifts (wkdate, wkshift, cabnum);

CREATE UNIQUE INDEX incikey
    ON incidents (wkdate, wkshift, cabnum);

CREATE UNIQUE INDEX maintkey
    ON maintenance (cabnum, maindate, maintype);
```

USING SQL TO LOCATE AND RETRIEVE DATA

SQL supports a very powerful command, **SELECT**, which is used to locate and retrieve data. The SQL **SELECT** is *not* the same as the select operation from the relational algebra. While the relational select retrieves data from all columns of one or more rows from a single table, the SQL **SELECT** command can retrieve from multiple tables (using a join), can project specific columns from the result, and can perform some computations. The ability to perform more than one relational algebra operation with a single command means that **SELECT** is based on the relational calculus, not the relational algebra. All or part of the **SELECT** syntax is used in a number of other SQL commands, including those to insert, modify, and delete data and to create views.

The general form of the **SELECT** command has a number of options:

```
SELECT  [DISTINCT]  column_name1  [,column_name2]...
      FROM  table_name  [,table_name2]...
      [WHERE  predicate]
      [ORDER  BY  column_name1  [,column_name2]...]
      [GROUP  BY  column_name1  [,column_name2]...]
      [HAVING  predicate];
```

SIMPLE SQL RETRIEVAL

In its simplest form, **SELECT** must specify which columns should be included in the output and the table from which they should come. The list of columns to be included in the result can specify all columns in the table by using an asterisk or can contain the names of the columns.

For example,

SELECT * FROM shifts;

will produce the output seen in Figure 8.1. All columns and all rows have been selected; the * indicates all columns, and the absence of **WHERE, GROUP BY**, and/or **HAVING** clauses allows all rows to be included. As mentioned in Chapter 6, the use of the wildcard * can be dangerous. If the number of columns in a table is increased or decreased, output with * will change.

To see only the days and shifts for which cabs have been reserved, use:

SELECT wkdate, wkshift FROM shifts;

```
SELECT * FROM shifts;

WKDATE       WKS  CAB  DRVN  W  ODOMRE  ODOMRE
15-JUL-86 day  1Ø4  ØØØ6  t  2Ø2662  2Ø2771
15-JUL-86 day  238  ØØ1Ø  t  21Ø965  2111Ø4
15-JUL-86 day  4Ø4  ØØ2Ø  t  319333  319487
15-JUL-86 eve  Ø45  ØØ11  f       Ø       Ø
15-JUL-86 eve  1Ø4  ØØØ1  t  2Ø2771  2Ø29Ø5
15-JUL-86 eve  144  ØØ12  t  35ØØØ2  35Ø19Ø
15-JUL-86 ngt  Ø45  ØØ16  t   4883Ø   4919Ø
15-JUL-86 ngt  1Ø8  ØØØ2  t   53885   539ØØ
15-JUL-86 ngt  215  ØØØ8  t   2Ø1Ø7   2Ø225
16-JUL-86 day  1Ø4  ØØØ6  f       Ø       Ø
16-JUL-86 day  238  ØØ1Ø  f       Ø       Ø
16-JUL-86 day  4Ø4  ØØ2Ø  f       Ø       Ø
16-JUL-86 eve  ØØ2  ØØØ4  f       Ø       Ø
16-JUL-86 eve  1Ø4  ØØØ1  f       Ø       Ø
16-JUL-86 ngt  ØØ2  ØØØ7  f       Ø       Ø
17-JUL-86 day  1Ø4  ØØØ6  f       Ø       Ø
17-JUL-86 day  238  ØØ1Ø  f       Ø       Ø
17-JUL-86 day  4Ø4  ØØ2Ø  f       Ø       Ø
17-JUL-86 ngt  1Ø8  ØØØ2  f       Ø       Ø
18-JUL-86 day  1Ø4  ØØØ6  f       Ø       Ø
18-JUL-86 day  238  ØØ1Ø  f       Ø       Ø
18-JUL-86 eve  ØØ2  ØØØ4  f       Ø       Ø
18-JUL-86 eve  Ø45  ØØ11  f       Ø       Ø
18-JUL-86 ngt  Ø45  ØØ16  f       Ø       Ø
18-JUL-86 ngt  1Ø8  ØØØ2  f       Ø       Ø
18-JUL-86 ngt  215  ØØØ8  f       Ø       Ø
19-JUL-86 day  1Ø4  ØØØ6  f       Ø       Ø
19-JUL-86 eve  1Ø4  ØØØ1  f       Ø       Ø
19-JUL-86 eve  238  ØØØ3  f       Ø       Ø
2Ø-JUL-86 eve  238  ØØØ3  f       Ø       Ø
```

Figure 8.1 SQL SELECT Command—Example 1

The output from this query appears in Figure 8.2.   This output contains duplicate rows, since the attributes WKDATE and WKSHIFT don't constitute an entire primary key. **SELECT** can be instructed to return only unique rows by adding the keyword **DISTINCT** to the query:

SELECT   DISTINCT   wkdate,   wkshift   FROM   shifts;

```
SELECT wkdate, wkshift FROM shifts;
```

WKDATE	WKS
15-JUL-86	day
15-JUL-86	day
15-JUL-86	day
15-JUL-86	eve
15-JUL-86	eve
15-JUL-86	eve
15-JUL-86	ngt
15-JUL-86	ngt
15-JUL-86	ngt
16-JUL-86	day
16-JUL-86	day
16-JUL-86	day
16-JUL-86	eve
16-JUL-86	eve
16-JUL-86	ngt
17-JUL-86	day
17-JUL-86	day
17-JUL-86	day
17-JUL-86	ngt
18-JUL-86	day
18-JUL-86	day
18-JUL-86	eve
18-JUL-86	eve
18-JUL-86	ngt
18-JUL-86	ngt
18-JUL-86	ngt
19-JUL-86	day
19-JUL-86	eve
19-JUL-86	eve
20-JUL-86	eve

Figure 8.2 SQL SELECT Command—Example 2

The resulting table can be found in Figure 8.3a.

The virtual table produced by a select can be sorted before it is displayed by using the **ORDER BY** clause. If the **ORDER BY** clause is not used, the contents of a virtual table will be displayed in the order in which they were entered. For example, in Figure 8.3a data are ordered by date and shift, but only because they were entered from the keyboard in that

```
SELECT DISTINCT wkdate, wkshift FROM shifts;
```

```
WKDATE       WKS
15-JUL-86 day
15-JUL-86 eve
15-JUL-86 ngt
16-JUL-86 day
16-JUL-86 eve
16-JUL-86 ngt
17-JUL-86 day
17-JUL-86 ngt
18-JUL-86 day
18-JUL-86 eve
18-JUL-86 ngt
19-JUL-86 day
19-JUL-86 eve
20-JUL-86 eve
```

Figure 8.3a SQL SELECT Command—Example 3a

manner. If, however, FTC's office clerk wishes to see the output by shift and then date, the **SELECT** command must be issued as:

> **SELECT DISTINCT wkdate, wkshift**
> **FROM shifts**
> **ORDER BY wkshift, wkdate;**

This query will produce the result in Figure 8.3b. Since the shifts are stored as text, they are ordered alphabetically in ascending order. The dates, stored as a SQL **date** data type, are ordered chronologically in ascending order.

Output may also be sorted in descending order by using the keyword **DESC** after any attribute which is to be sorted in that manner. For example, to produce Figure 8.3a in descending order by date:

> **SELECT DISTINCT wkdate, wkshift**
> **FROM shifts**
> **ORDER by wkdate DESC, wkshift;**

This query produces the table in Figure 8.3c.

```
SELECT DISTINCT wkdate, wkshift
FROM shifts
ORDER BY wkshift, wkdate;
```

WKDATE   WKS
15-JUL-86 day
16-JUL-86 day
17-JUL-86 day
18-JUL-86 day
19-JUL-86 day
15-JUL-86 eve
16-JUL-86 eve
18-JUL-86 eve
19-JUL-86 eve
2Ø-JUL-86 eve
15-JUL-86 ngt
16-JUL-86 ngt
17-JUL-86 ngt
18-JUL-86 ngt

Figure 8.3b   SQL SELECT Command—Example 3b

```
SELECT DISTINCT wkdate, wkshift
FROM shifts
ORDER BY wkdate DESC, wkshift;
```

WKDATE   WKS
2Ø-JUL-86 eve
19-JUL-86 day
19-JUL-86 eve
18-JUL-86 day
18-JUL-86 eve
18-JUL-86 ngt
17-JUL-86 day
17-JUL-86 ngt
16-JUL-86 day
16-JUL-86 eve
16-JUL-86 ngt
15-JUL-86 day
15-JUL-86 eve
15-JUL-86 ngt

Figure 8.3c   SQL SELECT Command—Example 3c

```
SELECT wkdate, wkshift
FROM shifts
WHERE drvnum = '0010';

WKDATE      WKS
15-JUL-86 day
16-JUL-86 day
17-JUL-86 day
18-JUL-86 day
```

Figure 8.4 SQL SELECT Command—Example 4

RESTRICTING ROWS WITH WHERE

Criteria for retrieving specific rows from one or more tables can be included in a **SELECT** command by using a **WHERE** clause. The keyword **WHERE** is followed by an expression that identifies which rows should be retrieved. The expression is known as a *predicate*. For example, to see all the shifts reserved for driver number 10:

```
SELECT wkdate, wkshift
FROM shifts
WHERE drvnum = '0010';
```

In this case, the predicate is a logical expression that contains a constant value against which the value of an attribute must be matched. Predicates may contain any of the standard logical operators (<, <=, =, >=, >). Multiple expressions may be included by linking single expressions with **AND** or **OR**; any expression or operator may also be inverted with **NOT**. The result of this query appears in Figure 8.4.

Suppose, however, that an office worker doesn't remember a driver's number, only the driver's name. The query must then begin in the DRIVER relation and follow the primary key–foreign key link between DRIVER and SHIFTS. SQL queries can perform the primary key–foreign key match if told to equate two attributes in different relations. The query might be issued as:

```
SELECT wkdate,wkshift
FROM driver,shifts
WHERE drvnam = 'Zilog, Charlie'
   AND driver.drvnum = shifts.drvnum;
```

The **FROM** clause lists all relations that must be used in the query. In the predicate, the names of attributes that appear in more than one relation are prefaced by the name of the relation and a period; **driver.drvnum**, for example, means the DRVNUM attribute from the

```
SELECT cabnum, make, model, year, curodom
FROM cab
WHERE licnum IN ('345 YAO', '111 ABC');

CAB MAKE              MODEL              YE CURODO
ØØ2 Checker           4-door sedan       73        Ø
105 Checker           4-door sedan       63 286ØØ3
```

Figure 8.5 SQL SELECT Command—Example 5

DRIVER relation. A row is created in the result table (which is exactly the same as the table in Figure 8.4) whenever two things are true: a row in DRIVER has a value of Zilog, Charlie for DRVNAM, and a row in SHIFTS has the same driver number as the driver number from the Zilog, Charlie row in DRIVER. SQL uses a join to implement queries of this type, though join itself is not a SQL operation.

As well as the standard logical operators, predicates in a WHERE clause may contain additional operators: **IN** and **NOT IN** (used to specify a set of values), **LIKE** and **NOT LIKE** (used for pattern matching), **BETWEEN** and **NOT BETWEEN** (used to specify a range), and **IS NULL** and **IS NOT NULL**.

For example, to retrieve data about the two cabs with license plates 345 YAO and 111 ABC, the SQL query could be written:

> **SELECT cabnum, make, model, year, curodom**
> **FROM cab**
> **WHERE licnum IN ('345 YAO', '111 ABC');**

This query produces the output seen in Figure 8.5. The **IN** operator is followed by a list of those values against which some attribute should be matched. The list is surrounded by parentheses and items in the list are separated by commas. **IN** is really a shorthand for multiple **OR** expressions dealing with the same attribute. In other words, this same predicate could have been written as:

> **licnum = '345 YAO' OR licnum = '111 ABC'**

NOT IN is shorthand for a series of negative **AND** expressions concerning the same attribute. Suppose, for example, that FTC's chief mechanic needs to see data on all cabs except cabs numbered 006, 108, and 378. That data can be retrieved with:

> **SELECT cabnum, make, model, licnum, curodom**
> **FROM cab**
> **WHERE cabnum NOT IN ('006', '108', '378');**

```
SELECT cabnum, make, model, licnum, curodom
FROM  cab
WHERE licnum NOT IN ('006','108','378');
```

CAB	MAKE	MODEL	LICNUM	CURODO
Ø02	Checker	4-door sedan	345 YAO	Ø
Ø45	Ford	LTD	867 POP	45999
1Ø4	Checker	4-door sedan	356 QLT	2Ø4998
1Ø5	Checker	4-door sedan	111 ABC	286ØØ3
144	Ford	LTD	29Ø AAQ	1Ø3245
215	Ford	LTD	776 IKL	23ØØØ
238	Ford	LTD	98Ø JAM	256256
4Ø4	Checker	4-door sedan	2Ø6 TTL	3214Ø9

Figure 8.6 SQL SELECT Command—Example 6

The result of this query can be seen in Figure 8.6. Only those rows from CAB that have a cab number not equal to any of the cab numbers in the list are included in the result. Just as the **IN** predicate could be rewritten as a series of **OR** expressions, the **NOT IN** could be rewritten as a series of **AND**s:

cabnum <> '006' AND cabnum <> '108' AND cabnum <> '378'

It is also possible to write this same predicate as a single negated **OR**:

NOT (cabnum = '006' OR cabnum = '108" OR cabnum = '378')

It is important to recognize that there is often more than one way to write a SQL query to obtain a desired result.

BETWEEN and **NOT BETWEEN** can also be used as shorthand for combinations of standard logical operators. To retrieve the names of all drivers who are scheduled to drive the day shift over a three-day period , a SQL query might be written:

> **SELECT drvnam**
> **FROM driver, shifts**
> **WHERE driver.drvnum = shifts.drvnum**
> **AND wkshift = 'day'**
> **AND wkdate BETWEEN '15-JUL-86' AND '17-JUL-86';**

The result, seen in Figure 8.7, contains only driver names. As discussed earlier, the names are retrieved by matching the driver number of all rows from SHIFTS that meet the other

```
SELECT drvnam
FROM driver, shifts
WHERE driver.drvnum = shifts.drvnum
  AND wkshift = 'day'
  AND wkdate BETWEEN '15-JUL-86' AND '17-JUL-86';
```

DRVNAM
Miller, Phyllis
Zilog, Charlie
Abelman, John
Miller, Phyllis
Zilog, Charlie
Abelman, John
Miller, Phyllis
Zilog, Charlie
Abelman, John

Figure 8.7 SQL SELECT Command—Example 7

criteria (day shift and an appropriate date) with the driver number in DRIVER. The predicate
can also be written as two logical inequalities linked with **AND**:

   wkdate >= '15-JUL-86' AND wkdate <= '17-JUL-86'

In a similar manner, a list of all drivers *not* scheduled to drive during that three-day
period can be obtained by simply negating the **BETWEEN** operator:

   SELECT drvnam
   FROM driver, shifts
   WHERE drvnum.driver = shifts.drvnum
      AND wkshift = 'day'
      AND wkdate NOT BETWEEN '15-JUL-86' AND '17-JUL-86';

The result of this query can be seen in Figure 8.8. The predicate, like the predicate using
BETWEEN, can be rewritten to obtain the same results as either:

   wkdate < '15-JUL-86' OR > '17-JUL-86'

or

   NOT (wkdate > '15'-JUL-86' AND wkdate < '17-JUL-86')

```
SELECT drvnam
FROM driver, shifts
WHERE driver.drvnum = shifts.drvnum
 AND wkshift = 'day'
 AND wkdate NOT BETWEEN '15-JUL-86' AND '17-JUL-86';
```

DRVNAM
Miller, Phyllis
Zilog, Charlie
Miller, Phyllis

Figure 8.8 SQL SELECT Command—Example 8

```
SELECT cabnum, maindate, maintype
FROM maintenance
WHERE maintype LIKE 'replace%';
```

CAB MAINDATE MAINTYPE
4Ø4 12-JUN-86 REPLACE REAR UPHOLSTERY
4Ø4 12-JUN-86 REPLACE REAR WINDSHIELD

Figure 8.9 SQL SELECT Commmand—Example 9

```
SELECT cabnum, maindate, maintype
FROM maintenance
WHERE maintype NOT LIKE 'replace%';
```

CAB MAINDATE MAINTYPE
ØØ2 18-MAY-86 new engine
ØØ2 18-MAY-86 tune-up
238 28-MAY-86 repack frnt whl bearings
238 28-MAY-86 tune-up
1Ø4 12-JUN-86 tune-up
215 12-JUN-86 tune-up
4Ø4 12-JUN-86 tune-up
ØØ6 15-JUN-86 tune-up
1Ø8 Ø2-JUL-86 tune-up
Ø45 14-JUL-86 tune-up
1Ø5 15-JUL-86 tune-up
378 15-JUL-86 tune-up
144 16-JUL-86 inspect damage

Figure 8.10 SQL SELECT Command—Example 10
```
```

The operators **LIKE** and **NOT LIKE** allow wild cards to be used as part of character constants in logical expressions. SQL supports two wild-card characters. When used in a quoted string, % (the percent sign) means that any characters may be substituted. For example, **Sm%** will match Smith, Smythe, Smithson, Smithers, and so on. In other words, it will match anything that starts with "Sm." (Don't forget that upper and lower case are significant between quotes.) The second wild card, _ (the underbar), holds the place of a single character. **Sm_th**, for example, will match Smith or Smyth, but not Smooth. The wild-card characters can appear anywhere within the quoted string.

If FTC's chief mechanic wishes to see information about all cabs that have had something replaced, the SQL query could be written as:

```
SELECT cabnum, maindate, maintype
FROM maintenance
WHERE maintype LIKE 'replace%';
```

The query returns the rows seen in Figure 8.9.

On the other hand, to retrieve information about all cabs whose maintenance involved something other than replacement, the query would be written:

```
SELECT cabnum, maindate, maintype
FROM maintenance
WHERE maintype NOT LIKE 'replace%';
```

The above version of the query produces the result in Figure 8.10.

The **IS NULL** and **IS NOT NULL** operators are fairly straightforward. For example, if FTC's office clerk needs to see the names of all drivers for whom there is no phone number, the query might be written:

```
SELECT drvnam
FROM driver
WHERE drvphone IS NULL;
```

In other words, the **IS NULL** and **IS NOT NULL** operators provide a way to retrieve rows with or without null values regardless of what is actually being stored in the base tables for null values. (Some DBMSs store blanks or zeros for null; others store the characters "NULL"; some give the user control over what is stored.)

SUBQUERIES

A *subquery* is a complete **SELECT** command used as part of a **WHERE** clause predicate. Like the **SELECT** commands already discussed, a subquery returns a table as its result. That result table is then used to evaluate the rest of the query. For example, a query to retrieve the cab and license numbers of all Checker cabs made before 1970 could be written:

```
SELECT cabnum, licnum
FROM cab
WHERE make = 'Checker'
   AND year = ANY (SELECT year
                   FROM cab
                   WHERE year < '70');
```

The subquery is the **SELECT** command that appears in parentheses. The result of the subquery is a table containing the year of manufacture of each cab that was made before 1970. The subquery table is a temporary table and is not displayed or stored in main memory for the user. It is important to understand that the subquery table includes only the YEAR attribute, but SQL is aware of which rows from CAB are included in that table. In other words, if the year of manufacture falls in the requested range, SQL can obtain the values of other attributes in the same row, even though the subquery table only contains the year.

The contents of that subquery table are used to evaluate the **year = ANY** portion of the WHERE clause predicate. **ANY** is a special operator used only with subqueries; it can be paired with any of the standard logical operators. As used in the above example, **= ANY** is equivalent to **IN**; this is true as long as only one attribute is being compared. If more than one attribute is involved, the operator must be **IN**. Rows will be included in the final result (Figure 8.11) only if their year of manufacture is equal to any of the entries in the table returned by the subquery and if they were made by Checker.

To see all reservations that were not driven on July 15, 1986, a query could be written as:

```
SELECT drvnam
FROM driver, shifts
WHERE driver.drvnum = shifts.drvnum
   AND wkflag = 'f'
   AND wkdate = ANY (SELECT wkdate
                     FROM shifts
                     WHERE wkdate = '15-JUL-86');
```

The subquery produces a temporary table that contains all shifts driven on July 15, 1986. Each row in that table is evaluated against the other two conditions in the **WHERE** clause. The condition involving WKFLAG selects only those reservations that haven't been driven; the condition equating DRVNUM in DRIVER to DRVNUM in SHIFTS provides the primary key–foreign key link that makes it possible to retrieve the driver's name. The resulting table contains only one entry, Erlich, Martin.

```
SELECT cabnum, licnum
FROM  cab
WHERE make = 'Checker'
  AND year = ANY (SELECT year
    FROM  cab
    WHERE year < '7Ø');


CAB LICNUM
1Ø4 356 QLT
1Ø5 111 ABC
378 771 TOW
4Ø4 2Ø6 TTL
```

Figure 8.11 SQL SELECT Command—Example 11

This query could just as easily have been written:

SELECT drvnam
FROM driver, shifts
WHERE driver.drvnum = shifts.drvnum
   AND wkdate = '15-JUL-86'
   AND wkflag IN (SELECT wkflag
                   FROM shifts
                   WHERE wkflag = 'f');

In this case, the subquery produces a table of all shifts with a WKFLAG of 'f'. Each row in that temporary table is checked for a WKDATE of July 15, 1986. The result will be exactly the same as the first version of the query (remember that **IN** is exactly the same as = **ANY**).

Does it matter, then, which way the query is written? In terms of performance, it can. The subquery table returned by the first version (WKDATE in the subquery), will generally return far fewer rows than the subquery in the second version (WKFLAG in the subquery); the further ahead FTC books cab reservations, the more this will hold true, since future reservations are by default assigned a WKFLAG of 'f'. Since each row in the subquery must be evaluated individually against the other portions of the predicate, the subquery table with the fewest rows will require the fewest comparisons and will therefore, in most circumstances, decrease the time needed to produce the result of the query.

The **NOT IN** and **!= ANY** operators can be used to answer questions phrased in the negative. For example, the SQL query to list all the cabs not reserved for a given day might be written:

   SELECT DISTINCT cab.cabnum
   FROM cab, shifts
   WHERE cab.cabnum NOT IN (SELECT cabnum
                            FROM shifts
                            WHERE wkdate = '15-JUL-86');

```
SELECT DISTINCT cab.cabnum
FROM cab, shifts
WHERE cab.cabnum NOT IN (SELECT cabnum
                          FROM shifts
                          WHERE wkdate = '15-JUL-86');
```

C A B
ØØ2
ØØ6
1Ø5
378

Figure 8.12   SQL SELECT Command—Example 12

The subquery retrieves the cab number of cabs that are reserved on the desired date. The **NOT IN** operator indicates that cab numbers should be included in the final result (Figure 8.12) only if a cab number from CAB is not contained in the subquery table.   Inside the subquery itself, the attribute CABNUM does not need to be prefaced by the name of the relation from which it should come; the subquery uses only SHIFTS.   However, outside the subquery, CABNUM alone is ambiguous, since it appears in both CAB and SHIFTS. To indicate that cab numbers from CAB are to be compared to the cab numbers retrieved from SHIFTS, the CABNUM following WHERE is prefaced with its relation. The same holds true for the cab numbers returned by the query; they are to be taken from CAB, not SHIFTS, and must be so indicated.

Subqueries can also be nested, one within the other. A nested subquery can be used to retrieve data about all drivers scheduled for a given day and shift:

```
SELECT DISTINCT drvnam, drvphone
FROM driver, shifts
WHERE driver.drvnum = shifts.drvnum
  AND shifts.drvnum IN (SELECT drvnum
                        FROM  shifts
                        WHERE wkdate = '15-JUL-86'
                          AND wkshift IN (SELECT wkshift
                                          FROM  shifts
                                          WHERE wkshift = 'eve'));
```

Like nesting loops within a programming language, nested subqueries must be completely contained within one another. The innermost subquery is evaluated first. In the previous example, the result of which appears in Figure 8.13, the innermost subquery returns rows from SHIFTS that correspond to the desired shift. That table is evaluated against the desired date in the outer subquery. The result of the outer subquery is a table containing rows for each shift reserved for the requested date *and* shift. Finally, the entries in the subquery table

```
SELECT DISTINCT drvnam, drvphone
FROM driver, shifts
WHERE driver.drvnum = shifts.drvnum
   AND shifts.drvnum IN (SELECT drvnum
                          FROM shifts
                          WHERE wkdate = '15-JUL-86'
                             AND wkshift IN (SELECT wkshift
                                             FROM shift
                                             WHERE wkshift = 'eve'));
```

DRVNAM	DRVPHONE
Erlich, Martin	ØØØ-ØØØ-ØØ11
Bailey, Max	ØØØ-ØØØ-ØØØ1
Eastman, Richard	ØØØ-ØØØ-ØØ12

Figure 8.13 SQL SELECT Command—Example 13

are used to identify which drivers are scheduled so that their names and phone numbers can be retrieved from DRIVER via the primary key–foreign key link.

Like many SQL queries, the previous query could be written in another way to produce the same result:

> **SELECT DISTINCT drvnam, drvphone**
> **FROM driver, shifts**
> **WHERE driver.drvnum = shifts.drvnum**
>   **AND shifts.drvnum IN (SELECT drvnum**
>   **FROM shifts**
>   **WHERE wkdate IN (SELECT wkdate**
>   **FROM shifts**
>   **WHERE wkdate = '15-JUL-86')**
>   **AND wkshift IN   (SELECT wkshift**
>   **FROM shifts**
>   **WHERE wkshift = 'eve'));**

In this version of the query, the conditions about both date and shift are expressed as subqueries nested within the outer subquery that produces the driver numbers associated with the required date and shift.

GROUPING QUERIES

SELECT can perform a number of summary functions on data, returning grouped information. For example, a table reporting the total number of miles driven in each day and shift contained in SHIFTS, can be obtained by using:

```
SELECT wkdate, wkshift, SUM(odomrdg2 - odomrdg1+1)
FROM  shifts
GROUP BY wkdate, wkshift;
```

WKDATE	WKS	SUM(ODOMRDG2-ODOMRDG2+1)
15-JUL-86	day	445
15-JUL-86	eve	325
15-JUL-86	ngt	51Ø
16-JUL-86	day	3
16-JUL-86	eve	2
16-JUL-86	ngt	1
17-JUL-86	day	3
17-JUL-86	ngt	1
18-JUL-86	day	2
18-JUL-86	ngt	3
19-JUL-86	day	1
19-JUL-86	eve	2
20-JUL-86	eve	1

Figure 8.14 SQL SELECT Command—Example 14

> **SELECT wkdate, wkshift, SUM(odomrdg2-odomrdg1+1)**
> **FROM shifts**
> **GROUP BY wkdate, wkshift;**

This query produces the result seen in Figure 8.14. **SUM** is a function. It performs the computation indicated in parentheses and then sums the values for each distinct pair of WKDATE and WKSHIFT, the attributes by which the data should be grouped. **AVG** (computes the average value of each group), **MAX** (returns the maximum value in each group), **MIN** (returns the minimum value in each group), and **COUNT** (returns the number of members in the group) may also be used in a **SELECT** command that includes a **GROUP BY** clause.

The table in Figure 8.14 contains some undesirable data, those single-digit numbers that correspond to rows for future reservations. To make the result more meaningful, we might wish to exclude all shifts that haven't been driven:

> **SELECT wkdate, wkshift, SUM(odomrdg2-odomrdg1+1)**
> **FROM shifts**
> **WHERE wkflag = 't'**
> **GROUP BY wkdate,wkshift;**

The addition of the **WHERE** clause restricts the rows to those with a WKFLAG of 't', producing the more meaningful table that appears in Figure 8.15.

```
SELECT wkdate, wkshift, SUM(odomrdg2 - odomrdg1+1)
FROM  shifts
WHERE wkflag = 't'
GROUP BY wkdate, wkshift;


WKDATE    WKS SUM(ODOMRDG2-ODOMRDG2+1)
15-JUL-86 day                    445
15-JUL-86 eve                    325
15-JUL-86 ngt                    51Ø
```

Figure 8.15 SQL SELECT Command—Example 15

The **HAVING** clause can be used to restrict which groups are included in the final table. For example, to report the average mileage for only the day and evening shifts:

> **SELECT wkdate, wkshift, AVG(odomrdg2-odomrdg1+1)**
> **FROM shifts**
> **GROUP BY wkdate, wkshift**
> **HAVING wkshift != 'ngt';**

Since no **WHERE** clause is present, data on all day and evening shifts currently in the database are included in the result (see Figure 8.16). To exclude shifts that have not been driven, a **WHERE** clause can be used in conjunction with **GROUP BY** and **HAVING**:

> **SELECT wkdate, wkshift, AVG(odomrdg2-odomrdg1+1)**
> **FROM shifts**
> **WHERE wkflag = 't'**
> **GROUP BY wkdate, wkshift**
> **HAVING wkshift != 'ngt';**

The above query produces the one line result in Figure 8.17.

CREATING VIEWS

A SQL view is a single virtual table created by selecting columns and rows from base tables and other views. Views are primarily used as security devices to restrict user access to data. As you will see in Chapter 12, when we discuss database security, it is possible to tailor table and view permissions precisely to individual users. They can also be used as a device to capture the tables produced by complex queries. In essence, the view assigns a

```
SELECT wkdate, wkshift, AVG(odomrdg2 - odomrdg1+1)
FROM  shifts
GROUP BY wkdate, wkshift
  HAVING wkshift != 'ngt';
```

WKDATE	WKS	AVG(ODOMRDG2-ODOMRDG2+1)
15-JUL-86	day	148.3
15-JUL-86	eve	1Ø8.3
16-JUL-86	day	1
16-JUL-86	eve	1
17-JUL-86	day	1
18-JUL-86	day	1
18-JUL-86	eve	1
19-JUL-86	day	1
19-JUL-86	eve	1
20-JUL-86	eve	1

Figure 8.16 SQL SELECT Command—Example 16

name to a table created as the result of a **SELECT**. The contents of the table are not stored on disk, but instead the definition of how it was created.

Views are created with the **CREATE VIEW** command:

> **CREATE VIEW view_name**
> **AS SELECT [DISTINCT] column_name1 [,column_name2]...**
> **FROM table_name**
> **[WHERE predicate]**
> **[GROUP BY column_name [HAVING predicate]];**

Each view is given a unique name that must conform to the rules for naming tables. Once the view has been created, its name can be used in any SQL command in place of a base table name. This means that views can be created from previously defined views as well as from base tables.

The contents of a view are determined by the result of a **SELECT** command. Remember that **SELECT** returns a table and that the table returned may be the join of other tables. For example, if FTC wished to create a view for their chief mechanic, it might include data from just the CAB and MAINTENANCE relations:

> **CREATE VIEW MrFixIt**
> **AS SELECT cabnum, licnum, maintype, maindate, mainodom**
> **FROM cab, maintenance**
> **WHERE cab.cabnum = maintenance.cabnum;**

```
SELECT wkdate, wkshift, AVG(odomrdg2 - odomrdg1+1)
FROM shifts
WHERE wkflag = 't'
GROUP BY wkdate, wkshift
   HAVING wkshift = 'ngt';
```

WKDATE	WKS	AVG(ODOMRDG2-ODOMRDG2+1)
15-JUL-86	ngt	255

Figure 8.17 SQL SELECT Command—Example 17

In this example, the **WHERE** clause is used to identify the primary key–foreign key relationship to be used for a join. It can also, however, be used to restrict the rows that appear in a view. The following view could simplify the job of the night shift dispatcher, since it only includes data about the night shift:

> **CREATE VIEW Nights**
> **AS SELECT drvnum,drvnam, cabnum,wkdate**
> **FROM driver, shifts**
> **WHERE driver.drvnum = shifts.drvnum**
> **AND wkshift = 'ngt';**

SQL views may be updated, but only with care. It is up to the person using a view to determine if the update can logically be propagated to the base tables from which the view was ultimately created. The point is that the DBMS will not verify that a view is updatable; therefore, SQL views are more commonly used only as retrieval devices.

INSERTING, MODIFYING, DELETING DATA

INSERTING DATA

The SQL command to enter data into a table, **INSERT**, comes in two formats: one to load a single row and the other to load multiple rows from some other table or view. To load a single row, the format is:

> **INSERT INTO table_name [(column_name1, column_name2...)]**
> **VALUES (value1, value2...);**

If values for all attributes in the row are to be added with a single **INSERT**, then the names of the columns in the table are not necessary. The data values must, however, appear in the value list (in parentheses after **VALUES**) in the same order in which the columns were defined. For example, to insert a row into the MAINTENANCE table:

>   INSERT INTO maintenance
>   VALUES ('002','18-MAY-86','new engine',0);

Null values, for those columns that have not been defined as **NOT NULL**, can be entered by using the characters "NULL" in the value list.

If, however, data for less than all attributes are to be loaded, then the columns must be specified:

>   INSERT INTO maintenance (cabnum, maintype, maindate)
>   VALUES ('045','tune-up','14-JUL-86');

The order of the columns need not be the same as the order in which they were defined in the table. SQL will match data in the value list with the attribute names by position.

The second **INSERT** format loads multiple rows of data from one relation or view to another:

>   INSERT INTO table_name1 [(column_name1, column_name2...)]
>   SELECT select_list
>   FROM table_name2
>   [WHERE predicate]
>   [GROUP BY column_name [HAVING predicate]];

The rows identified by the **SELECT** portion of the command are loaded into the target table listed on the first line of the command. The attributes in the select list must exist in the target table. This format might be used to permanently capture a virtual table created by a **SELECT**. For example, assume that FTC has created a new base table to contain the average mileage driven on each day and shift:

>   AVERAGES (WKDATE, WKSHIFT, AVGMILES)

AVGMILES is computed in a **SELECT** command that includes a **GROUP BY** clause. A unique index has been built on the primary key. Periodically, the AVERAGES table can be updated with the command:

>   INSERT INTO averages
>   SELECT wkdate, wkshift, AVG(odomrdg2-odomrdg1+1)
>   FROM shifts
>   WHERE wkflag = 't'
>   GROUP BY wkdate, wkshift;

The presence of the unique primary key index will ensure that no duplicate rows appear in AVERAGES, regardless of how often it is updated or how often SHIFTS is purged.

MODIFYING DATA

Data modification is performed with the **UPDATE** command:

```
UPDATE  table_name
   SET  column_name1  =  expression1
      [,column_name2  =  expression2]  ...
   [WHERE  predicate];
```

For example, to change Pat Miller's address:

```
UPDATE  driver
   SET  drvstr  =  '15 N. 55th',
      drvcsz  =  'Nowhere, US 00055'
   WHERE  drvnum  =  '0005';
```

The **WHERE** clause identifies the row which is to be updated. If only a single row is to be changed, then the predicate will, as in the previous example, include a primary key expression. New values are assigned to columns with **SET**; the expression to the right of the equal sign may be constants, other attributes, or may contain arithmetic operations (for **number** columns only), string operations (for **char** and **long** columns only), or date operations (for **date** columns only).

UPDATE commands without a **WHERE** clause can be dangerous; they will make the same change to an entire table. For example:

```
UPDATE  maintenance
SET  wkflag  =  't';
```

will change the value of WKFLAG to 't' in *every* row in the MAINTENANCE table.

DELETING DATA

Like **UPDATE**, the rows on which a **DELETE** command operates are specified with a **WHERE** clause:

```
DELETE  FROM  table_name
[WHERE  predicate];
```

Though the **WHERE** clause is technically optional, if it is left off the **DELETE** command it will remove every single row from the specified table. A **DELETE** is therefore the potentially most destructive SQL command.

To delete a single row, the **WHERE** clause should contain a primary key expression:

```
DELETE FROM incident
WHERE cabnum = '104'
   AND wkdate = '15-JUL-86'
   AND wkshift = 'day';
```

Since the above command contains all three parts of the primary key, it will delete exactly one row. If, however, FTC wishes to purge all reservations from SHIFTS that occurred before a specific date, the predicate will include only the date and not the shift or cab number:

```
DELETE FROM shifts
WHERE wkdate < '16-JUL-86';
```

Because SQL table definitions don't include primary key–foreign key relationships, it is possible to delete a primary key without removing all foreign key references to it. For example, if a cab is sold or otherwise removed from service and its row is deleted from CAB, all rows from SHIFTS, INCIDENTS, and MAINTENANCE that involve that cab must also be deleted. There is no way to do this deletion with a single **DELETE**; it requires a series of them:

```
DELETE FROM shifts
WHERE cabnum = '144';

DELETE FROM maintenance
WHERE cabnum = '144';

DELETE FROM incidents
WHERE cabnum = '144';

DELETE FROM cab
WHERE cabnum = '144';
```

SUMMARY

SQL (Structured Query Language) has been accepted by the American National Standards Institute as the standard for relational database query languages. SQL, developed by IBM, is available with a wide range of relational DBMSs, from IBM's *DB2*, which runs only on IBM mainframes, to *Oracle*, which will run on microcomputers as well as larger machines.

SQL provides commands to:

- Create tables
- Create views
- Create indexes to speed retrieval and enforce the uniqueness of primary keys
- Modify tables and views by adding columns or increasing the width of a column
- Load data into tables
- Modify data in tables
- Delete data from tables
- Retrieve data from tables
- Manage data security (details in Chapter 12)

SQL supports entity integrity by permitting columns to be defined as **NOT NULL**. Enforcing the uniqueness of primary keys requires the use of a unique index; the uniqueness of the keys is enforced in the index, not directly in the base table. SQL does not, however, have provisions for specifying primary key–foreign key references and therefore does not enforce referential integrity.

SQL databases support an on-line, dynamic data dictionary. The data dictionary can be queried by authorized users with the same syntax used to query data tables.

REFERENCES

ANSI/X3H2 Committee. (1984) *American National Standard Database Language SQL (X3H2-84-117)*. ANSI/X3/SPARC Project 363D. October.

Baker, Jerry. (1986) "SQL: a new standard." *Computerworld*. February 19: 55-58.

Cardenas, Alfonso F. (1985) *Data Base Management Systems*. 2d ed. Boston: Allyn and Bacon.

Chamberlin, D.D., M.M. Astrahan, K.P. Eswaran, P.P. Griffiths, R.A. Lorie, J.W. Mehl, P. Reisner, and B.W. Wade. (1976) "SEQUEL 2: a unified approach to data definition, manipulation and control." *IBM Journal of Research and Development*. 20:56-574. November.

Date, C. J. (1986) *An Introduction to Database Systems, Vol I*. 4th ed. Reading, MA: Addison-Wesley.

EXERCISES

Given the set of relations below from the University Archaeological Museum, write the SQL commands necessary to perform the operations that follow:

GRANT (GRANT-NUM, SOURCE, TOTAL, TOTAL-AWARD, PRINCIPAL-RESEARCHER)
BUDGETS (GRANT-NUM, COST-CENTER#, COST-CNTR-DESC, ORIG-ALLOC, AMT-AVAIL)
GRANT-PURCHASES (GRANT-NUM, COST-CENTER#, P-O-NUM, VENDOR, DATE, TOTAL-AMT)
DIG-MASTER (DIG, DIG-DESCRIPTION)
DIGS (GRANT-NUM, DIG)
ITEMS (P-O-NUM, ITEM, QUANT, COST-EACH, LINE-COST)
VENDORS (VENDOR, ADDRESS, PHONE)
GRANT-PAYROLL (GRANT-NUM, COST-CENTER#, DATE, ID#, GROSS-PAY, FED-TAX, SS-TAX, STATE-TAX, INSURANCE, NET-PAY)
EMPLOYEES (ID#, NAME, ADDRESS, PHONE, SSN, PAY-RATE, #DEDUCTIONS)
INS-PLANS (ID#, INS-PLAN, COVERAGE-TYPE)
INS-COSTS (INS-PLAN, INDIVIDUAL, FAMILY)
DIG-ASSIGNMENTS (DIG, ID#)

1. Create a table for each of the relations listed. Modify table and column names wherever necessary to conform to SQL naming rules. Use the table and column names from this problem for the rest of the exercises below.

2. Create the following views:

a. For purchasing, a view that might be used to record the contents of a purchase order (vendor information, overall purchase order information, line items on the purchase order)
b. For payroll, a view that might be used to process the monthly payroll
c. For personnel, a view that might be used to summarize the insurance plans to which museum employees subscribe
d. For personnel, a view that might be used yearly to produce W-2 forms
e. For principal researchers, a view that might be used to summarize all financial activity against their grants. This view should be customized to contain only data pertaining to one archaeologist (i.e., there will be one such view for each archaeologist who has grants in the database).

3. Answer the following requests for information:

a. Given the name of an archaeologist (a principal researcher), list all the grants and grant award amounts for that archaeologist that are currently active (i.e., currently in the database).

b. List the names of all archaeologists who have received grants of more than $50,000.

c. List the social security number and pay rate of each principal researcher.

d. Given a purchase order number, list the contents of that purchase order (i.e., the line items), including the name of each item, how many were ordered, and the unit cost.

e. Given a dig number, list the names of all employees working on that dig.

f. For each employee, list the total gross pay for any given period (e.g., six months or a year).

g. Find the total amount of a purchase order without looking in the GRANT-PURCHASES table.

h. Display a unique list of all insurance plans to which employees on a given dig subscribe.

i. Given a cost center number, list all charges that have been made against that cost center (something to consider: can this be done with only one SELECT?).

j. List the names of all vendors with whom orders for a single item costing over $5,000 have been placed.

k. Given a vendor name, list the name of the principal researcher for each grant to which that vendor has sold supplies.

l. List all employees who are *not* assigned to a dig.

m. Given a vendor name, list all grants to which the vendor has *not* sold supplies.

4. Make the following modifications to existing data:

a. Change an employee's address

b. Record that a purchase order has been filled by deleting all references to it from the database

c. Record charges made against a grant, either via purchase orders for goods or via payroll (will one SQL command suffice or will it require two?)

d. Purge the database of all references to a grant that has been terminated (Hint: be careful of the order that you delete data; don't destroy primary keys too early)

Oracle Ins and Outs

CHAPTER OUTLINE:

CHAPTER OBJECTIVES

After reading this chapter, you will:

1. Know how to use *Oracle*'s Interactive Application Facility to generate data entry/modification programs to enforce primary key constraints and referential integrity
2. Know how to format simple *Oracle* reports

ENFORCING KEY CONSTRAINTS

Though SQL does not store referential integrity rules in its data dictionary, *Oracle* provides a mechanism for enforcing them without writing an application program. A utility known as *IAG* (Interactive Application Generator) will produce a compiled data entry/ modification program that uses a custom-designed screen form and can perform referential integrity verification. While it is certainly possible to use C, the host language currently supported by the microcomputer implementation of *Oracle*, to write a program using IAG to enforce the key constraints, is both simpler and faster.

IAG conducts a dialog with the program developer. This dialog is saved in a text file with an *.INP* extension. The text file can be edited with any text editor (e.g., MS-DOS EDLIN) to make small changes and then recompiled. A user runs the compiled program with *IAP* (Interaction Application Processor). Together, IAG and IAP are known as *IAF*, the Interactive Application Facility.

An IAF application is made up of a set of blocks, each of which can perform data entry and/or modification on a single table. The dialog between IAG and the program developer therefore begins with questions about the application, followed by questions that pertain to blocks. Within each block, IAG requests field definitions and directions as to where they should be placed on the screen. The easiest way to understand how IAF can be used to enforce integrity constraints is to look at an example of an IAG dialog.

The dialog that follows was used to create a data entry and modification program for the relation SHIFTS. The screen form produced when the program is run appears in Figure 9.1. In the dialog, the questions asked by IAG are printed in boldface; the program developer's responses are printed in italics. Notes discussing the dialog appear in plain text.

Application Title:
Shift Entry

The application title is for programmer reference only.

ORACLE workspace size:
<cr>

The workspace size refers to the amount of workspace *Oracle* should allocate for the largest possible query used by this application. Workspace is measured in 1K increments from three to 12. Simply pressing the carriage return, as was done in this example, will select the workspace size assigned when *Oracle* was installed.

Block name / Description:
Shift Entry

As with the application name, the block name is for programmer reference only.

Table name :
shifts

> Each block supports a single table. View tables as well as base tables are acceptable, but, as discussed in Chapter 8, updating views can be risky.

Check for uniqueness before inserting Y/N:
Y

> A response of *Y* instructs *Oracle* to ensure that new rows do not duplicate existing rows in the table, enforcing the constraint that states that a relation consists of unique tuples.

Display/Buffer how many records :
1

> Each screen form can display data for more than one table row at any one time, limited by the amount of space on the screen. *Oracle* needs to know how many rows will be displayed so that main memory storage (buffers) can be allocated for the data. The form in Figure 9.1 displays only one row at a time.

```
                            Shift Entry


            Date:

           Shift:

           Cab  #:

        Driver  #:

          Driven? f

   Start  mileage:ø

     End mileage: ø
```

Figure 9.1 The Data Entry Form Produced by the Sample IAF Application

Field name :
wkdate

Each field in the screen form may correspond to an attribute in the base table or may be a local variable used later in the block to generate computed or concatenated values.

Type of field :
date

Fields may be **char**, **alpha** (only letters and spaces), **date**, **number**, **int** (integer), or **money** (dollars and cents format). Note that the **long** data type, which may be used for attributes in base tables, is not available and that the **alpha**, **int**, and **money** data types can be used in IAF applications but not base tables.

Length of field / Display length / Query length :
9

The length-of-field parameter specifies the maximum number of characters that can be entered for a field. Display length refers to the number of characters that will be displayed, while query length specifies the number of characters that can be entered when performing a query. If all three are the same, only one number needs to be entered.

Is this field in the base table Y/N :
Y

A *Y* response indicates that the field corresponds to an attribute in a base table.

Is this field part of the primary key Y/N :
Y

A *Y* response indicates that the field is all or part of the primary key. This information will be used to identify fields that should be concatenated and then checked for uniqueness. The uniqueness check performed by an IAF program is independent of the presence or absence of a unique primary key index.

Field to copy primary key from :
<cr>

If a primary key value is not entered directly into a field which corresponds to an attribute in the base table, it may be moved from that field to the base table attribute by listing the input field name in answer to this question. In this particular example, primary key values are entered directly into the base table attributes. The question is therefore answered with a carriage return.

Default value :
<cr>

> A response other than a carriage return to this question will enter a default value for the field.

Page :
1

> Each block within an IAF application can present more than one screen form (known as a *page*). A field can appear on only one page. Since this application creates only a single form, all fields will be located on page one.

Line :
7

> The position for the entry of each field on the screen is based on starting coordinates expressed in an 80-column-by-24-line grid. Space for entering the WKDATE field will begin be on line seven.

Column :
20

> Space for entering the WKDATE field will begin with column 20.

Prompt :
Date:

> The prompt is a short text string that will be displayed either above or to the left of the field's entry position.

Display prompt above field Y/N :
N

> A *Y* response will cause the prompt to be displayed on the line above the field's entry position. An *N* will display the prompt to the left of the entry position. In this case, the entry position must be offset far enough to the right to print the entire prompt; otherwise, the prompt will be truncated to fit.

Allow field to be entered Y/N :
Y

> A *Y* response will permit keyboard entry into this field. In those cases where a field is for display purposes only or where it is never displayed but used as the destination of a

computation or concatenation, an *N* response will prevent the user from entering data into that field.

SQL>
<cr>

SQL queries, in particular those that can check the existence of primary keys for foreign key values, can be entered at this point.   Examples appear later in this dialog. If no SQL query is to be performed on a field, the program developer enters a carriage return.

Is this field fixed length Y/N :
Y

A *Y* response will instruct IAP to check the number of characters entered for this field. If the number of characters entered doesn't match the full length of the field, an error message will be printed and *Oracle* will not commit the transaction.

Auto jump to next field Y/N :
Y

A *Y* response will cause the cursor to automatically jump to the next field on the screen when this field is filled.

Convert field to upper case Y/N :
N

A *Y* response for **char** or **alpha** fields will convert all characters in the field to upper case.

Help message :
<cr>

The help message is a short string of text that will be displayed if the user presses the help key while the cursor is in the entry space for this field.

Lowest value :
<cr>

Range checking will be performed if a value is entered for this and the following question.

Highest value :
<cr>

If a lowest value is entered above, then the value entered in response to this question forms the top of a range against which the value of this field will be checked.

Field name :
wkshift

The set of questions repeats for each field in the application.

Type of field :
char

Length of field / Display length / Query length :
3

Is this field in the base table Y/N :
Y

Is this field part of the primary key Y/N :
Y

Field to copy primary key from :
<cr>

Default value :
<cr>

Page :
1

Line :
9

Column :
20

Prompt :
Shift:

Display prompt above field Y/N :
N

Allow field to be entered Y/N :
Y

SQL>
<cr>

Is field fixed length Y/N :
Y

Auto jump to next field Y/N :
Y

Convert field to upper case Y/N :
N

Help message :
<cr>

Lowest value :
<cr>

Highest value :
<cr>

Field name :
cabnum

Type of field :
char

Length of field / Display length / Query length :
3

Is this field in the base table Y/N :
Y

Is this field part of the primary key Y/N :
Y

Default value :
<cr>

Page :
1

Line :
11

Column :
20

Prompt :
Cab #:

Display prompt above field Y/N :
N

Allow field to be entered Y/N :
Y

SQL>
select cabnum
from cab
where cabnum = :cabnum
<cr>

In the relation SHIFTS, CABNUM is a foreign key reference to CAB. The SQL query above performs a lookup to verify that the value entered exists as a CABNUM in CAB. The name of the field is prefaced by a colon to distinguish it from the attribute CABNUM.

Message if value not found :
Cab doesn't exist!

If the SQL query is unsuccessful, this message will be displayed across the top of the screen.

Must value exist :
Y

A *Y* response indicates that the transaction should not be committed unless the SQL query is successful. When used in this way, the combination of this question and the two preceding it act to enforce referential integrity.

Is the field fixed length Y/N :
Y

Auto jump to next field Y/N :
Y

Convert field to upper case Y/N :
N

Help message :
<cr>

Lowest value :
<cr>

Highest value :
<cr>

Field name :
drvnum

Type of field :
char

Length of field / Display length / Query length :
4

Is this field in the base table Y/N :
Y

Is this field part of the primary key Y/N :
N

Default value :
<cr>

Page :
1

Line :
13

Column :
20

Prompt :
Driver #:

Display prompt above field Y/N :
N

Allow field to be entered Y/N :
Y

Allow field to be updated Y/N :
Y

> This question appears only for non–primary key fields. A *Y* response allows that
> value in the field to be modified.

SQL>
select drvnum
from driver
where drvnum = :drvnum
<cr>

Message if value not found :
Driver doesn't exist!

Must value exist Y/N :
Y

Is field mandatory Y/N :
Y

> This question appears only for non–primary key fields (primary key fields are auto-
> matically mandatory, since they cannot be null). A *Y* response will instruct *Oracle*
> to verify that this field is not null before committing the transaction.

Is field fixed length Y/N :
Y

Auto jump to next field Y/N :
Y

Convert field to upper case Y/N :
N

Help message :
<cr>

Lowest value:
<cr>

Highest value:
<cr>

Field name :
wkflag

Type of field :
char

Length of field / Display length / Query length :
1

Is this field in the base table Y/N :
Y

Is this field part of the primary key Y/N :
N

Default value :
f

       WKFLAG is always false when a reservation is first entered into SHIFTS.

Page :
1

Line :
15

Column :
20

Prompt :
Driven?

Display prompt above field Y/N :
N

Allow field to be entered Y/N :
Y

Allow field to be updated Y/N :
Y

SQL :
<cr>

Is this field mandatory Y/N :
Y

Is this field fixed length Y/N :
Y

Auto jump to next field Y/N :
Y

Convert field to upper case Y/N :
N

Help message :
<σ>

Lowest value :
<σ>

Highest value :
<σ>

Field name :
odomrdg1

Type of field :
number

Length of field / Display length / Query length :
6

Is this field in the base table Y/N :
Y

Is this field part of the primary key Y/N :
Y

Default value :
0

Page :
1

Line :
17

Column :
20

Prompt :
Start mileage:

Display prompt above field Y/N :
N

Allow field to be entered Y/N :
Y

Allow field to be updated Y/N :
Y

SQL>
<cr>

Is field mandatory Y/N :
Y

Is field fixed length Y/N :
N

Auto jump to next field Y/N :
Y

Convert field to upper case Y/N :
N

Help message :
<cr>

Lowest value :
<cr>

Highest value :
<cr>

Field name :
odomrdg2

Type of field :
number

Length of field / Display length / Query length :
6

Is this field in the base table Y/N :
Y

Is this field part of the primary key Y/N :
N

Default value :
0

Page :
1

Line :
19

Column :
20

Prompt :
End mileage:

Display prompt above field Y/N :
N

Allow field to be entered Y/N :
Y

Allow field to be updated Y/N :
Y

SQL>
<cr>

Is field mandatory Y/N :
N

Is field fixed length Y/N :
N

Auto jump to next field Y/N :
N

Convert field to upper case Y/N :
N

Help message :
<cr>

Lowest value :
<cr>

Highest value :
<cr>

Field name :
<cr>

This carriage return signals that field definitions are completed for this block.

Block name / Description :
<cr>

This carriage return signals that block definitions are completed for this application.

: *<cr>*
: *<cr>*
:   *Shift Entry*
: *<cr>*

These four lines, each entered at IAG's colon prompt, appear as a heading on the screen form (two blank lines, the title, and another blank line).

: *%END*

The percent sign is a command to IAG; it will not be printed on the screen. **END** signals the end of the dialog. Other % commands, placed before **END**, can be used to place static text anywhere on the screen (these commands are documented in the *Oracle* manual). After **%END** is entered, IAG will automatically compile the application, producing a file with a *.FRM* extension.

To run the application, a user types:

   IAP application_name

The user will then be prompted for valid user name and password (see Chapter 12 for details on *Oracle* security control). Assuming the user has the appropriate access rights, the form will be displayed on the screen and data entry and/or modification can begin.

PRODUCING REPORTS

Oracle provides a pair of utilities which together provide virtually unlimited ability to format reports from a single database. The price of this power and flexibility is simplicity; producing *Oracle* reports requires some knowledge of programming logic. The two parts of *Oracle*'s report facility are the report formatter (*RPF*) and the report generator (*RPT*). RPF formats a text file that contains text, data, and formatting commands, sending output either to a file or directly to the printer. RPT executes data retrieval commands to produce the text file which RPF will format. The remainder of this chapter presents an introduction to both programs. The full range of RPF and RPT commands can be found in the *Oracle* manual.

The steps for creating an *Oracle* report are:

1. Create a source file using a text editor (MS-DOS's EDLIN will do if nothing else is available) containing text, RPT commands, and RPF commands. If you use a word processor, be sure to save the file as text only.
2. Process the file with RPT, producing an interim text file. This text file should be given an *.RPF* extension.
3. Process the text file with RPF to produce the final output.

RPT and RPF commands are prefaced by either a period or pound sign (#) to distinguish them from text that is to be printed on the report. To make it easier to see which command is of which type, the listings that accompany this discussion make use of the convention followed in *Oracle*'s documentation: RPT commands are prefaced with a period, RPF commands with a pound sign.

THE DRIVER ROSTER REPORT

The *Oracle* version of the driver roster appears in Figure 9.2. It was produced by the source code in Listing 9.1. That code employs text, RPT, and RPF commands to format the report. Let's look at the RPF commands first.

By default, a report page has 66 lines; this assumes that a printer is using 11-inch paper and printing six lines to the inch. Top and bottom margins for the report can therefore be set by indicating the top and bottom lines that are available for printing:

#page 6 58   (line four in Listing 9.1)

The word **page** is an RPF command. The first number after the command is the line on which printing should begin; the second number is the last line that can be printed on the page. This will provide one-inch margins if the printer is printing six lines to the inch.

Oracle views the width of a report as a table. The default table has one column that is 132 print positions wide. Any number of tables, however, can be defined. Generally, a one-column table is used to define the right and left margins:

```
1       #dt 1 17 63 #
2       #dt 2 1 5 8 32 35 46 #
3       #t 1
4       #page 6 58
5       #s 6
6       #cul Current Driver List #
7       #s 2
8       .DATABASE CABS
9       .DECLARE drvnum a4
10      .DECLARE drvnam a25
11      .DECLARE drvphone a12
12      .DEFINE seldrivers
13         SELECT drvnum, drvnam, drvphone
14         INTO drvnum, drvnam, drvphone
15         FROM driver
16      ..
17      .DEFINE body
18         .PRINT drvnum
19         #nc
20         .PRINT drvnam
21         #nc
22         .PRINT drvphone
23         #nc
24      ..
25      .DEFINE head
26         #t 2
27         Numbr #n ----- #nc
28         Name #n ----- #nc
29         Phone #n ----- #nc
30         #b
31         .body
32      ..
33      .DEFINE foot
34         #te
35      ..
36      .REPORT seldrivers body head foot
37      #te
38      .STOP
```

Listing 9.1 Source Code for the Driver Summary Report

#dt 1 17 63 #   (line one)

dt (define table) is followed by a table number and then pairs of numbers that specify the starting and ending print positions of the columns within the table. In this case, table 1 begins at position 17 and ends at position 63. Note that the command ends with a pound sign as well as begins with one.

<u>Current Driver List</u>

Numbr	Name	Phone
-----	----	-----
0001	Bailey, Max	000-000-0001
0002	Baker, Mary Ann	000-000-0002
0003	Lewis, John	000-000-0003
0004	Santiago, John	000-000-0004
0005	Miller, Pat	000-000-0005
0006	Miller, Phyllis	000-000-0006
0007	Phong, Quen	000-000-0007
0008	Wong, David	000-000-0008
0009	Young, Leslie	000-000-0009
0010	Zilog, Charlie	000-000-0010
0011	Erlich, Martin	000-000-0011
0012	Eastman, Richard	000-000-0012
0013	Kowalski, Pete	000-000-0013
0014	Mariott, Emily	000-000-0014
0015	French, Janice	000-000-0015
0016	Thieu, Lin Van	000-000-0016
0017	Jackson, Rafael	000-000-0017
0018	Wilson, Carter	000-000-0018
0019	Kolson, Jan	000-000-0019
0020	Abelman, John	000-000-0020

Figure 9.2 The Driver Roster Report

Once this table is opened, all other tables' column definitions will be relative to the left-most position in this table. For example,

#dt 2 1 5 8 32 35 46 #   (line two)

defines a table, numbered 2, with three columns. The first column begins at position 1 and ends at position 5. However, if table 1 above is open when table 2 is invoked, then the first column of table 2 will actually occupy print positions 17 through 21. Table 2 is used to actually place the driver number, name, and phone number on the report.

A table is opened with the command **t**:

#t 1   (line three)

Until the table is closed with **te** (table end), all tables opened subsequently will be relative to the right edge of this table.

Blank lines can be introduced into a report in two ways: **b** (see line 30) will produce a single b lank line; **s** *n*, where *n* is an integer, will insert *n* blank lines (see lines five and seven).

All printing occurs within the current column. Therefore, to center a heading on the report, table 1 should be open. (Remember that table 1 has a single column consisting of the entire printable width of the page.) The RPF command **cen** will center text; **cul** will center and underline it (line six). To print column headings, table 2 must be open (line 26). Each heading is to be left justified in its column; the absence of an RPF command will automatically left justify text (**r** will right justify). The headings are also underlined by placing a row of dashes on the line below the heading. The command **n** indicates that printing should continue in the same column on the line below. Therefore, the line

Numbr #n -----

will print the characters "Numbr" in the first column of table two. The **#n** causes RPF to drop down one line before printing the dashes. As it appears in Listing 9.1 (line 27), this line ends with **#nc** (new column), which moves to the next column right. If printing is already occurring in the right-most column, the current column becomes the left-most column. The roster's column headings are printed by lines 27–29.

The first RPT command that should appear in a report is **DATABASE** (line eight). This actually opens the database from which the report will be created. Then all variables used by the report must be declared. Variables that will be used to store data retrieved from the database may have the same names as attributes in the database. In that case, the variable names may need to be prefaced with an ampersand (**&**) in SQL statements to distinguish them from attributes. If necessary, local variables used only by the report can also be defined (see the driver summary report that follows for an example). The roster uses only three variables—**drvnam**, **drvnum**, and **drvphone**—each of which corresponds to an attribute in the database. They are declared with the RPT command **DECLARE** (lines 9–11). Each variable is given a type. **char** variables are listed as a*n*, where *n* is the maximum length string the variable will hold.

The actual work of retrieving data and placing it in its proper places in the text file that RPF will format is controlled by the **REPORT** command (line 36). **REPORT** takes up to four parameters, each of which is the name of a *macro*. The macros used by RPT are programming macros similar to those used in assembly language programming; they are not the same as keyboard macros used by many spreadsheet programs. A programming macro is a block of program statements that is given a name. The macro name is then used in the program code whenever the macro statements should be executed. When the program is processed (assembled or compiled, whichever is appropriate), the macro code is physically inserted into the processed program in place of the macro's name. This is known as *macro substitution*. It is unlike using a subroutine or function in that a macro actually generates repeated code.

The **REPORT** command must reference at least two macros: a **SELECT** macro that retrieves data and a body macro that prints the data retrieved by the **SELECT** macro. The header and footer macros are optional, though if one is present, the other must be as well. Macro definitions begin with the command **DECLARE macro_name** (lines 12, 17, 25, and 33) and end with a period. If periods are being used to signal RPT commands, then the last line in a macro definition will appear as two periods (lines 16, 24, 32, and 35).

A **SELECT** macro contains a SQL **SELECT** command to retrieve data from the database. Any SQL command, including those with subqueries, is acceptable. However, an additional line must be added to indicate the variables in which data should be placed. This line begins with the keyword **INTO** and is followed by the variable list. Values are placed into the variables by position. (The value of the first attribute in the **SELECT** list is placed in the first variable in the variable list, etc.) The driver roster needs only one **SELECT** macro (lines 13–15) to retrieve driver information.

The head macro in lines 26-31 (it can have any name; **head** is used only for convenience) opens table 2, prints the headings followed by a blank line, and then prints the first line of the body macro. (A macro is executed by simply using its name.) Body, header, or footer macros can contain any RPT or RPF commands as well as text.

The **PRINT** command inserts the contents of a variable into the text file produced by RPT. It is used by the body macro (lines 18–23) to display data retrieved from the database. The **nc** commands that follow each **PRINT** control placement of the text.

In this program, the footer is nothing more than a place holder (line 34). Though there is no text or data to print in the footer, it is required because the report uses a header. The footer's contents, the **te** command that closes table 2, could have just as easily been placed above line 37, which closes table 1. The final line in the program, **STOP** (line 38), is a signal to RPT to quit processing the file.

To understand just exactly what RPT does to a source file, look at Listing 9.2. It represents the interim text file produced by running RPT on the driver roster source code. Notice that all the RPT commands are gone; the RPF commands remain. There are no macro definitions and no variables. The file now contains a sequential listing of the RPF commands sandwiched between the data retrieved from the database by the **SELECT** macro. The commands in the body, header, and footer macros have been inserted repeatedly whenever the macro was used.

THE DRIVER SUMMARY REPORT

Producing the driver summary report in Figure 9.3 adds a bit of complexity to the report-generation process. Any report with groupings (e.g., the shifts are grouped by driver) is really a report within a report. The shifts for a given driver are printed within a listing of all drivers who had shift reservations within the report period. The source code to produce this report appears in Listing 9.3.

The driver summary report uses four tables. Table 1 (line 47 in Listing 9.3) is used to set left and right margins. Table 2 (line 48) contains one column to print the driver name. Table 3 (line 49) contains four columns for the remainder of the shift data. Table 4 (line 50) is used only to print column headings.

```
#dt 1 17 63 #
#dt 2 1 5 8 32 35 46 #
#t 1
#page 5 68
#s 5
#t 2
Numbr #n ----- #nc
Name #n ---- #nc
Phone #n ----- #nc
#b
ØØØ1
#nc
Baily, Max
#nc
ØØØ-ØØØ-ØØØ1
#nc
ØØØ2
#nc
Baker, Mary Ann
#nc
ØØØ-ØØØ-ØØØ2
#nc
ØØØ3
#nc
Lewis, John
#nc
ØØØ-ØØØ-ØØØ3
#nc
ØØØ4
#nc
Santiago, Jorge
#nc
ØØØ-ØØØ-ØØØ4
#nc
ØØØ5
#nc
Miller, Pat
#nc
ØØØ-ØØØ-ØØØ5
#nc
ØØØ6
```

Listing 9.2 The Driver Roster Report After Being Run Through RPT

```
#nc
Miller, Phyllis
#nc
ØØØ-ØØØ-ØØØ6
#nc
ØØØ7
#nc
Phong, Quen
#nc
ØØØ-ØØØ-ØØØ7
#nc
ØØØ8
#nc
Wong, David
#nc
ØØØ-ØØØ-ØØØ8
#nc
ØØØ9
#nc
Young, Leslie
#nc
ØØØ-ØØØ-ØØØ9
#nc
ØØ1Ø
#nc
Zilog, Charlie
#nc
ØØØ-ØØØ-ØØ1Ø
#nc
ØØ11
#nc
Erlich, Martin
#nc
ØØØ-ØØØ-ØØ11
#nc
ØØ12
#nc
Eastman, Richard
#nc
ØØØ-ØØØ-ØØ12
#nc
```

Listing 9.2 (cont.) The Driver Roster Report After Being Run Through RPT

```
0013
#nc
Kowalski, Pete
#nc
000-000-0013
#nc
0014
#nc
Mariott, Emily
#nc
000-000-0014
#nc
0015
#nc
French, Janice
#nc
000-000-0015
#nc
0016
#nc
Thieu, Lin Van
#nc
000-000-0016
#nc
0017
#nc
Jackson, Rafael
#nc
000-000-0017
#nc
0018
#nc
Wilson, Carter
#nc
000-000-0018
#nc
0019
#nc
Kolson, Jan
#nc
000-000-0019
```

Listing 9.2 (cont.) The Driver Roster Report After Being Run Through RPT

```
#nc
ØØ2Ø
#nc
Abelman,  John
#nc
ØØØ-ØØØ-ØØ2Ø
#nc
#te
#te
```

Listing 9.2 (cont.)   The Driver Roster Report After Being Run Through RPT

To make this report as flexible and as easy to generate as possible, the person run-ning the report should be able to enter the starting and ending dates for the report without having to use a text editor to modify the source code. The RPT command **ASK** will print a prompt on the screen and accept keyboard input into a variable during an RPT run. The for-mat of the command is:

> **ASK "prompt" variable_name**

Lines 53 and 54 are used to collect the dates for the driver summary.

An important note is necessary here with regard to variable data types. If you look at the **DECLARE** statements for **wkdate, startdate,** and **enddate,** you will notice that they are declared as nine character strings rather than date variables. Though RPT does support a date variable type, it is not the same as the data type **date** used with **CREATE TABLE;** columns designed for RPT date type variables must be **number** columns that are loaded by IAF applications. SQL **date** columns must be handled as strings when using RPT.

This report also uses numeric variables. Each position in a numeric variable is gen-erally represented by a nine (see lines five, eight, and nine), though formatting characters can preserve leading zeros and insert commas, decimal points, and dollar signs.

The driver summary report needs two **SELECT** macros, one to **SELECT** each driver that has reserved a shift during the report period and one to **SELECT** all shifts reserved by those drivers. Lines 12–18, **seldrivers,** will retrieve the driver information. Note that the keyword **DISTINCT** is essential in this **SELECT**; if it is not present, all of the data for each driver will be repeated completely for each shift the driver has reserved.

Shift data are retrieved by the macro **selshifts** (lines 19–26). The variables in the WHERE clause are preceded by ampersands to distinguish them from attribute names. Even though **startdate** and **enddate** do not duplicate attribute names, RPT will assume that they are attribute names unless the ampersand is present.

The report title and column headings are printed in lines 55–63. They could just as easily have been placed in a header macro, in which case a footer macro would have also been required. Since no header and footer are present, the **REPORT** command to print the overall

DRIVER SUMMARY REPORT

Driver	Date	Shift	Cab	Miles
------	----	-----	---	-----
Miller, Phyllis				
	15-JUL-86	day	1Ø4	149
	16-JUL-86	day	1Ø4	Ø
Zilog, Charlie				
	15-JUL-86	day	238	139
	16-JUL-86	day	238	Ø
Abelman, John				
	15-JUL-86	day	4Ø4	154
	16-JUL-86	day	4Ø4	Ø
Erlich, Martin				
	15-JUL-86	eve	Ø45	Ø
Bailey, Max				
	15-JUL-86	eve	1Ø4	134
	16-JUL-86	eve	1Ø4	Ø
Eastman, Richard				
	15-JUL-86	eve	144	188
Thieu, Lin Van				
	15-JUL-86	ngt	Ø45	36Ø
Baker, Mary Ann				
	15-JUL-86	ngt	1Ø8	148
Santiago, Jorge				
	16-JUL-86	eve	ØØ2	Ø
Phong, Quen				
	16-JUL-86	ngt	ØØ2	Ø

Figure 9.3 The Driver Summary Report

```
1        .DATABASE CABS
2        .DECLARE drvnam a25
3        .DECLARE wkdate a9
4        .DECLARE cabnum a3
5        .DECLARE miles 999
6        .DECLARE wkshift a3
7        .DECLARE startdate a9
8        .DECLARE odomrdg1 999999
9        .DECLARE odomrdg2 999999
10       .DECLARE drvnum a4
11       .DECLARE enddate a9
12       .DEFINE seldrivers
13             SELECT DISTINCT driver.drvnum, drvnam
14             INTO drvnum, drvnam
15             FROM driver, shifts
16             WHERE driver.drvnum = ANY (SELECT DISTINCT drvnum
17             FROM shifts)
18       ..
19       .DEFINE selshifts
20             SELECT wkdate, wkshift, cabnum, odomrdg1, odomrdg2
21             INTO wkdate, wkshift, cabnum, odomrdg1, odomrdg2
22             FROM shifts
23             WHERE drvnum = &drvnum
24             AND wkdate >= &startdate
25             AND wkdate <= &enddate
26       ..
27       .DEFINE outerbody
28             #t 2
29             #b
30             .PRINT drvnam
31             #te
32             #t 3
33             .REPORT selshifts shiftbody
34             #te
35       ..
36       .DEFINE shiftbody
37             .SUB miles odomrdg2 odomrdg1
38             .PRINT wkdate
39             #nc
40             .PRINT wkshift
41             #nc
42             .PRINT cabnum
43             #nc
44             .PRINT miles
45             #nc
46       ..
```

Listing 9.3 Source Code for the Driver Summary Report

```
47      #dt 1 15 65 #
48      #dt 2 1 25 #
49      #dt 3 27 35 37 41 43 45 47 51 #
50      #dt 4 1 25 27 35 37 41 43 45 47 51 #
51      #page 6 58
52      #t 1
53      .ASK "Enter start date:" startdate
54      .ASK "Enter end date:" enddate
55      #cul Driver Summary Report #
56      #s 3
57      #t 4
58      Driver #n ------ #nc
59      Date #n ---- #nc
60      Shift #n ----- #nc
61      Cab #n --- #nc
62      Miles #n ----- #nc
63      #te
64      .REPORT seldrivers outerbody
65      #te
66      .STOP
```

Listing 9.3 (cont.)   Source Code for the Driver Summary Report

body of the report (line 64) contains only the names of the **SELECT** macro and the body macro (**outerbody**).

Two things must be accomplished by **outerbody** (lines 27–35). It must print the driver name and then all the shifts reserved by that driver during the report period. The shifts reserved by the driver are really a report all their own. Therefore, a **REPORT** command appears within the **outerbody** macro (line 33). It executes the **selshifts** macro and then the body macro for the shifts, **shiftbody** (lines 36–46), which first computes the miles driven in a shift and then prints the data.

When looking at the source code for *Oracle* reports, it is important to realize that the order is which statements are actually executed does not necessarily correspond to the order in which they are placed in the listing. Macros must be defined before they are used. Therefore, though macro definitions are generally placed at the beginning of a source file, they are not executed until their name appears either by itself (an explicit execution) or as part of a **REPORT** command.

EXERCISES

The following exercises are based on this set of relations for the office of Margaret Holmes, D.M.D:

PATIENT-MASTER (PATIENT#, NAME, ADDRESS, PHONE, SSN, WHO-PAYS, REL-TO-WHO-PAYS, PAYMENT-SOURCE)

PAYERS (WHO-PAYS, HOME-ADDRESS, HOME-PHONE, PLACE-OF-EMPLOYMENT, WORK-PHONE, INSURANCE-CARRIER)

APPOINTMENTS (PATIENT#, APPT-DATE, APPT-TIME, APPT-FLAG)

VISITS (PATIENT#, DATE, PROCEDURE, COMMENTS)

COSTS (PROCEDURE, PRICE)

INCOME (PATIENT#, PAY-DATE, SOURCE, AMT, WHO-PAYS)

LEDGER (WHO-PAYS, TOTAL-AMT-OWED)

INV-MAST (ITEM#, ITEM-DESCR, REORDER-PT, REORDER-QTY, CURRENT-INV)

ORDERS (P-O#, DATE, VENDOR, TOTAL-AMT)

VENDORS (VNAME, VADDRESS, VPHONE, CONTACT-PERSON)

LINE-ITEMS (P-O#, ITEM#, QTY, UNIT-COST, TOTAL-COST)

OWED (VENDOR, AMT-OWED)

PAYMENTS (VENDOR, CHECK-DATE, CHECK#, AMT-PAID)

1. Use the SQL command CREATE TABLE to install the relations in Dr. Holmes' database. You may change table and column names wherever necessary to conform to SQL rules.

2. Using IAG, create programs for data entry and/or modification for the following list of tables. In each case, be sure to use SQL commands where appropriate to enforce referential integrity. Test each program with IAP using your own test data to be sure that it works. Your testing procedure should verify that all constraints are indeed enforced by the program.

    a. PATIENT-ENTRY
    b. APPOINTMENTS (Also enforce the constraint that appointment times must be between 8 a.m. and 12 noon and between 1 p.m. and 4:30 p.m.)
    c. VISITS
    d. LINE-ITEMS
    e. PAYMENTS (Also enforce the constraint that CHECK# must be between 1001 and 2000)

3. Write and implement the following reports:

a. A patient roster containing patient names and phone numbers.
b. A list of all patients who haven't been seen in the past year. The cut-off date should be entered from the keyboard.
c. An appointment calendar for any given day. The day required should be entered from the keyboard.
d. A summary of all procedures performed on all patients in the database, listed by patient. This will require a nested report similar to the driver summary report example.
e. A single purchase order as if you were printing on a purchase order form. Include:
   1. purchase order number
   2. vendor name and address
   3. for each line item, the item description, quantity ordered, unit cost, total cost
   4. total amount of the purchase order
f. A summary of all payments made to vendors, grouped by vendor, during a given time period. Include a subtotal of payments for each vendor (Hint: put it in a footer for the inner report). Then finish the report with the total payments made (put this in the overall report footer). Enter the time period for the report from the keyboard.

R:base System V

CHAPTER OUTLINE:

CHAPTER OBJECTIVES

After reading this chapter, you will:

1. Be able to install a relational schema using *R:base System V*
2. Understand the techniques needed to enforce integrity and key constraints
3. Be able to retrieve data from an *R:base System V* database

R:base System V is the latest release of the microcomputer database marketed by Microrim, Inc. Its predecessors include *R:base 4000*, which is no longer available, and *R:base 5000*, which is still widely used. *R:base 5000* databases are more or less compatible with *R:base System V*. Though *5000* files must be converted before they can be used with *System V*, very little program code must be changed. On the other hand, *5000* does not support user views. Defining and using views is discussed at the very end of this chapter, since the view definition command uses syntax from the major *R:Base* retrieval command, SELECT. *System V* can also be run as either a single- or multi-user database; *5000* is single-user only. The discussion in this chapter therefore generally applies to both *5000* and *System V* as far as the command interface is concerned; any minor differences will be noted as appropriate. On the other hand, there are major differences in the procedures used to create data entry forms and to create report formats.

TERMINOLOGY

The names of objects within an *R:base System V* database adhere closely to the terminology of relational database theory:

1. Relations may be referred to as *relations* or *tables*.
2. Attributes are referred to as *attributes*, *columns*, or *fields*.
3. Tuples are called *rows*.

Definitions of the tables in the database are contained in the *data dictionary*. The data dictionary uses a number of tables, including one to describe report formats, one to describe screen forms, one to hold integrity rules, and two to describe views. (The view-description tables are not found in *R:base 5000*, since that package doesn't support views.) These tables can be queried in the same way that a table containing data can be queried. This data dictionary therefore functions as a catalog. It can also be described as a *dynamic catalog*, since changes to the database structure are made to the data dictionary itself and then automatically propagated into the tables. On the other hand, although data dictionary tables can be queried like data tables, data cannot be entered or amended in the same way data are modified in data tables; *R:base System V* has a special series of commands for dealing with the data dictionary.

A complete *R:base System V* database consists of a set of tables, the data in those tables, and their associated indexes. Physically, it is implemented as three files. If the *R:base System V* implementation of the FTC database is given the name FTC, then the files supporting it will be:

1. FTC1.RBS (the data dictionary)
2. FTC2.RBS (the data)
3. FTC3.RBS (indexes on attributes which have been designated as keys)

Regardless of the size or complexity of an *R:base System V* database, the DBMS will always generate only those three files on disk.

THE *R:BASE* PROGRAMMING LANGUAGE

R:base System V programs, called *command files*, are used primarily to create turn-key systems for casual and/or unsophisticated users. This section contains an introduction to that language so that you can read the short program samples that accompany the rest of this chapter. If you are already familiar with the *R:base System V* programming language, you can easily skip this section.

During the development process, *R:base System V* programs are run under an *interpreter*, which translates the program into a form the computer can understand line-by-line from the source code file as the program is being run. Once the developer is certain that the programs aren't likely to change, they can be *compiled*. The compiler (*CodeLock*) is supplied with the *R:base System V* package (the *R:base 5000* compiler is called *RBCOMPILE*). It will permanently translate programs into machine-executable form (binary). Compiled programs run much faster than interpreted programs. They are also more secure, since users have no access to source code but only to the compiled, binary version of the program.

R:base System V command files consist of a combination of commands that can be entered at the **R>** prompt and special commands for manipulating variables, input, and output. Commands are embedded in control statements that determine when and how the commands will be executed. Command files can be compiled and combined into a *procedure file* to reduce the number of individual files supporting a particular application.

R:base System V provides a text editor for entering program code. To edit a new file, type:

R>rbedit

To edit an existing program, type:

R>rbedit command-file

R:base System V program files can take any name that adheres to MS-DOS constraints (maximum of eight characters followed by a period and a three-character extension). Therefore, if you give a program file name an extension, you must use that extension when referencing that file.

R:base System V programs are executed with the command **RUN** at the **R>** prompt. This command can also be issued from within a program to execute another program. Programs executed in this way are referred to as *subroutines*. Subroutines should end with the statement **RETURN**, which sends control back to the program or subroutine that called them.

R:base System V also supports parameter passing; up to nine parameters may be passed from a calling program to a subroutine:

RUN command-file IN procedure-file USING parameter-list

R:base System V programs, therefore, generally consist of many subroutines, each of which performs a single program function. For example, the code that prints an application program's main menu will be contained in a command-file; code to enter data into relations will require one subroutine per relation; each report will be printed by a separate subroutine. Designing programs in this way makes them easier to develop, debug, and modify.

VARIABLES

Like other high-level programming languages, the R:base System V language uses variables. Variables are assigned values with the **SET** command:

SET VAR variable-name TO variable-contents

as in:

SET VAR mdate TO 07/15/89

The expression following **TO** can consist of a constant, the name of another variable, an arithmetic or string expression, or an expression to retrieve data from a database table. For example, the following command will locate a single driver's name using the driver number (stored in the variable **.mdrvnum**) and assign it to the variable **mdriver**:

**SET VAR mdriver TO drvname IN driver WHERE drvnum eq   +
.mdrvnum**

When variables are used anywhere but directly after a command (e.g., **SET VAR**), R:base System V must be told explicitly to use the contents of the variable by preceding the variable name with a period (e.g., **.variable-name**, referred to as a *dotted variable*). Otherwise, R:base System V will view the variable name as a string to be assigned to some other variable. For example:

SET VAR newdate TO .olddate

This statement will assign the current contents of the variable **olddate** to the variable **newdate**.

An *R:base System V* variable assumes the data type of the first value assigned to it. However, the data type of a variable can be changed explicitly:

SET VAR variable-name data-type

This command will not only change the data type of the variable but will also attempt to convert the current contents of the variable to the new type. If the data conversion cannot be done, the variable will be given the new data type and a value of null.

Date conversions can be extremely useful. For example, later in this chapter you will see that WKDATE must be concatenated with one or more text attributes to form a composite key. If WKDATE is stored in date format, it must be converted to text before it can be concatenated. Assuming WKDATE is stored in the variable **mdate**, then the following statement will do the conversion:

SET VAR mdate TEXT

CONTROL STRUCTURES

As with other high-level languages, *R:base System V* programs execute statements in sequence, beginning with the first and moving from statement to statement, unless given instructions to do otherwise. There are three major ways to "do otherwise":

1. Use **RUN** to call a subroutine
2. Use **IF/ELSE/ENDIF** to choose between two possible sets of actions
3. Use **WHILE/ENDWHILE** to repeat actions

R:base System V supports a version of the CASE statement, but it is somewhat limited. The value of the test expression must be a single integer; only one executable expression can follow any given value, though the expression can be a call to a subroutine. *R:base System V* also supports an unconditional branch—**GOTO label**. In terms of well structured programming, however, the **GOTO** should be used sparingly, if at all.

IF/ELSE/ENDIF is an example of a program control structure that permits the selection of alternative actions based on the value of some expression. Assume, for example, that a program has been written to retrieve a FTC driver's phone number and print an appropriate response. The program must not only do the retrieval, but must handle the situation in which a driver doesn't have a phone. Part of that program might appear as in Listing 10.1.

In that listing, an **IF** statement first evaluates the expression following **IF**. (The contents of the variable **error**, which is being used to contain system error numbers, will be 0 if the operation was successful; it will be non-zero if some error occurred.) If the expression is true, then the statements between **IF** and **ELSE** will be executed; the statements after **ELSE** will be skipped; the program continues with whatever follows **ENDIF**.

```
SET ERROR VAR error                (*used to evaluate search*)
SET VAR mdrvphone TO drvphone IN driver WHERE drvnum eq .mdrvnum
IF error eq 0 THEN
    WRITE "The phone number is" & .mdrvphone AT 5 5
ELSE
    WRITE "That driver doesn't have a phone" AT 5 5
ENDIF
```

Listing 10.1 *R:base* Code Segment to Perform Selection

However, if the expression is false, the statements between **IF** and **ELSE** are skipped and the program executes those between **ELSE** and **ENDIF**.

Any logical expression can follow **IF**; the logical expression is always followed by **THEN**. Any executable statements can appear between **IF** and **ELSE** as well as between **ELSE** and **ENDIF**, even other **IF/ELSE/ENDIF** structures. The **ELSE** portion of the structure is not required. If there is only one alternative, one that should be executed if the expression after **IF** is true, then the structure may be written as:

```
IF error eq 0 THEN
    WRITE "The phone number is" & .mdrvphone
ENDIF
```

R:base System V has one way to do repetition, the **WHILE/ENDWHILE**. (It is possible to simulate the action of a **WHILE/ENDWHILE** using **IF/ELSE/ENDIF** and **GOTO**, but there is rarely any reason to do so.) Assume, for example, that you wish to execute a block of statements ten times. The following code will do so:

```
SET VAR count TO 0
WHILE count < 10 THEN
    SET VAR count TEXT                (*convert to text*)
    WRITE "This is iteration #" + .count
    SET VAR count INTEGER            (*convert back to integer*)
    SET VAR count TO .count + 1
ENDWHILE
```

The program will execute all statements between **WHILE** and **ENDWHILE** as long as the expression following **WHILE** is true. (Note that the expression is always followed by the keyword **THEN**.) The expression is evaluated at the top of the loop. Therefore, it must have a value of true before the **WHILE** statement is encountered for the first time; otherwise the loop will never execute at all.

The other important thing to remember is that there must be some action *within the loop* that eventually will cause the expression after **WHILE** to become false. That is the purpose of the statement **SET VAR count TO .count + 1**; after ten iterations of the loop, **count** will have the value of 10, which will make the expression **count < 10** false. Without that statement, the loop would repeat infinitely.

INPUT AND OUTPUT

The *R:base System V* programming language supports three commands that display something on the computer screen:

1. **WRITE**— displays a line of text on the screen. The general format is:

WRITE "some text" AT row column

2. **DISPLAY**—displays the contents of a screen file. Screen files contain information and text for the display of messages. They are most easily created with *Application EXPRESS*, the application generator that comes with the *R:base System V* package. Their most common use is to associate help screens with menus. The general format of the command is:

DISPLAY screen-file-name

3. **TYPE**—displays the contents of a text file. Any standard ASCII text file can be typed to the screen. Files displayed with type can be created with **rbedit** or any other word processor, as long as they are saved as text-only. The general format of the command is:

TYPE text-file-name

Four commands will both display something on the screen and read data from the keyboard:

1. **CHOOSE**—displays a menu from a menu file and accepts the menu choice from the keyboard. Menus for use by this command are created using *Application EXPRESS*. The general format of the command is:

CHOOSE input-variable FROM menu-file-name

2. **FILLIN**—prints a prompt on the screen and accepts data into a single variable. This command works exactly like the BASIC command INPUT:

FILLIN input-variable USING "prompt string" AT row column

3. **ENTER USING**—Displays a data entry form and adds new rows to a table. The simplest form of the command is:

ENTER USING form-name

4. **EDIT USING**—Displays a data entry form and edits existing data. The simplest form of the command is:

EDIT USING form-name

Both **ENTER USING** and **EDIT USING** look for a press of the ESC key as an indication that the user has finished entering data and that the data should be loaded into the base tables. (*R:base 5000* note: **ENTER USING** and **EDIT USING** function somewhat differently in the *5000* environment. Their behavior is closely tied to the type of form being used.)

One command accepts only input:

1. **PAUSE**—waits for the user to press any key to continue. **PAUSE** can be combined with a **WRITE** to freeze the screen:

WRITE "Press any key to continue" AT 24 15
PAUSE

INSTALLING A THIRD NORMAL FORM DATABASE

Installing a 3NF relational design with *R:base System V* usually involves the following steps:

1. Define attributes and assign them to tables. This can be done either with interactive commands in the Define mode or with *Definition EXPRESS*. (*R:base 5000* uses *Application EXPRESS*.)
2. Define integrity rules.
3. Create data entry forms for all tables.

Though these three steps have been listed as a sequential process, it is important to realize that the limitations surrounding the definition of integrity rules will often have an impact on the attributes which must be created.

While *Definition EXPRESS* can be used to define an *R:base System V* database, it is just as fast and often more convenient to do so using interactive commands. To begin the definition process, type:

R> **define database-name**

The R> prompt will change to D>, indicating that you are now in the Define mode.

The Define mode allows you to define four things—attributes, tables, rules (discussed in the next section), and passwords (discussed in Chapter 12). Therefore, *R:base System V* must be told which kind of definitions will follow. To begin entering attributes, simply type:

D> **attributes**

or

D> **columns**

The term **attributes** is a carry-over from *R:base 4000*. Most *R:base 4000* commands are recognized by *R:base 5000* and *System V*, though they are not mentioned in the documentation.

All attributes are entered into the data dictionary as they are defined. At this point in the process, they are not gathered into tables; they merely form a pool of attributes from which tables can be built. Attributes that are to be used in more than one table should nonetheless be entered only once.

The general format for entering an attribute is:

D> **attribute-name attribute-type length key**

Available attribute types are TEXT, INTEGER, REAL, DOUBLE (not available in *R:base 5000*), DATE, CURRENCY (DOLLAR in *R:base 5000*), TIME, and NOTE (not available in *R:base 5000*). The NOTE data type is used to hold blocks of text of up to 4,092 characters.

A length should be entered only for TEXT items. A length for any other item indicates that the item will have multiple values (i.e., it is an array or repeating group). This type of construct violates the basic concept of a relational table, which by definition has no repeating groups, and should therefore not be used. The term **key** at the end of an attribute definition instructs *R:base System V* to build an index on that attribute; it does *not* designate it as a primary key. Indexes should be built on all primary key attributes as well as any others that will be commonly used for searches. Once an index is present, *R:base System V* will automatically use it to optimize search requests.

R:base System V also supports computed attributes. In other words, it is possible to define a column that holds a value that is computed from other attributes already present in the table. (This capability is not available in *R:base 5000*.) For example, if FTC wished to store the number of miles driven during a shift in the SHIFTS relation, an attribute could be defined as:

D> **miles = (odomrdg2 - odomrdg1 + 1) integer**

ODOMRDG1 and ODOMRDG2 must, of course, be defined before MILES is defined. MILES will be assigned a data type by default based on the data types of the attributes from which it is computed.

The attributes used in the *R:base System V* implementation of the FTC database appear in Table 10.1. There are four attributes (SHIFTKEY, INCIKEY, MAINKEY, and DRVKEY) that are not present in the original design. All of these attributes have been added to compensate for a limitation in the definition of integrity rules: conditions within rules can contain references to only single attributes; concatenated (compound) attributes cannot be used.

The attribute SHIFTKEY will be used in the table SHIFT; its contents are obtained by concatenating WKSHIFT, WKDATE, and CABNUM. It can be defined as:

D> **shiftkey=(wkdate + wkshift + cabnum) text 14**

The + is the concatenation operator. (*R:base 5000* note: Derived attributes are not available with *R:base 5000*. The concatenated keys must be loaded with a program that accepts data

Table   10.1
Attributes Used in the *R:base System V* Implementation of the FTC Database

Attribute	Type	Length	Key?	Attribute	Type	Length	Key?
cabnum	TEXT	3	yes	licnum	TEXT	7	
cabstat	TEXT	1		maindate	DATE		
curodom	INTEGER			mainkey	TEXT	36	yes
details	TEXT	200		mainodom	INTEGER		
drvcsz	TEXT	25		maintype	TEXT	25	
drvkey	TEXT	15	yes	make	TEXT	15	
drvnam	TEXT	25		model	TEXT	15	
drvnum	TEXT	4	yes	odomrdg1	INTEGER		
drvlexd	DATE			odomrdg2	INTEGER		
drvlic	TEXT	15		purdate	DATE		
drvphone	TEXT	12		shiftkey	TEXT	14	key
drvstat	TEXT	15		wkdate	TEXT	8	
drvstr	TEXT	25		wkflag	TEXT	1	
incikey	TEXT	14	yes	wkshift	TEXT	3	
incitype	TEXT	15		year	TEXT	2	

into a variable form.) The drawback to this approach is that **wkdate** must be defined as a TEXT type attribute rather than a DATE type attribute. There is no function to convert a date to a text string and dates cannot be concatenated with strings. However, the only other alternative is to use a data entry form that accepts the primary key values into variables. In that case, the date variable can be converted to a text variable by using **SET VAR** as described earlier in this chapter. It can then be concatenated to the other parts of the key and finally loaded into the relation with the **LOAD** command. This procedure requires programming.

Date attributes are useful because they support date comparisons even if the dates are stored in MMDDYY format. If, however, dates are stored as text in YYMMDD format, date comparisons will work just as well. Since the latter approach is simpler (i.e., it requires no programming to implement concatenated keys), it was chosen for the FTC database.

DRVKEY (obtained by concatenating DRVNUM, WKDATE, and WKSHIFT) is also used in SHIFTS. While it is not the primary key, it can be used to ensure that a driver hasn't already reserved a given shift on a given day.

INCIKEY will be used in the table INCIDENT; its contents are obtained by concatenating WKSHIFT, WKDATE, and CABNUM (e.g., **incikey=wkdate + wkshift + cabnum**). MAINKEY will be used in the table MAINTAIN; its contents are obtained by concatenating CABNUM, WKDATE, and MAINTYPE. This approach does require extra disk space. However, the inclusion of these extra attributes (one for every table with a compound primary key) will make it possible to specify a complete set of integrity constraints within the data dictionary.

Once all attributes have been defined, they are grouped into tables. Table definitions are preceded with either:

D> **tables**

or

D> **relations**

Relations is another carry-over from *R:base 4000*.

Each table is defined by giving the name of the table and the names of the attributes it will include:

D> **table-name WITH attribute1 attribute2 attribute3...**

Remember to use a + as a continuation sign if the table definition command becomes longer than what will fit on one line.

Complete table definitions for the FTC database can be found in Table 10.2.

To leave the define mode and return to the **R>** prompt, type:

D> **end**

Table   10.2
Defining Tables for the *R:base System V* Implementation of the FTC Database

D> cab WITH cabnum make model year purdate licnum conditn cabstat curodom

D> driver WITH drvnum drvnam drvstr drvcsz drvphone drvlic drvlexd drvstat

D> shifts WITH wkdate wkshift cabnum drvnum wkflag odomrdg1 odomrdg2 shiftkey drvkey

D> incident WITH cabnum wkdate wkshift incitype details incikey

D> maintain WITH cabnum maindate maintype mainodom mainkey

R:base System V provides special commands for querying the data dictionary.

list   columns

will produce an alphabetical listing of all attributes, showing their type, length (if appropriate), whether or not they are a key, and the relations to which they belong.

list   tables

will produce an alphabetical listing of all relations, showing the number of columns and rows in each.

list   all

will produce an alphabetical listing of all relations, including their attributes and the characteristics of those attributes.

The *R:base 4000* versions of the above commands (**listatt, listrel, listatt all**) may be used as well.

DEFINING RULES TO ENFORCE PRIMARY KEY CONSTRAINTS

R:base System V can store rules to which data must conform within the data dictionary. The DBMS automatically enforces those rules whenever data are entered, modified, or deleted. Rules are stored in a table named RULES. That table can be queried using *R:base*'s **SELECT** command or with the special command **list rules**.

Rules are entered in the Define mode. Once in the define mode, type:

D> **rules**

to indicate that rule definitions will follow.

The general format of a rule is:

"Error message" attribute-name IN relation-name logical-condition

The error message is a string of up to 40 characters that will be printed on a data entry form whenever the rule is violated. The rule is therefore expressed in the positive; it states one or more conditions that must be met. Notice also that although each rule may contain more than one condition joined by **AND** or **OR**, each condition applies to one attribute in one relation. The concatenation operator cannot be used to create a compound attribute. As mentioned earlier, this is the reason an extra attribute must be stored in the relation itself to contain the concatenated key.

In order to completely enforce primary key constraints, two rules must be present for each primary key, one to ensure that the key is nonnull and another to ensure that the key is unique. In the relation CAB, for example, the rule to express entity integrity would be written as:

"You must enter a cab number" cabnum IN cab EXISTS

The operator **EXISTS** verifies that a given attribute has a value. Therefore, if CABNUM has no value (i.e., it is null), this rule will be violated and the error message will appear. *R:base System V* will not execute any data modifications if a rule has been violated.

A rule can also be written to verify that cab numbers are unqiue:

"Duplicate cab number" cabnum IN cab NEA cabnum IN cab

This rule will compare a new cab number against all cab numbers already stored in CAB. The rule will be violated if a match is found.

Rules for DRIVER, which also has a single-attribute primary key, are created in the same way as those for CAB. The other three relations in the FTC database, however, have compound primary keys. Entity integrity rules can be expressed in terms of single attributes. For example, this rule will work for the relation SHIFTS:

"You must have a cab, date and shift" cabnum IN shifts EXISTS +
AND wkdate IN shifts EXISTS AND wkshift IN shifts EXISTS

The rule to verify the uniqueness of primary keys is expressed as:

"Cab already reserved" shiftkey IN shifts NEA shiftkey IN shifts

Why is this concatenated key really necessary? Why won't it work to write the rule:

"Cab already reserved" cabnum IN shifts NEA cabnum IN shifts   +
AND wkdate IN shifts NEA wkdate IN shifts AND wkshift IN   +
shifts NEA wkshift in SHIFTS

The expression in this rule will be true so long as (1) the cab is reserved for any date and shift; (2) a reservation exists on any day and for any cab for the shift; and (3) a reservation exists on any shift and for any cab for the date. In other words, the logical expression is evaluated by first verifying the truth of the *parts* of the expression and then logically ANDing them together. The intention of the rule, however, is to perform the logical ANDing *before* the search. The only way to do this within the constraints of the DBMS is to use a primary key attribute that already contains the concatenated key.

DEFINING RULES TO ENFORCE REFERENTIAL INTEGRITY

A rule must exist for each foreign key–primary key reference. The following rule, for example, will verify that a shift reservation is for a cab that exists in the database:

"No cab by that number" cabnum IN shifts EQA cabnum IN cab

Rules can also be established for the concatenated primary keys. Since no incident should be reported for a shift that was never reserved, a rule might be written as:

"Cab not driven that shift" incikey IN incident EQA shiftkey IN   +
shifts

The complete set of integrity rules that supports the FTC database can be found in Table 10.3. Note that there is one rule (Rule 4) that can't be classified as a primary key constraint or a referential integrity rule. This rule makes sure that any given driver doesn't reserve more than one cab for any given date and shift. It is a good example of a rule that helps maintain overall data integrity, though it isn't really necessary to meet the demands of the relational model.

Table 10.3

Integrity Rules for the *R:base System V* Implementation of the FTC Database

Rule #	Rule	Message
1	drvnum IN driver nea drvnum IN driver	Duplicate driver number
2	cabnum IN cab nea cabnum IN cab	Duplicate cab number
3	shiftkey IN shifts nea shiftkey IN shifts	Cab already reserved
4	drvkey IN shifts nea drvkey IN shifts	Driver has reservation
5	incikey IN incident nea incikey IN incident	Incident already recorded
6	mainkey IN maintain nea mainkey IN maintain	Work already recorded
7	cabnum IN shifts eqa cabnum IN cab	No cab by that number
8	drvnum IN shifts eqa drvnum IN driver	No driver by that number
9	incikey IN incident eqa shiftkey IN shifts	Cab not driven that shift
10	cab IN maintain eqa cabnum IN cab	No cab by that number
11	cabnum IN cab exists	You must enter a cab number
12	drvnum IN driver exists	You must enter a driver number
13	cabnum IN shifts exists AND wkdate IN shifts exists AND wkshift IN shifts exists	You must have a cab, date, and shift
14	cabnum IN incident exists AND wkdate IN incident exists AND wkshift IN incident exists	You must have a cab, date, and shift
15	cabnum IN maintain exists AND maindate IN maintain exists AND maintype IN maintain exists	Enter date, type of work, & cab #

CREATING FORMS FOR DATA ENTRY AND INTEGRITY CONTROL

R:base System V does not provide default data entry forms, though a simple default form can be created quickly with *Application EXPRESS*. Custom forms, in particular forms for use with computed attributes, must be created by the database designer using *Forms EXPRESS*. A form will support data entry and modification in up to five tables. (*R:base 5000* note: *R:base System V* uses a single type of form for both single and multiple table data entry, but *R:base 5000* supports two distinct kinds of forms. *Table* forms are used for data modification on a single table. Data are entered directly into the attributes and stored directly into the table. *Variable* forms, however, may apply to one or more tables, since their data are entered into variables, rather than directly into attributes. While table forms can be used interactively (i.e, from the **R>** prompt), variable forms can only be used within a program. The way in which forms are created for use with *R:base 5000* is considerably different than the procedure used with *R:base System V*. Therefore, if you are using *R:base 5000* you should consult the program documentation for details.)

```
Press [ESC] when done

                        Form Characteristics


Assign passwords for this form? ...........................................[N/A]
  Read-only password:_____        Modify password:_____
Clear the screen before form use? ........................................[Yes]
Clear the screen after form use? .........................................[Yes]
Display a status line during form use? ...................................[Yes]
Do you want custom colors for the form? ..................................[No ]
 Foreground color: _____      Background color: _____
 Press [ENTER] for a color palette

Do you plan to use the form with the ENTER command? ......................[Yes]
  Do you want to change the menu? ........................................[No ]
 ┌──────────────────────────────────────────────────────────────────────────┐
 │  Add    Duplicate    Edit again   Discard    Quit                          │
 └──────────────────────────────────────────────────────────────────────────┘
Do you plan to use the form with the EDIT command? .......................[Yes]
Do you want to change the menu? ..........................................[No ]
 ┌──────────────────────────────────────────────────────────────────────────┐
 │  Edit    Save    Add new    Delete    Reset    Prev    Next    Quit        │
 └──────────────────────────────────────────────────────────────────────────┘

[ESC] Done    [F5] Reset    [F1Ø] Help    [ ↑ ] Up    [ ▼ ] Down
Form: cabntry        Customize form
```

Figure 10.1 Customizing an *R:base System V* Screen Form

```
Press [ESC] when done
                            Table Characteristics


Do you want to add new rows to the table? ............................[Yes]

Do you want to replace existing rows in the table? .........................[Yes]
  Is the replace automatic when the user leaves the row? ...................[Yes]

Do you want to delete rows from the table? ..............................[Yes]
  Restrict the delete to the current table? ..............................[Yes]

Is this table on the MANY side of a ONE to MANY relationship? .............[N/A]

Do you want to define a region? ...........................................[No ]
  Do you want a border around the region? ...............................[N/A]
  How many lines in the border - enter 1 or 2: ____
  Do you want custom colors for the region? .............................[N/A]
  Foreground color:_____  Background color: _____
  (Press [ENTER] for a color palette)


[ESC] Done    [F5] Reset    [F1Ø] Help    [↑] Up    [↓] Down

Form: cabntry       Customize table    Table: cab
```

Figure 10.2 Customizing a Table for an *R:base System V* Screen Form

Form definitions are stored in a relation named FORMS. It can be queried with *R:base*'s **SELECT** command.

To create a data entry form, enter:

R> **forms form-name table-name**

If no database is open, *Forms EXPRESS* will present a menu to select one. Once a database is open, forms can be created or modified. If no table name has been included in the command that invoked *Forms EXPRESS*, *Forms EXPRESS* will also prompt for the first table that is to be included in the form.

Assuming that the form name entered is new (i.e., it isn't in the FORMS table), *Forms EXPRESS* gives the designer the chance to customize the form. Figure 10.1 shows the form customization screen for the CABNTRY form which is used to enter data into the CAB relation. Default values appear in brackets at the right edge of each line.

The form creation process also allows customization of some table characteristics. The table customization screen appears in Figure 10.2. The question about the table with regard to a one-to-many relationship is not applicable to the first table defined for a form.

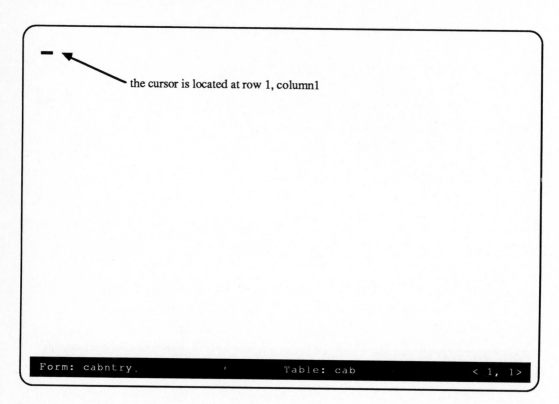

the cursor is located at row 1, column1

Form: cabntry.   '   Table: cab   < 1, 1>

Figure 10.3 The *R:base System V* Form-Definition Screen

The term *region*, as used by *Forms EXPRESS*, refers to a block on the screen that will be used to display more than one row from a given table at any one time.

After both the form and table characteristics have been customized, *R:base System V* presents the form designer with the Reports Definition menu. To actually design the layout of the form, select **Edit**. The Reports Definition menu will disappear, leaving a screen that is blank except for a status line at the bottom (see Figure 10.3). The current position of the cursor appears at the right of the status line.

Use the arrow keys to move the cursor about the screen. Static text (i.e., prompts) can be typed anywhere on the screen. However, lines 1 and 2 are used by *R:base System V* to display system prompts and messages. Forms will, therefore, generally look cleaner if they begin on line 3.

The data that are accepted into a data entry form are placed in *fields*. A field can be an attribute in a base table, a global variable (a variable whose contents are entered from the keyboard), or a lookup variable (a variable whose contents are retrieved from another base table in the database). To fix the screen coordinates where data for a field will be entered and/ or displayed:

```
Press [ESC] when done
                            Field Characteristics


Will new data be entered in the field? ...................................[Yes]

Can the user change the data displayed in the field? ....................[Yes]
  Restrict changes to the current table? .................................[Yes]

Do you want to display a default value in the field? ....................[No ]
Enter the default value OR #DUP to use the previous row value:
_____


Do you want custom colors for the field? ................................[No ]
  Foreground color:_____        Background color:_____
  (Press [ENTER] for a color palette)




[ESC] Return    [F1Ø] Help
Form: cabntry   Variable    Field: cabnum    Type: TEXT    Table: cab
```

Figure 10.4 Customizing a Field for an *R:base System V* Screen Form

1. Move the cursor to the left-most position of the area on the screen which will be set aside for the field.
2. Press [F6] (function key #6).
3. *R:base System V* prints a prompt at the top left of the screen:

   Enter column or variable name:

   Type either the name of an attribute in the base table or the name of a variable. Press [ENTER].
4. *R:base* prompts:

   Do you want to define an expression?

   Expressions are used to define global and lookup variables (examples can be found in the following section and in the section on reports, which use expressions in an identical manner). Since entering data into CAB requires no computations or lookups, each field will be the name of a column in the base table. No expressions will be used.

```
                              Cab Entry


    Cab number: S  E     Make: S            E    Model: S            E

    Year: SE             Purchase date: S ·      E

    License number: S       E

    Summary of cab's condition:

       S                        E

    Status ("t" = road-safe; "f" = not road-safe): E

    Current odometer reading: S    E



 [ESC] Return   [F3] Review   [F7] Prev Table   [F8] Next Table   [F1Ø] Help
 Form: cabntry                       Table: cab
```

Figure 10.5 The Cab Entry Form After All Fields Have Been Placed

     5. *R:base* prompts:

Do you want to customize the field characteristics?

An answer of yes will bring up the screen shown in Figure 10.4. This allows the designer to set default values, control whether a field can be updated, set custom colors, and so on.

6. Mark the starting position of the field on the screen by pressing **S**.

7. Mark the ending position of the field on the screen by pressing **E**.

Repeat steps one through seven for each field that is to be located on the form. Use [F8] to move to another table.

    After all fields have been located, the cab entry form appears as in Figure 10.6. Each field position corresponds to a column in a base table.

    To save the form, press [ESC] to redisplay the Forms Definition menu. Press [ESC] again and select **Save Changes**. If at a later time you wish to modify the form in some way, it can be recalled using:

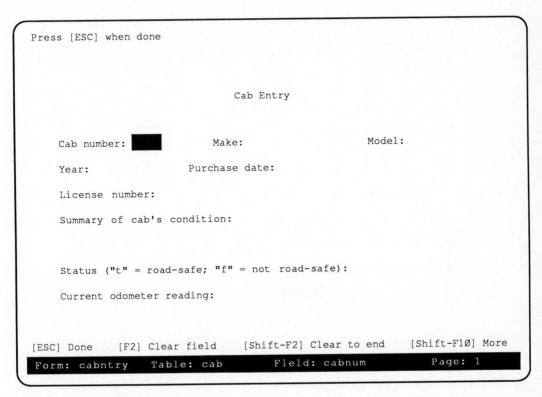

```
Press [ESC] when done



                            Cab Entry



     Cab number: ███████       Make:              Model:

     Year:              Purchase date:

     License number:

     Summary of cab's condition:



     Status ("t" = road-safe; "f" = not road-safe):

     Current odometer reading:


 [ESC] Done     [F2] Clear field     [Shift-F2] Clear to end    [Shift-F1Ø] More
  Form: cabntry     Table: cab        Field: cabnum          Page: 1
```

Figure 10.6 Using the Cab Entry Form

R> **FORMS form-name**

To use this form for data entry, type:

R> **ENTER USING form-name**

The form will appear on the screen along with the message "Press [ESC] when done" (Figure 10.6). This message is supplied by *R:base System V* to let the user know that only the ESC key will cause data entry. The RETURN and TAB keys can be used to move between data entry positions on the screen.

If no rules are violated, the ESC key will load the data into the appropriate table, clear the screen, and prepare to accept data for another row. However, if a rule is violated, *R:base System V* will print the rule at the top of the screen and not store the data. If more than one rule has been violated, only the message from the first one (i.e., the one with the lowest rule number) will be printed. For example, Figure 10.7 shows the cab entry screen after an attempt to enter a duplicate cab number.

```
┌─────────────────────────────────────────────────────────────────────┐
│  -ERROR- Duplicate cab number                    - Press [ESC] when corrected │
│                                                                       │
│                                                                       │
│                             Cab Entry                                 │
│                                                                       │
│                                                                       │
│      Cab number: 104      Make: Ford                Model: LTD        │
│                                                                       │
│      Year: 86             Purchase date: 10/31/86                     │
│                                                                       │
│      License number:  333 YOW                                         │
│                                                                       │
│      Summary of cab's condition:                                      │
│                                                                       │
│          Excellent; under warranty                                    │
│                                                                       │
│      Status ("t" = road-safe; "f" = not road-safe): t                 │
│                                                                       │
│      Current odometer reading:  15006                                 │
│                                                                       │
│                                                                       │
│   [ESC] Done    [F2] Clear field    [Shift-F2] Clear to end    [Shift-F1Ø] More │
│   Form: cabntry    Table: cab        Field: cabnum          Page: 1   │
└─────────────────────────────────────────────────────────────────────┘
```

Figure 10.7   Violation of an Integrity Rule When Using the Cab Entry Form

DATA RETRIEVAL

R:base System V supports three major ways to retrieve data:

1. Using the **SELECT** command to retrieve data from a single table based on a logical criteria. (**Beware:** this is a *retrieval command* and does not work exactly like a relational Select!) The result of a **SELECT** is a table that can be displayed on the screen or printed to obtain hard copy. **SELECT** is often combined with relational operations (e.g., **INTERSECT** or **JOIN**) in order to complete a query.
2. Using the **SET VAR** command qualified by a logical condition to assign a single value from a table to a variable.
3. Creating reports with *R:base System V*'s built-in report generator to produce batch output to either the screen or the printer.

By default, all *R:base System V* output is sent to the computer screen. To get hard copy, precede any output command with:

output printer

The result of any command issued after that point will be sent to the current primary printer (the LPT1: device). If **output printer** is issued from within a program, a message instructing the user to turn on the printer is usually a good idea, since the computer may "hang" if the printer isn't turned on when data are sent to it.

To return output to the screen, use:

output terminal

USING SELECT

SELECT is *R:base System V*'s primary retrieval tool. Like the relational algebra select, it extracts rows from a single table based on a logical criteria. However, the *R:base System V* **SELECT** also performs a projection, since it allows the user to specify which columns from the table should be included in the result. In fact, **SELECT** works very much like an operation from the relational calculus, since it performs several relational algebra operations with a single command. The table that is produced by **SELECT** is not a virtual table; it is displayed but not retained in main memory. The table can also be sorted on one or more attributes before display.

SELECT can be issued interactively or from within an application program. The general form of the command is:

SELECT attribute-list FROM table-name SORTED BY   +
**   attribute-list WHERE logical-condition**

The **SORTED BY** and **WHERE** clauses are optional. However, if no **WHERE** clause is included, every tuple in the table will be displayed.

The **WHERE** clause can contain any sort of logical condition as long as it applies to only one table. For example, the **SELECT** command:

R> SELECT drvnam FROM driver WHERE drvnum > "0015"

is acceptable, since the retrieval is based on the attribute **drvnum**, which is a part of the DRIVER relation.

Several conditions can can be linked together with the Boolean operators AND and OR:

R> SELECT drvnum FROM shifts WHERE wkflag = "f" AND   +
**   wkdate = .mdate**

This **SELECT** will display the driver number for all drivers who haven't driven their reserved shift on the date contained in the variable **mdate**. Note that the variable is used in its dotted form, indicating that this command appears *R:base* command file. A **FILLIN** command has been used to accept the date from the keyboard.

WHERE clauses can compare attributes to constants (e.g., **wkflag = "f"**), to the contents of variables (e.g., **wkdate = .mdate**), or to other attributes (e.g., **odomrdg1 >A odomrdg2**). Comparisons of two attributes require a special set of operators; the standard logical operators must be followed by the letter A.

SELECT formats its own output, complete with column headings. Text attributes which are too long to fit across an 80-column screen will be "wrapped." For example, Figure 10.8 shows the screen display produced by the command:

SELECT drvnum, drvnam, drvphone, drvstat FROM driver

This command is an easy way to create a Driver Roster. A printed copy can be obtained simply by changing the output destination from the terminal to the printer.

drvnum	drvnam	drvphone	drvstat
0001	Bailey, Max	000-000-0001	pay before
0002	Baker, Mary Ann	000-000-0002	pay after
0003	Lewis, John	000-000-0003	pay after
0004	Santiago, Jorge	000-000-0004	pay after
0005	Miller, Pat	000-000-0005	pay after
0006	Miller, Phyllis	000-000-0006	pay before
0007	Phong, Quen	000-000-0007	pay after
0008	Wong, David	000-000-0008	pay after
0009	Young, Leslie	000-000-0009	pay after
0010	Zilog, Charlie	000-000-0010	pay after
0011	Erlich, Martin	000-000-0011	pay before
0012	Eastman, Richard	000-000-0012	do not reserve
0013	Kowalski, Pete	000-000-0013	pay before
0014	Mariott, Emily	000-000-0014	do not reserve
0015	French, Janice	000-000-0015	pay after
0016	Thieu, Lin Van	000-000-0016	pay after
0017	Jackson, Rafael	000-000-0017	pay before
0018	Wilson, Carter	000-000-0018	do not reserve
0019	Kolson, Jan	000-000-0019	pay before
0020	Abelman, John	000-000-0020	pay before

Figure 10.8 The Result of: SELECT drvnum, drvnam, drvphone, drvstat FROM driver

As powerful as **SELECT** might be, it does have one major limitation. The following **SELECT** (an attempt to retrieve the names and phone numbers of all drivers who haven't driven a shift on a given day) will *not* work:

> **SELECT drvnam, drvphone FROM driver WHERE drvnum IN   +**
> **driver =A drvnum IN shifts AND wkflag IN shifts = "f" AND +**
> **wkdate IN shifts = .mdate**

SELECT will not perform cross-table lookups; the **WHERE** clause will not accept the qualifier **IN** to indicate that *R:base System V* should consult another table. This is the major difference between *R:base*'s **SELECT** command and the SQL **SELECT**. The *R:base* **SELECT** also cannot handle subqueries.

This limitation to the **SELECT** command can be handled by explicitly performing the relational operations needed to bring all the attributes required by a query into a single table. Though *R:base System V* supports a number of relational operations, the **INTERSECT** command is the most widely used. This command is *not* the same as the relational algebra operation intersect; it is a natural join! In its simplest general form, **INTERSECT** appears as:

> **INTERSECT relation1 WITH relation2 FORMING new-relation**

INTERSECT will automatically look for overlapping columns in the two relations and base the join on matching values in those columns. The matching columns will not be duplicated in the result. When used in this way, **INTERSECT** is a true relational natural join.

Implementing the query which attempts to retrieve the names of all drivers who have not shown up for their scheduled shifts on a given date therefore becomes:

> **INTERSECT driver WITH shifts FORMING temp**
> **SELECT drvnam, drvphone FROM temp WHERE wkflag = "f"   +**
> **AND wkdate = .mdate**
> **REMOVE temp**

The **REMOVE** command is used to delete the temporary table created by the **INTERSECT**. Tables created by **INTERSECT** are not virtual tables; they are created and stored as base tables (i.e., copies are made of all data and stored on disk). If temporary tables are not removed after they are used, the disk and data dictionary soon become clogged with them.

R:base System V 's **JOIN** command permits two tables to be joined on some basis other than matching values in overlapping columns. In other words, it performs joins other than the natural join performed by **INTERSECT**. The general form of **JOIN** is:

> **JOIN relation1 USING attrbute1 WITH relation2 USING   +**
> **attribute2 FORMING new-relation WHERE logical-condition**

The logical condition following **WHERE** specifies the relationship between the two attributes, which qualifies tuples for inclusion in the new table. While no Booleans (AND, OR) can be used to create a multiple condition, the relationships may be EQ (equal to, the default, which is assumed if **WHERE** is missing), GT (greater than), LT (less than), GE (greater than or equal to), LE (less than or equal to), or NE (not equal to).

R:base System V also supports a **PROJECT** command which acts as both a relational project and select:

> **PROJECT new-table FROM existing-table USING   +**
> **attribute-list SORTED BY attribute-list WHERE   +**
> **logical-condition**

The **SORTED BY** and **WHERE** clauses are optional. If no **WHERE** clause is present, all tuples from the original table will be included in the result.

PROJECT can be combined with *R:base's* **SUBTRACT** command to produce the cab availability screen (i.e., a listing of all cabs not reserved for a given date and shift). This type of output is always difficult, since it requires the listing of something which *isn't* present in a table (i.e., cab numbers in SHIFTS), rather than something that is.   **SUBTRACT** is similar to the relational algebra operation difference. It produces a resulting table that contains all tuples from one relation that are not in a second relation. However, the tuple matching is based on overlapping columns between the two tables. In other words, the relations do not have to be union compatible; they need only share at least one attribute. Like **INTERSECT**, **SUBTRACT** automatically looks for overlapping columns between the two relations. The general form of the command is:

> **SUBTRACT relation1 FROM relation2 FORMING new-relation**

The cab availability code could therefore be rewritten as:

> **PROJECT temp1 FROM shifts USING cabnum WHERE   +**
> **wkdate =   .mdate AND wkshift = .mshift**
> **SUBTRACT temp1 FROM cab FORMING temp2**
> **SELECT cabnum FROM temp2**
> **REMOVE temp1**
> **REMOVE temp2**

The first table listed is subtracted from the second table. Therefore, the second table should be the larger of the two, the one from which the "not equal" tuples should be pulled.

USING SET VAR

The **SET VAR** command is *R :base System V*'s way of assigning values to variables. It can be used to retrieve a single data value from an existing table for use within an application program. The general form of the command is:

> SET VAR variable-name TO attribute-name IN table-name +
>   WHERE primary-key-expression

For example,

> SET VAR cab TO cabnum IN shifts WHERE wkdate = '86/07/16' +
>   AND wkshift = "day" AND drvnum = "0010'

will retrieve the cab number for the cab which driver 0010 is scheduled to drive on July 16th.

While *R:base System V* will accept any logical expression following **WHERE**, **SET VAR** will perform reliably only if the expression specifies a primary key value. If it does not, there is no assurance that only one tuple will satisfy the expression. The variable can only hold one value at a time; it will be given the *first* value that meets the required conditions. Therefore, if the logical expression does not uniquely identify a single tuple, there is no way to be sure that the retrieval has located the correct value. For example,

> SET VAR cab TO cabnum IN shifts WHERE drvnum = "0010"

will assign a cab number to the variable **cab** for the first shift present for driver 0010 in SHIFTS. To obtain data about a single shift, the **WHERE** clause must include all parts of the primary key.

USING THE BUILT-IN REPORT GENERATOR

R:base System V's report generator, with its ability to do an unlimited number of lookups into tables other than the one on which the report is being created, can be used to create relatively complex output such as the driver summary report (the *R:base System V* version appears in Figure 10.9; shifts in the sample data which have not been driven have a Miles column figure of 0). Report formats are stored in a table called REPORTS, which can be queried with a **SELECT**. Entry and modification of REPORTS, however, should be made through the report generator.

The report generator, *Reports EXPRESS*, is invoked with:

> REPORTS report-name table-name

Reports EXPRESS is in many ways similar to *Forms EXPRESS*. If no database is open when *Reports EXPRESS* is invoked, you will be prompted to select one. If **report-name** is an existing report, *R:base System V* presents it for editing. Otherwise, the program assumes that you wish to define a new report format. Each report format is based on a single table or view, though data from other tables may be pulled in with lookup variables where needed. If no report or table name is present in the **REPORTS** command, *Reports EXPRESS* will prompt for them.

```
                        Weekly Driver Summary Report

Driver                    Date         Cab    Shift    Miles    Comments
-----------------------   -----------  ---    -----    -----    --------
0001 Bailey, Max          07/15/86     104    eve      134
                          07/16/86     104    eve      0
                          07/17/86     104    eve      0

0002 Baker, Mary Ann      07/15/86     108    ngt      15
                          07/17/86     108    ngt      0
                          07/18/86     108    ngt      0

0003 Lewis, John          07/19/86     238    eve      0
                          07/20/86     238    eve      0

0004 Santiago, Jorge      07/16/86     002    eve      0
                          07/18/86     002    eve      0

0006 Miller, Phyllis      07/15/86     104    day      149      Ticket
                          07/16/86     104    day      0
                          07/17/86     104    day      0
                          07/18/86     104    day      0
                          07/18/86     104    day      0
                          07/19/86     104    day      0

0007 Phong, Quen          07/16/86     002    ngt      0

0008 Wong, David          07/15/86     215    ngt      148      Ticket
                          07/18/86     215    ngt      0

0010 Zilog, Charlie       07/15/86     238    day      139
                          07/16/86     238    day      0
                          07/17/86     238    day      0
                          07/18/86     238    day      0

0011 Erlich, Martin       07/15/86     045    eve      0
                          07/18/86     045    eve      0

0012 Eastman, Richard     07/15/86     144    day      188      Accident

0016 Thieu, Lin Van       07/15/86     045    ngt      360
                          07/18/86     045    ngt      0

0020 Abelman, John        07/15/86     404    day      154
                          07/16/86     404    day      0
                          07/17/86     404    day      0
```

Figure 10.9 The *R:base System V* Version of the Driver Summary Report

The *Reports EXPRESS* main screen (Figure 10.10) makes the following actions possible:

1. **Edit**—placing page and column headings and footings as well as fields on the page
2. **Expression**—defining variables to hold both data that should be looked up in other tables and values that should be derived from data stored in tables
3. **Configure**—defining report characteristics and breakpoints
4. **Draw**—drawing borders on the report

Reports are made up of up to seven sections:

1. Report header (abbreviation RH): printed once at the start of the report. There is only one RH section per report.
2. Page header (abbreviation PH): printed once at the start of each page. Page headers are generally used to give headings to columns of data or to print page numbers. There is only one PH section per report.

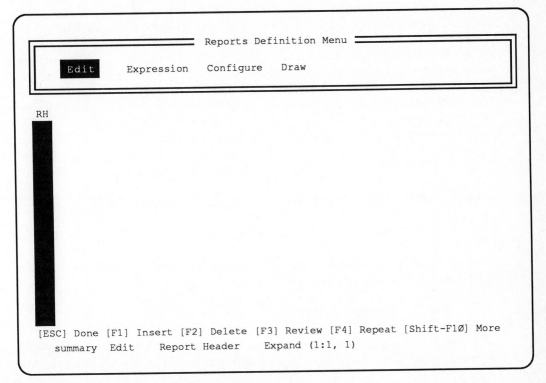

Figure 10.10 The *Reports EXPRESS* Definition Screen

3. Break header (abbreviation H#): printed once for each breakpoint value. Multiple, nested breakpoints are permitted. The # in the abbreviation is replaced with the number of the breakpoint.
4. Detail (abbreviation D): printed once for each set of data values. Detail lines form the body of a report.
5. Break footer (abbreviation F#): printed once for each breakpoint value
6. Page footer (abbreviation PF): printed once at the bottom of each page
7. Report footer (abbreviation RF): printed once at the end of the report

The section to which a line on the Report Definition belongs is indicated by the abbreviation that appears at the far left of the screen. (The area in inverse video is known as the *mark* area.) When a new form is created, as in Figure 10.10, the report header section is active.

When the expand mode is on (the word Expand appears in the bottom line of the screen, as in Figure 10.10), directional movements—the ENTER key or the cursor keys— add lines to the section. [F7] and [F8] move to the previous and next section, respectively. When the Expand mode is toggled off with [F9], directional movements move between sections without expanding them. [F7] and [F8] can still be used to move between sections.

Text, attributes, and variables are placed on the form just as they are when defining data entry forms. To locate text, move the cursor to the starting position and type. To locate attributes or variables, move the cursor to the starting position and press [F6].

Since the Driver Summary report uses data from other tables and must also compute the number of miles driven during a given shift, variables are required. When you enter something that isn't the name of an attribute in the table or view on which the report is defined, *Reports EXPRESS* assumes that it's a variable. An equal sign will appear to the right of the variable name, after which you should enter an expression that defines the contents of the variable.

Local variables, those for use in this report, are defined as:

variable-name = arithmetic-or-string-expression

Lookup variables, which pull in data from another table or view, are defined as:

variable-name = attribute IN table-name WHERE logical-condition

For example, if the variable **miles** is used to hold the number of miles driven during a given shift, its definition might be given as:

miles = odomrdg2 - odomrdg1

The problem with this formula is that it is accurate for shifts that haven't been driven (i.e., it produces a result of 0), but it is inaccurate for shifts that have been driven (i.e., a 1 should be added to the result).   To correct this situation, use one of *R:base System V*'s logical functions. These work very much like IF statements in a spreadsheet. For example:

miles = IFEQ(odomrdg1,odomrdg2,0,odomrdg2 - odomrdg1 + 1)

is the same as:

IF odomrdg1 = odomrdg2 THEN
miles = 0
ELSE
miles = odomrdg2 - odomrdg1 + 1
ENDIF

A driver's name can be retrieved with:

dname = drvnam IN driver WHERE drvnum = drvnum

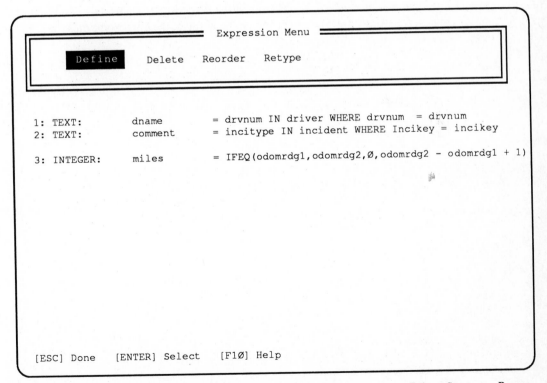

Figure 10.11 Variables Used to Create the *R:base System V* Version of the Driver Summary Report

The first **drvnum** in the **WHERE** clause refers to an attribute in **driver**, the second to an attribute in the table on which the report is being created. Using the same format, the type of incident reported for a given shift is retrieved with:

comment = incitype IN incident WHERE incikey = shiftkey

If no incident exists for a given shift, **comment** will be set to null.

Variables defined for a particular report can use data from other variables defined for that same report. However, variables used in expressions to define other variables must have been defined *before* they are used on the right-hand side of the equals sign in a variable definition expression.

Variables can also be defined by selecting the **Expression** option from the Report Definition menu. The Expression screen, seen in Figure 10.11 with all of the variables needed for the Driver Summary report, can also be used to view a variable summary.

The completed report format, with all text, attributes and variables placed appears in Figure 10.12. The report has two report header lines, three page header lines, and three page footer lines (all blank). Since the detail line data (data about a single cab driven on one date in a single shift) are grouped by driver, this report also has a breakpoint. The breakpoint header line contains the name of the driver, and the detail line contains data describing the shift. However, before a breakpoint header can be defined, the breakpoint must be configured.

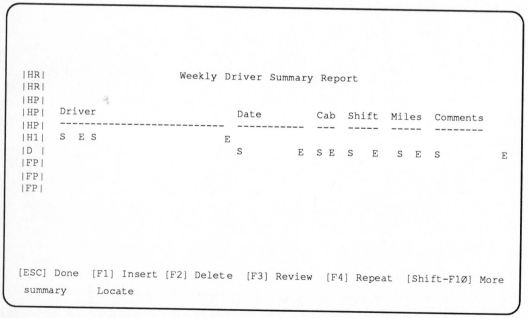

Figure 10.12 The Completed Driver Summary Report Layout

To configure a breakpoint, select **Configure** from the Report Definition menu. The configuration screen, seen in Figure 10.13, is used to specify up to ten nested breakpoints. The variable reset option should be changed to YES if the report contains variables for group subtotals. When the report is printed, the table or view on which it is based will be sorted on the breakpoint fields. This same configuration screen can also be used to control page ejects, the number of lines per page, and so on.

Break headers and footers can be used to print subtotals. Report footers can hold report totals. Assume, for example, that the Driver Summary report is being expanded to include the total miles driven by each driver during the report period and an overall total of all miles driven. Doing so requires defining two new variables, one for the subtotal and one for the overall total:

subtotal = **SUM(miles)**   ; subtotal variable
total = **SUM(miles)**   ; overall total

Though the definition of the two variables is identical, **subtotal** will be reset for each driver, and **total** will accumulate over the entire report. Both of these variables cannot be defined until after **miles** has been defined.

```
Lines Per Page . . . . . . . . . : 6Ø
Remove Initial Carriage Return . : [NO]
Manual Break Reset . . . . . . . : [NO]
Page Footer Line Number. . . . . : [ Ø]

              BREAKPOINTS                         FORM FEEDS
          Break     Variable          Header                  Footer
          Column    Reset         Before    After    Before    After

Report                              [NO]     [NO]     [NO]      [NO]
Page                  [NO]
Break1    drvnum      [NO]          [NO]
Break2    [NONE]      [NO]          [NO]
Break3    [NONE]      [NO]          [NO]
Break4    [NONE]      [NO]          [NO]
Break5    [NONE]      [NO]          [NO]
Break6    [NONE]      [NO]          [NO]
Break7    [NONE]      [NO]          [NO]
Break8    [NONE]      [NO]          [NO]
Break9    [NONE]      [NO]          [NO]
Break1Ø   [NONE]      [NO]          [NO]
```

Figure 10.13 Setting a Breakpoint from the Configuration File

The presence of a subtotal changes the definition of the breakpoint. In Figure 10.14, you will see that variables should be reset after each driver. (This was not essential with the first version of the report.) Changing Reset Variables from NO to YES does not automatically reset all variables. (If it did, there would be no way to obtain report totals.) Instead, you will be asked to select exactly which variables should be reset. In this case, it will be **subtotal**.

The Report Definition screen also changes. Figure 10.15 now shows a break footer line (F1) and a report footer line (RF), each of which contains data.

The finished report is printed by typing:

R> **PRINT summary WHERE wkdate >= '86/07/15' AND   +**
   wkdate <= '86/07/21'

If used within an application program, the starting and ending dates for the report can be entered by the user from the keyboard. A subroutine to accept the dates and to choose between screen and printer output appears in Listing 10.2. Note that this subroutine sets null to a blank before printing so that nothing will appear in the **Comments** column if no incident was recorded for any given shift.

```
Lines Per Page . . . . . . . . . : 60
Remove Initial Carriage Return . : [NO]
Manual Break Reset . . . . . . . : [NO]
Page Footer Line Number. . . . . : [ 0]

                BREAKPOINTS                      FORM FEEDS
             Break     Variable         Header              Footer
             Column    Reset      Before    After    Before    After

Report                             [NO]     [NO]      [NO]      [NO]
Page                   [NO]
Break1       drvnum    [YES]       [NO]
Break2       [NONE]    [NO]        [NO]
Break3       [NONE]    [NO]        [NO]
Break4       [NONE]    [NO]        [NO]
Break5       [NONE]    [NO]        [NO]
Break6       [NONE]    [NO]        [NO]
Break7       [NONE]    [NO]        [NO]
Break8       [NONE]    [NO]        [NO]
Break9       [NONE]    [NO]        [NO]
Break10      [NONE]    [NO]        [NO]
```

Figure 10.14 Making Sure Variables Are Reset When Computing Subtotals

```
|HR|                       Weekly Driver Summary Report
|HR|
|HP|
|HP|   Driver                           Date        Cab  Shift  Miles  Comments
|HP|
|H1|   -------------------------     -----------   ---  -----  -----  --------
|D |   S  E  S                    E
|F1|                              S           E  S E  S   E   S E  S             E
|FP|                                             Total:     S  E
|FP|
|FP|
|FR|                                            Total:  S    E



[ESC] Done  [F1] Insert [F2] Delete [F3] Review  [F4] Repeat  [Shift-F1Ø] More
   summary      Locate
```

Figure 10.15 The Driver Summary Report with Subtotals and a Total

DEFINING AND USING VIEWS

R:base System V implements user views as virtual tables. View definitions are stored in two system tables: VIEWS, which contains the columns included in views, and VIEWCOND, which contains any WHERE conditions applied to the view definitions. Views that are defined as a subset of a single base table can be updated, though new rows cannot be added. Views created from multiple base tables are not updatable in any way, but can be used for data retrieval. Any given view can contain data from up to five tables.

Since views created from multiple base tables cannot be updated, it may not be clear that they are at all useful. However, if often-used queries require data from multiple tables, you can save considerable time and effort by defining a view that assembles the needed data rather than explicitly performing a join to create a temporary table (a physical entity) each time the query is issued. The SELECT can be then performed on the view rather than the joined, temporary table.

To create a view, use the command:

VIEW view_name WITH attribute-list FROM table-list   +
      WHERE logical-condition

```
NEWPAGE
FILLIN StartDate USING "Starting date for Driver Summary Report: " AT 5 5
FILLIN EndDate USING "Ending date for Driver Summary Report:" AT 8 5
FILLIN dest USING "Send report to printer (P) or screen (S)?" AT 15 5
IF dest = "P" OR dest = "p" THEN
  OUTPUT PRINTER
ELSE
  NEWPAGE
ENDIF
PRINT summary WHERE wkdate <= .StartDate AND wkdate <= .EndDate
IF dest = "P" OR dest = "p" THEN
  OUTPUT TERMINAL
ENDIF
RETURN
```

Listing 10.2 An *R:base System V* Subroutine to Print a Report

For example, assume that FTC wishes to create a view that will contain the names and phone numbers of all drivers who haven't reported for a reserved shift:

VIEW NoShows WITH drvnum drvnam drvphone wkdate wkshift   +
FROM driver shifts WHERE wkflag = 'f'

This view can be queried in the same way that a base table is queried:

SELECT drvnam drvphone FROM NoShows WHERE wkdate =
'86/07/15' and wkshift = 'eve'

Note that the attribute DRVNUM does not appear anywhere in the query. It is essential, however, in the view definition. When a view defined on multiple tables is invoked, *R:base System V* will execute a join to create the view. In order to implement the join, one or more overlapping columns between the multiple tables must be present in the view definition.

EXERCISES

The complete database for the office of Margaret Holmes, D.M.D., is comprised of the following set of third normal form relations:

PATIENT-MASTER (PATIENT#, NAME, ADDRESS, PHONE, SSN,
    WHO-PAYS, REL-TO-WHO-PAYS, PAYMENT-SOURCE)
PAYERS (WHO-PAYS, HOME-ADDRESS, HOME-PHONE, PLACE-OF-
    EMPLOYMENT, WORK-PHONE, INSURANCE-CARRIER)
APPOINTMENTS (PATIENT#, APPT-DATE, APPT-TIME, APPT-FLAG)
VISITS (PATIENT#, DATE, PROCEDURE, COMMENTS)
COSTS (PROCEDURE, PRICE)
INCOME (PATIENT#, PAY-DATE, SOURCE, AMT, WHO-PAYS)
LEDGER (WHO-PAYS, TOTAL-AMT-OWED)
INV-MAST (ITEM#, ITEM-DESCR, REORDER-PT, REORD-QTY, CUR-
    RENT-INV)
ORDERS (P-O#, DATE, VENDOR, TOTAL-AMT)
VENDORS (VNAME, VADDRESS, VPHONE, CONTACT-PERSON)
LINE-ITEMS (P-O#, ITEM#, QTY, UNIT-COST, TOTAL-COST)
OWED (VENDOR, AMT-OWED)
PAYMENTS (VENDOR, CHECK-DATE, CHECK#, AMT-PAID)

1. Consider the 3NF relations listed above. What extra attributes must be added to which relations so that a complete set of integrity rules can be specified in an *R:base System V* implementation?

2. Install the schema with *R:base System V*.
    a. Change relation and attribute names as necessary to meet the *R:base System V* rules.
    b. Create indexes on all primary keys

3. Define rules to enforce integrity constraints. The complete set of rules should verify that primary keys are nonnull, that primary keys are unique, and that all foreign key values reference existing primary keys.

4. Design a data entry form to handle the entry of a new person into PAYERS. Is a program required to use this form? Why or why not? If not, what command will initiate the data entry process?

5. Design a data entry form to handle the entry of a new patient. (Don't forget the foreign key reference to WHO-PAYS.) Then write a short program that will use the form and enter data into the PATIENT-MASTER relation.

6. Formulate the *R:base System V* syntax necessary to answer the following requests for information:

    a. Given a patient number, identify the person responsible for paying that patient's bills.

    b. Given a patient number, display the patient's dental history (all visits present in the database for that patient).

    c. List the names and phone numbers of all patients who didn't keep their appointments (APPT-FLAG = "f").

    d. Given a patient name, display the patient's dental history.

    e. Display the item number and description of all inventory items that need to be reordered (i.e., the quantity on hand is less than the reorder point).

    f. Given a purchase order number, display the name and address of the vendor to whom the purchase order was issued.

    g. Given a purchase order number, display the items numbers, the item descriptions, the quantity ordered, and the unit cost for each item on the order.

7. Create a report to display the current contents of the dental office's supply inventory. For each item in the inventory, include:

    a. The item number

    b. The item description

    c. The quantity on hand

    d. The reorder point

8. Create a report that will show payments made to vendors of a specified period of time. (The period of time is specified in the command that prints the report.) The report should include:

    a. The name of each vendor

    b. The date, check number, and amount of each payment made to each vendor

    c. A subtotal of payments made to each vendor

    d. The total amount paid to all vendors

9. Create a report that print statements of patient accounts. The report should include the following for each patient:

    a. A heading containing the patient's name and address

    b. For each procedure performed on the patient, a listing of the date of the procedure, the type of procedure, and the cost of the procedure

    c. The total amount owed for all procedures performed

    Since statements are printed and mailed monthly, how should the report be printed to restrict the data in the report to a single month?

11

dBase III Plus

CHAPTER OUTLINE:

CHAPTER OBJECTIVES:

After reading this chapter, you will:

1. Be able to install a relational schema using *dBase III Plus*
2. Understand the techniques needed to enforce integrity and key constraints
3. Be able to retrieve data from a *dBase III Plus* database

TERMINOLOGY

Like most microcomputer database packages, *dBase III Plus* does not have the same names for objects within the database environment as those found in relational theory. The major differences are as follows:

1. Each relation is implemented as a single physical file and is called a *database file*.
2. Attributes are known as *fields*.
3. Tuples are known as *records*.

dBase III Plus also supports views and catalogs. While most of what is discussed in this chapter applies to *dBase III* as well as *dBase III Plus*, views and catalogs are unique to the latter package.

A *dBase III Plus* catalog is not the same as the catalogs described in relational theory. It is a database file with a fixed structure (see Table 11.1) that contains data to group together all the physical files that support a single database. Any file that is created or used while a catalog is open is automatically added to the catalog if it is not already a member. Relational catalogs, however, contain data about attributes, their characteristics, and the relationships between them; *dBase III Plus* catalogs deal only with files.

dBase III Plus views are similar in concept to the views described in relational theory. A view captures database files, indexes, filters (to define which fields in the database files should be available to the user), and relationships between the database files. Any given catalog can support a theoretically infinite number of views created from the same database, limited only by disk space and the upper limit on the number of records that can appear in a database file.

Table 11.1
Structure of a dBase III Plus Catalog File

Field	Field Name	Type	Width	Dec	Comments
1	PATH	char	70		Disk directory where file is located
2	FILE_NAME	char	12		File name including extension
3	ALIAS	char	8		Default is file name minus extension, though user can modify
4	TYPE	char	3		Same as file extension
5	TITLE	char	80		User supplied for database, format, report, and view files; key expression for index files
6	CODE	num	3	0	Assigned by *dBase* to group index, reports, and formats created from the same database file
7	TAG	char	4		Unused by *dBase*; user may insert comments

THE DBASE III PLUS PROGRAMMING LANGUAGE

In order to enforce database integrity and provide a turnkey system for casual and/or unsophisticated users, a developer working with *dBase III Plus* must write programs using the programming language supplied with the package. Therefore, this section contains an introduction to that language so that you can read the sample programs that accompany the rest of this chapter. If you are already familiar with the *dBase III Plus* programming language, you can easily skip this section.

During the development process, *dBase III Plus* programs are run under an *interpreter*, which translates the program into a form the computer can understand line-by-line from the source code file as the program is being run. Once the developer is certain that the programs aren't likely to change, they can be *compiled*. Compilers, available from several different independent vendors, permanently translate the program into machine-executable form (binary). Compiled programs run much faster than interpreted programs. They are also more secure, since users have no access to source code but only to the compiled, binary version of the program.

dBase III Plus programs are little more than a series of interactive *dBase III Plus* commands (those that can be entered at the dot prompt) embedded in control statements that determine when and how the commands will be executed. They also include special commands for painting the screen and reading data from the keyboard.

dBase III Plus provides a text editor for entering program code; it is invoked with the command:

.MODIFY COMMAND prog_name

Each program is stored as a separate physical file; the file name is given a **.PRG** extension. They are run with the command **DO**, which can be issued from the dot prompt or from within a program. That means that programs can run other programs. Therefore, *dBase III Plus* programs generally consist of many small **.PRG** files, referred to as *modules*, each of which performs a single program function. For example, the code that prints an application program's main menu will be in one module; code to enter data into relations will require one module per relation; each report will be printed by a separate module. Designing programs in this way makes them easier to develop, debug, and modify.

VARIABLES

Like other high-level programming languages, the *dBase III Plus* language uses variables. *dBase III Plus* refers to them as *memory variables* to distinguish them from fields.

Memory variables must be initialized before they can be used. That means that they must be assigned a value. For example,

mName = SPACE(30)

initializes a memory variable called **mName** that will contain a maximum of 30 characters. Memory variables that are first assigned a character value can only contain text. Their maximum length is equal to the length of the string first assigned to them. Memory variables that will hold data for logical and date fields should be initialized as character variables. (Dates can be converted with **CTOD()** when necessary.)

Memory variables that are designed to hold computational quantities are defined by giving them initial numeric values.

mQuantity = 0.0

sets aside a memory variable that will contain a real number with one place to the right of the decimal point.

mQuantity = 0

establishes a memory variable to hold an integer.

The use of memory variables presents a small problem when using **FIND**. The **FIND** command works without quotes around the index key value that *dBase III Plus* is to use in the search. How then, can *dBase III Plus* recognize that

FIND mName

is an instruction to search using the contents of the memory variable **mName** rather than the characters mName? If you preface a memory variable with **&**, as in

FIND &mName

dBase III Plus will use the contents of the memory variable rather than the characters in its name. This is what *dBase III Plus* calls *macro substitution*, and should not be confused with keyboard macros as supported by many spreadsheet packages. Although it is possible to assign a series of commands to a memory variable and then invokes them by placing an **&** in front of the variable, there is no easy way to assign that string of commands to a key sequence.

Because using **FIND** with memory variables is a bit clumsy, *dBase III Plus* also provides the **SEEK** command. **SEEK** works exactly like **FIND**; however, it assumes that a string of characters not surrounded by quotes is a memory variable and no **&** is needed. To get **SEEK** to use an explicit string of characters in an index search, surround the characters in quotes.

CONTROL STRUCTURES

As with other high-level language programs, *dBase III Plus* programs execute statements in sequence, beginning with the first, and moving from statement to statement, unless given instructions to do otherwise. There are four distinct ways to "do otherwise":

1. Use **DO** to execute another program
2. Use **IF/ELSE/ENDIF** to choose between two sets of possible actions
3. Use **DO CASE/ENDCASE** to choose between many sets of possible actions
4. Use **DO WHILE** to repeat actions

There is one significant omission from the list above—there is no GOTO. The *dBase III Plus* command **GOTO** refers only to moving the record pointer. It cannot be used to transfer control within a program.

Both **IF/ELSE/ENDIF** and **DO CASE/ENDCASE** are examples of program control structures that permit the selection of alternative actions based on some value. Assume, for example, that a program has been instructed to use an index to search for some value:

```
SEEK  mKey
IF  FOUND()
    ? mKey+" is in the database"
ELSE
    ? mKey+" is not in the database"
ENDIF
```

An **IF** statement first evaluates the expression following **IF**. (The function **FOUND()** will be true if the **SEEK** was successful; it will be false if the value stored in **mKey** was not present in the database file.) If the expression is true, then the statements between **IF** and **ELSE** will be executed; the statements after **ELSE** will be skipped and the program continues with whatever follows **ENDIF**. However, if the expression is false, the statements between **IF** and **ELSE** are skipped and the program executes those between **ELSE** and **ENDIF**, also continuing with the statements after **ENDIF**.

Any logical expression can follow **IF**. Any executable statements can appear between **IF** and **ELSE** as well as between **ELSE** and **ENDIF**, even other **IF/ELSE/ENDIF** structures. The **ELSE** portion of the structure is not required. If there is only one alternative, one that should be executed if the expression after **IF** is true, then the structure may be written as:

```
IF  FOUND()
    ? mKey " is present in the database"
ENDIF
```

DO CASE/ENDCASE is an extension of **IF/ELSE/ENDIF** that simplifies the task of selecting between multiple alternatives. Assume, for example, that you have created a menu for your users that presents them with five different alternatives. The selected alternative is stored in the memory variable **choice**. Code to select between them and take the appropriate action might be written as:

```
DO CASE
    CASE choice = 1
        DO program1
    CASE choice = 2
        DO program2
    CASE choice = 3
        DO program3
    CASE choice = 4
        DO program4
    CASE choice = 5
        EXIT
    OTHERWISE
        ? "That wasn't one of your choices.  Try again, please."
ENDCASE
```

The **CASE** statement is bracketed by **DO CASE** and **ENDCASE**. The lines that begin with **CASE** present a logical condition for *dBase III Plus* to evaluate. If the condition is true, the program will execute the statements between that **CASE** and either the next **CASE**, the **OTHERWISE**, or the **ENDCASE**. (Any executable statements are permitted.) If the expression after **CASE** is false, the program evaluates the expression after the next **CASE**. If all expressions after **CASE** are false, the program executes the statements following **OTHERWISE**.

Once the program has found a true expression and executed the statements that follow it, program execution continues with the statement below **ENDCASE**. **CASE** statements are evaluated from the top down; even if more than one of the expressions following **CASE** are true, only the statements following the first one encountered will be executed.

dBase III Plus has only one way to do repetition, the **DO WHILE/ENDDO**. Assume, for example, that you wish to execute a block of statements ten times. The following code will do so:

```
count = 0
DO WHILE count < 10
    ? "This is iteration number"+STR(count)
    count = count + 1
ENDDO
```

The program will execute all statements between **DO WHILE** and **ENDDO** as long as the expression following **DO WHILE** is true. The expression is evaluated at the top of the loop. Therefore, it must have a value of true before the **DO WHILE** statement is encountered for the first time; otherwise, the loop will never execute at all.

The other important thing to remember is that there must be some action *within the loop* that eventually will cause the expression after **DO WHILE** to become false. That is the purpose of the statement **count = count + 1**; after ten iterations of the loop, **count** will have the value of 10, which will make the expression **count < 10** false. Without that statement, the loop would repeat infinitely. For more extensive examples of controlling **DO WHILE** loops, see the sample code that accompanies the section on data retrieval later in this chapter.

CUSTOM SCREEN FORMATS

Custom screen formats can be created with the command **CREATE SCREEN**. **CREATE SCREEN** generates two files, one with a **.FMT** extension and another with a **.SCR** extension. If you examine a **.FMT** file, you will see that it consists of a series of **@ row,col SAY** and **@ row, col GET** commands.

@ row, col SAY displays a string of text on the screen at the coordinates specified by **row, col** (assuming the screen is a 24-x-80 grid). **@ row, col GET** positions the cursor to the **row, col** coordinates and establishes a place for the user to enter data. **GET** must be followed by the destination for the data, either a memory variable or a field. **GET** does not actually do data input; that is handled by **READ**. **READ** accepts data for all **GET**s that haven't been read since the last **READ** statement was encountered.

READ statements are generally not part of .FMT files. .FMT files contain only the series of **SAY**s and **GET**s needed to paint the screen. The format is invoked with

SET FORMAT TO .fmt_filename

and followed by a **READ** which initiates the data entry.

INSTALLING A THIRD NORMAL FORM DATABASE

Installing a 3NF relational design with *dBase III Plus* generally involves the following steps:

1. Open a new catalog for the database
2. Create one database file for each relation, each in a separate work area
3. Index each database file on its primary key

4. Establish as many foreign key–primary key relationships as the software will permit
5. Create a view from the environment (for developer use only)
6. Create any additional indexes the application may require

Doing so for the Federated Taxi Company database requires the commands that appear in Listing 11.1.

Assuming that a file named FTC.CAT doesn't already exist, the **SET CATALOG** command (line one in Listing 11.1) establishes a new catalog file. All files created or used from that point on will automatically be added to the catalog unless the user enters **SET CATALOG OFF** (prevents additions to the current catalog) or **SET CATALOG TO catalog_name** (closes the current catalog and opens a different catalog with the name **catalog_name**).

The next major task is to create the database files themselves, along with primary key indexes and foreign key–primary key links. Database files to which other database files will be related must be created and indexed first. Therefore, CAB and DRIVER must exist before SHIFTS or MAINTAIN; SHIFTS must be created before INCIDENT. (Note that two of the relation names have been shortened to eight characters; this is because MS-DOS restricts file names to eight characters plus a three-character extension.)

```
. SET CATALOG TO FTC                                            (1)
. SELECT 1                                                      (2)
. CREATE CAB                                                    (3)
. INDEX ON CABNUM TO CABNUM                                     (4)
. SELECT 2                                                      (5)
. CREATE DRIVER
. INDEX ON DRVNUM TO DRVNUM
. SELECT 3
. CREATE SHIFTS
. INDEX ON DTOC(WKDATE)+WKSHIFT+CABNUM TO SHFTKEY               (6)
. SET RELATION TO DRVNUM INTO DRIVER                            (7)
. SELECT 4
. CREATE INCIDENT
. INDEX ON DTOC(WKDATE)+WKSHIFT+CABNUM TO INCIKEY
. SET RELATION TO DTOC(WKDATE)+WKSHIFT+CABNUM INTO SHIFTS
. SELECT 5
. CREATE MAINTAIN
. INDEX ON DTOC(MAINDATE)+CABNUM+MAINTYPE
. SET RELATION TO CABNUM INTO CAB
. CREATE VIEW FROM ENVIRONMENT                                  (8)
. SELECT DRIVER
. INDEX ON DRVNAM TO DRVNAM                                     (9)
```

Listing 11.1 *dBase III Plus* Commands to Install the Federated Taxi Company Database

Each database file is created in a separate work area so that all will remain in use during the installation process. The command **SELECT**, issued, for example, on lines two and five in Listing 11.1, moves between the ten available work areas. **CREATE** (as in line three) invokes the full-screen database file definition process, creating the database file structure on disk (see Figure 11.1). The index on the primary key is created next (line four, for example). Generally, when index keys are a single field, the index file is given the same name as the key field.

The index for SHIFTS (line six) is based on a compound primary key consisting of the date, shift, and cab number. The key expression is created by concatenating all three fields. Note that the date field (WKDATE) must be converted to a character string with **DTOC()** before it can be concatenated into the key.

There are two foreign keys in SHIFTS—CABNUM, which relates to CAB, and DRVNUM, which relates to DRIVER. We would like to be able to permanently establish both relationships, but *dBase III Plus* supports only one relationship *out* of any work area. When this situation occurs, implement the relationship that will be most frequently used (line seven). In this case, FTC employees dealing with shift reservations are more often

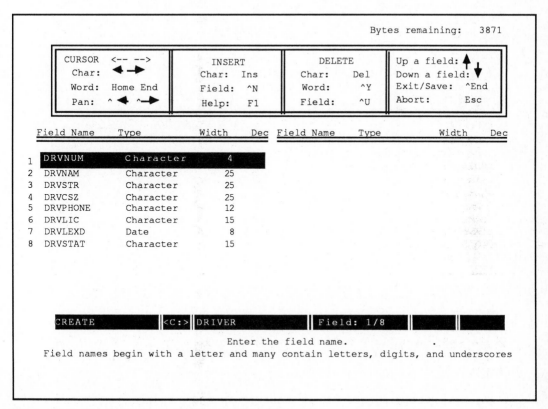

Figure 11.1 Creating a *dBase III Plus* Database File

Table 11.2
Structure of the FTC Database Files for a *dBase III Plus* Implementation

CAB.DBF

Field	Field Name	Type	Width
1	CABNUM	Character	3
2	MAKE	Character	15
3	MODEL	Character	15
4	YEAR	Character	2
5	PURDATE	Date	8
6	LICNUM	Character	7
7	CONDITN	Character	25
8	CABSTAT	Logical	1
9	CURODOM	Numeric	6

INCIDENT.DBF

Field	Field Name	Type	Width
1	CABNUM	Character	3
2	WKDATE	Date	8
3	WKSHIFT	Character	3
4	INCITYPE	Character	15
5	DETAILS	Character	200

DRIVER.DBF

Field	Field Name	Type	Width
1	DRVNUM	Character	4
2	DRVNAM	Character	25
3	DRVSTR	Character	25
4	DRVCSZ	Character	25
5	DRVPHONE	Character	12
6	DRVLIC	Character	15
7	DRVLEXD	Date	8
8	DRVSTAT	Character	15

MAINTAIN.DBF

Field	Field Name	Type	Width
1	CABNUM	Character	3
2	MAINDATE	Date	8
3	MAINTYPE	Character	25
4	MAINODOM	Numeric	6

SHIFTS.DBF

Field	Field Name	Type	Width
1	WKDATE	Date	8
2	WKSHIFT	Character	3
3	CABNUM	Character	3
4	DRVNUM	Character	4
5	WKFLAG	Logical	1
6	ODOMRDG1	Numeric	6
7	ODOMRDG2	Numeric	6

going to need details about a driver (e.g., name and phone number) than about a cab. The relationship between SHIFTS and CAB can be established temporarily by issuing a **SET RELATION TO** command within an application program when necessary.

The database file structures for the *dBase III Plus* implementation of the FTC database appear in Table 11.2.

After creating all five database files, their primary key indexes, and as many primary key–foreign key relationships as possible, the installation can be captured by giving the command **CREATE VIEW FROM ENVIRONMENT** (line eight). The major drawback to this approach is that a view created in this way cannot be modified with the full-screen **MODIFY VIEW** command. Therefore, it is best suited to creating the view that captures the entire database for developer use, rather than for creating user views. The details of this view can be seen in Table 11.3.

The last step in the installation process is to create any additional indexes that the database will need. Since some of the FTC applications require retrieval by a driver's name, an index on that field will speed the performance of application programs. The index is created on line nine.

Why is the driver name index created *after* the view is taken from the environment? The answer lies in the limitation imposed on the database by the number of files that can be open at any one time. *dBase III Plus* will permit 10 database files to be open simultaneously. (If a database file has a memo field, that memo field is counted as one of the 10

Table 11.3
A View Created from the Environment

Select area: 1. Database in Use: C:CAB.DBF Alias: CAB
  Master index file: C:CABNUM.NDX Key: cabnum

Select area: 2. Database in Use: C:DRIVER.DBF Alias: DRIVER
  Master index file: C:DRVNUM.NDX Key: drvnum

Select area: 3. Database in Use: C:SHIFTS.DBF Alias: SHIFTS
  Master index file: C:SHFTKEY.NDX Key: dtoc(wkdate)+wkshift+cabnum
  Related into: DRIVER
  Relation: drvnum

Select area: 4. Database in Use: C:INCIDENT.DBF Alias: INCIDENT
  Master index file: C:INCIKEY.NDX Key: dtoc(wkdate)+wkshift+cabnum
  Related into: SHIFTS
  Relation: dtoc(wkdate)+wkshift+cabnum

Select area: 5. Database in Use: C:MAINTAIN.DBF Alias: MAINTAIN
  Master index file: C:MAINKEY.NDX Key: dtoc(maindate)+cabnum+maintype
  Related into: CAB
  Relation: cabnum

database files as well.) The FTC database requires only five. However, there is a limit of a total of 15 open files for the entire implementation. Each index file, format file, report file, and program file is counted toward that total. Assuming that the catalog is closed once the initial view has been taken from the environment, then the FTC database is already using 10 files (5 database files and 5 index files; the view file is closed once the view is established). To leave the developer with the greatest flexibility, the initial view should therefore contain the minimum number of files possible.   The index on driver name is included in the catalog; it simply isn't part of the initial view.

The problem with the limit on total files being open isn't a trivial one. When you consider that a *dBase III Plus* application program will often have two levels of menus, several levels of program modules, and an active format file all open at the same time, then the 5 files left after the entire FTC database is installed aren't enough. The solution is to create a number of user views that contain only those parts of the database essential to a specific application.

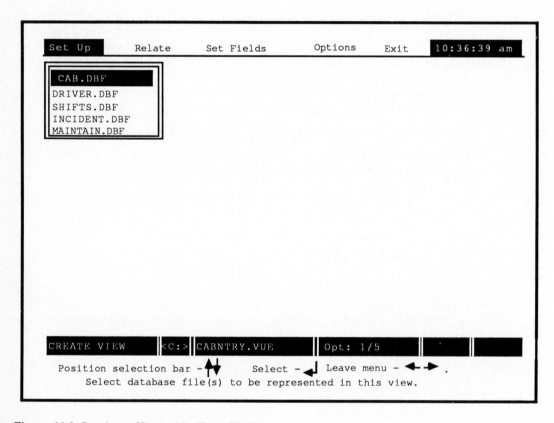

Figure 11.2 Creating a View with *dBase III Plus*

For example, the application that records reservations for shifts uses only three relations—CAB, DRIVER, and SHIFTS. A view including those three database files, their primary key indexes, and the index on driver name uses seven files rather than 10. The application program can then use eight files; this is usually a sufficient number to manage formats, reports, and program modules.

User views are most easily created with the full-screen, menu-driven **CREATE VIEW** command (see Figure 11.2.). The **Set Up** menu is used to select which database files in the current catalog are to be included in the view. The **Relate** menu takes the place of the **SET RELATION TO** command to establish foreign key–primary key links. **Set Fields** is used to select fields from the related database files for the view. Finally, **Options** can be used to install a filter, restricting the values of the fields.

The user views that are needed to support the FTC database appear in Table 11.4.

ENFORCING PRIMARY KEY CONSTRAINTS

Like many microcomputer DBMSs, *dBase III Plus* cannot automatically enforce primary key constraints (uniqueness and entity integrity). However, they can and should be maintained by application programs.

The uniqueness of primary keys cannot be enforced by creating a unique index on the key. An index created with the keyword **UNIQUE** does not prevent the addition of records with duplicate primary keys; instead, it will only index one occurrence of a given primary key. In other words, wherever records with duplicate primary keys exist in the database file, the unique index will only see the first one. Therefore, the only way to ensure that primary keys are unique is to explicitly check for a unique primary key value before adding a new record to a database file.

Entity integrity (ensuring that no attribute in a primary key has a null value) must also be maintained by explicit actions of an application program. The strategy is to accept data from the keyboard into memory variables rather than database variables so that the values in the memory variables can be verified before they are actually stored in a database file.

Consider, for example, the sample code in Listing 11.2, a module to add a new record to the CAB relation. The module accepts a cab number and then explicitly issues a command to determine if the cab number is already present in the database file (**FIND &mCABNUM**). A no-find condition (**EOF()** = true) indicates that the cab number stored in **mCABNUM** is not currently present in CAB. However, if *dBase III Plus* was able to find the **mCABNUM** value, **EOF()** will be false. In that case, the module prints a message indicating that the cab number already exists; the record is not added to the file.

The check for entity integrity is also explicit. The program verifies that **mCAB-NUM** actually contains some value other than blanks; if **mCABNUM** does contain blanks, the record will not be added to the database file. Note that this check for entity integrity means that the **DO WHILE** loop that controls the data entry cannot be stopped by a simple carriage return. The user must enter a specific end-of-data flag (**quit**).

Table 11.4

Views Needed to Support the dBase III Plus Implementation of the FTC Database

---

NEWCABS.VUE   /*Entering new cabs, printing roster*/

Select area: 1.   Database in Use: C:CAB.DBF   Alias: CAB
   Master index file: C:CABNUM.NDX   Key: cabnum

CABLINKS.VUE   /*Maintaining cabs*/

Select area: 1.   Database in Use: C:CAB.DBF   Alias: CAB
   Master index file: C:CABNUM.NDX   Key: cabnum

Select area: 2.   Database in Use: C:SHIFTS.DBF   Alias: SHIFTS
   Master index file: C:SHFTKEY.NDX   Key: dtoc(wkdate)+wkshift+cabnum
   Related into: CAB
   Relation: cabnum

Select area: 3.   Database in Use: C:INCIDENT.DBF   Alias: INCIDENT
   Master index file: C:INCIKEY.NDX   Key: dtoc(wkdate)+wkshift+cabnum
   Related into: SHIFTS
   Relation: dtoc(wkdate)+wkshift+cabnum

Select area: 4.   Database in Use: C:MAINTAIN.DBF   Alias: MAINTAIN
   Master index file: C:MAINKEY.NDX   Key: dtoc(maindate)+cabnum+maintype
   Related into: CAB
   Relation: cabnum

DRIVER.VUE   /*Entering drivers, printing roster*/

Select area: 1.   Database in Use: C:DRIVER.DBF   Alias: DRIVER
   Master index file: C:DRVNUM.NDX   Key: drvnum

DRVLINKS.VUE   /*Maintaining drivers*/

Select area: 1.   Database in Use: C:DRIVER.DBF   Alias: DRIVER
   Master index file: C:DRVNUM.NDX   Key: drvnum

Table 11.4 (cont.)

Views Needed to Support the *dBase III Plus* Implementation of the FTC Database

---

Select area: 2. Database in Use: C:SHIFTS.DBF Alias: SHIFTS
 Master index file: C:SHFTKEY.NDX Key: dtoc(wkdate)+wkshift+cabnum
 Related into: DRIVER
 Relation: drvnum

Select area: 3. Database in Use: C:INCIDENT.DBF Alias: INCIDENT
 Master index file: C:INCIKEY.NDX Key: dtoc(wkdate)+wkshift+cabnum
 Related into: SHIFTS
 Relation: dtoc(wkdate)+wkshift+cabnum

SHFTNTRY.VUE /*Making reservations, printing scheduling data*/

Select area: 1. Database in Use: C:CAB.DBF Alias: CAB
 Master index file: C:CABNUM.NDX Key: cabnum

Select area: 2. Database in Use: C:DRIVER.DBF Alias: DRIVER
 Master index file: C:DRVNUM.NDX Key: drvnum

Select area: 3. Database in Use: C:SHIFTS.DBF Alias: SHIFTS
 Master index file: C:SHFTKEY.NDX Key: dtoc(wkdate)+wkshift+cabnum
 Related into: DRIVER
 Relation: drvnum

SUMMARY.VUE /*Printing weekly driver summary—NOTE: uses driver name index*/

Select area: 1. Database in Use: C:DRIVER.DBF Alias: DRIVER
 Master index file: C:DRVNAM.NDX Key: drvnam

Select area: 2. Database in Use: C:SHIFTS.DBF Alias: SHIFTS
 Master index file: C:SHFTKEY.NDX Key: dtoc(wkdate)+wkshift+cabnum
 Related into: DRIVER
 Relation: drvnum

Select area: 3. Database in Use: C:INCIDENT.DBF Alias: INCIDENT
 Master index file: C:INCIKEY.NDX Key: dtoc(wkdate)+wkshift+cabnum
 Related into: SHIFTS
 Relation: dtoc(wkdate)+wkshift+cabnum

Table 11.4 (cont.)

Views Needed to Support the *dBase III Plus* Implementation of the FTC Database

PROBLEMS.VUE   /*Reporting incidents*/

Select area: 1.   Database in Use: C:CAB.DBF Alias: CAB
   Master index file: C:CABNUM.NDX   Key: cabnum

Select area: 2.   Database in Use: C:SHIFTS.DBF   Alias: SHIFTS
   Master index file: C:SHFTKEY.NDX   Key: dtoc(wkdate)+wkshift+cabnum
   Related into: CAB
   Relation: cabnum

Select area: 3.   Database in Use: C:INCIDENT.DBF   Alias: INCIDENT
   Master index file: C:INCIKEY.NDX   Key: dtoc(wkdate)+wkshift+cabnum
   Related into: SHIFTS
   Relation: dtoc(wkdate)+wkdate+cabnum

```
SET VIEW TO NEWCABS
mCABNUM = SPACE(3)
mMAKE = SPACE(15)
mMODEL = SPACE(15)
mYEAR = SPACE(2)
mPURDATE = SPACE(8)
mLICNUM = SPACE(7)
mCONDITN = SPACE(25)
mCABSTAT = SPACE(1)
mCURODOM = 0
SET FORMAT TO CABENTRY
READ
DO WHILE mCABNUM <> LCASE("quit ")
     IF mCABNUM = "   "
            CLOSE FORMAT
            CLEAR
            @ 5,5 SAY "You must enter a cab number"
            WAIT
     ELSE
            FIND &mCABNUM
            IF .NOT. EOF()
                 CLOSE FORMAT
                 CLEAR
                 @ 5,5 SAY "That cab number already exists"
                 WAIT
            ELSE
```

Listing 11.2   Verifying Primary Key Constraints for the CAB Relation

```
                  APPEND BLANK
                  REPLACE CABNUM WITH mCABNUM
                  REPLACE MAKE WITH mMAKE
                  REPLACE MODEL WITH mMODEL
                  REPLACE YEAR WITH mYEAR
                  REPLACE PURDATE WITH CTOD(mPURDATE)
                  REPLACE CONDITN WITH mCONDITN
                  REPLACE CABSTAT WITH mCABSTAT
                  REPLACE CURODOM WITH mCURODOM
            ENDIF
      ENDIF
      mCABNUM = SPACE(3)
      mMAKE = SPACE(15)
      mMODEL = SPACE(15)
      mYEAR = SPACE(2)
      mPURDATE = SPACE(8)
      mLICNUM = SPACE(7)
      mCONDITN = SPACE(25)
      mCABSTAT = SPACE(1)
      mCURODOM = 0
      SET FORMAT TO CABENTRY
      READ
ENDDO
RETURN
```

Listing 11.2 (cont.)   Verifying Primary Key Constraints for the CAB Relation

ENFORCING REFERENTIAL INTEGRITY

The **SET RELATION TO** command establishes a link between a foreign key and the primary key it references, but the link in no way ensures that a primary key occurrence exists for every foreign key occurrence; it only facilitates data retrieval. Therefore, referential integrity must be enforced through an application program. The code must not only verify that primary key references exist whenever a foreign key is added to a database file or modified, but it must also delete all foreign key records whenever the primary key is deleted from its database file.

Listing 11.3 contains a module that adds a record to SHIFTS. The module first verifies that values have been entered for cab, date, and shift (i.e., it verifies entity integrity) and then ensures that no reservation with those values already exists (i.e., it verifies that the primary key is unique). The memory variable **flag** is set to one if a reservation is already present; a non-zero value for **flag** will prevent a record from being appended to SHIFT.

If the reservation is not present, then the module attempts to find the cab number in CAB (**FIND & mCABNUM**). An **EOF()** value of true indicates that the cab number is not present. At that point, the user is given two choices—enter a record in CAB corresponding to the cab number or abort the attempt to make a reservation (**flag** is set to one).

```
CLOSE DATABASES
SET VIEW TO SHFTNTRY
SELECT SHIFTS
mCABNUM = SPACE(3)
mDRVNUM = SPACE(4)
mWKDATE = SPACE(8)
mWKSHIFT = SPACE(3)
flag = 0
choice = 0
SET FORMAT TO SHFTFMT
READ
DO WHILE mCABNUM <> LCASE("quit")
    IF mCABNUM = "   " .OR. mWKDATE = "        " .OR. mWKSHIFT = "   "
        CLOSE FORMAT
        CLEAR
        @ 5,5 SAY "You must enter a cab number, date, and shift"
    ELSE
        Lookup = mWKDATE + mWKSHIFT + mCABNUM
        FIND &Lookup
        IF .NOT. EOF()
            flag = 1
            CLOSE FORMAT
            CLEAR
            @ 5,5 SAY mCABNUM+" is already reserved for " + mWKSHIFT + " on" + WKDATE
            WAIT
        ELSE
            SELECT CAB
            FIND &mCABNUM
            IF EOF()
                CLOSE FORMAT
                CLEAR
                @ 5,5 SAY mCABNUM+" isn't in the database."
                @ 7,5 SAY "You may 1) Add the cab or 2) Abort the shift reservation"
                @ 9,5 SAY "Which one? " GET choice
                READ
                IF choice = 1
                    DO ADDCAB
                ELSE
                    flag = 1
                ENDIF
            ENDIF
            IF flag = 0
                SELECT DRIVER
                FIND &mDRVNUM
                IF EOF()
                    CLOSE FORMAT
```

Listing 11.3 Module to Add a Shift Reservation

```
                    CLEAR
                    @ 5,5 SAY mDRVNUM+" isn't in the database."
                    @ 7,5 SAY "You may 1) Add the driver or 2) Abort the shift reservation"
                    @ 9,5 SAY "Which one? " GET choice
                    READ
                        IF choice = 1
                    DO ADDDRVR
                    ELSE
                        flag = 1
                    ENDIF
                ENDIF
            ENDIF
        ENDIF
        SELECT SHIFTS
        IF flag = 0
            APPEND BLANK
            REPLACE WKDATE WITH CTOD(mWKDATE)
            REPLACE WKSHIFT WITH mWKSHIFT
            REPLACE CABNUM WITH mCABNUM
            REPLACE DRVNUM WITH mDRVNUM
            REPLACE WKFLAG with "F"
        ENDIF
    ENDIF
    mCABNUM = SPACE(3)
    mDRVNUM = SPACE(4)
    mWKDATE = SPACE(8)
    mWKSHIFT = SPACE(3)
    flag = 0
    SET FORMAT TO SHFTFMT
    READ
ENDDO
RETURN
```

Listing 11.3 (cont.) Module to Add a Shift Reservation

If the cab number exists in CAB (i.e., **flag** still has a value of 0), the module attempts to find the driver number in DRIVER (**FIND &mDRVNUM**). A no-find presents the user with the same choice he or she had for a missing cab number: add the driver to DRIVER or abort the reservation attempt.

The record is appended to SHIFTS only if the data entered by the user passes all four tests: values are present for cab, date, and shift; the record has a unique primary key; a record for the cab number exists in CAB; and a record for the driver number exists in DRIVER. WKFLAG is given a default value of F (false), since clearly a shift hasn't been driven at the time the reservation is made. The starting and ending odometer readings (ODOMRDG1 and ODOMRDG2) are left empty.

When a record is deleted from a database file that has foreign keys that reference its primary key, all foreign key references must be deleted from their database files as well. If this does not happen, then deleting the primary key record will leave the database in a state that violates referential integrity (i.e., foreign keys will exist that reference nonexistent primary keys).

Listing 11.4 contains a module that deletes a cab from the FTC database. This module would be used, for example, if a cab were sold or if a cab were destroyed in a traffic accident. In either situation, all reservations (past and future) that exist for the cab should be removed. Maintenance and incident records should also be be purged.

The module first locates the record for the cab in the relation CAB. If the record is present, it is flagged for deletion (**DELETE**). The module must then search each database file that may contain foreign key references to the cab. Since the database files containing the foreign key references aren't indexed on CABNUM, the only solution is to perform a sequential search using **LOCATE FOR** to find the first occurrence of CABNUM and then **CONTINUE** to locate all the others. Since the **DELETE** command merely flags records for deletion, the module finishes by giving the user the chance to pack the database files to physically remove the deleted records.

```
CLOSE DATABASES
SET VIEW TO CABLINKS
mCABNUM = SPACE(3)
SELECT CAB
CLEAR
@ 5,5 SAY "Cab number to delete:" GET mCABNUM
READ
DO WHILE mCABNUM <> " "
    FIND &mCABNUM
    IF EOF()
        @ 5,7 SAY "That cab isn't in the database."
        WAIT
    ELSE
        DELETE
        SELECT SHIFTS
        LOCATE FOR CABNUM = mCABNUM
        DO WHILE .NOT. EOF()
            DELETE
            CONTINUE
        ENDDO
        SELECT MAINTAIN
        LOCATE FOR CABNUM = mCABNUM
        DO WHILE .NOT. EOF()
            DELETE
            CONTINUE
```

Lising 11.4 Module to Delete a Cab

```
            ENDDO
            SELECT INCIDENT
            LOCATE FOR CABNUM = mCABNUM
            DO WHILE .NOT. EOF()
                  DELETE
                  CONTINUE
            ENDDO
        ENDIF
        SELECT CAB
        CLEAR
        mCABNUM = SPACE(3)
        @ 5,5 SAY "Cab number:" GET mCABNUM
        READ
ENDDO
choice = " "
@ 5,15 SAY "Pack the database files?" GET choice
READ
IF UPPER(choice) = "Y"
        @ 5,17 SAY "Packing will take a while ... please be patient"
        PACK
        SELECT SHIFTS
        PACK
        SELECT INCIDENT
        PACK
        SELECT MAINTAIN
        PACK
        @ 5,19 SAY "All done!"
        WAIT
ENDIF
RETURN
```

Listing 11.4 (cont.)   Module to Delete a Cab

DATA RETRIEVAL

INTERACTIVE RETRIEVAL

dBase III Plus has two major retrieval commands—**DISPLAY** and **LIST**. If used as relational operators, each will be qualified with **FOR** and some condition that identifies the records that should be retrieved. When used in that manner, they are equivalent. For example, to retrieve all current reservations for a given cab, a user could enter:

```
. SELECT SHIFTS
.DISPLAY WKDATE,WKSHIFT FOR CABNUM = "105"
```

or

```
.SELECT SHIFTS
.LIST WKDATE,WKSHIFT FOR CABNUM = "105"
```

DISPLAY and **LIST** can also be used to retrieve data from more than one relation. Assume that the SHFTNTRY view has been established. In that view, there is a relationship from SHIFTS to DRIVER. Then, to see the names of the drivers scheduled to drive on a given shift, a user could issue:

```
.SELECT SHIFTS
.LIST DRIVER->DRVNAM FOR WKDATE = 07/15/86 .AND ;
    WKSHIFT = "eve"
```

The **LIST** command will perform a sequential search on SHIFTS. For each record that meets the criteria (the evening shift of July 15, 1986), it will follow the DRVNUM to a record in DRIVER that contains a matching DRVNUM and retrieve the associated DRVNAM. Note however, that the predicate following **FOR** is restricted to a single database file (SHIFTS).

If relationships are established with **SET RELATION TO**, *dBase III Plus* will permit predicates that involve data from two different relations. Assume, for example, that FTC's clerk needs to know if a particular driver is scheduled to drive any shift on a particular date. The query could be expressed as:

```
.SELECT SHIFT
.DISPLAY WKSHIFT FOR WKDATE = 07/20/86 .AND.   ;
    DRIVER->DRVNAM = "Miller, Phyllis"
```

dBase III Plus will conduct a sequential search of SHIFTS, looking for all records with a WKDATE of July 20, 1986. For each record that meets the date criteria, it will take the driver number and use it to locate a matching record in DRIVER. It will use the value of DRVNAM associated with the matching DRVNUM to determine if the record in SHIFTS should be displayed. Remember, this query will not work unless a relationship has been established from SHIFTS into DRIVER on the driver number.

Conceptually, a number of relational operations underlie the previous query:

1. Select all tuples from SHIFTS where WKDATE = 07/20/86
2. Join the result of step one with DRIVER, using DRVNUM as the matching column
3. Select all tuples from the result of step two where DRVNAM = "Miller, Phyllis"

4. If the table created by step three is not empty, take a projection to include just WKSHIFT

5. Display the result of step four

dBase III Plus, however, does not use relational operations to implement the query. The **SET RELATION TO** command actually forces the following actions when the query is issued:

1. Search SHIFTS sequentially until a record is found with WKDATE = 07/20/86.

2. Using the value of DVRNUM from the record found in SHIFTS, **FIND** a record with that DRVNUM in DRIVER, using the index that has been built on DRVNUM. (This is why database files into which something is related must be indexed on the related expression.)

3. If the value of DRVNAM in the DRIVER record found in step one is equal to "Miller, Phyllis," display WKSHIFT from SHIFTS.

4. Repeat steps one to three until end-of-file is reached.

This process raises a couple of important points. First of all, if the database file into which something is related (e.g., DRIVER) doesn't have unique primary keys, then data retrieved via a **SET RELATION TO** linkage may not always be valid. The index lookup will always find the *first* occurrence of the key expression. If there are multiple occurrences of that same key expression, then there is no way to ensure that the record found is the correct one to associate with the record containing the foreign key.

Second, while the procedure may seem a bit clumsy and certainly doesn't strictly fit within the theoretical relational model, it has one major advantage over using a join; it doesn't create another database file. Microcomputer DBMSs generally do not use virtual tables; they don't have the main memory to store them. Operations such as join create new tables on disk, a problem in an environment where storage space may already be at a premium. The join is also a much slower operation than the index lookup.

DISPLAY and **LIST** are most useful in the interactive mode (i.e., when issued from the dot prompt). They display data in a default format that cannot be modified by an application program. The format cannot be modified because these commands do not create a virtual table. Each record that meets the search criteria is displayed immediately after it is retrieved; no more than one record is present in main memory at a time. Therefore, application programs that provide customized display and report formats resort to another technique to manage retrieval.

RETRIEVAL FROM WITHIN AN APPLICATION PROGRAM

If an application program needs to retrieve and print a small number of records that meet a specific criteria, it will use commands that locate records but do not display them. Those commands are **FIND** or **SEEK** (used when the retrieval is qualified by an expression on which the database file has been indexed) and the combination of **LOCATE** and

CONTINUE (used when the retrieval is based on an unindexed expression). Once the appropriate record has been located, it is displayed (either on the screen or on the printer) with either **@ row,col SAY** or **?**.

For example, consider the code in Listing 11.5. It contains a module to create the display screen presented in Figure 2.7, the Driver-Info screen. The data to create the display are located in two database files—DRIVER and SHIFTS. SHIFTS is related to DRIVER, but that relationship will not be of any use in this case. The relationship is designed to locate information about the driver of any given cab in any given shift. However, the relationship doesn't work both ways; it will not locate all shifts driven by a specific driver. That retrieval must be done explicitly.

```
SET VIEW TO SHFTNTRY
CLEAR
mKey = SPACE(25)
SELECT DRIVER
@ 5,5 SAY "Enter the driver number or the driver name:" GET mKey
READ
DO WHILE mKey <> " "
    IF SUBSTR(mKey,1,1) >= "0" .AND. SUBSTR(mKey,1,1) <= "9"
        FIND &mKey
        IF .NOT. FOUND()
            @ 7,5 SAY mKey+" isn't a valid driver number"
            WAIT
        ENDIF
    ELSE
        SET INDEX TO DRVNAM
        FIND &mKey
        IF .NOT. FOUND()
            @ 7,5 SAY mKey+" isn't a driver in this database"
            WAIT
        ENDIF
    ENDIF
    IF FOUND()
        CLEAR
        @ 2, 5 SAY "Driver: "+DRVNAM
        @ 2,40 SAY "Phone: "+DRVPHONE
        @ 4, 5 SAY "Status: "+DRVSTAT
        @ 7,38 SAY "SHIFTS"
        @ 9,30 SAY "DATE"
        @ 9,39 SAY "SHIFT"
        @ 9,45 SAY "CAB#"
        @ 9,50 SAY "DRIVEN"
        SELECT SHIFTS
```

Listing 11.5 Module to Create the Driver Info Screen

```
            LOCATE FOR DRVNUM = mKey
            IF .NOT. FOUND()
                @ 12,30 SAY "That driver has never driven for us"
                WAIT
            ELSE
                @ 10,20 SAY " "                    * positions cursor
                DO WHILE FOUND()
                    @ ROW()+1,30 SAY WKDATE
                    @ ROW(),40 SAY WKSHIFT
                    @ ROW(),45 SAY CABNUM
                    IF WKFLAG = .T.
                        driven = "yes"
                    ELSE
                        driven = "no"
                    ENDIF
                    @ ROW(),52 SAY driven
                    IF ROW() = 22
                        WAIT
                        CLEAR
                        @ 1,20 SAY " "             * positions cursor
                    ENDIF
                    CONTINUE
                ENDDO
                WAIT
            ENDIF
        ENDIF
        CLEAR
        SELECT DRIVER
        SET INDEX TO DRVNUM
        mKey = SPACE(25)
        @ 5,5 SAY "Enter driver number or driver name:" GET mKey
        READ
ENDDO
RETURN
```

Listing 11.5 (cont.) Module to Create the Driver Info Screen

The Driver Info screen module allows the user to locate the driver by either driver number or driver name. There is no need to ask the user which one he or she wishes to use; if the first character of the memory variable **mKey** is a digit, then it is reasonable to assume that a driver number has been entered (human names generally don't start with numbers). The module then uses the appropriate index (DRVNUM or DRVNAM) to **FIND** the DRIVER record. Note that **SEEK** could be used in place of **FIND**; the only difference in this case is that **SEEK** would not require the **&** (the macro substitution character).

If the **FIND** is unsuccessful (i.e., **FOUND()** = false) then the module prints an appropriate error message and gives the user another chance to enter a driver name and number.

If the find is successful, the module displays information about the driver using a series of **@ row,col SAY** commands to position the cursor.

Information about the driver's shift reservations is contained in SHIFTS. The module must perform a sequential search to retrieve *all* entries pertaining to the driver in question. Even if SHIFTS were indexed on DRVNUM, it would not be of any use in this instance, since both **FIND** and **SEEK** locate the first occurrence of an index expression; repeated **FIND**s and **SEEK**s will continue to retrieve the same record. Therefore, the module uses the sequential search provided by **LOCATE** and **CONTINUE**.

The module uses **LOCATE** to retrieve the first occurrence of a shift reserved by the driver. If the driver has never driven any shifts, then an appropriate message is printed on the screen and the display finishes at that point. However, if at least one record for the driver is present in SHIFTS, then the module enters a loop which displays the data. After executing the display statements (a series of **@ row, col SAY**), a **CONTINUE** causes *dBase III Plus* to search for the next record that matches the driver number.

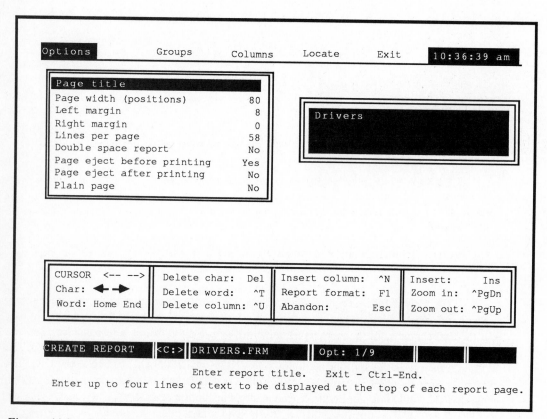

Figure 11.3a Setting the Page Configuration for a *dBase III Plus* Report

Since it is likely that the data for a driver will fill more than one screen, the module must also keep track of where the cursor is on the screen. The function **ROW()** returns the current row. When that value reaches 22 (there are 24 rows on most computer screens), the module freezes the screen with **WAIT**, which halts program execution until the user presses any key. The module must then clear the screen, reposition the cursor, and continue display and retrieval. Note that *dBase III Plus* has no command that simply positions the cursor on the screen. Therefore, in order for the relative addressing of **ROW()+1** to function properly, a dummy **@ row,col SAY** command is used to place it one row above where output should begin on each screen.

On occasion, it is necessary to process a relation in a sequential manner. In other words, the application needs to access every tuple in order. Common uses of that strategy are to print mailing labels, to print statements from accounts receivable data, or to print checks from accounts payable data. Such batch operations may be run at night when the system is not being heavily used for on-line retrieval.

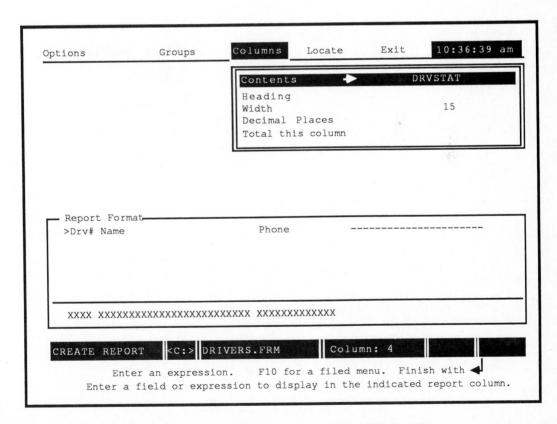

Figure 11.3b Indicating Where Data Should Be Printed for a *dBase III Plus* Report

The simplest way to produce a batch report is to use a report format designed with *dBase III Plus*'s built-in report generator. Invoked with **CREATE REPORT**, it presents the user with a menu-driven procedure that can be used to define the layout of the report.

Assume, for example, that the Federated Taxi Company wishes to print a roster of all drivers currently in the system. Since this is a very simple report, the report designer will need to use only three of the menus—**Options, Columns,** and **Exit.** The **Options** menu configures the general size and layout of a printed page (Figure 11.3a). The **Columns** menu establishes the attributes whose data will be printed in the body of the report (Figure 11.3b). **Exit** is used to save the report format on disk (Figure 11.3c).

While it is possible to print the report from the dot prompt with the command **REPORT FORM report_name**, the report can also be invoked from within an application program. Sample output from the report appears in Figure 11.4. Note that the report is printed in driver-number order, since the driver-number index was the primary index at the time the report was printed.

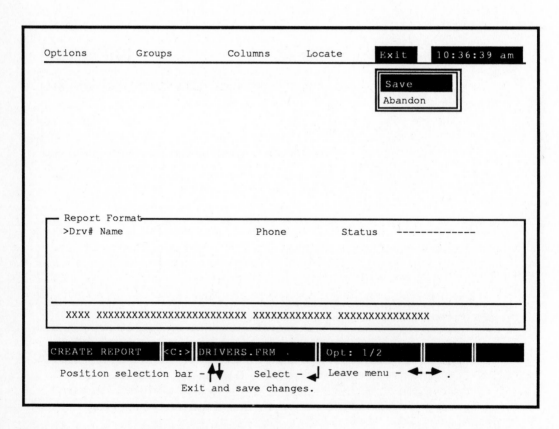

Figure 11.3c Saving a *dBase III Plus* Report Format

Page No.   1
10/18/87
                              Drivers

Drv#   Name   Phone   Status

0001   Bailey, Max   000-000-0001   pay before
0002   Baker, MaryAnn   000-000-0002   pay after
0003   Lewis, John   000-000-0003   pay after
0004   Santiago, Jorge   000-000-0004   pay after
0005   Miller, Pat   000-000-0005   pay after
0006   Miller, Phyllis   000-000-0006   pay before
0007   Phong, Quen   000-000-0007   pay after
0008   Wong, David   000-000-0008   pay after
0009   Young, Leslie   000-000-0009   pay before
0010   Zilog, Charlie   000-000-0010   pay after
0011   Erlich, Martin   000-000-0011   pay before
0012   Eastman, Richard   000-000-0012   do not reserve
0013   Kowalski, Pete   000-000-0013   pay before
0014   Mariott, Emily   000-000-0014   do not reserve
0015   French, Janice   000-000-0015   pay after
0016   Thieu, Lin Van   000-000-0016   pay after
0017   Jackson, Rafael   000-000-0017   pay before
0018   Wilson, Carter   000-000-0018   do not reserve
0019   Kolson, Jan   000-000-0019   pay before
0020   Abelman, John   000-000-0020   pay before

Figure 11.4 A *dBase III Plus* Roster of FTC Drivers

Listing 11.6 contains a module to print the driver roster using the standard *dBase III Plus* report format. The module is quite simple. It sets the required view (DRIVER, which contains only the relation DRIVER), establishes DRVNAM as the index so that the report will print the driver names in alphabetical order, tells the user to ready the printer, and then invokes the report format. Using report formats created by *dBase III Plus*'s report generator is therefore the easiest way to produce batch output.

However, situations may occur in which the report generator isn't flexible enough to produce a required report. Consider, for example, the Weekly Driver Summary report (Figure 2.12). The data in that report come from three relations—DRIVER, SHIFTS, and INCIDENT. *dBase III Plus* will permit only one relationships *out* of a given database file. Assuming that the Weekly Driver Summary report is based on SHIFTS, it requires relationships to both DRIVER and INCIDENT, a situation that cannot be handled through the report generator.

```
SET VIEW TO DRIVER
SET INDEX TO DRVNAM
CLEAR
ready = " "
@ 5,5 SAY "Turn on the printer.  Press any key when ready."  GET ready
READ
REPORT FORM DRVLST TO PRINT
RETURN
```

Listing 11.6   Module to Print a Roster of Drivers Using a *dBase III Plus* Report Form

The Driver Summary report also requires a format too complex for the report generator to handle; not only is the driver name printed only once for each driver but the driver name is used to group the shift data. Therefore, the only way to produce this report is to print it completely within an application program.

The *dBase III Plus* commands that perform qualified retrievals (**FIND, SEEK, LOCATE, and CONTINUE**) can't be used to execute a batch operation such as the one required by the Driver Summary report, which requires stepping through a database file, record by record. Batch processing must be done in a very nonrelational manner; the application program must explicitly manipulate the record pointer. The basic technique is to set the pointer to the beginning of the database file being processed by either issuing a **GO TOP** command or by **USE**ing the database file. The application program then processes the record and uses **SKIP** to advance the record pointer to the next record. The processing/ **SKIP** continues until the end-of-file (**EOF()** = true) is reached. While this procedure explicitly violates Codd's rules for a fully relational database (it violates Rule 12, the non-subversion rule), it is the only way to do batch processing with *dBase III Plus*.

The module that prints the Weekly Driver Summary report appears in Listing 11.7. There is certainly more than one way to assemble this report, but perhaps the simplest way is to work from the relation DRIVER, since the index DRVNAM will ensure that the drivers appear in alphabetical order. Therefore, the module works its way through DRIVER, record by record. For each driver, it consults SHIFTS to see if the driver has driven any shifts during the period requested by the user. For each shift that meets the criteria, the module checks to see if an incident was recorded.

For its basic structure, the module has two **DO WHILE** loops. The outer loop, which steps through DRIVER, stops when end-of-file is reached. The inner loop identifies the shifts for each driver by conducting a **LOCATE/CONTINUE** search on SHIFTS until the **CONTINUE** is unsuccessful (**FOUND()** becomes false), searching for any shift reservations present for that driver that fall within the time period bounded by **start** and **end**. For every shift that meets the criteria, the module searches INCIDENT to determine if an incident was recorded for that shift.

After retrieving the data for a single shift, the module computes the number of miles driven during that shift. Note that the computation is not performed if a driver did not drive a shift for which he or she had a reservation.

```
SET TALK OFF
SET VIEW TO SUMMARY
CLEAR
choice = " "
start = SPACE(8)
end = SPACE(8)
miles = SPACE(6)
@ 5, 5 SAY "Send output to screen (s) or printer (p)?" GET choice
@ 7, 5 SAY "Print summary for period beginning:" GET start
@ 9,10 SAY "and ending:" GET end
READ
start = CTOD(start)
end = CTOD(end)
IF UPPER(choice) = "P"
  SET PRINT ON
ENDIF
?
? SPACE(33)+"Driver Summary"
? SPACE(30)+start+" to "+end
?
?
? "Driver"+SPACE(20)+"Date"+SPACE(5)+"Shift Cab Miles Comments"
?
NumbOfLines = 7
first = "T"
SELECT DRIVER
dName = DRIVER
DO WHILE NOT EOF()
  SELECT SHIFTS
  LOCATE FOR DRVNUM = DRIVER->DRVNUM .AND. (WKDATE >= start .AND. WKDATE <=end))
  DO WHILE FOUND()
    LookUp = DTOC(WKDATE)+WKSHIFT+CABNUM
    SELECT INCIDENT
    SEEK LookUp
    IF FOUND()
      comment = INCITYPE
    ELSE
      comment = SPACE(15)
    ENDIF
    IF WKFLAG
      miles = RIGHT(STR(ODOMRDG2 - ODOMRDG1), 6)
    ELSE
      miles = SPACE(6)
    ENDIF
    IF first = "T"
      ?
      ? dName+" "+DTOC(WKDATE)+" "+WKSHIFT+" "+CABNUM+"   "+miles+ comment
```

Listing 11.7 Module to Print a Weekly Driver Summary

```
       first = "F"
    ELSE
       ? SPACE(16)+DTOC(WKDATE)+" "+WKSHIFT+" "+CABNUM+"   "+miles+ comment
    ENDIF
    NumbOfLines = NumbOfLines + 1
    IF UPPER(choice) = "P"
       IF NumbOfLines >= 60               * one inch bottom margin
          EJECT
          ?
          ? SPACE(33)+"Driver Summary"
          ? SPACE(30)+start+" to "+end
          ?
          ?
          ? "Driver"+SPACE(20)+"Date"+SPACE(5)+"Shift Cab Miles Comments"
          ?
          NumbOfLines = 7
       ENDIF
    ELSE
       IF NumbOfLines = 22
          WAIT
          CLEAR
          NumbOfLines = 0
       ENDIF
    ENDIF
    SELECT SHIFTS
    CONTINUE
  ENDDO
  first = "T"
  SELECT DRIVER
  SKIP
  dName = DRVNAM
ENDDO
IF UPPER(choice) = "P"
  EJECT
  SET PRINT OFF
ENDIF
RETURN
```

Listing 11.7 (cont.)   Module to Print a Weekly Driver Summary

At that point, the module can print a single line of the report. A memory variable, **first**, is used as a flag to determine whether or not this is the first shift data printed for the driver. If it is the first (**first** = true), then the driver's name is printed. Otherwise, the field for the driver's name is left blank.

If a module is using *dBase III Plus* 's built-in report generator, then there is no need to worry about breaking the report between pages; that is handled automatically. However, custom reports must count the number of lines printed and explicitly manage page breaks. Reports that are printed to standard 8 1/2-by-11-inch paper (six lines per inch) get 66 lines per page; reports that are displayed on the screen count each of the 24 screen rows as a line.

Printed reports generally issue an **EJECT** after counting 60 lines to give a one-inch margin at the bottom. Listing 11.7 uses the memory variable **NumbOfLines** to keep track of how much of a page has been used. Note that the module reprints the headings at the top of each new page.

Reports that display on the screen tend to display data down to row 22. Then the program issues a **WAIT** (which displays its prompt on row 24) to freeze the screen before proceeding. Once the user satisfies the **WAIT** by pressing any key, the program clears the screen and continues with the display. While this module does not redisplay the headings with successive screens, there is no reason that could not be done.

EXERCISES

The complete University Archaeological Museum database consists of the following sets of 3NF relations:

1. SLIDE LIBRARY MANAGEMENT

    SLIDE (DIG, SEQ-NUM, DESCRIPTION)
    SUBJECTS (SUBJECT, DIG, SEQ-NUM)
    BORROWED (DIG, SEQ-NUM, BORROWER, DATE-DUE, RETURN-
        FLAG)

2. GRANT ADMINISTRATION

    GRANT (GRANT-NUM, SOURCE, TOTAL-AWARD, PRINCIPAL-
        RESEARCHER)
    BUDGETS (GRANT-NUM, COST-CENTER#, CONST-CNTR-DESC,
        ORIG-ALLOC, AMT-AVAIL)
    GRANT-PURCHASES (GRANT-NUM, COST-CENTER#, P-O-NUM,
        VENDOR, DATE, TOTAL-AMT)
    DIGS (GRANT-NUM, DIG)
    ITEMS (P-O-NUM, ITEM, QUANT, COST-EACH, LINE-COST)
    VENDORS (VENDOR, ADDRESS, PHONE)
    GRANT-PAYROLL (GRANT-NUM, COST-CENTER#, DATE, ID#,
        GROSS-PAY, FED-TAX, SS-TAX, STATE-TAX, INSURANCE,
        NET-PAY)
    EMPLOYEES (ID#, NAME, ADDRESS, PHONE, SSN, #DEDUCTIONS,
        INS-PLAN1, INS-PLAN2, INS-PLAN3)
    INS-COSTS (INS-PLAN, INDIVIDUAL, FAMILY)
    DIG-ASSIGNMENTS (DIG, ID#)

3. ARTIFACT INVENTORY

> ARTIFACT-LOG (<u>ARTIFACT-NUM</u>, DIG, GRID-NO, DATE-FOUND,
> DEPTH-FOUND, DESCRIPTION, ID#, SHELF-NUM)
> ARTIFACTS-OUT (<u>ARTIFACT-NUM</u>, BORROWER, DATE-BORROWED,
> LOCATION, DATE-DUE, RETURN-DATE)

1. Considering *dBase III Plus*, explain why it makes sense to break this database into three parts. Are the three parts completely independent? (Are there any foreign key–primary key relationships between them?)

2. Using *dBase III Plus*, implement the three parts of the University Archaeological Museum database. For each part, do the following:

   a. Create a database file structure for each relation. Adjust relation and attribute names to meet *dBase III Plus* rules.
   b. Establish as many foreign key-primary key links as possible with **SET RELATION TO**.
   c. Create primary key indexes. For the GRANT ADMINISTRATION portion, keep in mind that only 15 files can be open at one time; you will have to make choices about which indexes should be present in your initial view.
   d. Create an initial view from the environment.
   e. Create any additional indexes you will need.

3. Two relations, EMPLOYEES and VENDORS, contain no foreign key references. Data entry into those relations therefore requires only checks for unique, nonnull primary keys. For each:

   a. Use CREATE SCREEN to design a data entry form.
   b. Write a program to handle data entry. Use the code in Listing 11.2 as an example.

4. The GRANT relation contains one foreign key reference—the PRINCIPAL-RESEARCHER must be an employee (i.e., it must match a value of NAME in EMPLOYEES). To manage GRANT, do the following:

   a. Use CREATE SCREEN to create a data entry form.
   b. Write a program for data entry. Use the code in Listing 11.3 as an example.
   c. Write a program for deleting a grant. The code in Listing 11.4 will provide an example.

5. Create a view that will permit a user to manage purchases made against grant funds. Using that view, formulate the *dBase III Plus* syntax necessary to answer the following requests for information:

    a. Given a grant number, display all the cost-center numbers and cost-center descriptions for that grant.
    b. Given a grant number, display all the purchase orders that have been cut for that grant.
    c. Given a purchase order number, list the name, address, and phone number for the vendor.
    d. Given a purchase order number, display the items, their unit cost, the number ordered, and the line cost for all items on the purchase order.

6. Using the view created in exercise five, design a report format to summarize grant-purchasing activity for one month. The report should:

    a. List purchase order numbers and total amounts for each purchase order.
    b. Compute a subtotal of expenditures for each grant.
    c. Compute a total of expenditures for the entire month.

How should GRANT-PURCHASES be indexed to ensure that the report prints properly? What command syntax will print the report?

7. If necessary, create an additional view to manage the artifact inventory. Then, using that view, develop the *dBase III Plus* syntax necessary to answer the following requests for information:

    a. Given an artifact number, display its shelf number.
    b. Given an artifact number, determine if that artifact has been removed from its shelf.
    c. Given an artifact number, display the number of all artifacts stored on that shelf.
    d. Given an artifact number, display the number and description of all artifacts stored on that shelf.
    e. Display the names of all artifacts that are overdue.
    f. Given the name of a borrower, display the numbers and descriptions of all artifacts checked out by that borrower.

Which of these queries might work better as part of an application program? Which are better suited to on-line, ad hoc retrieval?

8. Create a report format, using a suitable view, that will provide a summary of artifacts that have been removed from their shelves in the warehouse (i.e., those that have been checked out but not yet returned). The report should include:

   a. The artifact number
   b. The artifact description
   c. The borrower
   d. The location to which the artifact was taken
   e. The date the artifact is due

How will indexing affect the appearance of the report? What command will be needed to print the report?

12

Managing a Database System

CHAPTER OUTLINE:

CHAPTER OBJECTIVES:

After reading this chapter, you will:

1. Be familiar with database security considerations, including unintentional data damage and intentional damage and disclosure
2. Understand the responsibilities and functions of a database administrator

DATABASE SECURITY

Security wasn't much of an issue when it was possible to put your data on a single floppy disk and carry it away to be locked safely in a drawer. However, the introduction of large-capacity hard disks and multi-user microcomputer DBMSs has raised the question of how sensitive data can be protected. If you are administering a database system, you must be concerned with both intentional and unintentional, unauthorized modification and disclosure of data.

UNINTENTIONAL DATA DAMAGE

Unintentional modification or destruction of data can happen in a number of ways. It may be the result of hardware problems, either media failure (e.g., a disk head crash) or a power loss. It may also be caused by the misbehavior of applications programs that have not been properly debugged.

Backup

The best insurance against hardware problems is to keep backup copies of data along with paper documents for all activity against the database that has occurred since the backup was made. These can be used to restore the database once the hardware problem has been corrected. The generally accepted practice is to keep three sets, or generations, of backups (this is known as a *grandparent-parent-child* scheme). Having three generations of backups helps to ensure that a failure while attempting to restore the database from a backup isn't catastrophic.

How often should backups be taken? That depends on how active a database is. In very active environments, databases are backed up every day. However, the database must generally be idle (i.e., no activity in process) while the backup is being taken. For a single-user database, that presents no problem, but scheduling backups for multi-user databases does take some care.

On the whole, backing up a database is a time-consuming, bothersome procedure. Unless someone insists, system operators may simply "forget" to take backups. This, however, is a potentially dangerous (read "costly") situation. Consider what happened to a lazy independent contractor a few years ago.

This contractor was using an old Apple II+ with a 10 Mb Bernoulli Box (a high-capacity disk drive with changeable media cartridges) to maintain a mailing list of over 5,000 names. The *dBase II* database file stored on the Bernoulli Box cartridge was eight times larger than a standard Apple II+ floppy disk. Backing up the file required manually splitting the database file and downloading the data to floppies. The entire process took about two hours.

Like many people, the contractor was lazy and decided to take a chance. No backup of the database file was taken for over a year. Then the worst happened: while printing a set of mailing labels, the cartridge failed. (Bernoulli Box cartridges use high-density floppies that are more susceptible to damage than hard disks.) The contractor had two choices: re-enter all 5,000 names from hard copy or attempt to recover the data. So the cartridge was mailed to the manufacturer of the disk drive in the hopes that the database could be recovered.

You can decide for yourself if the contractor was lucky. The drive manufacturer was able to recover all but three of the 5,000 records. However, the price tag for the recovery process (labor and the cost of a new cartridge) was over $250. As you might guess, the first thing the contractor did when the recovered cartridge arrived was to make a backup copy.

Application Programs

Damage caused by bugs in application programs cannot always be avoided. Even the most carefully tested program may contain code that will behave unexpectedly in rare circumstances. However, application *development* should not take place using actual data. To protect the database from errors caused by programs not yet completed, all testing should occur against a special test database set aside for that purpose. The test database is usually a subset of the real database that can be regenerated from the real database at any time.

INTENTIONAL DATA DAMAGE AND DISCLOSURE

The simplest way to secure a database system against willful tampering is to restrict physical access to the computer. Placing a computer in a locked room and keeping tight control over who has the keys, for example, can be an effective way to control who has access to a database. However, if the computer handles remote users (either over telephone lines or through a network) or if the computer is shared by many different applications, then physical security is not enough. Security measures must be implemented while the user is on-line.

Identifying the User

The first step in on-line security is to identify the user. In multi-user environments, this is handled by the operating system. When a user attempts to log on to the system, he or she must enter a user name and an associated password. Anyone who cannot supply a recognizable user name–password combination is not permitted access to the computer. Once the user is on the system, the computer must assume that the user is the individual for whom the user name and password were created. To ensure the integrity of a password system, users must be encouraged not to share their passwords, not to write them down, and to change them frequently.

Single-user microcomputer operating systems generally do not have individual user accounts or work areas. The computer assumes that anyone who has access to the keyboard is authorized to use the machine. Security must therefore be handled at a lower level by the DBMS itself.

Internal DBMS Security

A fully relational DBMS handles security through what is known as an *authorization matrix.* Conceptually, an authorization matrix is a table that records which users can perform which kinds of activity against which data objects. Figure 12.1 contains a sample authorization matrix for the Federated Taxi Company database. Rights are granted to a specific user by relation and by operation. For example, the Kellys have all rights to every relation in the database. However, the chief mechanic can only view the cab reservation data; he cannot change it. By the same token, the scheduling clerk can view the cab maintenance data, but cannot change it.

A DBMS uses an authorization matrix in the following way: when a user makes a request for data retrieval or modification, the DBMS checks the user name against the relation name in the matrix. If the user has the appropriate access rights, then the operation will be allowed to proceed. If not, the user request will be denied.

Microcomputer databases, however, vary greatly in the degree of security they provide as part of their program code. Many, such as the single-user *dBase III Plus,* have no features specifically designed to ensure data security. (Although the single-user *dBase III Plus* has no security features, the LAN pack provides considerable capabilities for securing a database environment.) Some, such as *R:base System V*, provide password protection for major operations and data objects. Others, such as *Oracle*, use an authorization matrix.

USER	CAB	DRIVER	SHIFTS	INCIDENT	*MAINTAIN
Accountant	RETRIEVE	RETRIEVE	RETRIEVE	RETRIEVE	RETRIEVE
AKelly	ALL	ALL	ALL	ALL	ALL
Clerk	MODIFY	MODIFY	MODIFY	MODIFY	RETRIEVE
ChiefMechanic	RETRIEVE	RETRIEVE	RETRIEVE	RETRIEVE	MODIFY
Dispatcher1	RETRIEVE	RETRIEVE	MODIFY	MODIFY	NONE
Dispatcher2	RETRIEVE	RETRIEVE	MODIFY	MODIFY	NONE
Dispatcher3	RETRIEVE	RETRIEVE	MODIFY	MODIFY	NONE
Dispatcher4	RETRIEVE	RETRIEVE	MODIFY	MODIFY	NONE
Dispatcher5	RETRIEVE	RETRIEVE	MODIFY	MODIFY	NONE
Dispatcher6	RETRIEVE	RETRIEVE	MODIFY	MODIFY	NONE
OtherMechanics	RETRIEVE	NONE	NONE	RETRIEVE	MODIFY
QKelly	ALL	ALL	ALL	ALL	ALL

Notes:

1. MODIFY rights imply RETRIEVE rights
2. ALL rights include the right to change the rights of another user

Figure 12.1 An Authorization Matrix for the FTC Database

If you wish to learn more about the issues surrounding database security, see Fernandez, 1981; Denning, 1983; Griffiths, 1976.

SECURING AN *ORACLE* DATABASE

Oracle provides security at two different levels. Initially, a user must supply a recognized user name–password combination in order to be admitted to the *Oracle* system; *UFI*, *IAF*, and *RPT* will not execute without an authorized user name–password. Once a user has been admitted to the system, the rights that an individual user has to data objects and the activities that a user can perform are handled by an authorization matrix.

The single SQL command, **GRANT**, is used to assign rights to both the database system and objects within it. The SQL command **REVOKE** is used to remove those rights. When *Oracle* is first installed, it has only one authorized user name–password, SYSTEM/MANAGER. The SYSTEM user has DBA (database administrator) privileges. Any user with DBA privileges can:

1. Establish other user name–password combinations
2. Create and modify tables and their contents without restriction
3. Retrieve data without restriction
4. Grant and revoke the rights of other users

Any user with DBA privileges can grant DBA privileges to any other user, but in practice you may not wish to do so. In most installations, there is only one user with DBA privileges and its user name–password are guarded carefully.

To log on to *Oracle*, a user must at least have CONNECT rights:

GRANT CONNECT
TO NewUser
IDENTIFIED BY MyPassword;

This command will establish a user name of **NewUser** and an associated password of MyPassword. **NewUser** can now log on to *Oracle* but can neither create tables nor access existing tables or views.

Alternatively, a user who must not only be able to **CONNECT** to *Oracle*, but one who must be able to create and drop tables as well, is granted **RESOURCE** rights along with **CONNECT** rights:

GRANT CONNECT, RESOURCE
TO NewUser
IDENTIFIED BY MyPassword;

Users with **RESOURCE** rights can only drop tables that they have created themselves.

It is also possible, though not necessarily desirable, to create another user with **DBA** privileges:

GRANT DBA
TO NewUser
IDENTIFIED BY MyPassword;

Once a user has been granted **CONNECT, RESOURCE,** or **DBA** rights, other rights are granted to give the user access to needed data objects. The types of rights available are:

> 1. ALL (all of the rights below)
> 2. SELECT (retrieval only)
> 3. INSERT (add data)
> 4. UPDATE (modify data)
> 5. DELETE (delete data)
> 6. ALTER (add or expand columns)
> 7. INDEX (create indexes)

Any of these rights can be applied to a single table for a single user. **SELECT, INSERT, UPDATE,** and **DELETE** rights can be applied to views.

The general syntax for granting rights on data objects is:

GRANT right1 [,right2...]
ON table-name/view-name
TO user-name1 [,user-name2...]
[WITH GRANT OPTION];

For example, to give **NewUser** the right to query to CAB relation:

GRANT SELECT
ON cab
TO NewUser;

If the **WITH GRANT OPTION** is included, then **NewUser** will be able to grant his or her rights to other users. However, if **NewUser** did not create the table to which he or she is granting rights, then the table name must be preceded by the creator's user name. For example, assume that **NewUser** wishes to grant **SELECT** rights to CAB to **OldUser**:

GRANT SELECT
ON system.cab
TO OldUser;

The name of the user that created a table is separated from the table name by a period. In this case, CAB was created by SYSTEM.

In some cases, you may wish to grant a particular kind of right to all *Oracle* users. In that case, replace the name of the user following **TO** with the keyword **PUBLIC**. For example, to let all of FTC's users see the DRIVER table:

```
GRANT  SELECT
ON  driver
TO  PUBLIC;
```

More than one type of access right can be granted with a single **GRANT** command. To give **NewUser** the right to retrieve from and add data to CAB:

```
GRANT  SELECT,  INSERT
ON  cab
TO  NewUser
WITH  GRANT  OPTION;
```

The above command also gives **NewUser** the right to grant **SELECT** and **INSERT** rights to CAB to other users.

Rights can be taken away from users by using **REVOKE** to reverse the grant process. In general, the **REVOKE** command appears as:

```
REVOKE  right1  [,right2...]
ON  table-name/view-name
FROM  user-name1  [,user-name2...];
```

This same syntax can be used to revoke rights to data objects or to revoke rights to the *Oracle* system. To prevent **NewUser** from inserting records into CAB:

```
REVOKE  INSERT
ON  cab
FROM  NewUser;
```

NewUser will keep his or her **SELECT** rights to CAB, but loses **INSERT** rights. Rights can be revoked only by the user who granted them.

The command:

```
REVOKE  CONNECT
FROM  NewUser;
```

will remove **NewUser** from the *Oracle* system entirely. In doing so, all rights granted by **NewUser** will also be automatically revoked.

SECURING AN *R:BASE SYSTEM V* DATABASE

R:base System V provides two levels of password protection, on the database and on individual tables. While anyone can **OPEN** any database from the **R>** prompt, the types of activities that the user can perform are limited by the passwords he or she is able to supply.

An owner password controls access to the database structure. Once a database is assigned an owner password, the **DEFINE**, **RELOAD**, and **UNLOAD** commands are restricted to those who enter the correct password. The command

OWNER first_password

establishes an owner password. It can be issued either at the **R>** prompt or in the Define mode. Changing the owner password requires:

RENAME OWNER first_password TO second_password

To supply an owner password and gain access to the database structure, the user enters:

USER   owner_password

Passwords can also be assigned to tables. Tables can be given modify passwords (MPW), which restrict alteration of data in the table; or they can be given both modify and read (RPW) passwords. Read passwords prevent data retrieval from a given table and are not valid unless the table has also been assigned a modify password. Each table can be given one MPW and one RPW.

Any user who supplies the proper password receives all rights associated with that password. What that means is that while *R:base System V* table passwords do not necessarily have to be unique; if more than one table is assigned the same password, then a user entering that password gains rights to *all* tables with that password.

Table passwords are assigned in the Define mode.

D> PASSWORDS

tells *R:base* that the commands that follow will establish table passwords. The general syntax of the command to actually assign the passwords is:

RPW
or   **FOR table_name IS table_password**
MPW

Table passwords are reassigned by simply reissuing this command for the same table with a different password.

Users gain access to tables that have been given passwords in the same way that owners gain access to the database structure:

USER table_password

An *R:base System V* application that is running from an application program can also use a table as an authorization matrix in the manner described in the next section for *dBase III Plus*. Access to the matrix can be restricted with both a MPW and a RPW.

SECURING A *DBASE III PLUS* DATABASE

The Single-User Environment

While it is true that the single-user *dBase III Plus* has no features specifically designed for data security, it is possible to impose some measure of safety through an application program.   It is important, though, to keep in mind that there is nothing that will keep a knowledgeable user who has been granted admittance to the computer by the operating system from running *dBase III Plus* and issuing unrestricted interactive commands at the dot prompt.

In many businesses, however, *dBase III Plus* users have not been trained to work directly with the DBMS. Instead, they use an application program that presents a menu-driven interface and custom screen forms. In that case, users can be required to supply a password which governs whether or not they will be permitted to run the program. As an example, consider the following sample code:

```
TrialPassword  =  SPACE(30)
Password = 'TOP SECRET'
CLEAR
@ 5,5 SAY "Password:"   GET TrialPassword
READ
IF Password <> TrialPassword
   CANCEL
ENDIF
```

The **CANCEL** command will close all open files and return to the dot prompt.

There are two drawbacks to this approach:

1. The password is hard-coded into the program. Someone must edit the command file to change it.
2. The password applies to all users and all operations.

A more satisfactory approach is to create a special database file that serves as an authorization matrix. The file will include a field for the user name and one field for each data object on which the program wishes to enforce security. For example, an authorization matrix for the Federated Taxi Company database would have the structure that appears in Table 12.1.

    There is one field for the user name and one for each relation in the database. The relation fields contain a single-digit code corresponding the type of rights each user has to the relation. While the coding scheme is arbitrary, in this example the codes are assigned as follows:

> 0 = no rights
> 1 = read only rights
> 2 = append rights
> 3 = modify rights
> 4 = append and modify rights
> 5 = append, modify, and delete rights (all rights)

Append, modify, and delete rights imply retrieval rights.

Table 12.1
Structure of a *dBase III Plus* Database File for Use as an Authorization Matrix

Field	Field Name	Type	Width	Comments
1	USER	Character	15	Holds character string which user must type in order to be identified by the database system
2	PASSWORD	Character	15	Holds character string which must match the value of USER
3	CAB	Character	8	Holds character string specifying which rights a user has to the CAB relation
4	DRIVER	Character	8	Holds a character string specifying which rights a user has to the DRIVER relation
5	SHIFTS	Character	8	Holds a character string specifying which rights a user has to the SHIFTS relation
6	INCIDENT	Character	8	Holds a character string specifying which rights a user has to the INCIDENT relation
7	MAINTAIN	Character	8	Holds a character string specifying which rights a user has to the MAINTAIN relation

The authorization matrix file can be maintained by a separate application program (preferably protected by a password) or manipulated manually from the dot prompt.

An application using the authorization matrix must first identify the user:

```
USE Matrix INDEX User
UserName = SPACE(20)
mPassWord = SPACE(20)
CLEAR
@ 5,5 SAY "User ID:"   GET UserName
READ
@ 10,5 SAY "Password: " GET mPassWord
READ
FIND &UserName
IF EOF() .OR. PassWord <> mPassWord
   @ 15,5 SAY "Unrecognized User ID or password"
   WAIT
   CANCEL
ENDIF
*continue with the program
```

As mentioned earlier in this chapter, once the user has supplied a recognized user ID and password, the computer must assume that the user is the individual to whom the ID and password were assigned. From that point on, the application program must consult the authorization matrix file before performing any action requested by a user.

For example, assume that FTC's office clerk wishes to add a reservation for a shift. An application program would process the request in the following manner:

```
SELECT Matrix
FIND &UserName
IF SHIFTS < 2 .OR. SHIFTS = 3
   CLEAR
   @ 5,5 SAY "You are not authorized to add data"
   WAIT
   RETURN
ENDIF
* process the Append request
```

The major drawback to using a database file as an application matrix is the overhead it places on program execution; programs will run more slowly. However, it is the most flexible way to maintain data security in the single-user environment.

The Multi-User Environment

The *dBase III Plus* multi-user environment is considerably different from the single-user in terms of security. The LAN pack provides user accounts with passwords through a utility called *dBase ADMINISTRATOR*.   The same utility can be used to specify which users have access to individual data objects. Access restrictions can be applied at both the file and field level. The DBMS handles access requests through an authorization matrix.

Using *dBase ADMINISTRATOR*, a user can be assigned a security classification level. (*dbase III Plus* calls them *access levels*)   The access level assigned to a user is returned by the **ACCESS()** function and can be used by an application program to determine if a user should be permitted to perform a particular action against the database. It is important to recognize that access levels are merely assigned by *dBase*; the DBMS does not enforce them. The access levels are also not affixed to objects within the database. The way in which access levels are used, therefore, must be determined by database designers and implementation within application programs.

For example, a user might be given an access level between one and five, indicating whether that user has rights to view and/or modify unclassified, restricted, secret, top-secret, or eyes-only data objects. The organization has decided that users can view and/or modify data objects at the same or lower access levels. An application program that displayed the contents of a database file whose contents were determined by the organization to be top-secret (access level four) might manage access in the following manner:

```
IF  ACCESS()  >=  4
   { display  the  data }
ELSE
   ? 'Database error.  Requested  action  cannot  be  performed'
ENDIF
```

Note that the message returned to a user without a sufficient access level doesn't indicate explicitly that a security breach has occurred. Since someone may really be attempting to breach database security, it is unwise to alert a user that they have encountered a place where security controls are in force.

As an additional security feature, the multi-user version of *dBase III Plus* also provides file encryption. Encryption systems use an algorithm to transform data into some form of code. Unauthorized users who might look at the files on disk (i.e., they are not working within the DBMS and/or its supporting application programs) will not see meaningful data; the encrypted files will look like nonsense.

DATABASE ADMINISTRATION

As mentioned in Chapter 1, a database administrator (DBA) is someone who is responsible for managing a database installation. Though the DBA function is most commonly referred to as if it were performed by a single individual, the job may be shared by more than one person, especially in large database environments.

The job description also varies widely from business to business. It generally, however, includes some or all of the following areas of responsibility:

1. System planning and design
2. Application program development (including employee supervision)
3. Design (data dictionary) maintenance
4. Security
5. Public relations

SYSTEM PLANNING AND DESIGN

If a business is going to "do it right," a database administrator will be the first person hired after the organization makes the commitment to install a database system. The DBA will work closely with a systems analyst to evaluate the business' information needs and will often have the responsibility of designing the schema for the database. This aspect of the job has implications for the kind of educational background and/or experience a DBA should have.

In order to design an effective schema, a DBA must have technical database knowledge and experience. In the past, this has meant that some database administrators were promoted into that position from the data processing department. They followed by career path of programmer → programmer analyst → analyst → database administrator.

However, if a database system is to serve an organization for more than a short time, its design must be based on more than just immediate needs; it must allow for growth and change. In other words, the DBA needs to know something about upper-level management's plans for the future. Upper-level management has, in some cases, been most comfortable sharing that sort of information with an individual who has management experience. Therefore, some database administrators have been middle managers who made a lateral move from another department.

Both middle managers without technical expertise and data processing specialists without management experience tend to find a DBA's job difficult. Ideally, a database administrator should have education and/or experience in both data processing (including systems analysis techniques) and management. During the past decade, undergraduate and graduate programs have been developed that provide exactly that combination of studies. These programs are often called Computer Information Systems, or just Information Systems.

APPLICATION DEVELOPMENT

A DBA may have supervisory responsibility for programmers and programmer/analysts who develop applications programs for the database system. This aspect of the job is more than just a managerial responsibility; the DBA must be concerned with program standards as well.

Standards for applications programs are essential. These standards include:

1. Performance—the speed at which a program responds to the user
2. User interface—the type of interface (e.g., menu vs. command driven)
3. Programming style—how the program should be structured
4. Testing procedures—how new programs should be tested and who will verify the tests

Performance

How long are you willing to wait for a computer to respond to a command you type? Not very long. When you're staring at a CRT, 30 seconds is an eternity. To force programmers to design and code efficient applications programs, a DBA will often establish standards that specify the maximum amount of time that may be permitted to elapse between the carriage return that terminates user input and the display of a response on the screen.

User Interface

Left alone, many programmers will create command-driven programs that provide little or no information to the user. That kind of interface is adequate if the program is only going to be used by highly trained, technologically sophisticated individuals. However, in most database environments, the majority of users are not computer professionals. Rather, they are people trained in other areas who are using computers to help them do their jobs.

User interface standards will therefore often prescribe when menu-driven systems are required and describe data entry screen formats. They may also require programmers to make an effort to make sure their programs are easy to use by placing the bulk of the work on the program rather than on the user.

For example, assume that an applications programmer is writing a data entry program. There are two ways to control the program loop that allows the user to enter repeated sets of data. The first way is to ask the user how many sets of data he or she plans to enter and then to have the program code count, stopping the program when the requested number of records have been entered. This, however, places too great a burden on the user. The second technique for controlling the loop—using an end-of-data flag—is far better in terms of user interface. The user doesn't have to know how many sets of data are to be entered. When the user has finished, he or she simply enters the end-of-data flag and exits the program.

Programming Style

Database administrators may establish standards that regulate how programs will be logically structured and in what style they should be written. While at first this might seem to take away a programmer's creativity and freedom, it is essential if programs are to be easy to maintain. In fact, in environments where a database system has been implemented for a period of time, more than 80 percent of the programming activity that takes place involves maintaining existing programs rather than creating new ones.

Often, the person maintaining the program will not be the same as the person who originally wrote it. If all programs have a consistent structure and style, it will be significantly easier for someone who wasn't the original author to understand and therefore modify a program.

Testing Procedures

As mentioned earlier in this chapter, one of the prime sources for accidental destruction of data in a database is the testing of new applications programs that have not been thoroughly debugged against "real" data. The problem is easily solved by establishing a separate database for testing. This test database contains a subset of the real database and can be easily regenerated if an application program destroys any data.

Who, then, should decide when an application program is ready to be run on actual data? Generally, it's not wise to let programmers decide for themselves. The author of a program knows the code very well; he or she may inadvertently continue to interact with the program in such a manner that hidden bugs never appear. A better test is to let someone completely unfamiliar with the program source code interact with it. It is the DBA's responsibility to establish standards as to who will do the testing and the levels of performance a program must achieve before it can be run against the database.

There are two important implications of all these standards. First of all, they must be documented. If a new programmer is hired, some sort of document must exist that can be given to the new employee to read; you can't expect someone to adhere to standards if they don't know what they are. Secondly, standards must be enforced. It is the DBA's responsibility to monitor programmer performance and determine if established standards are being met. As a manager, the DBA must also take corrective measures if variation from the standards is beyond a tolerable level.

DESIGN MAINTENANCE

Regardless of how thorough the needs assessment is that leads to a database design, the time will come when the database no longer adequately meets the needs of an organization. Perhaps the users have become more sophisticated and are making requests for information that was not captured in the original design. Perhaps the activities of the organization have changed, bringing different requirements for data analysis. Whatever the cause, a database must change with the needs of its users. It is therefore the responsibility of the DBA to set procedures for and manage changes in the design of the database.

Making a change in a database schema is not always a simple matter. For example, suppose that Small Bank does decide to go from five-digit to nine-digit zip codes. Who will the change affect? Which applications are affected? For Small Bank, any applications programs that print materials for mailing as well as CRT data entry forms will feel the impact of the change. How much will it cost to implement the change? How much reprogramming is involved? If it will cost a great deal in programmer time to change output formats to accommodate the longer zip code, savings in postage may be overridden by programmer salaries.

In large database environments, where many different departments share the same database, requests for changes to the database schema are made in writing to the DBA. The DBA then circulates the proposed change to all those who are potentially affected by the change, asking for their opinion. Generally, the DBA reviews the responses and makes a decision on whether or not to allow the modification. If the modification is allowed, the DBA or an authorized person on the DBA's staff will make the change in the data dictionary.

This procedure for managing design changes has given database administrators a reputation for always saying no. It has also given rise to one of the worst "light-bulb" jokes of all times (included here so you can have at least one database joke to tell your friends):

QUESTION: How many database people does is take to change a light bulb?

ANSWER: Three: one to write the insertion program, one to write the removal program, and a database administrator to make sure that no one else changes it while the first two are working.

SECURITY

A database administrator has the responsibility for establishing and monitoring security standards and procedures. This includes not only the security measures discussed earlier in this chapter but also deciding who has access to what data. Making decisions as to which users will be permitted to access which data is not a trivial problem. Humans, as a rule, are very possessive of their privileges; anything that makes a person feel that he or she is less privileged than another is a possible source of contention.

Consider this not-so-farfetched scenario: You are hired as a database administrator for a small college. After performing your needs assessment, you determine (in concert with the systems analyst and management) that the first department to be handled by the new database system will be Personnel.

Currently, personnel files are kept in a set of three filing cabinets. Although the cabinets lock, a physical lack of space has forced them to be kept in the main reception area. The receptionist has always kept the key; the cabinets are unlocked whenever anyone needs a file. No one has ever had much trouble with the arrangement, though it is apparently well known among the clerical staff that the receptionist "peeks," always having juicy gossip to share over coffee.

Once the database system is installed and tested, the paper personnel files are removed to storage. It makes more room in the reception area, but the receptionist is furious. Access has been limited to the personnel portion of the database that is the schedule for on-campus interviews and no rights to look at any individual's data have been provided. Now the receptionist is in your office, standing in front of your desk, demanding to know why the data are unavailable.

As a manager, you've made the correct decision not to give the receptionist rights to personnel data. That job includes answering the phone, making appointments, and verifying that people show up for scheduled appointments. It in no way involves data stored about current employees. However, you must still deal with the interpersonal problem that has arisen from someone feeling offended because privileges have been reduced.

No matter how good a DBA's interpersonal skills, situations like the one just described do occur. They can't always be resolved just between the DBA and the individual making the complaint. Many organizations will therefore have a committee whose sole purpose is to evaluate access requests and either grant or deny them. Rather than taking authority away from the DBA, such a committee, more often than not, supports the DBA by giving him or her a place to turn for arbitration.

PUBLIC RELATIONS

A database administrator often functions as a liaison between the database staff and the rest of the world. The DBA must interact with system users, management, and people outside the organization. In this role, he or she walks a very fine line, since the wishes of the data processing staff must be balanced against the demands of users and top-level management.

As an interface between top-level management and the database staff, the DBA must ensure that management doesn't set unrealistic goals for systems development projects. This function has serious implications as to where the DBA should be placed in the organizational hierarchy.

In some businesses, DBA's are placed on project development teams at the same organizational level as the programmers and analysts. However, DBA's who are part of the data processing staff tend to have a difficult time getting management to listen to them. If a DBA is going to be effective as a management–DP liaison, then he or she has to be someone with some managerial clout. Not only must a DBA be able to enforce standards, but he or she must also be comfortable, if not in the board room, at least in the CEO's office. A DBA should therefore report directly to someone at the vice-presidential level (preferably a vice-president for data processing) or, in a smaller organization, directly to the CEO.

The DBA's responsibility as the interface between management and data processing personnel goes two ways. While the DBA protects the DP staff from unreasonable management demands, he or she must also realize that the DP staff may be capable of producing more work in a shorter amount of time than they claim. Once system development goals have been established, it is the DBA's responsibility to supervise the process and make sure the goals are met.

The DBA must also act as an interface between users and the database. End users require training. Sometimes, they may want to understand why a particular type of output that they requested cannot be produced. They need someone to whom they should direct their suggestions for system modifications. The DBA and his or her staff will therefore be responsible for designing and conducting user training sessions as well as fielding any queries users might have.

In some organizations, the database administrator is expected to act as a spokesperson for his or her employer. The DBA may be asked to speak about the organization's database system at professional meetings, or to describe the system for other businesses considering the installation of a similar system.

SUMMARY

Data stored in databases must be secured against both intentional and unintentional disclosure, alteration, or destruction.

Unintentional damage disclosure can be caused by hardware failures (e.g., media failure or power outage) or by application programs that contain errors. There are two major strategies for securing a database against those kinds of damage:

1. Keeping backup copies of the database. (If the database is damaged, it can be restored from the backup copy.)
2. Establishing procedures for testing new application programs. (New programs are run against a sample database until they are free of errors.)

Databases are secured against willful tampering by restricting access to the computer. Merely restricting physical access to the machine is only sufficient if the machine cannot be used via telecommunications lines (dial-up access over telephone lines and/or multi-user). In that case, the first line of defense lies with the computer operating system. Before a user gains access to the computer, he or she must supply a user name and matching password.

This type of security is not generally available with single-user microcomputers. Security must therefore be handled by the DBMS itself. Relational databases use authorization matrices to record the rights of individual users to data objects. Generally, relational databases are secured at the the table level. The term "database administration" refers to the activities involved with managing a database environment. The database administrator (DBA) may be a single individual or a group of individuals.

Although the duties of the DBA vary considerably from organization to organization, in its fullest sense, the job involves the following areas of responsibility:

1. Coordinating system planning and design: The DBA serves on the system design team and works closely with systems analysts to develop an effective database schema.
2. Supervision of application development: The DBA establishes standards for application program performance, for the user interface, for programming style, and for program testing procedures.
3. Coordinating design maintenance: The DBA supervises and authorizes changes to the schema.
4. Security: The DBA establishes and maintains security standards and procedures.
5. Public relations: The DBA functions as a liaison between the database staff and people inside and outside the organization.

REFERENCES

Denning, D.E. and P.J. Denning. (1983) *Cryptography and Data Security*. Reading, MA: Addison-Wesley.

Durell, William R. (1985) *Data Administration: A Practical Guide to Successful Data Management*. New York: McGraw-Hill.

Everest, Gordon C. (1985) *Database Management*. New York: McGraw-Hill.

Fernandez, E.B., R.C. Summers, and C. Wood. (1981) *Database Security and Integrity*. Reading, MA: Addison-Wesley.

Griffiths, P.P. and B.W. Wade. (1976) "An authorization matrix for a relational data base system." *ACM Transactions on Database Systems*. 1(3).

Martin, James. (1983) *Managing the Data-Base Environment*. Englewood Cliffs, NJ: Prentice-Hall.

Tillman, George D. (1984) "Data administration versus data base administration - there is a difference." *InforSystems*. 31:98-102. February.

Weldon, J.L. (1981) *Data Base Administration*. New York: Plenum Press.

Zmud, Robert W. (1983) *Information Systems in Organizations*. Glenview, IL: Scott, Foresman.

THINGS TO THINK ABOUT

1. One way to secure a database system against damage from power failures is to install a stand-by power supply that provides enough battery power for a computer operator to save all activity to disk and perform an orderly shutdown. Is this a sufficient hedge against power failure? Why or why not? If not, what else should be done?

2. It takes three hours for the Quality Mail-Order Company to back up their order entry database. However, the backup procedure means that the database can't be used while the backup is being made. QMOC advertises that they will accept orders 24 hours a day, seven days a week except for national holidays. The manager has therefore scheduled backups on holidays. Is this enough? Why or why not? If not, when should the manager schedule the backups? Is there going to be an optimal time to do it?

3. You are working for a small but exclusive investment firm. Data about client portfolios are kept on a single microcomputer that has a hard disk. Your boss thinks that the best way to secure the data is to put the computer in a small, windowless room and keep track of who has the keys. Is this a good idea? Why or why not?

4. You are a software reviewer who has been assigned the evaluation of a new DBMS. As you read the documentation, you find that it uses an authorization matrix to secure tables. The people who comprise the audience for your review won't understand the term "authorization matrix," much less how one works. Write the portion of the review that will explain the technique for your readers.

5. List the skills and personality traits that, in your opinion, characterize the ideal database administrator. Is this a job you would like to have? Why or why not?

6. A database administrator can be placed at many levels in an organization's job hierarchy. A DBA might be assigned to each systems development team, or the DBA might be a staff position that reports to a corporate vice-president. What are the advantages to each approach? What are the disadvantages? Formulate your answer in terms of the responsibilities of the DBA job.

7. Imagine that you are the DBA for a good-sized grocery chain (over 100 stores in a three county area). The Board of Directors wants to install UPC scanners in all of the stores. The software that will handle the cash registers and the inventory is to be written by the chain's in-house DP staff. Management says that the scanners can be delivered and installed in the stores in four weeks. They want you to make sure the software is ready at the same time. However, your experience tells you that you have more than six months of programming time ahead of you. What will you tell the Board of Direc-

tors? Should the installation of the scanners be delayed? If so, what arguments can you make to convince them to accept the delay?

8. You are the DBA for a mail-order company that specializes in sporting goods, camping equipment, and above-ground swimming pools. The manager of the swimming pool division wants to change the domain for the shipping weight of merchandise. (Currently the domain is numbers from 0.1 pounds to 99.9 pounds.) As DBA, how will you proceed with this request for change? What criteria will you use to make the decision about whether or not to allow the change?

9. You are still the DBA for the mail-order company in question eight. In response to a request from the sporting goods division manager, you have assigned a team of programmers to create an application program that will categorize and summarize sales for each quarter. Three weeks later, the lead programmer appears in your office, grinning from ear to ear. "All done," he says, "two weeks ahead of schedule. We've put it on the system for that sporting goods fellow." After hearing this, you get very upset.

   a. What's wrong with what the programming team did? What problems might their activities cause?
   b. Outline some procedures that might be used to avoid the potential problems created by your programming team.

10. Imagine that you are the DBA for a county library system. Every library employee has the right to retrieve data from the database that has replaced the card catalog. However, only the technical services librarians have the right to make changes. This restriction angers some of the library service technicians, who had formerly made changes themselves to the card catalog. How will you answer their demands for the right to modify the database?

PART

III

Appendices

The Office of Margaret Holmes, D. M. D.

1. Transcript of a conversation between Dr. Margaret Holmes and a systems analyst:

DR. HOLMES: Thanks for coming. I know it's late, but I really need your help. The paperwork around this place is really getting out of hand.

ANALYST: How do you mean?

DR. HOLMES: I started my practice three years ago—from scratch, mind you! I'm a good dentist; I really take good care of my patients, but nobody at dental school ever talked about how you *manage* a practice. We sure could have used a class in keeping patient records, hiring staff, firing staff, billing, inventory, patient scheduling—you name it. I seem to be swimming in paper in this office.

ANALYST: Let's see if we can narrow down your problems a bit. First of all, how many employees do you have?

DR. HOLMES: Just two, a clerk-receptionist and a dental assistant.

ANALYST: Who's responsible for the paperwork?

DR. HOLMES: The receptionist. She makes appointments and is supposed to keep track of patient records.

ANALYST: What about the financial end of things?

DR. HOLMES: I have an accountant.

ANALYST: Does the accountant do the billing?

DR. HOLMES: Yes. Actually, she's my sister. She comes in once a week and picks up all the payments we've received. Then she balances the checkbook, pays all the bills, and does whatever accountants do with the ledger sheets. Once a month she comes up with a summary of patient charges and amounts people owe. Then she makes a listing for the receptionist, who does the typing and mailing of the statements.

ANALYST: Do you pay your sister?

DR. HOLMES: As much as I can. Considering all the work she's doing, it's really not enough.

ANALYST: So you can either pay her more, cut down on the amount of work you ask her to do, or both.

DR. HOLMES (laughing): Well, if you can help me, I can cut down on her work-load. If we can also get more accurate billing information, then I can make more money and pay her more, too.

ANALYST: More accurate billing? What's the problem there?

DR. HOLMES: I suppose it's the fault of the way I record patient charges. I keep a history card for each patient. Whenever I see a patient, I write down whatever I did and note the charge. I give the card back to the receptionist, who's sup-posed to log the fact that I saw the patient in a notebook. Then the card gets filed.

ANALYST: The notebook you just mentioned—is that what your sister uses to fig-ure out the billing?

DR. HOLMES: That and the history cards themselves. You see, when a patient makes a payment or when we get a payment from an insurance company for a patient, the receptionist pulls the patient's card and marks the payment on the card. The log tells my sister who's been in the office, but the history card actually records what the patient still owes.

ANALYST: Since you say there's a problem with billing, the system obviously isn't working.

DR. HOLMES: All sorts of things go wrong. Sometimes, the patient history cards get misfiled. My sister can't find them when she needs to see how much someone really owes us. Then we're faced with either letting it go and hoping the patient has insurance to cover the cost, or running the risk of angering a patient by billing them for something that's already been paid.   Other things go wrong, too. Sometimes payments aren't recorded, or they get credited to the wrong patient.

ANALYST: How do you organize the patient files?

DR. HOLMES: By name.

ANALYST: Hmm. What happens if you have two patients by the same name?

DR. HOLMES: Then the receptionist is supposed to look at the address.

ANALYST: Well, here's a simple suggestion—something you can do right now, even before we get to installing a computer system for you. Why not assign each patient a number? Put that number on the statements as they go out and ask your patients to write the number on their check. That should make cross-referencing payments and patients much easier.

DR. HOLMES: Now why didn't I think of that?

ANALYST (smiling): I hope it helps. Now, does your sister also handle payroll?

DR. HOLMES: Yes. It's not difficult, considering that there's only the two employees. I pay her as a consultant.

ANALYST: And you get whatever's left over?

DR. HOLMES: More or less. Some of the profit goes back into the business for equipment and the like.

ANALYST: Let me summarize just a bit here, so I can be sure that I understand everything we've talked about so far. You're having trouble with patient billing, but the major underlying cause of that trouble is the system you use to keep records about patients. Both patient history and patient billing records are kept on the same card. If the cards are misfiled or lost, then the patient billing data may be inaccurate.

DR. HOLMES: Exactly. Can a computer help?

ANALYST: In both cases, yes. I think you need to consider keeping patient history data and patient billing data separate—not on two computers or in two different programs, but logically separate. If you request a copy of a patient's dental history, for example, you needn't see the financial history as well.

DR. HOLMES: You mean I should have one system to record financial information and one to record medical information?

ANALYST: They can be the same system, but they are two distinct functions that share some data. I think part of what has gotten you into trouble up to this point is mixing the two.

DR. HOLMES: I think I see what you mean.

ANALYST: What about patient scheduling? Is that a problem?

DR. HOLMES: Not at all. The receptionist has one of those oversized scheduling books. She just writes a patient's name in the right spot when an appointment is made. A liberal application of whiteout is enough to cancel an appointment. If we've got to choose something that doesn't need to be computerized, it can be patient scheduling.

ANALYST: OK. There's one more thing you mentioned—inventory.

DR. HOLMES: I haven't got one. I mean, I order supplies and drugs, but I haven't any written record of what there is.

ANALYST: How do you decide when to reorder?

DR. HOLMES: My dental assistant and I just look at the shelves in the storeroom; if we see that something is low, we put it on the list for the receptionist to order.

ANALYST: Is that a satisfactory procedure?

DR. HOLMES: Are you kidding? We always seem to be running out of one thing or the other.

ANALYST: Well, a computer can help you keep track of inventory levels, but you'll have to determine your own reorder point.

DR. HOLMES: Reorder point?

ANALYST: The minimum quantity of an item that you will accept before placing an order for more.

DR. HOLMES: You're telling me that this computer won't be much more than a record-keeping device, that it won't make decisions.

ANALYST: That's more or less true. It can make decisions of a sort, if the rules are laid out clearly. For example, if you let the computer know the reorder point for items in your inventory, it can decide whether or not an item needs to be reordered by comparing the quantity on hand to the reorder point you've established.

DR. HOLMES: I see. I guess I should have had a computer course as well as an office management course.

ANALYST: An introductory course at a community college, or through the continuing education department of a college or university, wouldn't hurt. In fact, you might want to send your employees as well, since they'll be using whatever system we install for you.

DR. HOLMES: If nothing else, it'll make us less afraid of the machine.

ANALYST: That's exactly it ...

2. Transcript of a conversation between the analyst and the receptionist for Dr. Margaret Holmes:

ANALYST: Dr. Holmes tells me that you're in charge of most of the paperwork in this office.

RECEPTIONIST: And answering the phone, and opening the mail, and calming frightened kids, and calling people to remind them about appointments ...

ANALYST: I'm afraid I can't help you with answering the phone or the frightened kids, but Dr. Holmes has asked me to see what can be done to clean up the record keeping.

RECEPTIONIST: First of all, we need to do something about those patient record cards. I mean, I try really hard to make sure that they get put back in the right place, but I'm only human. Sometimes I make mistakes. And it gets so busy in here. I'll have two dozen of those stupid cards on my desk, three people with six noisy kids waiting out here, the phone'll be ringing, and then the mailman will come in and dump a sack of letters on top of everything. Man, those cards have got to go. I mean, once one gets lost, then we're dead!

ANALYST: I'm hoping that we can come up with some solution, but in order to find one, I need to get some information from you about how you do things.

RECEPTIONIST: Like what?

ANALYST: Why don't you pretend that a patient has just walked through the door. Tell me, step by step, exactly what *you* do until the time that patient leaves.

RECEPTIONIST: OK. First, I get the person's name. Then I check him off in the appointment book, just so I know that he's come in. I've already pulled his card from the file. I pull the cards for all the day's patients first thing in the morning, so all I have to do is find it in the pile on my desk. When she's ready, Karen—that's the dental assistant—comes out and calls the patient. After that, I don't do anything until both Dr. Holmes and Karen are through. Whoever was the last to see the patient gives the card back to me. They've written down what they've done. I use my chart to figure out how much to charge the patient, and I write the numbers on the back of the card. See, here's charges and payments for the patient, all right here on the cards. Sometimes, if the charge isn't the regular fee, Dr. Holmes writes me a little note, so I have to look carefully. Before the patient leaves I make another appointment, either for more work or a six-month checkup. At the end of the day, I write the name of every patient that we saw in this notebook; that's so Susan knows who might need to be billed. Then I file all the cards.

ANALYST: What happens then, when the mail comes in?

RECEPTIONIST: I separate it. I set aside bills we have to pay to give to Susan, the accountant. I take the checks that have come in and pull the cards for each person who sent a payment. Then I write down the payment and subtract that amount from what the person owes. Dr. Holmes got me a calculator so my figures would be right. Insurance companies sometimes send us one big check for several patients; then I have to read the letter that comes with the check very carefully, to make sure that I credit the right patients with the right amount. Oh, yeah, I have to leave out all the cards that have recorded payments for Susan; otherwise, she won't know who's paid. It can get pretty tricky.

ANALYST: I bet it can. I think I've got a pretty good feeling for how the record-keeping part of your job works. Now that I think of it—don't you also take care of ordering supplies?

RECEPTIONIST: Yeah. I just write down everything that Dr. Holmes and Karen tell me to order. Then once a month I type up purchase orders and mail them out.

ANALYST: How do you figure out how much to order?

RECEPTIONIST: If it's something I haven't ordered before, I ask Dr. Holmes. Otherwise, I just order the same amount I did last time, unless Karen or Dr. Holmes tells me exactly how much they want.

ANALYST: How do you figure out where to order from?

RECEPTIONIST: If it's something new, Dr. Holmes or Karen will tell me. Otherwise, I order from the same place as I did before, unless, of course, I'm told to do it differently.

ANALYST: OK. I want to thank you very much for talking with me.

RECEPTIONIST: What's going to happen next?

ANALYST: I'm not sure. I need to talk to Karen and Susan. Then I'll make a report to Dr. Holmes and see what she wants to do from there.

3. Transcript of a conversation between the analyst and Dr. Holmes' dental assistant:

ANALYST: I'd like you to tell me about your part in keeping patient records and in working with the supply and drug inventory.

DENTAL ASSISTANT: Well, I write on the patient history cards, just like Margaret does.

ANALYST: Where do you get the cards?

DENTAL ASSISTANT: From the corner of the receptionist's desk. I'm the one who gets the patient from the waiting room. I get him settled in a chair and then either leave him for Margaret, or go ahead and do whatever work I have to do. Like, if they need a cleaning or X-rays, I'll do that before Margaret sees the patient. As soon as I'm done, I write down whatever I did on the card; I leave it on the counter for Margaret.

ANALYST: Does every patient see Dr. Holmes?

DENTAL ASSISTANT: Actually, no. Sometimes we do have people who just come in for a cleaning. For example, if they're taking a drug like tetracycline that precipitates stains on the teeth, they might need to be cleaned once a month or so.

ANALYST: What happens to the card in that case?

DENTAL ASSISTANT: Then I take it back to the receptionist. Even if I forget, I get all cards back to her by the end of the day. I always make a check of the treatment rooms before I go home.

ANALYST: What if the receptionist goes home before you do?

DENTAL ASSISTANT: Then I leave the cards on her desk anyway. She takes care of it in the morning.

ANALYST: OK. I think I understand how it works. So, let's talk about the supplies.

DENTAL ASSISTANT: There's not much to say. We've got that storage room you saw when Margaret gave you the tour. If we need anything, we just go in and get it.

ANALYST: What do you do when things run low?

DENTAL ASSISTANT: Tell the receptionist. She keeps a list. Once a month, she sends out orders.

ANALYST: Do you have any problems with having too much of something or too little?

DENTAL ASSISTANT: Oh, every so often we run out of something, but it's not a big problem. I'll tell you—I think the problem with those patient history cards and the screwy billing system is far more serious than running out of cotton wadding.

ANALYST: I hear you.

4. Transcript of a conversation between the analyst and Susan Holmes, Margaret Holmes' sister and accountant:

SUSAN HOLMES: Did you know that it was my idea that Margaret call you in?

ANALYST: No.

SUSAN HOLMES: Well, it was. She didn't have any idea how bad things were. She wasn't working with the figures! I've been trying to keep her books, but this crazy system she's come up with for recording patient charges and payments is a major problem. If she'd ever had a course in basic bookkeeping she'd know what she's doing to me.

ANALYST: What sort of system are you using right now?

SUSAN HOLMES: A one-write system. I've got a checkbook and cash-disbursements journal, and a cash-receipts journal. I also have a very small payroll system and an accounts payable system that's based on ledger cards. But accounts receivable? It's all on those stupid cards. I haven't been able to convince her that she needs to keep separate records about patient finances.

ANALYST: Let's start with accounts payable. How do you manage that part of the business?

SUSAN HOLMES: I get copies of purchase orders from the receptionist. I use those to create accounts payable entries. The receptionist gives me all the bills as they come in. I write the checks and post the payment on the ledger cards. I have complete control over accounts payable entries, so it works quite well.

The same is true, by the way, for payroll. Margaret tells me how much to pay everyone. I write the checks, pay the IRS, et cetera. Since there's so few people, I also do the W-2 forms at the end of the year. What I really want to talk about, though, is accounts receivable. My sister doesn't even know what that term means!

ANALYST: Why don't you tell me how it works, then.

SUSAN HOLMES: Well, when a payment comes in, the receptionist records the amount credited to a patient's account on the patient history card. Then she sticks the card in a pile that's supposed to be given to me once a week, so I know who's paid what. But there are so many of those stupid cards laying around the outer office that they go astray. I really wish Margaret would realize that she needs a separate set of accounts receivable records. Then the checks could come straight to me. I wouldn't mind keeping track of what people owe her.

ANALYST: What about the billing?

SUSAN HOLMES: Talk about clumsy systems. Once a month, I get a list of all the patients that have been seen. That list is people who *might* be billed. I have to check each person in that list against his or her cards to see exactly what they owe. But who knows where the card is? It might be in the file, it might be in the pile of cards that have posted payments that week, it might be lost somewhere. Who knows? At any rate, once I decide what people really owe, I make up a billing sheet. The receptionist actually types the statements and sends them out.

ANALYST: There's something that's eluding me here. How do you catch overdue bills?

SUSAN HOLMES: It's very difficult. The only way to figure out who's account isn't up-to-date is to go through all those history cards. When Margaret's practice was small, it wasn't a problem. The receptionist did it during slack times. But now she's too busy with just keeping the office going. We're losing revenue there, for sure. Look, I've told my sister that if she doesn't put in a computer system to keep patient records and do accounting, I'm going to quit. I think you're going to get this contract, because she certainly won't find another accountant who'll work as cheaply as I do!

ANALYST: I don't think I'd better comment on that.

The University Archaeological Museum

1. Transcript of a conversation between a systems analyst and the museum's director:

ANALYST: I enjoyed the tour, but somehow I think that looking at the objects you have on display is giving me an overly simplistic view of what your museum does.

DIRECTOR: Now that I think of it, you're right. We do many more things than just display the artifacts our researchers have discovered in the field.

ANALYST: Why don't you tell me about your other activities.

DIRECTOR: Well, first of all, we have a rather large slide collection. We record the history of all of our digs that way.

ANALYST: Who's in charge of the slide collection?

DIRECTOR: We have a graduate student working part time as the slide librarian. He labels the slides as they come in and is responsible for seeing that they are filed. Unfortunately, the collection has grown rather large. The graduate student changes every year and it's getting harder and harder to find things.

ANALYST: Just exactly how are the slides used?

DIRECTOR: Most of the time they're used as parts of lectures.

ANALYST: So it's the researchers themselves who later come for the slides taken at their digs?

DIRECTOR: Exactly. They're supposed to return the slides once the lecture is over—the slides do belong to the museum—but at this point, we really have no way of verifying that everything comes back.

ANALYST: Besides the slide collection, what other activities does the museum have?

DIRECTOR: We actually administer our own digs. The museum staff writes grant proposals. When we are fortunate enough to get one funded, we hire research staff, including the archaeologists, student help, and support staff.

ANALYST: Who takes care of the grant monies? I mean, who does the purchasing and the payroll?

DIRECTOR: When it's our grant, we do.

ANALYST: What sort of staff does it take to handle the grants?

DIRECTOR: We have two full-time grant writers, an accountant, a purchasing clerk, and a payroll clerk. The grant writers act as administrators for the grants once they're funded.

ANALYST: They report to you?

DIRECTOR: Yes, they do. I get monthly summaries of all financial activity on each grant.

ANALYST: Who prepares the summary?

DIRECTOR: The accountant.

ANALYST: Are there any other activities I should know about? I haven't forgotten your artifacts, but let's leave them for last.

DIRECTOR: We do maintain a small library. It has copies of all the papers and books our researchers have written about our digs as well as several thousand books about archaeology. The library also carries subscriptions to the major archaeological journals.

ANALYST: Do you have a librarian?

DIRECTOR: Not full-time. A graduate student from the Library School works there 20 hours a week. You see, the collection doesn't grow very fast. A card catalog gives us access to the books. We keep the journals in alphabetical order by journal title and then by date. Usually, when someone is looking for a journal article, they already have the citation. The student catalogs new books as they come in, files the magazines, and checks books in and out. Actually, the library works very well right now.

ANALYST: OK. Now we ought to talk about your artifacts. Tell me, are all of them on display?

DIRECTOR: Hardly. We have an entire floor in the archaeology classroom building full of items that we either don't have room to display or that aren't ready for display. Actually, it's the state of that lab of ours that prompted me to call you. I'm not as concerned with the problems with the slide collection, or the amount of work it's taking to generate weekly accounting summaries, as I am with what appears to be a loss of valuable artifacts.

ANALYST: Loss? Do you think artifacts are being stolen, or are they simply being misplaced?

DIRECTOR: I'd like to think that they're being misplaced, but there's no way to tell until we come up with a better way to keep track of them.

ANALYST: How are they handled now?

DIRECTOR: Artifacts are tagged and numbered in the field. For each artifact, someone fills out a card, indicating the item's number, where it was found, and when it was found. The cards are supposed to be brought back to the lab with the artifacts. Then they're filed numerically by dig. Somehow, not all of the cards get back. We end up with artifacts with no cards, which means the artifacts are nearly useless, since we don't know anything about the environment in which they were found. What's worse, we often have cards without artifacts. Even more seriously, researchers will insist that a particular specimen was found for which we have neither the card nor the artifact.

ANALYST (thoughtfully): A computer isn't necessarily going to solve the problem of disappearing artifacts, especially if the computer is located here at the museum. If it merely replaces your card file, it's not going to help you much, except in reducing the amount of paper you keep over in the lab. At least on the surface, it sounds like you need to bring your controls closer to the dig. You may wish to consider using computers at dig sites. However, no computer by itself can force your field personnel to record data as it is generated.

DIRECTOR: I see your point. I like the idea of taking computers to the dig and recording data about the artifacts as the artifacts are unearthed. But we're also going to have to redefine our field procedures and institute some fairly tight controls. That's my job, isn't it?

ANALYST: Primarily. But we certainly can work together on it.

2. Transcript of a conversation between the systems analyst and the slide librarian:

ANALYST: Why don't you show me how you organize the slides.

SLIDE LIBRARIAN: Well, each slide gets a number. That number has two parts. The first part identifies the dig on which it was taken. The second part is just a sequence number. Look at this one; its number is 14-089. That means that it came from dig number 14 and is slide number 89. Once the slides are numbered, I just file them by number.

ANALYST: Do you keep some record of the subject of the slides?

SLIDE LIBRARIAN: Yes, here in this notebook. You see, there's an entry for each slide. I write a few words describing what's in each slide right by the slide number.

ANALYST: OK. Now, tell me what happens when someone comes to you and wants to borrow a slide.

SLIDE LIBRARIAN: First, we go to the notebook I just showed you to find the slide's number.

ANALYST: That must take a while.

SLIDE LIBRARIAN: You bet. If the person doesn't know exactly what slide they want, then it means looking through all the descriptions. You know what we could really use—some sort of index. Then we could find slide not only by dig, but by topic.

ANALYST: That's a big project, but certainly something that could be done.

SLIDE LIBRARIAN: I think it would be worth it, especially since I'm not here all the time. I mean, I wrote the descriptions of slides that came since I've been here, and those are the only ones I really know well. I wouldn't mind taking the time to put standardized subject terms on all the slides.

ANALYST: Be sure you know what you're volunteering for!

SLIDE LIBRARIAN: I hear you.

ANALYST: Now, let's assume that you've identified the slides that someone wants to borrow.

SLIDE LIBRARIAN: I go to the drawer and pull out the slides. Then I make a note in this other notebook about who's taking what slides.

ANALYST: And when the slides come back?

SLIDE LIBRARIAN: I check them off.

ANALYST: How do you determine when slides are "overdue"?

SLIDE LIBRARIAN: I just sort of look in the notebook. But it's a mess; sometimes I can't read my own writing. And, as you can see, there are so many entries that it's really hard to tell what's been returned and what hasn't.

ANALYST: Just one more question. Can people get into the slide library when you're not on duty?

SLIDE LIBRARIAN: No, they have to wait for me.

ANALYST: Good. That at least eliminates one source of possible problems.

3. Transcript of a conversation between the systems analyst and the museum accountant:

ANALYST: From my conversation with the Director, I understand that you are responsible for preparing monthly reports about the grants the museum administers. What reports do you prepare?

ACCOUNTANT: The monthly report is a summary of grant activity that lists the major line item expenditures for each grant. The Director doesn't really want all the details, like how much each individual was paid. He just wants to know how much was expended for salaries, supplies, transportation, and the like. The report compares the expenditures to the budget for the grant. But that monthly report is just for internal use; it's really the simplest document we produce.

ANALYST: Oh?

ACCOUNTANT: Each agency that grants us money has its own set of reporting rules. Some agencies, like most of the private foundations, are satisfied with a level of detail similar to the internal monthly summary. However, the government needs very detailed records. Therefore, we tend to keep records with as much detail as we can. It's easier to summarize than it is to try to break down an already summarized quantity at some later date!

ANALYST: That's certainly a smart way to do things. Tell me, how do you handle your data now?

ACCOUNTANT: We're using the university's main computer. Someone in the computer science department set up a database for us. The trouble is, since we didn't create it, we don't exactly understand how it works. The person who wrote it is long gone and we need some changes. I don't like the idea that we don't have closer control of this data.

ANALYST: What kind of changes do you need? What doesn't your current system do for you?

ACCOUNTANT: Well, it primarily has to do with how we classify costs. When the original system was written, all of our grants came from the federal government. The government had a single way of numbering costs centers; that numbering system was built into the database design. But since federal funds have dried up, we've pursued and received a number of grants from private sources. Some don't care how we report to them, but others have their own schemes for classifying expenditures.

ANALYST: So you're looking for something flexible and something on-site, something that you can control.

ACCOUNTANT: That's it exactly. I think we could manage our own data here in the office if we had a microcomputer with a large hard disk.

ANALYST: That sounds reasonable. What about purchasing with grants funds?

ACCOUNTANT: Now that you mention it, it would be useful to tie an accounts payable system into the grant record-keeping system. I mean, wouldn't it be great if every time we encumbered some grant money on a purchase order, that amount was automatically entered into the appropriate grant and the appropriate cost center?

ANALYST: You're not asking for anything that can't be done with today's hardware and software. Is there anything else besides the grant expenditures that you'd like to handle locally?

ACCOUNTANT: I'd like to put the museum's operating expenses on the machine as well. Just the bookkeeping right now, though. We've been sending payroll out and it works quite well. The accounts payable for the museum itself are fairly limited, since most of our purchasing is tied up with the grants. That part of things could also be left alone.

ANALYST: What do you want the operating expense system to do for you?

ACCOUNTANT: Primarily general ledger. I'd also like it to generate monthly balance sheets. Like most museums, we are always short of money and we have to keep a close watch on our cash flow.

ANALYST: In order to do this for you, I need to know exactly what kinds of data you keep for both the grants and the museum. And I'd like to know generally how you classify it.

ACCOUNTANT: OK, let's start with the grants. First of all, we keep data on the people who are being paid by the grant. I mean, it's a payroll application. We collect the data and send a tape to the service bureau that computes the pay and prints the checks.

ANALYST: So you keep things like name, age, social security number, number of dependents ...

ACCOUNTANT: Sure, as well as data about insurance plans. It's not just health insurance, either. Some of the digs can get dangerous, so many of the grants make provisions for life insurance as well.

ANALYST: What else do you track besides people?

ACCOUNTANT: Grant expenses fall into two big categories—things that support an actual dig and things that support administrative costs. Dig costs include supplies like tents, food, tools, electrical generators, and sometimes even jeeps. Grant monies also can cover office supplies that a dig might use, like notebooks and tape recorders. Many include transportation costs for the staff to and from the dig and lodging while they're traveling. Administrative costs include overhead paid to the museum for providing accounting and other administrative services, for storage space in the warehouse, and things like that.

ANALYST: You really can't predict, then, exactly what things will be purchased for any given grant.

ACCOUNTANT: That's true. I'd like a system that has big broad categories like supplies, and salaries, and transportation. Then we could associate some sort of text with each broad category that would describe exactly what the money was spent for. I'd also like to be able to associate a cost center number with each expenditure, but it shouldn't be built into the system. A human is going to have to assign cost center numbers, since they vary from grant to grant. Can that be done?

ANALYST: I think it can.

4. Transcript of a conversation between the analyst and the museum librarian:

LIBRARIAN: I don't know why you want to talk to me. Everything works just fine here.

ANALYST: Do you have a backlog of work?

LIBRARIAN: Heavens, no. I get the cataloging done right away. For most books I can either order catalog cards from a library supply house or use the cataloging in publication data in the book itself. It only takes a few minutes to process new books. As for the journals, I just stick them on the shelf as they come in.

ANALYST: What about keeping track of what people borrow? The slide library seems to have problems.

LIBRARIAN (with a shrug): We work on an honor system. Journals don't leave the library. We've got a copy machine so that if people need a copy of an article, they can just make one. If they want to take out a book, they put their name on the card and stick the card in a box.

ANALYST: What happens if a person wants a book that isn't on the shelf?

LIBRARIAN: Then I look in the box to see who has the book. I call that person and ask for the book. Sometimes we have to negotiate a bit, but it works. You have to understand that there's only 30 or so people who use this library regularly, so it's not a big problem.

ANALYST: Aren't there any archaeology students?

LIBRARIAN: Sure there are—lots. But they don't use this library. Most of this collection is duplicated in the main university library. We support this little library with grant funds for the convenience of the researchers.

ANALYST: Ah ...

5. Transcript of a conversation between the analyst and a field researcher:

ANALYST: I'm curious about what happens when an artifact is recovered.

RESEARCHER: Why? What does that have to do with a computer system for the museum?

ANALYST: At this point, I'm not sure. The Director is concerned about losing track of artifacts. Until I know how artifacts are handled, I can't even decide if the problem is one that can be helped by a computer or whether it's a procedural problem.

RESEARCHER: I see what you mean. Well, I can tell you how I manage my digs. Not everyone does it exactly the same way, however.

ANALYST: OK.

RESEARCHER: Before we start the dig, I hold a meeting with the students who will be doing the work. The dig is laid out in a grid. I show the students how to identify anything they find by the grid coordinates and also by the depth at which the item was found.

ANALYST: How is that data recorded?

RESEARCHER: I use 3-by-5 cards. Each artifact gets a number; usually it's written
on a tag tied to the artifact. The number is put in one corner of the note card.
Then the date and location of the find is written on the card. There's also room
to write notes about the item.

ANALYST: Does the card include a description of the artifact?

RESEARCHER: Not usually.

ANALYST: Hmm. Just a suggestion, perhaps a description would make it easier to
match cards and artifacts if an artifact lost its tag.

RESEARCHER: That's a thought ...   So far no computer, eh?

ANALYST: Not yet. Tell me, do you have trouble keeping track of the cards?

RESEARCHER: Well, one or two always get lost along the way. We're not talking
about your standard laboratory here; we're talking about people living and
working in tents in remote, primitive locations.

ANALYST: Are cards always written?

RESEARCHER: Except in rare instances. If we find out that a student isn't following the procedures for logging in an artifact, we'll fire the kid from the dig.

ANALYST: I've talked to the Director about using computers at the dig sites. From
what you tell me, it might help you in a couple of ways.

RESEARCHER: How's that?

ANALYST: You can store your artifact data on floppy disks rather than on cards. If
you keep several copies of the data disk, there's little chance that you'll lose
any data. In other words, data won't go astray in the same way individual
cards are prone to. Computers also have a strong motivating effect on young
people; a student who thinks it's too much trouble to fill out a 3-by-5 card is
likely to look forward to entering the data into a computer. So a computer at
the dig may also cut down on the number of artifacts that are never recorded.

RESEARCHER: I like the idea. We just need to work out the logistics, I suppose.
What about power?

ANALYST: It's less of a problem than you might think. You can run a portable computer off solar cells. Two of them, each about a foot square, will do the trick.

RESEARCHER: All right ... I'm game to try it. I think I'm going to take another look at my grant budget to see if I can squeeze out enough money for the equipment!

ANALYST: I'm glad you're enthused, but hang on for a bit. We've got a long way to go in the design process before we come up with software that's going to work well for you.

6. Transcript of a conversation between the analyst and the supervisor of the archaeology lab and warehouse:

ANALYST: I see that you store artifacts on these open shelves. How do you keep track of what's where?

SUPERVISOR: The shelf locations are numbered. When we get artifacts in from the field, we assign each one to a location. The location is written on the card that comes with the artifact.

ANALYST: Where do you store the cards?

SUPERVISOR: In drawers. We bought card catalog cabinets—like they use in libraries—because we have so many cards.

ANALYST: How are the cards organized?

SUPERVISOR: In two ways. The original cards are filed by dig. We also make a copy of the card which we file by shelf location.

ANALYST: How, then, do you locate a specific artifact?

SUPERVISOR: Usually, it's a researcher who comes in looking for something. He just plows through all the cards for his dig until he finds what he's looking for. Then he can go to the shelf and get the thing. It's too bad there isn't some way to use a description of the artifact to make finding the card easier.

ANALYST: I've been talking to one of the field researchers about that very thing. It should be possible to come up with a set of descriptive words that can be applied to most artifacts. If all the researchers assign descriptions from a standardized list of terms as well as numbers to the artifacts, then those descriptions could be used to speed the search for one artifact.

SUPERVISOR: Could the computer system you're going to put in do that?

ANALYST: Yes, it could. In fact, that's one of the things computers do very well. If you were to work with descriptions in your card system, you'd have to make a third copy of each card. However, it's reasonable to expect a computer to locate information about an artifact based on its location here in the warehouse, the number assigned to it at the dig, its description, the date and place where it was found, or any combination of those characteristics.

SUPERVISOR: Y'know, so much of what the Director thinks is "lost," isn't really. It's all here in the warehouse; we just can't find it.

ANALYST: I'll tell you what I told the Director. A computer can't solve procedural problems; all it can do is help you keep good records. If you don't insist that artifacts are returned to their assigned locations on the warehouse shelves, the best computer system in the world can't help.

SUPERVISOR: I understand. Could we set up some sort of system where each time an artifact is taken from its shelf, we record its destination in the computer?

ANALYST: You mean, is it in the museum or in the lab?

SUPERVISOR: Exactly. And I'd like to know who took it, as well.

ANALYST: There's no reason we couldn't do that. Remember, though, that the computer will be only as good as the people who put data into it. A computer isn't going to insist that a lazy person enter data nor can it prevent intentional theft.

SUPERVISOR: We used to think that a computer would solve all our problems, but I really see what you mean. The computer can keep our records and give us access to them in ways we could never have with our card file system, but it's up to us to design procedures to control human behavior.

ANALYST: You've just expressed an attitude that virtually ensures that a database system will work well for you. I'm looking forward to designing a system for your museum.

C

Glossary

All key: A relation is all key if it contains no non-key attributes. In other words, every attribute in the relation is required to make a unique primary key.

Application program: An application program is a computer program that does useful business work. Application programs are often contrasted with systems programs, which work to make the computer more efficient.

Attribute: An attribute is a data item that describes an entity about which data is to be stored in a relational database.

Attribute inheritance: Attribute inheritance refers to the situation in which the data items that are part of a record type in a network or hierarchy apply to related record types at lower levels in the hierarchy or network as well.

Authorization matrix: An authorization matrix is a table that contains information about user access rights to data. The columns in the table correspond to objects within the database; the rows correspond to users.

Bachman diagram: A Bachman diagram is a graphic tool used to show the relationships between record types in a network or hierarchy.

Backup: Backup is the act of making a copy of a database as a hedge against some sort of system failure.

Base table: Base tables are tables whose contents are physically stored on disk by a relational DBMS. See also **virtual table.**

Batch processing: A technique for processing data that groups together activities against a file for execution at one time. The group of activities is referred to as a *batch*.

Binary search: A binary search is a search technique that works on an ordered relation or an index to a relation. It is conducted by dividing the relation in half and then determining if the tuple being sought is above or below the middle. The process of bisecting the relation continues until either the tuple is found or it is clear that the tuple is not present. Binary searches are generally very fast, especially if the relation contains many tuples.

Candidate key: A candidate key is any set of attributes that meet the criteria to be a primary key. Every relation has at least one candidate key (the one selected as the primary key); some have more than one candidate key.

Catalog: A catalog is a data dictionary for a relational database.

CODASYL database: A CODASYL database is a simple network database based on the recommendations of CODASYL's (Committee on Data Systems Languages) Database Task Group (DBTG).

Command-driven: A command-driven system is one in which program actions are selected by typing a command at the keyboard. Because the user has to learn a set of commands, command-driven systems are best suited for highly trained users who make consistent use of the system.

Complex network: See **Network data model**.

Concurrent use: A DBMS permits concurrent use if more than one user can simultaneously interact with the same centralized database. This does not imply, however, that concurrent users can simultaneously use the same piece of data.

Constraints: Generally, constraints are lists of rules that describe how the data within a database environment interact. More specifically, constraints refer to strict rules that govern the behavior of data in a relational database; they are rules to which the data must adhere.

Cycle: In a network or hierarchy, a cycle occurs when a record type is related to itself.

Data dictionary: A data dictionary is the place where the definition of a database schema is recorded.

Data disintegrity: Data distintegrity occurs when multiple copies of what should be exactly the same piece of data are no longer the same.

Data inconsistency: Data inconsistency occurs when data which represent the same thing are not stored in the same way throughout a file management system.

Data-flow diagram: A data-flow diagram is a graphic tool used to show the flow of information through an organization. Typically, data-flow diagrams use three different symbols: a square for sources of data, a circle for processes applied to data, and a rectangle for places where data are stored.

Data model: A data model is a framework used to describe the logical relationships between data in a database.

Database: A database is a collection of data stored in physical files along with the definitions of the relationships between the data in those files such that the data are perceived as a unified, logical whole, without regard for the physical storage structures.

Database administration: Database administration is the function within an organization that manages and supervises a database installation.

Database administrator: A database administrator is one or more individuals whose responsibility it is to manage a database installation.

Database management: Database management is a technique for storing, organizing, and retrieving data stored in a database.

Database management system (DBMS): A database management system is a piece of software that acts as an interface between a user and the physical storage of data in a database. The user issues requests to the DBMS, which in turn takes care of storing and retrieving the data.

Database navigation: In a network or hierarchical database, navigation refers to threading through the relationships between record types to locate required information.

Deadlock: Deadlock, or a deadly embrace, is a condition within a multi-user database in which one or more users are frozen because (1) the data they need are locked by another user and (2) they hold locks on data needed by another user. The most common way to break deadlock is to force one user to release all locks.

Deletion anomaly: A relation has a deletion anomaly if, when a tuple is deleted, data that should be retained are inadvertently lost.

Determinant: A determinant is an attribute upon which some other attribute is functionally dependent.

Domain: A domain is the set of possible values for an attribute.

Domain/Key normal form (DK/NF): Domain/Key normal form is the theoretical design objective for relational databases. While its concepts are simple, there is still no way to place a relation in DK/NF, nor is it clear that all relations should be placed in that normal form.

Entity integrity: Entity integrity is a constraint on a relation that states that no part of a primary key can be null.

Exclusive lock: A user in a multi-user database is given an exclusive lock on a data object after indicating an intent to update that object. Once an exclusive lock is placed on a data object, no other user can update or even view that data until the exclusive lock is released.

Field: A field is a single piece of data that describes an entity.

File: A file is a physical entity generally located on either a magnetic tape or a magnetic disk. It has a name and may contain the text of a document, the code for a computer program, or data organized in some known structure.

File management: File management is a technique for storing, organizing and retrieving data that are stored in individual, isolated physical files. There is no logical pooling of the data. Each file supports its own application program.

First normal form: A relation is in first normal form if it is depicted as a two-dimensional table with columns and rows and no repeating groups. All relations are therefore in first normal form.

Foreign key: A foreign key is one or more attributes in one relation which reference (are the same as) a primary key in another relation. See also **Referential integrity**.

Fourth-generation language: See **On-line query language**.

Full functional dependency: A full functional dependency exists between two attributes or groups of attributes, A and B, if a functional dependence exists (i.e., A determines B) and the determinant is comprised of the smallest number of attributes necessary to establish the determinance.

Fully relational: A relational DBMS is fully relational if it meets the 12 rules for a fully relational DMBS.

Functional dependency: A functional dependency exists between two attributes or groups of attributes, A and B, if, at any given time, only one value of B is associated with any given value of A. B is determined by A, or B is functionally dependent on A.

Grandparent-parent-child: Grandparent-parent-child processing is a scheme for data backup that keeps three sets of backup copies at all times to ensure that, if the system fails during the backup process, there will be another backup copy available.

Hierarchical data model: The hierarchical data model views logical relationships between data as an inverted tree. Each node in the tree can be related to many nodes below it (its children) but only one node above it (its parent).

Impossible output: Output from a database system is impossible if it simply cannot be generated from the database, regardless of resources expended.

Index: An index is a table that is used to logically change the order of tuples within a relation. An index contains the key values on which the table is to be ordered and pointers to where the associated tuples in the relation can be found.

Infeasible output: Output from a database system is infeasible if it would consume amounts of resources disproportionate to its value.

Insertion anomaly: A relation has an insertion anomaly if data cannot be added to the relation when needed because the data to form a complete primary key are not available.

Instance (of a data item): See **Occurrence**.

Intersection data: See **Intersection record**.

Intersection record: In a network, an intersection, or link, record is a special record type introduced to reduce a simple complex (many-to-many) relationship to two simple (one-to-many) relationships. It can also be used to capture data that have meaning only in terms of the relationship between two entities (intersection data).

Input-Process-Output (IPO): Input-Process-Output is a general problem-solving model that is based on the assumption that it isn't possible to identify the input to a problem until the desired outcome has been expressed. The final step in the process is to specify the process that transforms the inputs to the outputs.

Link record: See **Intersection record**.

Locking: Locking is a technique to prevent the lost-update problem in a multi-user database. A user who indicates the intent to update a data item is given exclusive rights to that item, preventing another user from even viewing the data item until the update is complete.

Logical-physical data independence: If a system has logical-physical data independence, then it is possible to change the physical structure of the files without changing any application programs that use the data in those files.

Loop: In a network or hierarchy, a loop is a relationship between record types where a record type on a lower level is the parent of a record type on a higher level.

Lost update: A lost update occurs when two users update the same data item in a multi-user database one after the other. The second update, based on the value of the data item before the first update, erases the first update (i.e., it is lost) and may introduce bad data into the database.

Menu-driven: A menu-driven system is one in which program actions are selected by making a choice from a menu. Users generally enter the letter or number that corresponds to their menu choice, though some systems are equipped to let the user press a button. Menu-driven systems are easy to learn and are well suited to casual or minimally trained users.

Multi-user: A DBMS is multi-user if it permits more than one user to simultaneously have access to the data in a centralized database. See also **Concurrent use**.

Network compatible: A DBMS is network compatible if it can be used on a local area network, allowing remote users access to a centralized database.

Network data model: The network data model depicts logical relationships between data in a database as a hierarchy that permits any given record to be related to more than one record above it (i.e., it can have multiple parents). In a **simple network**, the multiple parents must be of different record types. In a **complex network**, the multiple parents may be of the same, or different, record types.

Normal forms: Normal forms are a set of increasingly strict rules that govern the way in which attributes can be arranged into relations.

Normalization theory: Normalization theory is the theory behind the arrangement of attributes into relations.

Null: If an attribute has a value of null, its true value is unknown. Null is not equivalent to zero or a blank; it is a specific value with the meaning "unknown."

Occurrence (of a data item): An actual piece of data (a value) is referred to as an occurrence, or instance, of a data item to distinguish it from the generic term describing the nature of the data item.

Occurrence diagram: An occurrence diagram shows the relationships between actual occurrences of data in a hierarchical or network database. Most commonly, occurrence diagrams show occurrences of record types, not of individual data items.

On-line query language: An on-line query language is a special set of commands that a DBMS understands. A user enters the commands one at a time from the keyboard; the DBMS executes each command immediately. A full-featured query language allows a user to define database structure, to enter, edit, and delete data, to retrieve data, and to format and print reports.

One-of-a-kind request: A one-of-a-kind request is a requirement for information that arises at the spur of the moment, cannot be predicted, and in all likelihood will never be repeated.

Path dependency: A path dependency exists in a hierarchical or network database when a record type has no meaning without knowing the record to which it belongs at the level above it in the hierarchy or network.

Parallel implementation: Parallel implementation is a technique for introducing a new computer system into an organization. Both the old system and the new system are run together, in parallel, through at least one business cycle. This helps to verify that the new system is working properly and provides an up-to-date alternative should the new system have to be shut down.

Plunge implementation: Plunge implementation is a technique for introducing a new computer system into an organization. The old system is discontinued in favor of the new. Plunge implementations have serious consequences if the new system is unsatisfactory in any way, since no up-to-date alternative exists within the organization if the new system must be shut down.

Primary key: A primary key is comprised of one or more attributes whose values uniquely identify each tuple in a relation.

Record: A record is the unit within a data file that contains a collection of data describing a single entity.

Record type: In a hierarchical or network database, the term "record type" refers to a collection of data items that describes either (1) a single entity about which the database is storing data or (2) a relationship between entities about which the database is storing data.

Redundant data: Redundant data occurs within a computer system when the same data about the same entity is stored more than once; multiple copies exist of the same data.

Redundant primary key: A primary key is redundant if it contains more attributes than necessary to make a unique identifier for the relation.

Referential integrity: Referential integrity is a constraint on a relation that states that all foreign key values must reference existing primary key values. No foreign key value can exist in the database unless the primary key it references is also present.

Relation: A relation is a two-dimensional table made up of columns and rows. The term comes from mathematical set theory.

Relational algebra: The relational algebra is a set of operations for manipulating relations. Each operation performs a single function. It is therefore often necessary to use a sequence of operations from the relational algebra to complete an information request. The eight basic operations of the relational algebra are select, project, join, union, difference, intersect, product, and divide.

Relational data model: The relational data model views the data within a database as if they were stored in a set of logically separate, two-dimensional tables. Relationships between the data are established by including duplicate columns in tables that are related.

Relational calculus: The relational calculus is a system for expressing operations against a relational database using the notation of formal logic theory. Complex operations can be combined into a single command.

Relationally complete: A DBMS is relationally complete if it supports five operations from the relational algebra: select, project, join, union, and difference.

Requirements document: A requirements document is the end product of the needs assessment phase of a systems development project. The document contains, in detail, the requirements of a new or improved information system. It may contain data-flow diagrams, lists of data items, and/or samples of required system output.

Schema: The schema is the overall, global logical organization of a database. It contains definitions of all the data items that the database will contain as well as the relationships between those data.

Second normal form: A relation is in second normal form if it is in first normal form and all non-key attributes are fully functionally dependent on the primary key.

Sequential search: A sequential search is a search technique that begins at the logically first tuple in a relation and proceeds by examining each tuple in the relation in order until either the required tuple is found or the entire relation has been searched. Sequential searches can be very slow on relations which contain many tuples.

Set: A set is the basic structure of a CODASYL database. Sets are two-level trees, with one record type as the parent (owner) and one or more children (members).

Shared lock: A shared lock is used in a multi-user database to prevent a user from changing data while another user is viewing it. Many users can hold a shared lock on the same data object. However, no user can obtain an exclusive lock until all shared locks are released.

Simple network: See **Network data model**.

Sorting: Sorting refers to physically reordering a relation so that the tuples are ordered by some key values. Sorting usually requires making a duplicate copy of the relation being sorted.

Systems analysis: Systems analysis is the process of evaluating an existing information system and then assessing user needs to determine where the system should be modified to better meet user needs. A systems analysis will often end with proposals for new and/or improved systems.

Systems analyst: A systems analyst is a person who is trained to evaluate information systems and propose alternatives for changing them so they will better meet user's needs.

Systems development cycle: The systems development cycle is a set of activities used to develop computer information systems. The steps in the cycle include performing a needs assessment to define needs, formulating and evaluating alternative solutions, designing the new system, and implementing the new system.

Subschema: A subschema is a logical subset of a database schema for use by a specific application; it is a user's view of the database. It includes only as much of the schema as the application requires. A single schema can theoretically support any unlimited number of subschemas.

Third normal form: A relation is in third normal form if it is in second normal form and all non-key attributes are mutually independent.

Transaction: A transaction is a unit of work. In the database field, the term refers to a single activity against a database. Transaction based DBMSs (generally multi-user DBMSs) support commands that mark the beginning and ending of transactions.

Transitive dependency: A transitive dependency exists in a relation when AttributeA $\rightarrow$ AttributeB $\rightarrow$ AttributeC and AttributeA is the primary key in the relation. Relations with transitive dependencies will have insertion and deletion anomalies as well as update problems.

Tuple: A tuple is a row in a relational table.

Turnkey system: A turnkey system is a computer system that a user can operate by simply pressing a few buttons, making menu selections, or entering a few simple commands. Turnkey systems are usually designed for users who are not technically sophisticated.

User-friendly: A system is considered to be user-friendly if it presents a non-threatening, easy to learn and use interface to the user.

View: A view is a subset of a relational database for use by a specific application. It is equivalent, in concept, to a subschema.

Virtual table: A virtual table is a temporary table created in main memory by a relational DBMS as the result of some relational operation. Unless the user specifically instructs otherwise, virtual tables are not written to disk.

Index